Elusive Togetherness

———————————————

PRINCETON STUDIES IN CULTURAL SOCIOLOGY

Paul J. DiMaggio, Michèle Lamont, Robert J. Wuthnow, Viviana A. Zelizer

A list of titles in the series appears at the back of the book.

Elusive Togetherness

CHURCH GROUPS TRYING TO BRIDGE AMERICA'S DIVISIONS

Paul Lichterman

PRINCETON UNIVERSITY PRESS

PRINCETON AND OXFORD

Copyright © 2005 by Princeton University Press
Requests for permission to reproduce material from this work should be sent to Permissions,
Princeton University Press
Published by Princeton University Press, 41 William Street, Princeton, New Jersey 08540
In the United Kingdom: Princeton University Press, 3 Market Place, Woodstock, Oxfordshire
OX20 1SY

Library of Congress Cataloging-in-Publication Data

Lichterman, Paul.
Elusive togetherness : church groups trying to bridge America's divisions / Paul Lichterman.
p. cm. — (Princeton studies in cultural sociology)
Includes bibliographical references and index.
ISBN 0-691-09650-3 (cl. : alk. paper) — ISBN 0-691-09651-1 (pb. : alk. paper)
1. Religion and social problems—United States.   2. Social action—United States.   3. Volun-
tarism—United States.   4. Associations, institutions, etc.—United States.   5. Small groups—
Religious aspects.   I. Title.   II. Series.

HN65.L455 2005
306.6′18′0973—dc22   2004058458

British Library Cataloging-in-Publication Data is available

This book has been composed in Minion type
Printed on acid-free paper. ∞
pup.princeton.edu

Printed in the United States of America

1   3   5   7   9   10   8   6   4   2

CONTENTS

TABLES AND FIGURES

ACKNOWLEDGMENTS

I WISH I COULD name the people who let me follow them, participate alongside them, and interview them. Maintaining the confidentiality I promised, I heartily thank the Urban Religious Coalition and especially its tireless, exquisitely thoughtful director Donald and board member Pastor Ed Lindstrom for welcoming me and talking at length with me about the URC. I deeply appreciate, too, all the members of the Justice Task Force, Park Cluster, and the Humane Response Alliance for allowing me to observe and participate for what must have seemed like a very long time. Members of the Lakeside Methodist and Lakeburg Presbyterian church outreach committees greeted my research sorties with good humor; thanks to their pastors for welcoming me. The directorship of the Urban Religious Coalition changed, but the participant-observer was still there, listening, trying to figure it out. I'm grateful to the URC's succeeding director who, like the first, made me feel not just tolerated but valued. Very much the same goes for the Adopt-a-Family project, and director Evan, to whom I'm extremely grateful for introducing me to the project and inviting me to observe. I admire the members of the Community in Christ and Lakeside Reformed church groups for their openness in welcoming a researcher to observe their new kind of community service. Pastor Nick surprised me by offering me a research site before I even had asked to be invited. He and his church group members offered me human warmth and humor; I appreciated both greatly.

Academic thinking toward this book began during a wonderful fellowship year at the Annenberg School for Communication, University of Pennsylvania. I thank program director Elihu Katz and fellow visiting scholars for conversations I still think about.

In the Sociology department at Wisconsin, Pamela Oliver first suggested that the Urban Religious Coalition might be an interesting organization to study; I can hardly thank her enough for the suggestion. Pam read multiple iterations of this project closely and insightfully, talked me up, or down, as need be, and helped steward me through assistant professorhood to tenure in the department with grace, unending forbearance, and support of my work, for which I'm deeply grateful. Adam Gamoran was a perceptive reader and wonderful chair. Jerry Marwell cheerfully endured cascades of professional questions; Erik Wright and Myra Marx Ferree offered wonderfully incisive comments and treated me to lively conversation about earlier chapter drafts. Thanks also to Jane Piliavin, Phil Gorski, Mitch Duneier, and Doug Maynard for helpful observations. Living with this project would have been a lot harder without the companionship of Mark Suchman and Mustafa Emirbayer. I learned from my advisees and seminar students and have plenty more to learn; thanks especially to Kelly Besecke, Mimi Schippers, Susan Munkres, Lyn Macgregor, Gianpaolo Baiocchi, Scott Hoffman, and Jesse Norris.

I feel fortunate for a rich variety of mentors and intellectual compatriots who contributed much as this project unfolded. A fellowship year at Princeton University's Center for the Study of Religion enabled me to finish the first draft of the manuscript. Robert Wuthnow, Center director, was an extremely thoughtful reader, and a sensitive and supportive listener who always seems to have pursued the questions that compel me, years before I embrace them. The fellows and staff at the Center made for a delightful year of conversations that deepened and broadened my thinking about religion and civic life. Thanks especially to Marie Griffith, Anita Kline, Gus Niebuhr, and Philip Ziegler, and to Princeton University for supporting the Center and a fabulous intellectual environment around it. For comments on chapter drafts, for seasoned advice, for conversations that I hope never are finished, for being a marvelous audience from the earlier stages of this project onward, or for all of these things and more, profuse thanks to Michèle Lamont, Robert Bellah, Penny Edgell, Lyn Spillman, Jeffrey Alexander, Ann Swidler, James Hunter, Richard Wood, Mitchell Stevens, John Evans, Ed Lehman, Verta Taylor, and Ann Mische. I am grateful too to people who kept me and my ideas company, gave me useful feedback, and helped in all sorts of ways as I got closer to the end of writing; they include Marcel Fournier, Yolande Cohen, Sid Tarrow, Daniel Kleinman, Jane Collins, Rhys Williams, Nancy Ammerman, Suzanne Staggenborg, Sharon Hays, Sarah Corse, Bethany Bryson, Courtney Bender, Doug Mitchell—even though I went with one of his competitors—Tom Streeter, Ron Jacobs, Jeff Olick, Francesca Polletta, Anne Kane, Steve Hart, Mark Chaves, Neil Gross, John Wilson, Stan Katz, Rob Smith—who played subway-chase with my runaway manuscript, uptown and downtown, and finally won—Matteo Bortolini, Adam Seligman, Daniel Cefai, Pierrette Hondagneu-Sotelo, Mike Messner, Jon Miller, and Don Miller.

I regret I cannot thank by name all the people who heard talks on some part of this project and offered helpful suggestions, thought-provoking questions, and intriguing insights. Gleefully, however, I thank the Center on Religion and Democracy, at the University of Virginia, for hosting the best five-day intellectual sleepaway camp ever—a writer's workshop. I'll long remember mulling over book manuscripts with writer colleagues; thanks especially to Chuck Mathewes, Pam Cochrane, Steven Jones, and James Hunter for making possible a set of conversations that enriched my book and my imagination. I'm grateful to the Lilly Endowment's Louisville Institute and its winter seminar for grantees, where James Lewis and Nancy Ammerman brought together senior and junior scholars who created together in so little time a lively community of inquiry. Thanks to the Endowment for a summer research grant that enabled me to figure out what was religious about Park Cluster.

Thanks indeed to my research assistant, Brady Potts, who tamed the wilds of my reference and footnote sections, and offered expert computer assistance with a smile, no less. I am grateful to Ian Malcolm at Princeton University Press for supporting this project, fielding my many questions, and finessing the manuscript through the editorial process. Comments from reviewers and the Press's own editorial board helped make this a stronger book.

Nina Eliasoph knows this book awfully well. A very long-running friendly argument with her goaded me to start the fieldwork. She as well as our kids, Olivia and Leo, were sympathetic sojourners; I knew that the book had become a familiar inhabitant in our home when Olivia began asking whether the latest conversation she had overheard was about one of my pseudonymous church volunteers. Nina has been an intellectual companion extraordinaire all the way through. It is hard to imagine carrying off this project without being able to share tenuous insights in the making with a brilliantly quirky partner who could sift and ponder with me, and make it all feel worth it. Nina was a muse who shined warm light on this project, and my life. Long may we collaborate in pondering society's perplexities.

Elusive Togetherness

INTRODUCTION

IT WOULD have been hard to guess from the beige linoleum tile floor, the white cinderblock basement walls, or the big aluminum coffee pots labeled "regular" and "decaf" standing at attention near the doorway. You would not know it from scanning the people in the room, either. Here were late middle-aged, white church volunteers in cotton shirts and tan slacks. Neither the scene nor the people would look very remarkable to many middle-class people in the American midwest. But soon after the director of the Urban Religious Coalition opened this meeting in the basement of Lakeburg Presbyterian Church, on September 18, 1996, it struck me that something historic was happening. Lakeburg's religious community was going to define caring in a new, ambitious way. Church groups were going to build new relationships with social service providers and community action groups, as they responded to the drastic social welfare policy reforms that President Clinton recently had signed into law.

I was at my first meeting of the Humane Response Alliance. People in the audience were worried about what welfare reform was going to mean for kids, people in nursing homes, recent immigrants. One volunteer walked us through the facts and figures in her elaborate handouts, trying to make the impending policy changes more concrete for us. Each month, 3.5 percent of the state's welfare caseload would be dropped from the rolls. Some of these "cases" would be people with compounded problems, another volunteer reminded us. He pointed out that some of these people had chronic medical conditions they could not afford to treat. They would not have had much schooling. Some would have a drug habit. We could not expect these people to move easily into the workforce, no matter how rosy the job market was just then. The volunteer spoke descriptively, not judgmentally. He was somber. "Not to be doomsday, but this is not trivial. It's an incredible challenge to the community."

How different this all sounded from what else I had heard about welfare reform. The Lakeburg daily paper had quoted state officials sporting an easy confidence with the policy changes. It would be a "walk in the park," the governor said. Outside this room, I had not heard anyone ask what would happen to poor immigrants or sick people who could not work. Urban Religious Coalition executive director Donald sounded urgent. Invoking the words of a presidential hopeful of that election season, Donald told us, "We need to look for new solutions. Bill Bradley says we need to find new ways to link the private and public sector." We in the Humane Response Alliance would try to "reconnect the caring community."

Neither Donald nor anyone else in this sprawling basement meeting-room sounded happy about the strict new limits on welfare payments. No one said that church groups could or should take over social service as state-sponsored services shrank. At the same time, Donald was saying that people of faith had civic obligations to the community at large, and needed to figure out new ways to practice them.

I was starting a new study of religiously based community service groups. I had been interested in changing styles of public involvement in the United States. Research for an earlier book had taught me that "being involved" could mean very different things to different people, with different consequences for collective action. I wanted to learn more about what being involved in local community life meant to religious people. Church-based volunteer groups were an oddly understudied part of community life in the United States, and this was a fascinating time to begin studying them.

So I followed a variety of church-based community service groups and projects, over three and a half years. I chose groups from the Protestant religious majority in the United States. I listened in as the Humane Response Alliance tried to strengthen civic bonds and build new ones in the wake of welfare reform. I listened in and joined in with other groups, some of them originally sponsored by the Humane Response Alliance. One of these produced educational workshops for local churches on the politics of welfare reform. Members of another cosponsored a public health nurse and an "eviction prevention" fund for apartment residents in a low-income neighborhood of African Americans, southeast Asian, and Spanish-speaking immigrants. Others put on evening events for "at-risk" teenagers, housed and fed homeless people in church basements as part of a revolving shelter program in Lakeburg, or kept elementary schoolers busy during a two-week summer camp. There was also a coalition of pastors, liberal and conservative, who met monthly to publicize their stand against racism in Lakeburg; some of the pastors figured that racial tensions would only increase as welfare reform left more people with fewer means of survival. I studied a theologically conservative Protestant network that organized different church groups to "adopt" families and support them as their breadwinners tried making the transition from welfare to work. I attended executive board meetings, meetings to plan special public events, and meetings of county social service workers, too. My earlier book had treated different kinds of activists. This time I hoped to learn about community groups of a sort I had not studied before, ones that make up a big part of ordinary civic life in the American cultural mainstream.

I especially wanted to find out how these groups created relationships beyond the group. How would people in my groups reach out to people they wanted to help, to other community groups, or to state agencies? How would they negotiate social inequality, religious and cultural diversity? Would the groups encourage members to spiral outward into relationships with people they would never meet otherwise? I listened carefully as the groups tried to create bridges outward. Would these groups do what so many theorists and commentators had argued, and hoped, they would do—build a greater community?

My discoveries became this book. I saw how hard it was for well-intentioned groups to go out and create civic community. I learned that the different *customs* which kept the groups themselves together strongly influenced the kind of relationships group members could try to create in the larger community. I found that it took a very flexible, willingly self-critical kind of group, one with particular customs, to create bridges across big social divides. Deep caring was good but not nearly enough. The support of state agencies was important, but not enough. It was not enough to have the "right" civic-minded ideas, the right discourse, either. My focus on customs contributes a different perspective to the ongoing conversation about civic engagement in America, at a time when America's social contract is being rewritten.

How would these religious groups bring religion into the civic arena? Would their very identity as religious groups promote divisiveness in Lakeburg's community life or create friction with county social service agencies? In fact I did not hear a great deal that was obviously religious at all in these groups, outside the conservative Protestant network. If we imagine bringing religion into the civic arena, often we imagine people praying in public or expounding on what sacred texts say about what other people should do or not do. I found a different way in which people bring religious meanings into the civic arena: Simply by following their customary group routines, they signal to themselves and others that they are religious people. These quiet signals of religious identity sometimes help people carry out civic obligations together. Different ways of signaling religious identity also can widen divisions inside community groups, even when members agree on the religious beliefs behind their group goals.

In the time since I started on my research rounds in Lakeburg, many studies of both secular and religious voluntary groups have used the concept of social capital. In these studies, social capital refers to the social networks, norms, and mutual trust that keep citizens working together on common projects. When I began, I had been fascinated by political scientist Robert Putnam's historical study of civic life in Italy; he used the concept of social capital to grasp the civic traditions that he argued were strong in some Italian regions and weak in others. I wanted to study the civic traditions of the United States. Like many sociologists, I read Putnam's succeeding study of American civic life, which found that civic group memberships had been dropping precipitously for three decades starting at the end of the 1960s. America was losing its stock of social capital, Putnam argued. A tremendous scholarly debate ensued, just as I started going to Humane Response Alliance meetings, as some scholars became alarmed at the possibility that democracy and social solidarity in America were disintegrating. The debate has continued at the same time that Putnam's version of the social capital concept has diffused widely.

As my own study continued I became convinced that the social capital concept could not address some of the core questions motivating the whole debate. Didn't we need to know more about different kinds of ties, and the meanings of those ties, if we were going to understand what civic groups can and cannot contribute to a greater civic togetherness in America? This study will not catalogue all the social ties that people in the Lakeburg groups created. That was not my goal. My goal was to understand how different meanings that groups gave to ties might influence the relationships they could create as they reached out beyond the group.

Some scholars have argued that the recent attention to local voluntary associations is dangerously misplaced. Americans need to confront our problems with national politics, they say. Securing more affordable housing or jobs that pay a living wage will take far more than helping hands and caring hearts in the local world of church-basement homeless shelters and food pantries. These critics argue that people who exhort Americans to join more voluntary organizations only deflect attention from the cold, hard necessity of political work.

While this is not a book about how to change society, little in it would challenge the role of political work in addressing social problems justly. To study local civic groups is not to imply that these groups can answer all or even most of a complex society's problems. Studying local civic groups teaches us a lot, however, about how and why ordinary citizens distinguish "political" from "charitable but not political" activities; the lines are neither natural nor always so obvious. I learned in Lakeburg that drawing a sharp distinction between politics and charity can disempower critical political discussion while narrowing a caring sensibility. For readers interested in the political potential of civic groups, this book points out that a group needs much more than an incisive, articulate analysis of social problems in order to be a good conduit of consciousness raising. Groups need the *customs* that can welcome people to social criticism instead of scaring all but those already convinced. Lacking those customs, groups may remain critical, prophetic, and sincere, but small and lonely.

Having read about religion's place in American civic life, I supposed that church-based volunteers might have a well-rooted sense of social responsibility that would promote enduring, community-building responses to welfare reform. I did meet people with a noble, self-sacrificing sense of social responsibility. Yet many were frustrated a lot of the time, not just with the new political context but with their own efforts. I saw and heard much more disappointment and self-doubt than I had expected. This book's scenes from the field show hardworking people of goodwill getting frustrated, because that is what I saw and heard as a participant-observer. We can learn a great deal from following closely how they constructed their groups and how they tried to create relationships with other people beyond the group. While one group was succeeding, on its own terms, in creating new bridges to people outside the group, the others were not—or else were not trying to create new civic ties at all, even though some sociological writings would impute that goal to them. I learned that volunteering often did not build community.

As a citizen and sometimes fellow volunteer, I can say easily that all of the groups and projects showed their participants to be people of goodwill, often forbearing people, sometimes very open-minded people. As a sociologist, I find the groups were constrained as well as empowered by cultural customs that no single person changes immediately at will. Cultural customs played a subtle, important role in making a broader togetherness elusive for most of the groups.

A Message to People of Faith

Some group members wondered why a Jewish sociologist wanted to study Christian community groups. The answer was easy: In a largely Christian country, one whose religious groups have been considered a major bulwark of democracy, it is important to study Christian community groups.

It is also fascinating. Ever since Durkheim, sociologists have pondered the relations between religion and social togetherness. But as a non-Christian, I consider myself particularly well disposed to learn how those relations work in the groups I studied, by taking as interesting what other scholars raised as Christians might take for granted. Having introduced myself as a sociologist and Jew to the groups, I hoped that members might relate to me as a sympathetic and interested outsider. When they did so, I learned a great deal. After one meeting of an ecumenical antiracism coalition, for instance, an evangelical pastor confided to me that his "mainline colleagues" made him uncomfortable because they were willing to include nature worshipers in a multicultural celebration. If I were a mainline, liberal Protestant, or if I had put myself off as completely hip to the differences between strands of Protestant Christianity, the pastor might not have ventured this far with me. Of course I had read studies of different kinds of Protestant faith before setting out with this project. But my outsider identity probably made my participant-observer's refusal to take things for granted all the more comprehensible to the people I studied. Parts of my relationship to the groups had little to do with religion.

I was also an academic amongst people sometimes wary of academics; a man in his late thirties amongst women and men in their fifties, sixties, and seventies; a short person with dark, curly hair and a prominent nose amongst people whose features more often than not bore out a Scandinavian or German heritage. I did not look, or sound, like a typical member. Yet, I was also a parent, like most of the people in this study; a citizen who read a local newspaper; a political progressive, like some though certainly not all of the group members. Not all my relationships in the field were relationships across religious or ethnic lines. Once we start to think about it, we will always find that researchers and the researched alike carry multiple identities, some more salient than others, some far more incumbent upon us than others. Being sensitive to multiple identities can help researchers understand the researched. That does not mean researchers can or should zero in on similarities and affect an easy identification with the people we study. It does mean there are potentials for creating connections, slowly and painfully perhaps, that help us think or feel *something* like what the people we study think and feel, *some* of the time.

A MESSAGE TO PROGRESSIVE SCHOLARS

Historian Michael Kazin has observed that the American left is often more wary of religion than intrigued by it. Students of religion and politics agree that religion only rarely gets recognized for its power to inspire movements for peace and social justice—though that is starting to change. It would not be surprising if politically progressive scholars wondered why they should be interested in religious community groups. Aren't these groups part of the problem? Don't they counsel politeness rather than protest, the hereafter rather than the here-and-now? Unless religious community groups are sites of critical consciousness raising, why should political progressives care about them?

Few theorists of progressive political change have written more perceptively on consciousness raising than Antonio Gramsci. And Gramsci has sensitized many social researchers to care about civic activity outside of political groups. Our standpoint on the social world, no matter what political valence, develops not only in school and at work but in civic interaction, as we participate in neighborhood associations, sports leagues, religious congregations, service organizations, or activist groups. Anyone interested in the potentials for popular, progressive thinking in the United States should be interested in religiously based groups that occupy such a substantial part of the American civic arena.

Chapter One

IN SEARCH OF THE SOCIAL SPIRAL

LISTENING TO CIVIC GROUPS REACH OUT

"Feelings and ideas are renewed, the heart enlarged, and the understanding developed only by the reciprocal action of men one upon another."[1] Social observers quote few sentences more frequently than this one, written by the famous nineteenth-century observer of American life, Alexis de Tocqueville. He was describing what could happen when people participate in civic groups. Many theorists and commentators cite Tocqueville's paean when they argue that civic groups help people spiral outward: By participating in civic groups, people's horizons expand so that they come to care more about people not only in the group, but in the wider community. The idea is that civic groups thicken the ties that bind society. They do more than introduce people to new ideas or help them accomplish goals. In this view, civic groups act as local workshops of social solidarity.

This is a study of what people say and do together in local civic groups. How if at all does participating in these groups create connections to the wider community? What does it mean to people when they "connect to the wider community" in a diverse, unequal, complex society? For over three years, I observed and participated alongside religiously based, community service groups in the midwestern U.S. city of Lakeburg as they responded to the historic welfare policy reforms of 1996. All the groups tried to reach out and bridge different kinds of social divides. With Tocqueville's famous claim in mind, I watched and listened closely to see how everyday interaction inside these groups might open up, or shut down, opportunities for members to build ties to diverse individuals, groups, or state agencies beyond the groups.

Though relatively few social scientists have observed civic groups up close, many care about them.[2] Routinely they say these groups are places in which people learn to deliberate about public issues, and to look out for each other and the wider world—to become citizens and members of society.[3] "Civic groups" include community centers, service clubs, citizen advocacy groups, social movement organizations, town hall forums, volunteer associations, e-mail discussion groups, churches, synagogues, mosques, and religiously based alliances. In everyday conversation Americans often distinguish "civic" from "religious," but religious groups are civic groups in widely accepted social-science terms. They turn out to be central to civic life in the United States.

As my long list suggests, American civic groups can take very different shapes. Some of these have become far more common while others have become less typical. Fifty years ago, many American civic groups were local chapters of national federations. People joined a local chapter, organized by other unpaid members, and they saw themselves as serving a locale in general, or sometimes a religious or ethnic group in the locale. They joined groups like the Elks clubs, Moose clubs, League of Women Voters groups, or B'nai Brith chapters, which still exist today. Increasingly, civic groups are professionally run, highly specialized, and loosely connected to larger networks and short-term coalitions of many sorts. Members see themselves as pursuing particular issues, or a particular social agenda, with like-minded others. Good examples are the Gray Panthers, Mothers Against Drunk Driving, feminist health collectives, Greenpeace, or the Lesbian and Gay Task Force.[4] Whatever shape these organizations take, social scientists have looked to them as generators of "feelings and ideas," as Tocqueville put it, that keep citizens talking and working with each other.

With that perspective, sociologists group together this wide variety of groups, associations, and networks and say that these constitute "civil society." In the simplest terms, civil society is the voluntary realm of social life outside the family, the economy, and the state.[5] I will use the term sparingly because it connotes an easily defined sector of society that would defy reality. For my purposes "civic" describes a kind of social relationship, not a sector of society. As a shorthand phrase, "civic groups" means groups in which people relate to each other and to the wider society *primarily* as citizens or members of society, rather than as subjects of state administration or as consumers, producers, managers, or owners in the marketplace. They relate to each other "civic-ally." Civic relationships sometimes develop inside or in conjunction with state institutions or commercial enterprises.[6]

The Lakeburg religious organizations and projects I studied easily count as "civic groups." Most of them belonged to one of two networks made up of churches. One was a mostly liberal or "mainline" Protestant, urban service network, and the other was a smaller, mostly conservative or evangelical Protestant network of churches.[7]

In this variety of groups and projects, I heard people renewing ideas, "enlarging the heart," in very different ways. But enlarged horizons did not often result in an outward-bound spiral of social bonds.

In the Humane Response Alliance (HRA), volunteers and social service professionals became more alarmed the longer they talked about how the city of Lakeburg should respond to the new welfare policy reforms. The HRA network leaders met monthly, hoping to create new relations between churches and social service groups. They wanted to piece together a social safety net. They incubated lots of new ideas. One pastor said churches should buy old hotels and convert them to low-income housing. A family services administrator said that volunteers needed to "have a spiritual experience that gives them ownership of the community." The HRA director talked about field hospitals—simple health-care centers housed in local churches—for people who could no longer afford medical attention. Families were already starting to camp out in the family ser-vice administrator's office hallway. I pictured sick and hungry people with no place to go. I always left these meetings feeling grim and agitated. Dreading a cascade of social fallout from the new policies, one pastor declared, "I'm think-ing of the Holocaust, the tremendous power of people to do ill to one another. It could get much worse."

Members brought to the alliance more than their deep concerns and deep foreboding. Each had years of experience running or volunteering in commu-nity groups. County officials said over and over that they were open to new state-civic partnerships. Sometimes they admitted that they did not know what to plan for these new times.

As much as they cared and as hard as they tried, the HRA had a hard time imagining, let alone building, ties with the social service agencies and churches they hoped would help them "reconnect the caring community" as Donald had put it. The longer they talked, the more desperately they worked to define tasks for volunteers to carry out, and the more frustrating the entire HRA effort be-came to them. After a valiant year, the HRA network dissipated. Counter to the Tocquevillian thesis, I found that there was a disconnect between the style of in-teraction in the group and the broader, civic-minded relationships they hoped to create.

During the same year, eight evangelical Protestant churches each committed a volunteer group to participate in an Adopt-a-Family program, a very differ-ent response to welfare reform. These mostly white groups from suburban churches would learn how to offer "Christ-like care" to mostly African Ameri-can, low-income families whose breadwinner was making the transition from welfare benefits to paid work. Following one of the groups closely, I found that their contacts with their "adopted" family widened their horizons, at least in some ways. Some of the group's members had never seen neighborhoods like their adopted family's. Said one, "There were bad spirits there. . . . I saw op-pression. . . . I saw depression all around." The group's leader described this member's experience as culture shock; she agreed. Members reminded each other not to be judgmental, not to suggest breastfeeding to a new mother who already had decided on bottles, not to make family members feel obligated to attend their church services. The group tried to develop a close, compassionate relationship with its family. Members treated one another's ideas about serving the family with goodwill.

Yet the more the group met, the more distant their relationship-building goal became. Members tried harder and harder to practice Christ-like care, and other ways of defining their relationship to the family dropped out of the picture. Members became less convinced that they needed each other in a group at all if they wanted to go out and serve people compassionately. The group faded away after seven months; the entire Adopt-a-Family program dissipated. Again, I found that there was a disconnect between the style of interaction in the groups and the relationships the groups hoped to create.

Another local church-based group, the Justice Task Force, had a still different response to welfare reform in Lakeburg. Task Force members put together statistics on America's growing income gap with a role-playing exercise and created an educational workshop to take to local churches. They were going to teach churchgoers the politics of wealth, poverty, and taxes. Group leader Catherine, a lawyer and director of a statewide peace and social justice network, made it her mission to spread the word that welfare reform served corporate interests. Welfare reform appealed to middle-income taxpayers, she said, because they were smarting from a huge shift in the tax burden over the past forty years, from corporations to individuals. I marveled at consciousness raising in action one night, as Catherine previewed some workshop materials with Task Force members, most of whom were less familiar with the terms of strident social criticism than Catherine. Upon hearing that low- and middle-income people suffered the tax burden more than the wealthy, one woman spontaneously cried out, "*That's not fair!*" Members were saying things they were afraid to say in their own churches, and they were enjoying it. They learned a lot of new things about corporate wealth. The group was fast becoming convinced that America's growing economic divide needed to be publicized at Lakeburg churches.

Once again, group members' "feelings and ideas" were renewed, as Tocqueville would have put it. Despite their passion for the issue, though, members learned little about how to communicate it to others in their own church circles. Few members signed up to put the welfare reform workshop on their churches' Sunday adult education programs. The host of a radical local radio talk show came to a Task Force meeting once and could hardly contain his frustration; he did not return. The educational workshops finally slid off the group's monthly agenda. Again, I discovered a disconnect between the style in which feelings and ideas were renewed in the group and the relationships that the group wanted to create.

Park Cluster, an alliance of churches that was first envisioned in the HRA, had different experiences. Original Cluster members, churchgoers with professional backgrounds, were people from outside the low-income, multiracial Park neighborhood. They drove in to tutor kids, volunteer in a summer camp, or help the local social worker serve pupusas and egg rolls at Park's annual multicultural festival. Over a rocky eighteen months, they did create relationships they had hoped to create with the Park neighborhood center and its black nationalist director. The more they met and talked about difficult, awkward relationships with surrounding people and groups, the more they treated the local social worker as a consultant rather than a director. The group's sense of its own place on the larger social map changed. Toward the end of the study it had begun to create relationships with community notables and school district officials who were not part of their smaller, original circle of volunteer contacts. They were spiraling outward. I discovered that the group's style of interaction itself encouraged members to spiral outward and establish new bridges between Park Cluster and other groups.

Comparing such different kinds of church-based groups, I do not attempt to explain all their frustrations and successes. I set out to hear how members of these groups interacted and how they tried to connect in some way with the wider, diverse social world. I looked for patterns. What made Park Cluster different? I wanted to see if any patterns I discovered in the field would help me address the long-standing argument about civic participation and broad social connections.

A Social Spiral?

Since Tocqueville, many writers have claimed that civic groups promote broad social ties beyond the group. Sometimes it is called the Tocquevillian or neo-Tocquevillian argument about civic life. Yet Tocqueville made many arguments—about civic groups, political groups, institutions, the cultural conditions of the United States—and people read Tocqueville in different ways. So we need a more specific name.

I will call it the social spiral argument: When individuals join a civic group, the *meanings they develop by talking to one another* encourage them to spiral outward, so that they create enduring relationships not only with other group members but with individuals and groups outside the group. As group members, they may create new relationships with sorts of people they would not meet otherwise, people who come from different backgrounds. In the simplest terms, the claim is that the style of interaction inside civic groups affects the kinds of relationships that members can cultivate outside. It is an extremely prominent but not very well specified argument. Phrases like "tend to" are appropriately vague. That the social spiral argument's terms are vague is only more reason to investigate it carefully, because it continues to motivate prominent research and theoretical writing today.

One other, even broader claim often accompanies the first one, so I consider it a part of the social spiral argument too. It is that the broader ties cultivated by civic groups help to empower civil society. This happens when those ties ultimately increase the collective decision-making responsibilities people carry in their capacity as *citizens,* responsibilities that otherwise would belong entirely to agents of the state or else dissolve into individual choices in the marketplace. Put briefly, participation in civic groups would create greater *social self-organization.* Much of each case chapter in this book will investigate the first, core claim about the social spiral. At the end of the case chapters, I will step back and ask, with the second claim in mind, how if at all it makes sense to say that the group empowered social self-organization locally.

Different versions of the social spiral argument conceive social connections and social self-organization in different ways. They recognize that some groups open themselves only to narrowly defined categories of members and exclude everyone else. Those groups do not spiral very far outward at all, and they do not care about helping to steer the larger society. Not all groups care to reach out, but proponents of the social spiral argument suppose that many groups do, and can.

I stress that the social spiral argument is about *meanings* people develop by talking and working together. "Social spiral" does not refer just to the fact that people in community groups create ties; that is no surprise. The point matters because some scholars today laud civic groups for the social ties they create, without asking about meanings. Studies in this vein truncate the social spiral logic that made civic groups matter to Tocqueville, and other social thinkers, to begin with. There is no doubt that people who join groups are physically available for new potential relationships beyond the group. But as the scenes from civic groups in Lakeburg suggest, copresence is not enough. The meanings that group members develop together shape their possibilities for spiraling outward. They are not the only factor, but as this book will demonstrate, they matter greatly.

At the outset, it makes sense to think that at least some civic groups could make people more broad-minded and more interested in broad ties to fellow citizens, too. There are still relatively few systematic studies which can show that civic groups make people think or act in civic-minded ways. Research on the consequences of volunteering, one popular form of civic engagement in the United States, has begun only recently.[8] Sociologist Jane Piliavin summarizes (2003) that few studies can say whether or not adults experience psychological growth or learn new things in voluntary groups. Still, members of volunteer groups do learn the skills of civic participation, and are more likely to become politically active than nonvolunteers (Verba, Schlozman, and Brady 1995). Studies of young people suggest that community service can cultivate civic-mindedness. A study of Minnesota high schoolers showed, for instance, that volunteering heightened the students' sense that community involvement is important. Scholars of volunteering have said that when students combine community service with reflection on that service, the resulting "service-learning" experience can make the students appreciate diverse groups in society more.[9] Appreciating diverse groups is not the same as creating relationships with them, but these studies are suggestive at least.

This book takes a next step. To see if theorists and researchers are right about the horizon-broadening, community-enhancing power of interaction in local civic groups, we have to make the vague, old, influential social spiral argument tractable to investigation today.

ADDRESSING THE QUESTION EMPIRICALLY

How Do They Do Things Together?

On his travels through America, Tocqueville was impressed, sometimes amused, by the ways Americans did things together. He marveled at the contrast with his fellow French citizens: Americans did not think they needed to wait for a body of local notables to tell them what to do. If a road needed improving, local residents formed a group to improve it. Americans seemed to trust each other, and themselves, to take initiative and act together for some greater good. Americans did all sorts of things together in this egalitarian and voluntary way. They built roads, governed towns, pledged each other to sobriety.

By being involved in civic life over time, Tocqueville thought, Americans would come to define themselves and their interests differently. They would learn to do things together *with a widening circle of people.* A social spiral would take shape. In Lakeburg, I watched and listened to how religious community-service group members did things together not only with other members but with people and groups outside the group, to see if Tocqueville and his theoretical descendants were right. Tocqueville's America was vastly different in some ways from today's, and that simple fact influenced the kinds of interactions I focused on most.

Look for Bridges

American civic groups today do things together and reach out in a society we can characterize as economically unequal, racially segregated, and densely packed with large organizations and networks. So it makes good sense to study how civic groups try to bridge different kinds of social and organizational divides. Tocqueville did not say specifically that civic groups could or should create relationships across social inequality, cultural difference, or organizational complexity. The civic realm Tocqueville envisioned was inhabited by townspeople and yeoman farmers who would be relatively homogeneous, socially and culturally, carrying on most of their civic affairs in very local groups.[10] But there is little point in using these nineteenth-century reference points, myopic even for their own time, if we want to assess the social spiral argument now.

The groups in this study all defined for themselves different kinds of bridge-building challenges. There are many kinds of social division. Instead of imposing one criterion for relationships that count as bridges across social divides, I watched to see how the groups defined their own projects of reaching out, how they acted on their own definitions. I listened to groups trying to create the bridges they wanted to create. The variety in this study does a good job of representing different challenges facing U.S. civic groups today. The theoretical background to the customs concept, laid out in the next chapter, supports my research strategy.

The strategy makes sense for a broader reason too. Social scientists are interested in narrow as well as inclusive groups, but few worry whether Americans are *capable* of developing relationships with other individuals or groups that are very similar to themselves. Recent research I discuss below shows how good Americans have been at creating narrowly defined, narrowly self-interested groups. That is not what Tocqueville had in mind. Tocqueville did not think that civic groups alone would create ties that knit society together, and it would be just as foolish to think they can do that now. But if Tocqueville's thinking is at all applicable today—and many contemporary researchers assume it is—then civic groups will have to spiral out beyond themselves and do some amount of bridging too. In terms of my metaphor, any social spiral that does not bridge some social divide is likely to be a short one.

Watch Relationships with the State

Recent theorists of civic life point out that some of the most important relationships that voluntary groups can create are ones with state agencies. Sometimes the state supports civic—that is, participatory, citizen-driven—projects, sometimes because of popular pressure.[11] Increasingly, civic participation means participating in short-term coalitions and alliances between state agencies and nonprofit groups.[12] As sociologists Boltanski and Thévenot (1991) would point out, this mixed institutional environment makes it all the more interesting to ask which logics citizens use to figure out who they are in relation to other people and groups on their social map. How would they decide—and what do the decisions tell us about the power of citizens? I paid close attention to the Lakeburg groups' relationships with state agencies, instead of treating civic groups as isolated, citizen-led efforts.

My Argument in a Nutshell

The social spiral argument needs rethinking. It would have a hard time accounting for how the styles of interaction in the Lakeburg groups often *stunted* the possibilities for spiraling outward and building enduring civic bridges. The social spirals I watched unfolding in the field were often frustratingly short and narrow *in group members' eyes.* Most of the groups, I will suggest, did little to empower civil society, to enhance social self-organization.

Yet, the argument is not simply wrong: Among the Lakeburg groups, the meanings shared inside Park Cluster did help the Cluster spiral outward and create ongoing ties to outside groups—ties that members themselves had not predicted. The social spiral argument deserves credit, too, for the idea that there *is* a relationship between the character of interaction inside a civic group and the kinds of relationships the group can cultivate with the world outside of the group—even if the argument describes that relationship inadequately a lot of the time. I do not reject the social spiral argument altogether; no study of a small number of groups can do that anyway. Instead, through *reconstructing*[13] the argument I suggest a new theory that is more precise, much more qualified, and more useful for further research.

A Paradox of Civic Engagement, a Better Theory of Groups

I discovered that instituting bridges beyond a group often, though not always, threatened dominant definitions of good membership in the group. Reaching outward threatened the solidarity of the groups—even groups that defined themselves as bridge-builders. That is a paradox in light of Tocquevillian thinking. To explain the paradox we need a better theory of group life. My findings lead me to propose that a community group's own togetherness shapes the kind of togetherness it can try to create with the world beyond the group. That does not mean that a society with more tightly knit groups is a society with more togetherness over all. Rather, the different *kinds* of togetherness within civic groups shape the possibilities for spiraling relationships outward.

A theory of group togetherness is the conceptual heart of this study. My theory highlights the power of group-building customs. *Group-building customs are routine, shared, often implicit ways of defining membership in a group.* These customs are themselves meaningful and have their own influence on social action. I name them group-building customs because I want to highlight that there are different, routine, or customary ways to sustain groups. Group-building customs played a crucial role in shaping the Lakeburg groups' potentials for spiraling outward. While mindful that there are many kinds of cultural customs, when I refer to routine, shared ways of defining group membership, I will use the shorter term "customs" for felicity's sake. Different groups in the study followed different customs.

Social Reflexivity

Comparing scenes from the Lakeburg groups alongside evidence from other studies, I suggest that it is easier for a group to build the bridges it wants to build if the group can practice *social reflexivity.* Groups practice social reflexivity when they talk reflectively, self-critically, about their relations with their wider social context—the people, groups, or institutions they see on their horizon. A group can practice social reflexivity when its customs *welcome reflective talk about its concrete relationships in the wider social world.*[14]

Reflexive conversation may seem simply ordinary, utterly unremarkable for a civic group. Yet my experience with the Lakeburg groups suggests that kind of conversation may actually threaten the customs of many civic groups. Groups cannot simply discuss anything at all that may interest individual members privately. Customs set parameters on group discussion. In my study, only Park Cluster sustained social reflexivity for any length of time, and it was the only group that succeeded at the bridge-building it wanted to do. By reflecting, sometimes painfully, on its external relations, the Cluster opened up possibilities for spiraling ties across social differences, and in a modest way it empowered Park residents and churches as decision makers. I heard social reflexivity surface in the other groups occasionally, and usually I heard it cut off. It threatened the groups' customs.

I am saying that *communication about* social ties matters a lot for *creating* social ties. Many of us are accustomed to thinking differently about social ties. Social scientists have often thought of social ties or networks as the "hard," structural facts of social life that strongly shape the "soft," malleable flow of communication between people. That perspective illuminates many important questions, but not my questions. As I will explain in chapter 2, recent writings on social ties and culture are taking a different perspective. They are emphasizing that relationships do not exist outside communication. Rather, a group creates and sustains social ties *through communication.* From this perspective, a group's communication does not simply reflect something else that is more "real" in social relationships. Listening closely to group communication is crucial if we want to understand *how* a group creates bonds, *how* the group spirals outward.

I stress that my argument about social reflexivity emerges from what I discovered in the field about the Lakeburg groups, pictured in chapters 3, 4, 5, and 6. Taken together, those groups' experiences suggested patterns, which I summarize at the end of chapter 6. In appendix I, I consider the potentials and limits of using groups from the city of Lakeburg to discern patterns like these.

Writings by pragmatist thinkers John Dewey and Jane Addams corroborate what I discovered, and sensitized me to interesting exchanges between members, recorded in my field notes. Both writers described, and promoted, something very much like social reflexivity; Addams pictured it colorfully, drawing on her settlement house experiences in Chicago one hundred years ago. The next chapter brings these two practical philosophers into my story. Their insights and Tocqueville's, along with contemporary sociological research, help me theorize customs and social reflexivity. While Dewey's and Addams's writings prefigure what I heard in the field, I ground my findings in contemporary scholarship on culture, groups, and social ties.

The Central Claims and Their Challenge to Current Thinking

Mine is an alternative to the social spiral argument, then. It has four main claims. First, civic groups maintain distinctly different customs—not just "civic-minded" or "anti-civic-minded" customs—and these give groups different styles of reaching out. The customs exist apart from the beliefs or ideologies that groups hold. Second, those customs influence the kinds of conversations a group can have; they can welcome or discourage social reflexivity. Third, social reflexivity enhances a group's ability to create or strengthen enduring, civic bridges across a variety of social differences.

Finally, the Lakeburg groups' experiences lead me to an argument about *how* people bring religion into public life. We often think of people making religion public by proclaiming religious teachings about what is good, or bad, to do. I found that groups can also bring religion into civic life in a much quieter way, by using religious meanings to understand their civic role in the wider world even if they rarely or never expound on religious teachings. Apart from influencing a group's stated *goals,* religious meanings influence customs; they provide some of the building blocks for a group identity in the wider civic arena. Scenes from the field in Lakeburg showed me, too, that religion is not necessarily a divisive force in civic life as we sometimes think. But when it is, the divisiveness may come from religious influences on customs, rather than religious influences on members' beliefs about social issues.

Group-building customs and reflexivity are not *enough* to create bridges beyond the group. Others already have argued that external, social-structural, and political conditions strongly influence what kinds of ties groups can build. My accounts of the Lakeburg groups incorporate this big, important point. At the same time this study highlights the powerful contribution of group culture in a way that others do not. Tocqueville's writings do not capture the variety of civic group cultures in the United States today, but he recognized that power of group culture more than do some of his contemporary champions.

A skeptic might ask what difference it makes if I argue that bridge-building goes more successfully when civic groups reflect on their social relationships. Who would dispute the value of reflection? My argument, first, is quite different from prominent, existing arguments about civic engagement. Some scholars say that it takes the right governmental policy or the right institutional framework to foster broad, civic-minded ties; customs and qualities of communication play little part in their thinking.[15] Along parallel lines some might suggest that these ties develop only when there is a congenial structure of political opportunity.[16] Some scholars of institutional change might suggest that social service bureaucracies define narrow slots for civic groups that would strongly determine the customs and probably preclude much social reflexivity.[17] And from a still different angle comes a communitarian argument, that civic groups need to ratify core moral values instead of enduring the open-ended questioning of social reflexivity, if they are going to create broad civic ties.[18] Case study chapters will elaborate on these viewpoints, mining their potential contributions. Still they show that these other viewpoints are inadequate to the task of explaining what I discovered about civic groups and relationships beyond the group. We may not be used to thinking that talk itself is the sort of "big" force that makes things happen in society; the case chapters illuminate the crucial role of talk.

There is more: Practicing social reflexivity is not the same as talking a *lot*, nor is it just another phrase for "talking about public issues" or "talking in a caring way." Chapter 2 lays out the conversational substance of social reflexivity in more detail, and describes how I identified it in my groups. And there is a broader message in my story about social reflexivity: If the civic arena is the realm in which citizens can exchange ideas freely and expand their horizons, as many theorists have argued, it is an odd thing that socially reflexive talk would be so rare there. It is odder still that, in a time when social scientists are discovering reflexivity in modern politics, in everyday understandings of the self, and even in religion, reflexivity may exist in theory much more than fact in contemporary American civic life.[19] With the cases in view, the concluding chapter returns to this perplexing observation.

My story about group interaction is different from others, too. This is a book not only about how civic groups work but how culture works. Many studies are analyzing culture in civic and political groups—at historic rallies and protests, in church committee meetings, on television talk shows. Insisting, as I do, that meanings matter, these scholars analyze communication—in discourses, vocabularies, or collective action frames, to name a few current analytic terms. Scholars of religious groups follow suit, analyzing vocabularies of compassionate service or discerning biblical symbolism in a group's definition of injustice. Different as these approaches to meaning are, they all abstract ideas or communication from the everyday settings in which people communicate. The assumption is that group settings are simply a container or a launch pad for the discourses or symbols or frames that do the work of making meaning.

While I paid attention to the words and phrases the Lakeburg groups used, I heard how the customs of particular group settings gave words and phrases particular meanings. These meanings opened up some lines of action and made others nearly unthinkable. The next chapter lays out this new approach to culture and collective action. Following chapters will show how it illuminates puzzles in the Lakeburg groups that would bedevil other approaches. To spiral outward, groups need more than civic-minded ideas, then. They need to know how to create settings that allow people to think and talk about spiraling outward without threatening the group's own togetherness.

Practical Consequences of the Argument

Paying close attention to ordinary civic groups does more than speak to social theory. Durable customs of group interaction make a very practical difference in what civic groups can and cannot accomplish, independent of opportunities that powerful institutions open for them. These differences mattered to group members themselves, and they matter to people who have studied groups like mine:

Differences in customs gave groups different potentials for collecting and distributing resources. In Park Cluster, for instance, one very vocal member assumed that a good group of churchgoing volunteers is one that funnels lots of donations to needy individuals and supports social workers who do not have enough hours in the day to do everything they would like to do. Most other members came to define a good group as one that builds ties to a neighborhood by helping sponsor public goods the neighborhood wants. Customs clashed in the Cluster. The outcome would determine how the Cluster served the Park neighborhood. Would the Cluster relate to its member churches as aggregates of private individuals who leave old coats and canned vegetables in donation barrels for Park residents, or would it pool collective church resources to support the salary of a public health nurse for the neighborhood?

Obviously both ways of supporting people in a low-income neighborhood can be valuable, but they are quite different ways of organizing resources. It is customary within many churches to define community service as an aggregate of individual, charitable donations and volunteer time; I listened to these customs at work in church outreach committees. Yet, in a time when many churches feel financially strained,[20] congregants may decide that a more collective-oriented approach is more efficient at meeting some needs in low-income neighborhoods. As chapter 6 will show, each way of shepherding resources entailed a different politics of relationship between church volunteers and the neighborhood they wanted to serve.[21] Neighborhood residents noticed the difference.

Scenes from the Adopt-a-Family project highlight the influence of customs on how a group uses or passes up expertise, too. Members of church groups in this project included social workers, even a high-level welfare agency administrator. At first, I heard social service workers trying to draw on their professional know-how to figure out how middle-class church groups could create relationships with their low-income, minority "adopted" families. But speaking with one's professional "hat" on was against the custom in play. Knowledge that might have been useful in a different setting was inappropriate in settings where people customarily defined themselves as humble servants in the spirit of Christ.

Differences in customs and social reflexivity contributed to different kinds of collaboration with county agencies. Customary ideas about the role of volunteers steered the HRA toward what its director himself considered an unsatisfying relationship with the county's welfare administration. Those ideas were reinforced by county social workers' own ways of doing things, but as I will argue, county agents did not just create those ideas on their own and force them on the HRA.

Civic groups need not always fill slots exactly as county officials define them. As Park Cluster's dominant customs changed, members became more and more reflexive about their own place in the civic arena. They related more self-consciously to other groups as partners, less as helpful adjuncts. They applied their "partnership" mode of acting to their relation with the county family services employee who attended their meetings. To her surprise, they argued with her over how to administer a program in the Park neighborhood's interest. Increasingly, research on civic-state partnerships is asking how the state can promote civic empowerment and responsibility "from above." The autonomous power of group-building customs, apart from formally instituted policies, may play an important part in the story.[22]

COMMUNICATING SOCIAL CRITICISM IN RELIGIOUS SETTINGS

One kind of civic "bridge" has mattered to generations of social theorists and researchers, from Antonio Gramsci to Pierre Bourdieu. It is the bridge that activists with critical viewpoints try to create with audiences whom they hope to convince. Activists and the sociologists who study them wonder what kinds of wording, what kinds of symbolism, make "consciousness raising" successful. Chapter 4 pictures critical-thinking churchgoers who want to share their righteous anger over welfare reform with fellow churchgoers. Making few inroads in their own churches, the Justice Task Force actually scared away like-minded potential supporters. The group's customs, not just its critical ideology, made crossing this particular bridge extremely difficult. Justice Task Force members often wondered why the biblical social justice message seemed difficult to discuss in their churches. Their response was to style themselves as critical prophets, standing up to mass-mediated common sense and hostile opinion. Ironically, as much as the group wanted to communicate morally inspired social criticism, vocal members customarily distanced themselves socially from would-be audiences, for the sake of the group's own solidarity as a band of critical thinkers. The Justice Task Force was hardly the first activist group that ever scared off curious visitors and marginalized itself, but my focus on customs offers a different angle on groups styled this way.

Students of American politics and civic life often say that religious groups are important sites for discussing politics and learning civic skills.[23] What kinds of discussions do they allow? Do these settings allow churchgoers to draw a variety of political viewpoints from their moral worldviews, or are some connections harder than others to make? In the case of mainline Protestants, recent scholarship finds a disconnect between biblically grounded, critical viewpoints publicized by denominational headquarters and opinions "in the pews." Denominational leaders wonder why the ideas they publicize in white papers and at press conferences do not percolate more deeply into local churches.[24] Focusing on group-building customs in churches and in church-based advocacy groups may help explain the gap.

CRAFTING MULTIRACIAL ALLIANCES

Focusing on customs also teaches us a lot about quiet barriers that can trip up the most sincere efforts by whites and people of color to work together. Scenes from Lakeburg's religious community service groups showed me that sounding and acting unprejudiced, or even proactively antiracist, was not nearly enough to bridge racial divides. In chapter 3, mostly white church volunteers give their time to chaperone evenings of dancing and indoor games put on for mostly minority "at-risk" teenagers. Surrounded by kids from neighborhoods unlike their own, the volunteers keep up a friendly, affirming demeanor but learn little if anything about the teens or how to create relationships with them. In chapter 5, self-sacrificing white church groups try hard to care deeply about African American former welfare-receiving families without regard to their race. But race will not go away despite their best intentions, and frustrations mount. In chapter 6, a progressive white community leader from Urban Religious Coalition acts stridently and selflessly in the interest of low-income, minority Park residents. Yet acting on other people's presumed interests turns out to be a problem itself that Park Cluster works to overcome. In each of these cases, white, majority culture people failed to bridge racial divides because their assumptions about group life—their customs—got in the way, even while they were decrying injustice or daring to reach out and care.

Social activists have tried piecing together alliances across racial lines to oppose racism, expand civil rights, and fight for equal protection from environmental hazards. Sociologists have tried to understand what makes these efforts conflicted and short-lived. Differences in ideology, leadership style, or understandings of collective identity are important; I would add customs to the list.[25] Customs that keep majority and minority groups from talking self-critically about their relations to one another can have very disappointing, practical consequences for would-be bridge builders.

The Historical Context for This Study

A New Social Contract? The New Attention to "Faith-Based" Community Groups

Front-page news was making religiously based community groups compelling to study when I went to the kickoff meeting of the HRA. In 1996, Congress drastically altered social welfare policy in the United States, and passed on to states the responsibility for putting the new policies into practice. The welfare reform legislation subjected most Americans to a lifetime limit of five years on welfare payments.[26] States could pass their own additional requirements. What would replace a governmentally guaranteed safety net? Some Americans—especially some politicians—hoped that religiously motivated, civic impulses would fill in as government's responsibilities shrank. No matter what political stance I held on welfare reform, it was an interesting time to start studying religious community service groups.

Religiously based volunteer and advocacy groups have been prominent players in American community life, from colonial times onward (Skocpol 2000; Thiemann, Herring, and Perabo 2000). But welfare reform legislation, and its aftermath, heightened the prominence of religious community service groups. The "charitable choice" provision of the 1996 welfare reform package requires government to consider religiously based groups when it contracts with organizations outside of government to provide social services. Charitable choice was supposed to encourage faith-based groups to apply for these contracts.[27] Some of the political rhetoric surrounding welfare reform coincided with the long-standing idea that religious faith promotes healthy social ties in America.[28] No single political position owns the idea: In the 2000 presidential race, candidates of both major parties endorsed an important role for local faith-based groups in the overall social contract with a shrunken federal government.

Policy makers as well as scholars of different political bents have had high hopes for faith-based community groups. None of the groups in this study applied for grants under the charitable choice provision during the time I spent in the field, though toward the end of that time, one of their sponsoring networks hosted a panel of local leaders to address the topic. Studies of religious groups running new social service programs are starting to come in from the field. Though the Lakeburg groups did not run government-funded programs, my study does contribute a distinctive perspective on the larger question of how religiously based community groups can or cannot contribute to a new social contract still being written.

Great Fears, Great Expectations

The study's stakes are high for social scientists and Americans in general as well as for policy makers. When I began going to group meetings in Lakeburg many people, and not just academics, were wondering whether and how American civic groups spiral ordinary citizens into community life. Throughout the 1990s and into the new millennium, social scientists continued to wonder about civic engagement in America. Sociologist Theda Skocpol (1999), for instance, worried that democracy itself was at stake if ordinary citizens allowed professionally run, narrowly defined interest groups to determine citizens' political agendas for them. She has proposed (2000) that religiously based civic groups have a role in a new social contract that would guarantee basic needs for everyone. But what kinds of ties are Americans willing to create, and what kinds will hold the social fabric together? Sociologist Robert Wuthnow found (1998) that many Americans prefer "loose" civic connections instead of enduring ties. Short-term, plug-in style volunteer work helps to keep community life alive in a highly mobile society. For Wuthnow it is an open question, though, whether or not this in-and-out style of civic engagement can bridge social diversity and empower citizens to steer society. Robert Bellah and his research team (1996, 1985) argued more pessimistically that many Americans sequester themselves in enclaves of the like-minded, instead of taking responsibility for more encompassing communities. Communitarian theorist Amitai Etzioni contended (1996) that Americans have indulged in narrow-minded identity politics instead of working together for the common good, and now desperately needed to "remoralize" civil society by dedicating themselves to core values. As public policy scholar Francis Fukuyama saw it (1999), Americans' "radius of trust" was shrinking. None of these writers said that local civic groups, secular or religious, could strengthen the social fabric by themselves. But all hoped that these groups could play a part in regenerating social ties that would empower citizens together.[29]

Political scientist Robert Putnam's stark, much-discussed findings on civic engagement put this ongoing discussion of togetherness in America on a new empirical footing. Writing in 2000, Putnam found that Americans joined far fewer civic groups, socialized less, and trusted public officials less than they had just three decades earlier. Americans have been losing social connections, Putnam concluded. Without those connections, it is harder to work together for the greater good. Putnam's work energized a wide-ranging national debate about American community life, what happened to it, how to regenerate it—if it needs regenerating. The claims of Putnam and other scholars resonated in everyday conversation, as many Americans told researchers and pollsters that they worried about weakening community ties.[30] Mine is not an historical study, so I will not weigh in on whether or not civic groups generate the social spiral less often than they used to. What matters is that Putnam's widely adopted framework presupposes the social spiral argument, even if his own terms of analysis are the wrong ones for testing it out in everyday life.

We need to revisit a classic source of the social spiral argument—Tocqueville—to understand what is missing in prominent contemporary arguments. I want to point out a few of Tocqueville's basic insights that motivate contemporary studies yet elude those studies' own methods and concepts.

A CLASSIC SOURCE

The most frequently cited source is the account of "civil associations," or civic groups, in Tocqueville's *Democracy in America*. To appreciate his account, we need to put aside the popularly received Tocqueville who said that civic groups are the fundamental expression of American democracy and a model to the world. Tocqueville understood American civic relationships to be more tenuous, part of a difficult, in some ways peculiarly American balance of competing and mutually reinforcing tendencies for which he found no long-term guarantees. *Democracy in America* pictured two sets of American public "mores" in tension with each other. One of these was not very civic minded at all: Americans had the custom of withdrawing into their small private circles. Political liberty, and in Tocqueville's view, relatively equal material conditions, freed up individuals to withdraw from public affairs and carve out private lives with a few, close, similarly minded others. "Each citizen isolate[s] himself from the mass of his fellows and withdraw[s] into the circle of family and friends. . . . he gladly leaves the greater society to look after itself."[31] If Americans had the custom of "forever forming associations" (p. 513), it was mainly because they were savvy enough to realize that groups could advance private interests more effectively than individuals alone. Egalitarian group effort made sense in a society of individuals willing to accept each other as social equals. It made sense, also, because in their expressly *political* groups, Americans already would have practiced the arts of association for a common interest, which they could then apply to civic projects (pp. 521–24).

Through interaction in civic groups—"the reciprocal action of men one upon another"—*people would change.* Their imaginations and "hearts" would grow bigger for their fellow citizens. The mores of narrowly self-interested action would expand into "self-interest properly understood," and these citizens would develop the habit of serving others outside their own small circles (p. 513). That does not mean Americans would cease to have particular interests. But by engaging in civil associations, Americans would stretch their social horizons, seeing a good beyond their immediate, private good. Civic associations would counterbalance a "natural" inclination to private pursuits with likeminded friends. Americans perpetually would feel tugged in two directions. But civic groups, Tocqueville hoped, would stretch the narrow social horizons that a commerce-driven society otherwise would cultivate. They would help people develop new meanings for social ties: "self-interest properly *understood*" (emphasis mine), he wrote. Tocqueville implied that civic group interaction had a qualitative dimension.

And with the right qualities of interaction, Tocqueville implied, civic group members would develop not just broader imaginations but *relationships*—ties to others, potentially others beyond the group. *Democracy in America* discussed the horizon-broadening powers of civil associations in the context of a contrast between aristocratic institutions and the "individualism" of democratic societies. "Aristocracy links everybody, from peasant to kin, in one long chain. Democracy breaks the chain and frees each link": Read in this context, Tocqueville was prescribing civic groups as the antidote to the atomizing effects of individualism, the salutary source of "a thousand continual reminders to every citizen that he lives in society" (pp. 508–9, 512). Ideally then, members of civic groups would do more than bond tightly to other members; they might in small ways contribute to refashioning a horizontal "chain" of interdependence appropriate to a democratic society. Like sociologist Robert Wuthnow (1999c), I interpret Tocqueville as arguing that civic groups potentially would encourage relationships with people of diverse stations, outside as well as inside the group. With their discussions of civic "bridging," neo-Tocquevillians such as Robert Putnam reiterate this theme in contemporary language.

There were always countervailing pressures. Between civic-minded service, private material striving, and the liberty to choose either, the democratic balance would be precarious. An ambitious leader might take advantage and grab power while citizens are burrowing deeper and deeper into private life. This oft-recited cautionary scenario embodies the second claim of the social spiral argument: Without the influence of civic groups, busily striving Americans might allow a despot to arise and organize society for them. Narrating it as a more gradual development, Tocqueville predicted that if centralized administration expands, "the more will individuals lose the idea of forming associations and need the government to come to their help" (p. 515). Civic groups generated a civic-minded imagination and social connections; if people stopped forming them, not only would they lose social ties, but their responsibility for organizing society itself would weaken as government agents acquired greater responsibility.

Conservative social thinkers today invoke this specter of creeping despotism to criticize social welfare programs or "big government" in general (Berger and Neuhaus 1977). But we do not need to read Tocqueville as a social conservative;[32] he does not necessarily advocate the commonsense, individualizing connotations of "responsibility," as in "your poverty is your own responsibility." When citizens are taking more ownership of social arrangements, they are taking more "responsibility," yet as sociologist Theda Skocpol points out (2000, 1999), they are not necessarily disempowering government, weakening governmentally guaranteed rights, or saying that only individual failings cause individuals' troubles. Social conservatives, radical democrats, liberals, and a variety of advocates for stronger community life all have anchored some of their claims about civic groups in Tocqueville's writings.[33] As political theorist Mark E. Warren observes, *Democracy in America* has set the terms of discussion for much of the literature on civic associations.[34] So it is worth considering what legacy Tocqueville actually left, and which parts of it motivate current work.

Tocqueville implied that social ties could *mean* different things. He distinguished civic ties born of calculating interest from ties driven by a taste for serving others. He contrasted the sense of social connection in aristocracies with the more flexible and tenuous sense of connection that individualism in a democracy cultivated. It is all very vague; and the potential of civic groups remained vague, too. Realistically speaking, how far and how broadly should we expect the social spiral to unfurl for individual members of any group? How, exactly, would interaction inside the group make ties spiral outward? Tocqueville implied that both imagined relationships—"a thousand continual reminders that he lives in society"—and concrete relationships were important, but he did not specify how the two related to one another.

For a sociologist who wants to know how civic groups work for society, Tocqueville's allusions to meanings and relationships are an intriguing warrant for closer examination. Currently prominent studies that claim Tocqueville's mantle undercut rather than clarify the important if vague role Tocqueville gave civic-minded meanings.   The most influential, current version of the social spiral argument, and the lively critiques of it, offer much more specific terms of inquiry. But they do not inform us enough about the social spiral argument, because they do not pay attention to what ties mean.

NEO-TOCQUEVILLIANISM AND THE REACTION TO IT:
THE ELUSIVE ROLE OF INTERACTION

The Social Spiral as Social Capital

Robert Putnam's (2000, 1996, 1995) argument about civic decline in late-twentieth-century America has greatly popularized the notion that civic groups generate social ties that weave the larger society together. Other neo-Tocquevillians such as Francis Fukuyama (1999) share the thinking. Putnam's social spiral argument depends on his own version of the concept "social capital," which differs from that of James Coleman, Pierre Bourdieu, and others.[35] Three components constitute Putnam's social capital: social networks, norms of reciprocity, and trust. The conceptual troika has diffused phenomenally among both followers and critics of Putnam's work.[36] Figures on declining civic group memberships should trouble us, Putnam argues, because these groups generate social capital, and social capital does many things: It enables citizens to work more easily together on community projects and cross-group alliances; it underwrites the risks of new business enterprises; it eases the way for interest groups to organize themselves; it safeguards the power of civil society to hold government accountable.[37] The first item on this list concerns Putnam greatly, and motivates a distinction between the "bonding" social capital that strengthens cohesion within a group and "bridging" social capital that helps a group connect to other individuals and groups across social differences.[38] The social spiral engages when groups cultivate bridging social capital.

Any concept that proposes to illuminate so much invites criticism. The social capital concept has provoked a great deal of it. Part of the trouble is that social capital is a very heterogeneous category. Many different acts and relationships indicate social capital in Putnam's use of the term: signing a petition, attending a public hearing, becoming a leader of a citizens' organization, attending church regularly. Defined so broadly, it is hard, too, to tell what institutional or social conditions promote social capital; scholars have argued over whether it is political institutions, government policy, the broader culture, or something else that facilitates the social capital in civic groups.[39] Then there is a more fundamental logical problem in using the concept: The same relationships that are consequences of a group's social capital, like a community organizing campaign for better housing, are also sources of the group's social capital, and indicators of it too. The U.S. civil rights movement must have required a lot of social capital, but it also *is* social capital (Putnam 2000, p. 23). Critics have alighted on the circularity problem already (J. Wilson 2001; Portes 1998), but it is acute for anyone who wants to understand *how* if at all the social spiral works; the social capital concept will not help us pinpoint different stages in the outward-bound process.

The social capital framework thrives by assimilating criticisms of itself. It sprouts new subcategories and dimensions: Proponents of the framework are distinguishing more types of social capital beyond the "bonding" and "bridging" variants: There is formal and informal social capital, thick and thin social capital, inward-looking and outward-looking social capital (Putnam and Goss 2002, pp. 9–11). Social capital researchers realize "bridging" itself is very vague, and suggest four different types of bridging social capital (Warren, Thompson, and Saegert 2001). These all are useful refinements for some research purposes. But as I discovered in Lakeburg, people develop qualitatively different kinds of "bridging" relationships, very different social spirals with different potentials for crossing social differences or empowering civil society.

Social capital researchers can say reasonably enough that these qualitatively different relationships all fit into the conceptual box of social capital. But if we want to know *how* civic groups work, how groups cultivate and use what researchers call social capital, we need a different concept. We need a framework that can recognize different styles of relationship from the start, instead of trying to convert them into different denominations of a single social "capital."[40]

Implicitly, some social capital researchers want to understand the ties that constitute social capital in qualitative terms. That is why only certain kinds of civic or political groups counted in Putnam's *Bowling Alone.* These do not include the many mass-membership interest groups such as the American Association of Retired Persons or professional nonprofit groups that develop global food policy or advocate civil rights in developing countries. In many of these groups, being a member means paying dues, receiving a quarterly update, maybe signing an e-mail petition. Members write checks; they do not often interact with other members. Virtual civic interaction won't count either; Putnam considers "Perot-style electronic town hall meetings" to be sorry substitutes for real civic community. Critic Debra Minkoff contends (1997) the virtual identities that national interest groups promote can produce a valuable sense of connection for marginalized people, lesbians and gay men for instance, who might otherwise fear "there is no one like me" in their own locales. In the neo-Tocquevillian account, professionally run interest groups and new forms of electronic democracy all lack an ill-specified *quality* of relationship. They are not deeply civic-minded, and less likely to promote an enriching, democratic experience, than are face-to-face groups.

The social capital concept itself is much bigger than the Tocquevillian tradition. It does not need a Tocquevillian heritage to do interesting work for social science.[41] But like Tocqueville, Putnam does *assume* that democratic ties spiral outward from meanings shared in face-to-face local groups, even if the social capital concept cannot distinguish meanings. *Bowling Alone* affirmed its roots in Tocqueville explicitly: It associated social capital with the older concept of civic virtue; it lauded civic groups for cultivating habits of public spiritedness; it quoted the same famous sentence that began this chapter. Tocqueville implied these were matters of meaning. Other social capital scholars, in turn, acknowledge the influence of Putnam's unquestionably important work.[42] Implicitly then, the neo-Tocquevillian social capital framework affirms that civic meanings matter. But it treats the "trust" or "norms" of social capital as quantifiable entities abstracted from meanings. A group, or a society, has more or less social capital; measures of social capital depend heavily on group membership and social participation statistics.

These statistics can be fascinating, and worrisome; they raise a variety of interesting questions. When it comes to researching the social spiral, though, focusing intently on these statistics misses the point altogether. By themselves the statistics do not inform us on how the "feelings and ideas" generated in civic groups will set the social spiral in motion; they do not tell us about the meanings of ties. The neo-Tocquevillian social capital framework has Tocquevillian aspirations but cannot live up to them.

To be fair, Putnam's main goals in both the United States and earlier Italian research (1993) were to offer broad historical overviews of nationwide civic engagement. Embarking on a long historical tour across entire nations, it makes sense to pack lightly, and rely on a concept that is flexible enough to accommodate all the local variation. The social capital concept offers a valuable bird's eye view of some big trends in collective life. We simply should recognize its limits, and not fall into the trap of asking only those questions about civic engagement that the concept can answer. Social capital is a conceptual telescope. The social spiral argument requires a microscope.

The Critical Response: Contentious Groups, Illiberal Groups, Racist Groups

Critics of neo-Tocquevillian thinking already have challenged the value of civic groups. They point out that these groups do not always cultivate a civic-minded spiral outward. Sometimes they screen out social diversity and endanger democratic government. These critics' historical studies show the limits of civic groups as workshops of solidarity. Sobering and valuable, they give good grounds for skepticism about the social spiral argument . They do not weigh in on it directly, though, since they do not examine group interaction. Their criticisms have informed my ethnographic inquiry; a brief look at them highlights what is distinctive in my study.

Some readers draw from *Democracy in America* that civic groups characteristically promote social harmony and liberal governance. Sociologist Michael Young (2002, 2001) takes sharp aim at the first assumption. He argues that some of the most important civic associations in the antebellum period just after *Democracy in America* was written were aggressive cultural warriors, literally fighting to impose an expansive organizational style and an abstract vision of God's country on the nation as a whole. Young's history of sometimes bloody episodes of Christian organization building does not bear directly on the social spiral argument, but does usefully remind us that civic associations may spiral outward in rivalry with other associations, not in concert with them. Political scientist Sheri Berman (1997) makes trouble for the second assumption. Berman argues that Germany's vibrant civic group life of the late-nineteenth and earlier-twentieth centuries fragmented society into group-based fiefdoms, disempowering a liberal state. Shorn of civic support, the weakly institutionalized political structure of the Weimar republic stood by, unable to block Nazi advances. Berman was not investigating civic groups' ability to spiral outward and thicken civil society itself, but her history poses an intriguing challenge to the social spiral argument: Civic organizations, she found, often catered to particular political and social constituencies. " [S]ocialists, Catholics, and bourgeois Protestants each joined their own choral societies and bird-watching clubs. . . . They tended to hive their memberships off from the rest of society" (Berman 1997, p. 426). They created social tunnels, not social spirals. Watching and listening closely, we can discover how processes inside civic groups, and not only the surrounding political context that Berman investigates, influence how much bridging the groups can accomplish.

Civic groups are just as capable of building moats as bridges. That is one of the central messages in sociologist Jason Kaufman's (2002) study of American civic clubs between the Civil War and World War I. Like Berman, Kaufman tells a story of segmentation that would challenge the thrust of the social spiral argument if applied on a national scale. In a decades-long fit of "competitive voluntarism," Americans of different ethnic, religious, and class backgrounds formed their own social clubs and mutual aid societies, emulating the successful organizations formed by their foes and competitors. Kaufman proposes that the growing field of civic associations entrenched social and cultural differences rather than bridging them. He deduces "a stark challenge to the argument that associationalism can help bridge gaps in the social fabric, joining disparate populations together in fellowship and solidarity" (2002, p. 8), the argument he associates with Robert Putnam.

The critics reveal an unsavory world of culture-warring, politically escapist, racist, and religiously bigoted groups. Critics have focused on the kinds of groups that would give neo-Tocquevillian arguments the most trouble, the "exceptions" to their general claims. Some groups draw brittle boundaries around narrowly defined identities. If a group's by-laws exclude blacks, Catholics, and Jews, for instance, we might assume we do not need to look any further into how group process orients the group's reach into—or recoil from—the wider society.

Though some civic groups were, and are, uncivil by widespread current standards, it does not follow that the social spiral argument never describes reality. Neo-Tocquevillians need not always be wrong. Putnam has focused mainly on the less socially toxic groups and consigns those like the Ku Klux Klan to a "dark side" of civic life (2000). Who would dispute that? But the rhetorical style here only boosts my contention that neo-Tocquevillians harbor a qualitative understanding of civic bonds that the social capital concept cannot accommodate. Critics score the limits in neo-Tocquevillian generalizations without offering an alternative to the social capital concept. The core, classic insight goes unexamined. The role of group interaction remains *elusive in the entire debate.*

In contrast, I have addressed the social spiral argument on its protagonists' chosen turf. Neo-Tocquevillians highlight local community service groups— ones very much like those pictured in this book. On the basis of their everyday experiences, I work toward a conceptual framework that can accommodate groups that do spiral outward and build bridges, and groups that try to but fail, as well as those that intend to reach out only narrowly or not at all.

From Capital to Conversation: Listening Up Close

Listening closely to ordinary people in unglamorous community service groups may be a counterintuitive thing to do. But if the phenomenal popularity of Putnam's social capital concept is any indication, many researchers and many Americans in general are concerned about mundane civic relationships. For some of the most basic and practical questions about those relationships, the social capital concept is the wrong research tool to use. In the past decade, researchers are starting to take to heart a simple truth that Mark E. Warren observes: "In contrast to markets and bureaucracies, association is the form of social organization that thrives on talk" (2001, p. 39). We do not fully understand civic groups unless we listen closely to that talk.

Some scholars are listening in because they want to know which kinds of groups host the freewheeling, wide-ranging political conversation upon which democratic citizenship is supposed to depend.[43] Some want to hear how people define what makes a good activist or a good volunteer. They ask: What traditions, symbols, or forms of common sense do people bring to civic life?[44] Others listen in on civic groups without using the category of "civic" at all: Some students of volunteering have listened to how volunteers relate to the people they serve or the people who manage them.[45] Some social movement scholars have followed the interactions that lead to strikes and switches in movement strategy or the ones that cultivate communities of dissent and resistance.[46] This study adds to the growing body of work on interaction in civic life. One of the things I listened to closely was how religion informed the Lakeburg groups.

CAN RELIGION HELP PEOPLE REACH OUT?

Religion and Civic Engagement

Religion figured large in Tocqueville's arguments about the virtues of civic life. Tocqueville argued that even in a very individualistic society, religious sentiments would turn people outward, putting some moral brakes on their pursuit of individual gain. It did not matter if Americans fervently believed Christian precepts, he reasoned. By expecting of each other at least a lip-service faith in a good larger than their own private good, Americans would keep alive a sense of connection to the wider society. The American historical record does suggest that faith-based groups sometimes have valued social togetherness (Skocpol 2000; Casanova 1994; Demerath and Williams 1992; Wuthnow and Hodgkinson 1990; McCarthy 1999). Is this true today, when many Americans are sensitive to, and wary of, religion's public presence at all? And how do religiously based groups create bonds—and barriers?

It is reasonable to think that Tocqueville could be right about American religion. The scriptures of both Christians and Jews contain potent images of communal cohesion, care for strangers and the socially marginal.[47] Some of these images are familiar to religious people, religiously indifferent people, and antireligious people; they would be hard to escape for anyone who has spent some time in the American cultural mainstream. The Exodus story, for instance, is a story of *shared* revelation, *shared* fate, interdependence. It might be easy enough for contemporary, Christian volunteers or activists to draw metaphors from biblical images of communal cohesion: From African American slaves to white European colonists, people of all sorts have pictured themselves as latter-day Israelites, bound together as a community with a common fate.[48] The "body of Christ" is another powerful, communal image—an image of shared responsibility to uphold Christian faith *as an interdependent community.* Jews and Christians alike also speak of a "covenant" with God, a collective obligation that must be nurtured.[49] Some contemporary Christian theologians affirm that Christian faith offers the resources for reaching out broadly to other members of society.[50]

People in this study did symbolize the connections between people with religious imagery. When the Ku Klux Klan threatened to march in Lakeburg, a coalition of local pastors organized a multicultural celebration, timed to coincide with the march, with the theme "All in the image of God." A similar idiom accompanied the Adopt-a-Family Project's kick-off program: We are all "Children of God," said our orientation program materials. And the program at the annual Council of Churches conference I attended quoted both the Hebrew bible and Christian scriptures on the importance of civic obligation. The message was that people have a duty to connect with each other in public life.

People also can use religious idioms to damn other people instead of connecting with them. During my study I heard one Protestant minister and candidate for Congress issue his audience a darkly foreboding jeremiad: Lakeburg would be judged and condemned if it continued to tolerate deviation from the Word of God; one of his competitors in the congressional race was a lesbian. Still, in the American context, at least, religious faiths can be a powerful inspiration for embracing the stranger, the other.

Most of the people in this book affirm Christian faith in their own lives. As Cnaan and his colleagues (2002) put it, religious congregations are "the most common and widespread institution in our society." Probably more than half of all Americans are active members of a local congregation (Finke and Stark 1986). Churches and synagogues also are the most widespread, and egalitarian, sites of civic engagement in the United States (Warner 1999, p. 238, derived from Ammerman 1997). Religious congregations and networks of congregations are hard to miss if we are looking for community service groups: They house homeless adults and runaway teens, shelter battered women and children, serve hot meals to hungry people, donate clothing, and assist victims of natural disasters. They also advocate—for cheaper housing, neighborhood development, environmental protection, educational opportunity, or gay and lesbian rights.[51] Almost half of Americans' association memberships are church related, and half of our volunteering takes place in a religious context.[52] In the United States, religious organizations are rich, widespread sources of social networks that nurture volunteering and social activism.[53] Religious commitments lead some Americans to civic engagement *beyond* their own religious congregations.[54] In the secular contexts of academic life, it is easy to ask, "Why study religious community groups?" By the numbers alone, one may as well ask why *not* study religious community groups.

Yet until quite recently, sociologists tended to assume that religion was mostly a private affair in the modern United States. On this "privatization thesis," even if religious values stir people to public action, the values would remain private.[55] The privatization thesis complements a commonly invoked distinction between religious and "civic" (i.e., secular) spheres. Americans often refer to religion as "private," not public, because the U.S. Constitution protects religion from many forms of state regulation. A long-standing, underappreciated tradition of community studies depicts religious congregations woven into the fabric of local American life, nurturing and sometimes threatening local ties.[56] Only in the past decade, though, are sociologists making religion's public force into a major research theme (Smith 1996).

Already interested in religion's public force, I chose religiously based groups partly because sociologists have given them comparatively little close-up attention. Recent work is starting to redress the gap. From studying community organizers up close, Stephen Hart (2001) concludes that people are wrong to think that religion unites people only for narrow, divisive aims. In their own work on faith-based community organizing, sociologists Mark R. Warren (2001) and Richard Wood (2002, 1999, 1994) show how shared religious discourse and ritual helps pastors, laypersons, and organizers to trust one another, and motivate one another, as they fight for better housing, new schools, and more control over urban development. Like my own study, these are asking how civic groups create social ties beyond the group as well as inside it. Warren and Wood want to understand what enables grass-roots, religious activists to win social justice battles, and bring more low-income people into the political process, at least temporarily. Relationships that contribute to successful grass-roots political struggles "count" as social capital in these works. We could say the studies are concerned with a particular kind of social spiral.

In contrast, my study examines different kinds of community groups trying build different kinds of bridges. I discovered how interaction inside the group relates to ties beyond the group, whether or not group members (or sociologists) deem the ties "political," or successful. Rather than ask which relationships facilitate grass-roots community organizing, and privilege those as social capital, I focused on links between diverse meanings inside the groups and diverse sorts of relationships groups were able to build outward.

Changes in social welfare policy, along with the continuing debate about America's civic health, are motivating more survey and ethnographic work on religious community service groups.[57] In the wake of welfare reform, researchers (Bartkowski and Regis 2003) find that church-based groups are serving dinners at churches, distributing bags of groceries, "adopting" former welfare-receiving families—all forms of service I found among my Lakeburg groups too. In Bartkowski and Regis's study of Mississippi churches, racial mistrust and denominational differences stalled or preempted churches' efforts to collaborate in poverty-relief work. The authors concluded that church-based social service would be driven by "bonding" as much as "bridging" social capital. Somewhat more optimistically, Ram Cnaan (2002) deduced from his survey of 251 American congregations that these local institutions are impressive storehouses of social capital. They help to keep their own members from needing to seek governmental assistance, and they offer the larger society something more, too. "Norms" constitute one term in the troika by which Robert Putnam defined social capital, and many American churches, Cnaan argued, cultivate a norm of civic engagement that explains their members' eagerness to get involved better than would members' theological beliefs. To join a church is to learn the norm of getting involved in the community.

How Religion Works

Some people, including some in the Lakeburg groups, fear that religion does just the opposite of encouraging people to spiral outward. They say religion fragments the civic arena and circumscribes the ties people can create. Yet sociologists have been finding that this "culture wars" argument describes professional advocates and publicists better than ordinary Americans.[58] A variety of social scientists, policy scholars, and theologians—Theda Skocpol, Robert Putnam, Mary Jo Bane, Brent Coffin, Ronald Thiemann, Robert Bellah, and others—all argue that religiously based community groups might potentially strengthen social ties in society at large.[59] None advocates that the United States become a "Christian nation." They argue that, given American culture and history, there are *widely shared* religious traditions that would help people create social bonds.

This book lays out a new argument about *how*, if at all, religion influences the social spiral. By no means denying the power of religious discourse and ritual, chapter 7 will suggest a subtler, still powerful way that religion influences civic life. Rather like Cnaan, I found that being a member of a congregation is itself meaningful, a source of shared norms, apart from the teachings of any particular religious tradition. But once again, the cover-all term "social capital" that Cnaan invokes only obscures differences that matter. Being a congregational member can mean very different things, and the different meanings have important consequences for action beyond the congregation.

Let me describe where and how I carried out the study.

Studying the Field of Religious Community Service Groups

Where I Listened: The Groups and Agencies

The two networks I studied were responding to welfare policy reform and, to a lesser extent, racial antagonisms. Both were independent of any single church or denomination. Both were nonprofit organizations, in which volunteers did much of the organizations' work under the guidance of a few paid staffpersons. I chose predominantly Protestant-based community groups simply because most social scientists would agree that Protestant Christian religion has shaped American culture and society as much or more than any other family of religious traditions. It is also still the largest such family in the United States. The Lakeburg groups occupied different places on the Protestant spectrum, from theologically liberal mainline Protestant denominations to theologically conservative evangelical Protestantism.

"Mainline" and "evangelical" are social categories, not biblical or theological ones.[60] They represent social scientists' and church members' own efforts to identify overarching commonalities and differences between Protestant churches whose particular histories have occupied many, many lifetimes of research and commentary. Though not the only branches of Protestantism alive today, these two influence contemporary American life strongly, in different ways. Each has developed partly in relation to the other. Mainline Protestants in the late-nineteenth and the twentieth centuries became increasingly identified with a progressive "social gospel" of social reform. Evangelical Protestants, reacting both to mainline Protestantism and the strict fundamentalism of some conservative Christians early in the twentieth century, advocated an "engaged orthodoxy" that highlights personal piety and holds a personal relationship with Jesus Christ to be the driving force of all life's endeavors. Adherents to both would affirm, by huge margins, the basic Christian belief that God was revealed in Jesus Christ. The two branches tend to relate to that belief in different ways.[61]

For the sake of a thumbnail sketch, it makes sense to distinguish the two by their members' typical stances toward religious pluralism and certainty. Among mainline Protestants, the majority takes the Bible as the inspired Word of God but say they do not take everything in it literally. A majority of mainliners hold that there are truths in other religions, and even that other religions can be equally good approaches to knowing God.[62] Their regard for pluralism may come from a sense that Christian understandings of God are available to all who seek God, more than from a purely relativist sense that religions are "really all the same underneath" or "all do the same things." Still, these trends in belief among mainliners contrast strikingly with tenets common to evangelical Protestants.

Since the 1940s, evangelical Protestantism in the United States has developed as a religious identity that emphasizes the singular truth of God as revealed in Jesus Christ. To be an evangelical is to carry a kind of identity, one that sustains strong boundaries between Christian truths and other religious or secular beliefs. To be evangelical is to make religious *certainty* a core part of one's identity—certainty about what one's beliefs are, and that they are true. Evangelicals usually think of their Christian identity as their most basic, life-defining one—an identity that grows not from birth but from the moment when an individual explicitly states the intent to commit his life to Jesus Christ.[63]

This "two-party" sketch of American Protestantism vastly simplifies distinctions between and within churches (Jacobsen and Trollinger 1998). Comparing Protestants in this way, however, follows authoritative arguments about religious change since World War II.[64] Mainline Protestant and evangelical Protestant group members consistently talked about themselves in terms of two camps, even while acknowledging differences within them. The broad generalities took on a factlike quality in everyday life, and usually mattered far more for everyday interaction in the Lakeburg groups than distinctions inside either category.

I tried out the social spiral argument in relation to groups from both of these branches of the faith. Given the contemporary map of civic life I sketched earlier, I wanted to study interchurch networks rather than focusing mainly on individual churches. I was happy to find one such network from each theological branch.

THE URBAN RELIGIOUS COALITION

Urban Religious Coalition (URC) was a mostly mainline-Protestant based network. The most actively involved of its fifty-two associated churches were Episcopal, United Methodist, Presbyterian (USA), United Church of Christ, and Lutheran (ELCA), but board members also attended a Catholic church and a

Unitarian society. The vague term "associated" reflects the URC's loose membership structure. While the URC board hoped that churches would send empowered representatives, it left it up to churches to decide how to become involved. Mostly, people got involved in URC projects as churchgoing individuals, not as church representatives. They would learn about URC projects through their own church's newsletters or announcements at Sunday services, or by becoming members of the URC and receiving the URC's bimonthly newsletter. Long intending to be an interfaith network, the URC elected a member of a local synagogue to its executive board during this study. At the start of the study, the Urban Religious Coalition was about to celebrate its twenty-fifth anniversary. Since the early 1970s, it had been sponsoring volunteer service programs for children and elderly people, supporting antiracism campaigns and interracial group dialogue in Lakeburg, and holding community forums and speaker series. Its statement of mission, "standing with the hurting, planting the seeds of social change," remained the same throughout my study. These groups and projects had to transcend specific denominational, theological traditions; they challenged themselves to be "faith-based" amidst a diversity of faiths. Their challenge, in microcosm, is the challenge for liberal religion in a diverse society.

In all, I studied eight different groups or volunteer projects that the URC sponsored or assisted with administrative support, financial support, or both. Four are each the *main* representative of a different set of customs, while a fifth serves the study by depicting a clash between liberal mainline and evangelical group customs (see table 1.1 at the end of this chapter). The "groups" endured over time and had easily identifiable core members. The "volunteer projects" were shifting collections of people who gathered on occasion to carry out a set of community service tasks usually defined by networker groups or individuals. The groups and projects were:

- Humane Response Alliance (HRA)—a citizen-initiated group of networkers[65]—church group leaders, nonprofit, and county agency personnel devising a church-based response to welfare reform.
- Fun Evenings—affiliated with HRA, a citizen-initiated project of nighttime entertainment events for "at-risk" teenagers; a Lakeburg county youth support agency took over direction of the project from its initial, solo networker.
- Justice Task Force—affiliated with HRA but met and acted autonomously; a group of churchgoers publicizing social justice perspectives on welfare reform and prison policy.
- Park Cluster—a group of churchgoers and pastors, sometimes joined by county agency workers, volunteering in and sponsoring public goods for a low-income, minority neighborhood; originally affiliated with HRA, the group met and acted autonomously by the time of my study.
- Religious Anti-racism Coalition—a citizen-initiated group of mainline

Protestant and evangelical Protestant pastors, along with several laypersons of other faiths, publicizing opposition to racism in Lakeburg through several public events and a monthly speaker series at coalition meetings.

Two volunteer projects, much less central to the study, serve as short comparison cases that bolster my arguments about the central cases. They are:

- Summer Fun Camp—run by Park Cluster with volunteer camp counselors, for elementary-school-aged children, two weeks every summer.
- Interfaith Shelter—a project of church volunteers organized by a paid networker to house and serve meals to homeless people in participating churches' shelters. Volunteers came predominantly from URC-affiliated churches, but the Shelter was a separate, nonprofit organization.

I also studied Lakeburg Religious Forum, a public, monthly discussion series organized by URC staff. At the forums, members of liberal URC-associated congregations and members of a few conservative Christian congregations discussed social issues, usually in church meeting halls. Forums carried titles such as "Sexuality: What's My Story?" "Are We All Really Created Equal?" and "What Makes a Family?" The forums sensitized me to the religious vocabularies Lakeburg churchgoers used to talk about social issues, and helped me understand how they perceived themselves on a wider social map. The book will not use any of these observations formally, because the forums were very different from all of the other groups. They consisted of small group discussions among different groups of people every month.

I also attended executive board meetings, and meetings to plan special events, like the multicultural alternative to the KKK march. I observed and participated alongside the various URC groups and projects over a period of three and a half years.

TUMBLING WALLS

The other community service network I studied is Tumbling Walls, whose member churches were almost entirely evangelical Protestant. The most active churches included a nondenominational congregation that identified itself as both evangelical and charismatic, an evangelical Reformed church, and a Vineyard Christian Fellowship. A pamphlet described Tumbling Walls this way:

Tumbling Walls is a local, non-profit, interdenominational ministry supported by area Christians and churches. We believe God has drawn us together for a purpose—to break down the walls that separate us so we can work together to build communities where God's love, wisdom and power are known. We believe we're being called to play a strategic role in uniting the Church so it can be more effective in offering Biblical answers to the problems of our day. . . ."

Tumbling Walls did not have formal, dues-paying members the way the URC did, but like the URC it survived on individual donations, church donations, and grants. It sponsored outdoor prayer meetings, set up forums for touring Christian speakers, and carried out a door-to-door giveaway project in Lakeburg, distributing five thousand free videos about Jesus Christ.

The largest program in Tumbling Walls, and the one I studied, was the Adopt-a-Family program I pictured already. The director of Tumbling Walls got groups from twelve churches to participate in befriending former welfare families during the life of the program. I observed and participated alongside two of these church groups over two years—with intensive participant-observation in one group for seven months. I also observed planning meetings with Tumbling Walls staff. And I observed Tumbling Walls-associated pastors at the anti-racism coalition and the monthly dialogue series, both convened through the URC. I also studied a free-meals project organized by two evangelical women for Park neighborhood residents, so I could compare them with Park Cluster and Adopt-a-Family. Their customs were similar to Adopt-a-Family's.

COUNTY AGENCIES AND OTHER GROUPS

More briefly, I studied groups or projects surrounding the URC and Tumbling Walls. These include: a county welfare task force whose participants included county welfare administrators and community leaders; a county-level family support agency made up of social workers, school district, and public health department employees; a local electoral organization that got involved in the Park neighborhood's school politics. I also over a year's time observed selected committee meetings inside two churches that core Park Cluster members attended.

Studying this wider field mattered for several reasons. First, as Robert Wuthnow has observed (1998), much of contemporary volunteering happens in conjunction with professional service organizations whose staff define "slots" for volunteer assistance. Though the cultural mainstream often pictures volunteering as a selfless act of individual compassion, much of this compassion is socially organized. How would these arrangements influence the social spiral? The cases in this book will show that while social service agencies shape opportunities for community service, volunteers may respond to those opportunities in more than one way. Studying the church committee meetings clarified to me how individual churches do and don't influence their members' group interaction in different settings.

The study did not set out to answer "What motivates individuals to volunteer?" or "What makes individuals more broad-minded?" Had these worthwhile questions been *this* study's questions, it might have made sense to compare religious and secular community service groups, in order to test out the notion that religion makes a difference. Not having done so, I will not claim that explicitly faith-based groups are more or less likely to succeed in reaching out than secular groups. This study pictures substantial variety already among groups that explicitly identify as religious.

Restricting the study to religiously identified groups makes sense for another reason: Comparing religious and secular groups would presuppose we know what goes into making a group religious. This was not a good assumption to make. At the start of this study, sociologists did not know clearly what it meant for group that is not a religious congregation to be a faith-based group. It was not clear what might count as a religious influence.[66] It was better to explore the volunteers' own meanings of "faith-based." Once having charted the breadth of faith-based community groups, comparisons with secular groups would be instructive. Given the place of religious groups in American civic life, and the current social-scientific and policy debates about their public role, I reasoned that listening to these groups closely would be a worthwhile thing to do.

How I Listened: Participant-Observation and Interviews

Participant-observation was the best method for charting the social spiral. During 1996–2000, I spent roughly eighteen months observing and participating alongside the Justice Task Force and Park Cluster. I spent twelve months observing the Humane Response Alliance; the Alliance went dormant soon after my last fieldwork session with it. I attended and participated in fourteen months of URC-sponsored Religious Anti-racism Coalition meetings. I followed the Adopt-a-Family project from its beginnings, including ten months of meetings. I participated in a year's worth of monthly dialogues in the URC's public forum series. And I volunteered to help staff four different Fun Evenings events for teenagers; the three year's spread of evenings enabled me to see if the program would change as its sponsorship passed from the URC to a Lakeburg county agency.

Focusing on everyday interaction in a study of religious groups might strike some readers as counterintuitive: Studying religious people commonly means studying what sacred texts or denominational traditions would say about what people do. That is not my main goal. I do not treat these community groups as direct representatives of biblical or denominational categories. It was more important to understand how the groups imagine their relation to society than how they imagine themselves in the nuances of Christian theology. As historian David Hall has recently pointed out (1997) scholars often write as if religious people are acting out theological dictates inside a culture-free bubble—as if theological or denominational teachings are their *only* context. Yet, as Hall insists, religious action happens only through a larger cultural context (see also Bender 2003; Ammerman 2003). I wanted to see and hear different kinds of religious people acting in their cultural context. Groups, not denominations or texts, were the acting subjects I followed.[67]

Broad differences between evangelical and mainline Protestant traditions are important in the story, because these were the striking *religious* differences that I heard most often. Beyond that, it would be unwise and perhaps impossible to divine "which denomination mattered more" for what the mostly mainline

Protestant, URC-sponsored groups did. Partly, this is because these groups were ecumenical. But I found, too, that people from the same church—and even the same individual participants—practiced different styles of engagement in different group settings. I could discover more about the *ways* that religion weaves into everyday life by noticing what people said and did, rather than assuming a priori that what religiously identified people say and do is determined in the last instance by the denomination with which they identify currently. I intentionally took a very "empiricist" approach, close to the ground of everyday life. I sought to identify patterns of communication and action. To do otherwise would risk an "essentialist" fallacy that makes a person's religious identity the default determinant of that person's speech or action.

The study also draws on interviews with thirty-five core members of these groups. Interviews enabled me to hear group members talk about why, if at all, a faith-based community service group differs from one that is not explicitly faith based. From interviews I could learn more about group histories, and individuals' histories within them. And I could learn about religious commitments that might not surface in group meetings.

THE CHAPTERS AHEAD

Chapter 2 develops my definition of a "bridge" and my concept of group-building customs, and shows how I used these to investigate the social spiral argument. Chapters 3, 4, 5, and 6 portray the main case groups identified in the table below. I describe the dominant customs in each group, showing how they promoted particular kinds of relationships while discouraging or ignoring others. The case chapters view the groups' experiences in light of alternative explanations and concepts—the role of the state; the power of shared discourses or ideologies apart from customs; social capital; the prejudices of members. Chapter 6 also compares the preceding cases with Park Cluster, to support my contention that social reflexivity is important for bridge-building. Chapter 7 uses the case of Park Cluster, with others as comparisons, to make a new argument about how people bring religion into civic life; scenes from the URC-sponsored Religious Anti-racism Coalition help make the case for studying religious identities apart from religious worldviews. With the cases all in view, chapter 8 deduces lessons and charts new directions for sociologists of civic life, and for anyone who wants to understand the limits and possibilities of civic groups. Appendix I discusses my methodological choices: I show how I pursued theoretical goals with evidence from one metropolitan region; I explain how Lakeburg worked as a site for generating tentative theory well as improving existing theory. Appendix II complements chapter 2, offering a more in-depth treatment of how I conceptualized customs, and how I found evidence of customs at work in the Lakeburg groups.

TABLE 1–1
Summary of the Lakeburg Groups and Projects

Customs	Group or Project	Bridge as Defined by Group	Social Reflexivity	Results of Reaching Out, as Perceived by Group
Networker		*intergroup:*		
	Humane Response Alliance leadership group	across churches between URC and county agency	little	failed
Volunteer		**not attempted**		
	Fun Evenings		little	for each project: brief
	Summer Fun Camp		little	interpersonal exchanges,
	Interfaith Shelter		little	some rewarding, some frustrating
Social Critic		*consciousness-raising:*		
	Justice Task Force (Economic justice workshops)	between political critics and other churchgoers	little	frustrating, workshop program folded
Social Servant		*deeply interpersonal:*		
	Adopt-a-Family	between church volunteer groups and members of former-welfare receiving families	little	frustrating, failure to develop close relations
	Free meals project	between private individuals and residents of Park neighborhood	one episode	frustrating at first, then project's future unclear
Partner		*intergroup:*		
	Park Cluster	between Cluster churches, low-income minority neighborhood and service agencies	increasingly frequent and central to group process	bridges develop, new opportunities open; frustrating and rewarding work
A Clash				
	Religious Anti-Racism Coalition	not examined here	not examined here	not examined here

Chapter Two

STUDYING THE SOCIAL SPIRAL

A COMMUNICATION-CENTERED APPROACH TO SOCIAL TIES

Follow the Interaction

On Tocqueville's trail, I set out in pursuit of the social spiral. Tocqueville supposed that something about interaction in local groups would promote broad ties to the world beyond the group. Increasingly, sociologists are coming to appreciate a similar insight: People create social ties *in interaction.*

It may seem like an odd thing to say—to emphasize that people *create* social ties. At first blush, it seems just obvious. On the other hand, haven't sociologists produced generations of studies teaching us that social ties constrain what individuals say and do together? The constraining and enabling force of social ties is a fundamental insight for sociology, after all—a challenge to the popular, commonsense thinking that makes individuals rather than relationships the core reality, and sees relationships as products of individual will. But we can appreciate that social ties shape interaction while recognizing, too, the role of interaction in perpetuating ties and creating new ties. We do not need to treat social ties as purely "structural" facts in a reality completely apart from the world of communication. Communication itself is a creative force. Eminent sociologist Charles Tilly puts it well: "Conversation in general shapes social life by altering individual and collective understandings, *by creating and transforming social ties* [emphasis mine], by generating cultural materials that are then available for subsequent social interchange, and by establishing, obliterating, or shifting commitments on the part of participants" (2002, p. 122). Scholars such as Tilly like to point out that people's private ideas will not result in collectively bound action if people never communicate those ideas.[1]

Maintaining ties to other people or groups takes more than physical proximity. Ties between individuals or groups can mean different things, and we communicate the meanings directly or indirectly.[2] This chapter lays out a communication-centered method of studying social ties: Following that method, I listened to the Lakeburg groups discussing their relationships with the world beyond the group; I heard how different customs shaped those discussions; I watched over time to see what kinds of discussion, and which customs, contributed to bridge-building, or cut it short. Of course, successful bridges depended on more than customs and communication. Appreciating the role of interaction in creating social ties, however, makes good sense in light of the Lakeburg groups' experiences.

Until recently, sociologists have not paid a lot of attention to the cultural, communication dimension of social ties.[3] Researchers have tended to conceive social ties as "hard" structures that shape the "soft" stuff of everyday interaction into enduring patterns. In this view, "cultural forms . . . flow through previously structured networks, leaving primary causal force with the structural properties of the relational system. The networks take on a substantial, reified quality, removed from the actual dynamics of interaction" (Mische 2003, p. 4). That is a useful model of social life for some sociological questions and has led to valuable discoveries. Sociologists have found, for instance, that given the right social network, people are more likely to join social movements, take big risks as activists, or carry on the struggle from one social movement to the next.[4] With this way of thinking about social ties, listening closely to group interaction would seem like a waste of time. The whole question of the social spiral and how, if at all, it works would drop out of the picture.

New thinking about social ties and networks gives the question of the social spiral a good sociological grounding. Network scholars such as Harrison White and colleagues (White 1992; Mische and White 1998) are understanding networks as clusters of relationships with stories and signals that organize those relationships and distinguish them from other clusters. Looking at it this way, networks are not preexisting "hard" conduits for "soft" interaction or culture. Rather, interaction helps to create network relations *in culturally patterned ways*. Social-structural power and resources shape networks (and vice versa), too. Resources, power, and culture come together in real life; sociologists separate them conceptually to understand better how processes like the social spiral work, if they work.[5]

Following everyday interaction, we can learn what roles these different social forces play. How could I tell which interactions would matter most?

What Counts as a Bridge? Follow the Group's Definition

I wanted to see how the Lakeburg groups reached out beyond their usual milieus—how they tried to build "bridges" beyond their own groups. That was the best way to reconstruct the social spiral argument in light of contemporary American social realities. Since reaching out meant different things in different groups, I followed the groups' own definitions, their own ways of defining the "we" on one side of the bridge and the "they" on the other side.

I could have proceeded differently. There are many kinds of social division in the United States, of course, but race, ethnicity, religion, or social class would come immediately to mind for many people. It might have made sense to count as bridges only relationships that groups develop across those lines, and to score groups that do not cross those lines as racist, class-biased, or religiously exclusive. Critics of neo-Tocquevillianism already have pointed out that civic groups often have excluded people by race, ethnicity, religion, or class, either explicitly or by default, or else reached out only to other groups of socially similar people (Kaufman 2002; Berman 1997). Knowing about exclusion in civic groups, important as it is, still does not tell us all that ties mean to people.

Alternatively, I might have distilled a single criterion from research on "bridging" social capital. The terrain is not well charted. As sociologist Robert Wuthnow observes, there are many possible kinds of bridges, including the ties that congregations create with social service agencies or the relationships that members of one civic group create by participating in other groups (2004, p. 89); this study observed these and other kinds of ties. Social capital scholars have been especially interested in bridges between groups or individuals separated by wide social or geographical distances.[6] Specific examples vary greatly. Putnam (2000) points to the modern American civil rights movement. At its broadest, it was a national, interracial, cross-class congeries of grass-roots activist groups, city improvement alliances, national coalitions, and interest groups. Other manifestations of bridging social capital include regional coalitions of faith-based community organizations for low-income people (Wood 2002; Mark R. Warren 2001), interracial ties in local neighborhoods (Briggs 1998), relationships between school personnel and parents (Noguera 2001), or individual friendships between ordinary citizens and powerful or wealthy people (Wuthnow 2004). Bridges can be inside a group, or between individuals in different groups, or between groups as collectivities (Putnam 2000; Wuthnow 2004). A single formula for defining a "bridge" would be unproductive, and only reify the reductions already suffered by translating qualitatively different relationships into the quantities of capital.

My decision to follow my groups' own definitions of reaching out makes sense given the still-early stage of scholarly discussion. The best research strategy would assess neo-Tocquevillian claims without taking a lot of untested generalizations onboard. It would avoid equating "bridging" with political ends, or nonpolitical ends. In this study's simple, working definition, a bridge is a *routinized* relationship that a civic group has to individuals or groups that it perceives as outside the group. Contemporary scholars do not worry that American groups cannot create contingent, very-short-term liaisons to serve their own interests; in Tocqueville's terms, they are concerned about Americans' willingness to practice "self-interest properly understood," to work over time for a greater good that eventually will benefit them too. My approach opened the study to the very different styles of civic relationship that the Lakeburg groups tried to create—more or less interpersonal, more or less political, more or less task driven—rather than assuming political or cultural biases that could rule out some groups from the start.[7] Keeping the definition broad and letting the style vary, I could step back then and ask as a sociologist what kinds of relationships empower civil society.

All of the Lakeburg groups tried to build bridges of some kind; all tried to relate to an "other." Park Cluster, representing Lakeburg church committees, worked hard to create ongoing relationships with leaders and groups in the so-cially and sometimes geographically distant Park neighborhood. White and middle-class Adopt-a-Family volunteers reached out to African American, for-mer welfare-receiving families they likely would never have met otherwise. Hu-mane Response Alliance members tried to create a food pantry network that not only would benefit low-income pantry patrons but would generate new ties be-tween different churches and between churches and the HRA; alliance members spoke of churches as surprisingly distant "others" with whom they hoped the al-liance could create a relationship. And the Justice Task Force wanted to create consciousness-raising relationships with churchgoers whom they experienced as very different from themselves, "others" in political terms. In other studies, signs of a bridge include ongoing transfer or sharing of material resources, cul-tural power and knowledge, political legitimacy, or leverage.[8] In different ways, the Lakeburg groups offered to transfer or share resources, power, or knowledge, too. Park Cluster was the only Lakeburg group that succeeded on its own terms in bridge-building. Exactly what kind of communication made these bridges possible?

Talking through Togetherness: Social Reflexivity

A Definition

Comparing the groups in table 1.1 at the end of chapter 1, a pattern emerges. Taken together, the Lakeburg groups' experiences suggest it is easier for a group to create bridges if it can practice social reflexivity in members' normal course of working together. A group practices social reflexivity when members engage in *reflective talk about the group's concrete relationships in the wider social world*. By engaging in that reflective talk, groups can open up possibilities for bridges across social differences.

In Park Cluster, the group that succeeded in building bridges outward, white and middle-class church volunteers opened themselves to pain and embarrass-ment as they pondered the Cluster's civic role in relation to a low-income, mi-nority neighborhood. They dared to listen to and learn from neighborhood leaders—not always quickly enough. They talked through the group's relation-ships to the wider locale, again and again, *as* they went about their work at monthly meetings. They practiced social reflexivity.

It should not be so strange an idea: People often say that you cannot take re-sponsibility for a relationship without daring to talk about it even if that hurts. In much of the American middle-class mainstream, common sense says that in-dividuals need to talk about their personal relationships in order to keep them healthy (Lichterman 1992; Carbaugh 1988). It should be all the more true for civic relationships between groups, which are hard if not impossible to point to directly. A group has to imagine itself in the relationship, picture who it is and who the other groups are, and picture the kind of relationship that holds them together.

Other Ways to Imagine Being Together

Yet social reflexivity is less familiar than, and quite different from, other ways that Americans conceive themselves within a broader social whole. One approach—I heard different versions of it in some of the Lakeburg groups—is to try ignoring social inequalities and differences, and affirm the common humanity of all individuals. As one homeless shelter organizer said, we need to reacquaint ourselves of our own flesh. That is how to build bridges. The man spoke as director of a church-sponsored network of shelters; he was saying we all are children of God. The secular version of the message resonates widely in American political culture: All individuals share equally the inherent rights and dignity of humankind. It is a noble sentiment; it is different from social reflexivity: When we all are *one,* there are not different social groups, or positions, or identities, with which we have relationships that we might discuss.

Another approach insists on cathartic self-exploration, self-critique. On this view, white bridge-builders need to set aside time to unlearn racism and learn new stories about their individual complicity in a racist society. This approach is, for majority groups, a chastening form of what observers call identity politics.[9] Castigated as "political correctness" by its detractors, it made the rounds in Lakeburg too: Some members of the largely middle-class and very largely white Lakeburg groups attended racial awareness workshops.

I heard a Christian-inflected version of this personal scrutiny in the Religious Anti-racism Coalition pictured in chapter 7. Coalition members bravely declared their need to confess the sin of their own racism. After that, they held a lengthy sharing session at one meeting, during which all present took turns talking about the role of race relations and cultural diversity in their own lives. Individually, members reflected thoughtfully on encounters with people or situations they identified as different from who or what they were accustomed to. It was reflection for sure; it just was different from social reflexivity.

The difference is important to recognize because increasingly civic leaders and activists make sharing sessions like these a component of their community-building projects.[10] The monthly public, small group "dialogues" sponsored by the URC are one example. Director Donald originally devised these dialogues in response to what he perceived as culture wars between religious liberals and conservatives that threatened to destroy civic community in Lakeburg. In these dialogues as well as the example from the antiracism coalition above, sharing sessions were not about how a preexisting civic group relates to other people or groups in the wider social world. Rather, the talk was personal, confessional, biographical—about people's formation as individuals, not about how a group might form itself in relation to its civic context.[11]

Sometimes personal scrutiny leads people to reject their own backgrounds and tightly embrace some other identity. The impulse has a long history in progressive American grass-roots politics.[12] I heard this approach in Lakeburg also, as when two members of the Justice Task Force said that their experiences in a much less affluent country made them reject their materialistic American culture and have as little contact as possible with what they considered the typical American lifestyle. Clearly the two had reflected on their place in the world. Their comments imply that they would have liked, at least symbolically, to reject the relationships they have as Americans rather than continue reflecting on those relationships in a complex, differentiated social world. Again, it may be a noble or at least heartfelt sentiment; it is different from social reflexivity. After all, the two did not cease being Americans.

Social reflexivity is a collective practice of imagining; it requires talking about differences and similarities straightforwardly, in the midst of forging relationships beyond the group. It is a deceptively simple concept, worth exploring further. So let me introduce two more classic sources—the writings of social philosophers John Dewey and Jane Addams. Each writer articulated a version of the social spiral argument. Dewey, whose writings are enjoying a renaissance of interest, has influenced prominent contemporary social theorists. Addams is just now receiving long-overdue credit as a social theorist in her own right. Like Tocqueville, Dewey and Addams wrote accounts that were normative as much as descriptive; I borrow their insights without taking their terms of discussion uncritically. Unlike Tocqueville they were quite explicit about the role of reflective, self-critical communication in civic life. They offer some more metaphors to help us picture what people are doing when they practice social reflexivity.

"Interacting Flexibly"

Decades after Tocqueville, John Dewey revisited Tocqueville's questions about the social moorings of a fast-paced, far-flung society. In *The Public and Its Problems,* (1927) he famously asked how a technologically advanced Great Society could bind itself into a Great Community. Just as for Tocqueville, civic-minded group interaction would play a big role—though in *Public* Dewey was even less clear than Tocqueville on the character of the groups. Even in a technologically complex Great Society, "vital and thorough attachments are bred only in the intimacy of an intercourse which is of necessity restricted in range" (p. 212). Very different from today's proponents of electronic town halls and electronic mail-generated social movements, Dewey insisted that face-to-face groups needed to anchor any great community that was going to be democratic.[13] But these groups would not take old, insular, communal customs for granted. Instead, groups of citizens would "interact flexibly and fully in connection with other groups," (1927, p. 147) so that individuals could develop their potentials to the fullest. Dewey was proposing his own version of the social spiral argument: Civic interaction would encourage citizens to develop themselves by reaching out and relating to groups in the wider civic world.

"Interacting flexibly" means building relationships *reflexively.* That is why Dewey distinguished between association as a physical fact and a moral fact. He was not saying simply that people who belong to groups have more opportunities for social contacts than people who don't. That is the logic of some contemporary arguments about social ties. Groups beget more groups, regardless of how members communicate; social capital has its own, silent dynamic, one might say. It is true: Presence in a group makes individuals available when other members ask them to get involved in new projects, increasing the chances they will meet new people too.[14] But association itself was not enough to constitute the civic community that Dewey hoped associations could bring into being. People would have to reflect upon the community they were building. "Association or joint activity is a condition of the creation of a community. But association itself is physical and organic, while communal life is moral, that is emotionally, intellectually and *consciously* [emphasis mine] sustained. . . . [N]o amount of aggregated collective action of itself constitutes a community" (p. 151).

Some proponents of grass-roots democracy have said that citizen groups do not need to reflect a lot on what they are doing. Local communities solving their own problems democratically is good already; it adds up to a greater political participation nationwide.[15] But if democracy in the full sense of the term *is* community, as Dewey wrote in *Public,* then civic associations could not contribute to the greater community for which Dewey longed if they did not reflect "emotionally, intellectually, and consciously" on their own community and its connections with other groups and communities.[16] Dewey was characteristically vague about the social relationships that would knit together his Great Community, but his prognosis does not make much sense if local groups do not reflect critically on who they are in relation to whom.[17]

The Great Community is an abstract, disembodied metaphor. Philosopher Judith Green has argued (1999) we need to reconstruct Dewey's ideas, color them in, if we want to grasp how diverse groups of people can cocreate a common democratic life today. While Dewey's writings are suggestive and might be reconstructed in this vein, Jane Addams wrote much more specifically and colorfully about democracy and diversity. For Addams just as for Dewey, democracy was not just a form of government but a way of life. Democratic politics without a democratic community was hollow and self-defeating.[18]

Addams hoped that the very experience of relating to diverse others would strengthen people's social ties beyond their small circles of socially similar friends. In *Democracy and Social Ethics* (2002 [1902]) she wrote that affluent people needed to "[mix] on the thronged and common road where all must turn out for one another and at least see the size of one another's burdens" (p. 7). Aloof bystanders would only risk "grow[ing] contemptuous of our fellows, and consciously limit[ing] our intercourse to certain kinds of people whom we have previously decided to respect" (p. 8). Such a citizen would fail at "interacting flexibly," as Dewey would have put it. Only through social engagement could affluent people, like Addams herself, learn new styles of relating to other people and create respectful relationships across yawing social divides. Addams no less than Dewey held out for a social spiral.

Dewey liked the metaphor of flexibility. Civic groups would interact "flexibly," he wrote (1927, p. 147). Local organs of public opinion in his Great Community would respond "flexibly" to the public's shifting concerns (1939, p. 161). What would promote flexibility to begin with? Dewey held that *perplexity* in the midst of problem solving spurred people on to reflect,[19] and this too resonated with Addams's thinking. For Addams, perplexity was the core experience that promotes habit-changing, relationship-changing reflection.

Togetherness Hurts: Perplexity as a Learning Experience

If Addams is a more grounded guide to social reflexivity than Dewey, it is partly because Addams drew on her experiences as a settlement-house organizer. Portraits of awkward, halting relationship-building in Addams's writings still can make readers squirm uncomfortably. We do not just see the perplexity but feel it ourselves as we watch well-meaning people trying to reach out, and learning slowly, painfully, how clueless they have been about people unlike themselves.

A splendid example is Addams's searching, searing look at the "charity visitor." A college-educated woman who feels bad for the urban underprivileged, the charity visitor calls at poor people's homes. She is perplexed to learn that parents control children dictatorially, send them off to factories at a young age, and pocket their meager pay. Earnest and self-righteous, the charity visitor holds forth on the "horrors of the saloon," only to learn that the family head regards his local bar as the place where he borrows money, enjoys camaraderie, and eats a free lunch. The charity visitor discovers nothing can be taken for granted. She is frustrated, disappointed. "If she is sensitive at all, [she] is never free from perplexities which our growing democracy force upon her" (2002 [1902], p. 31).

Perplexity might move her to give up altogether, or else to *reflect* on her experiences and change, rather than beating the customary path. Through painful social experience, abstract moral certainties might yield before perplexing contacts with other people's worlds. In that way the charity visitor, or any citizen who wants to "help the needy," sojourns with fellow citizens toward what Addams considered a more democratic way of life. "[W]ider social activity, and

contact with the larger experience, not only increases her sense of social obligation but at the same time recasts her ideals. She is chagrinned to discover that
in the actual task of reducing her social scruples to action, her humble beneficiaries are far in advance of her. . . . She has socialized her virtues not only
through a social aim but by a social process" (p. 33). Well-off people's experience with people unlike them could promote painful *discoveries* rather than
hard reliance on customary assumptions more appropriate to another social
class or another era. Those discoveries could make the customary terms of charity seem newly inappropriate. Taking less for granted, learning social life all over
again, the charity visitor learns to recognize her own social station in relation to
the very different station of her would-be beneficiaries.

Addams advocated difficult awakenings motivated by curiosity and compassion. Discovery, born of experience, would put builders of democratic community—at least women builders—in touch with their nobler, innate impulses.
Bridging relationships resonate with something deep in the human psyche, Addams implied, something that a "good college education" trains out of women
even as they learn the value of spiraling outward in the abstract.[20]

Addams did not transcend all of her social myopia. Contrasting the affluent
charity visitor's outlook with "the more emotional and freer lives of working
people," insisting on their natural sense of charity (2002 [1902], p. 21, for instance), Addams's own reflexivity sounds limited by sentimental, reverse value
judgments. Her disquisition on the woman charity worker might read as a realistically gendered, even feminist portrait of the late-nineteenth century college-
educated volunteer social worker. It might also read as insufficiently feminist for
failing to ask if only women should or do act on the "finer impulses" of social
compassion. We underappreciate Addams's contributions as a pragmatist theorist of democracy, a feminist and cultural radical if we cast her as nothing more
than a meliorist.[21] We can learn from her writings on civic relationships without taking onboard her entire vision of society and politics, any more than those
of the more canonical theorists Tocqueville or Dewey.

A Guide to Discovery in the Field

Dewey and Addams used metaphors that help us identify social reflexivity. Since
often it is groups that do things in civic life, not just lone individuals, I am interested in how people practice social reflexivity collectively. Addams's and
Dewey's metaphors and contemporary writings on reflexivity in general helped
me scan my field notes for these concrete signs that a group is practicing social
reflexivity:[22]

- it discusses reflectively the group's relationships to surrounding groups,
  individuals, or social categories of person; it challenges taken-for-
  granted assumptions about those relationships;

- it discusses reflectively why other individuals or groups do what they do, challenging taken-for-granted assumptions about what they do;
- it discusses reflectively its self-understanding; it challenges taken-for-granted assumptions about who the group is or should be.

What makes groups willing to host flexible, perplexing discussions about their place in the social world? What made these discussions so rare in most of the Lakeburg groups? Addams supposed that individual curiosity or compassion could compel social reflexivity. Dewey hoped that social scientists might help citizens practice the reflexivity that could turn a technologically advanced Great Society into a morally supple Great Community, but he was not very clear on what would make either social scientists or their fellow citizens able or willing to do that. Both Addams and Dewey thought that taken-for-granted customs stood in the way of reflexivity. My argument is that customs derived from the larger culture condition both the possibilities for and the constraints on social reflexivity.

The Quiet, Ambivalent Power of Customs

> There is a social pathology which works powerfully against effective inquiry into social institutions and conditions. It manifests itself in a thousand ways . . . which depress and dissipate thought all the more effectively because they operate with subtle and unconscious pervasiveness.
> —John Dewey, *The Public and Its Problems,* 1927

> Our conceptions of morality, as all our other ideas, pass through a course of development; the difficulty comes in adjusting our conduct, which has become hardened into customs and habits, to these changing moral conceptions.
> —Jane Addams, *Democracy and Social Ethics,* 1902

They broaden people's horizons. They pull people beyond small circles of like-minded friends. They stifle people's thinking about the bigger picture. They harden empathic citizenship into a dull rote. These all are claims about the power of ordinary customs in public life. Tocqueville put forth the optimistic view. Dewey and Addams held the more wary view. Customary habits, they worried, had the power to shut down reflection on social relationships—unless critical reflection itself could become customary.[23] Tocqueville, Dewey, and Addams all would have hit on something important about customs in the Lakeburg groups. Sometimes, customs did shut down critical reflection, and undercut expansive visions of togetherness. Occasionally, customs could encourage group members to spiral into the wider community, creating relationships they would not have predicted themselves.

Tocqueville, Dewey, and Addams all grasped something more basic about group life, too, and I have followed their insight: A group's shared customs have a reality of their own, a power apart from that of separate individuals' beliefs or traits. It is easy to think of individuals who seem different in a group from what they are like outside it. Groups call forth abilities, perspectives, even deeply held beliefs that individuals may not exercise outside the group. Social science research provides many examples,[24] and this study adds more. In chapter 5, volunteers with years of social work experience drew little if at all on their expertise when they joined other volunteers to figure out how to serve former welfare-receiving families in the Adopt-a-Family project. They were wearing different hats then; it was as if they did not know any more about social service clients than anyone else in the project. Sounding like an expert bureaucrat was not customary in their volunteer groups, and would have been offensive.

That is why this book focuses on groups and the customs of groups, instead of highlighting individuals or character types. Portraying how people do things together is the best way to address the social spiral argument and all of its hopes for civic life. Ethnographic studies often portray individuals, their hopes, fears, struggles, in compelling detail. The leading individuals in the Lakeburg groups will be hard to miss in the case chapters, and a different sort of study might have highlighted their biographical details. Fascinating as that can be, this book has different things to do: I want to introduce the quietly powerful customs of group settings that, in sometimes surprising ways, *make* us into distinct kinds of people in those settings, even when we are different outside.

Lakeburg groups' customs did seem to operate with an "unconscious pervasiveness" at least some of the time. Recent sociological work clarifies how this influence works. Customs often kept the Lakeburg groups from practicing social reflexivity—because doing so would have threatened the groups' own solidarity.

How People Do Things Together in Groups: Customs

Reintroduction

I have introduced group-building customs already: They are routine, shared, often implicit ways of defining membership in a group. My concept of group-building customs, or simply "customs," is more specific than Tocqueville's somewhat analogous notion of "mores,"[25] and more precise than Dewey's or Addams's own concepts of custom.

Different customs produce different kinds of group togetherness, not just more or less togetherness. For this study's purposes, groups do not make up their togetherness from scratch. Patterns of group togetherness are part of the larger culture upon which civic groups draw. The customs I discovered in Lakeburg are recognizable in other studies of civic groups, but the character and power of these patterns has not been clearly conceptualized previously. These customs have their own influence on social action. They are not simply derivatives of a group's formally stated purpose or beliefs.

Sociologists already have started showing how routine group practices shape the way members talk and act in the group and in the world outside the group. Different religious congregations follow different models of how to be a congregation, for instance—even within the same denomination. They have different ways of defining "who we are" and "how we do things here," as sociologist Penny Edgell Becker (1999) succinctly puts it. Congregations did not make up these models from scratch; they came from a broader repertoire. Similarly, sociologist Nina Eliasoph found out (1998) that "activist" and "volunteer" groups defined a good member in very different ways; the meanings of membership affected how if at all members could discuss political issues, apart from group members' beliefs about the issues themselves. My own studies of social activists (Lichterman 1995b, 1996, 1999) showed that the clashing definitions of group membership could make alliances between activists difficult, even when they all agreed on the issues. Environmentalist groups had a hard time working together on a campaign against industrial pollution, even though they all agreed with the ideology that minority locales are unfairly burdened with toxic dumpsites on account of "environmental racism." Different customs of group membership led to miscommunication and missed connections. Again, groups did not make up the meanings of membership from scratch; they came from the broader culture.

These studies drew on different theoretical traditions.[26] They already were suggesting what I found to be the case in the Lakeburg groups: Customs powerfully shape a group's relation to the social and cultural world outside the group.

Three Dimensions of Customs

There is no ready-made catalog of American group-building customs. We have to discover them inductively. Since "being a member" could mean different things in different groups, sociologists have looked for patterns in group life, identifying them with clues from previous research.[27] When I went to the Lakeburg groups, I listened to the ways members talked about or implied what makes a good, responsible member. I listened to the way the groups mapped themselves into the world of groups and institutions outside the group. And I listened for the genres of speech that seemed acceptable, mandatory, or unacceptable in the groups. A new, sensitizing framework (Eliasoph and Lichterman 2003) organized this listening-and-analyzing process in light of previous research; my Lakeburg cases further substantiated the framework.[28]

Using the framework, I listened for patterns of interaction that reveal shared assumptions about:

group boundaries: how group members should define what a group's relation to the wider world is;

group bonds: how group members should define mutual obligations in the
group; and

speech norms: what the appropriate genres of speech are in the group; what
the act of speaking itself is supposed to mean.

Using these dimensions as a guide makes it easier for researchers to notice and
document customs, and to compare across different kinds of groups. The following chapters will show how boundaries, bonds, and speech genres work together in the different groups I studied. Chapter 7 will show how religious traditions influenced the customs I saw and heard.

It takes no special intuition to discern customs. Readers who want to know
more about how I conceptualized customs and studied them should consult appendix II. There, I identify the supporting research literature for the concept,
and show how I studied it. Appendix II also describes how I avoided the potential logical problems that can arise when we want to identify customs at work in
everyday interaction.

Customs and Social Reflexivity

Jane Addams warned that relationships in a diverse, socially unequal society
would be perplexing only as long as we allowed our styles of relating to "become
hardened into customs and habits." But I found that there were particular customs that promoted bridging relationships, as well as customs that stymied
them. In the following chapters I show how customs shaped the possibilities for
social reflexivity in the Lakeburg groups.

The following chapters will show customs affecting reflexivity in interactions
separate from the ones I used to establish the existence of a custom. Otherwise
I would risk a kind of circular reasoning that I worked to banish from the study,
as I describe in appendix II. If customs operate as I have argued, they will influence conversations relevant to social reflexivity, and conversations not so obviously relevant. Scenes from early in the groups' histories helped me determine
what the customs were, which customs were jelling as the dominant ones. I use
scenes from later in the groups' histories to show how members shut down reflexivity or passed up obvious opportunities to practice it. In Park Cluster, I
heard one prominent member try to shut down the reflexivity that other members felt obligated to practice.

Breaches were good clues.[29] I heard how reflexivity threatened to *breach* the
customs that sustained the groups a lot of the time. To give one illustration from
the Adopt-a-Family project: One man suggested that his church group might
relate to its adopted family as people who lived in a specific neighborhood,

rather than as needy individuals in general. He was starting to say that church group members should reflect critically on their place on the social map, think of themselves as an "outsider" group "coming in" to a neighborhood that might have its own sense of cultural turf. The project director—usually voluble, articulate, and instructive—grinned quietly and awkwardly, and mumbled. No one else in the room took up the issue. The topic never came up again, the volunteer dropped out, and Adopt-a-Family continued to define itself as a collection of deeply compassionate volunteers relating to hurting individuals.

Where Do Customs Come From?

Culture

How do people figure out how to work together in groups, what to say, and what not to say? Do they make it up as they go along? Some parts of group life are innovative, idiosyncratic. Many groups develop in-jokes, nicknames, shared secrets, idiosyncratic ways of doing things that reflect the group's experience together. As sociologist Gary Alan Fine beautifully describes (for instance, 1987), groups work out "idiocultures." Sometimes idiocultures diffuse to other groups; Fine draws examples from Little League baseball teams.

The Lakeburg groups each had an idioculture: Members of one of my Adopt-a-Family church groups, for instance, shared stories, again and again, about how hard it was to make contact with the family's mother. The volunteers had not worked together before on a community project like this. They shared a novel set of circumstances; the jokes and stories they retold were not the same as the ones I heard in other Adopt-a-Family groups, not to mention other Lakeburg groups in this book. These were part of that group's own, idiosyncratic culture—and they carried emotionally charged meaning for the group.

I focused on a different level of culture in the Lakeburg groups.[30] As many sociologists of culture would put it, culture is a set of publicly shared, symbolic patterns that *enable and constrain* what people can say and do together. Sociologists have named these patterns discourses, vocabularies, traditions, codes, practices, schema, and other terms—each signaling a different theoretical approach to these symbolic patterns. From this viewpoint, culture *structures* people's ability to communicate. Culture exists beyond any single interaction. Using the cultural level of analysis we see and hear how culture shapes the possibilities in any one interaction.[31] Culture gives us the vocabularies, images, codes, or styles of interaction that organize ideas and experience into communicable form. People do not develop ideas and then put them into words that reflect the ideas transparently. Rather, communication is structured from the start by cultural forms—patterns—that the cultural level of analysis allows us to see or hear.

Material resources or institutional opportunities also shape a group's ability to talk about things of course. Still, forms of communication do not pop out automatically given the resources or opportunities a group has at hand. Under the enabling and constraining effects of resources or opportunities, cultural patterns organize what we can say—and as I will show, what we can do together.

In one powerful example, sociologist Robert Wuthnow found (1991) that while many millions of Americans do volunteer work in their locales every year, there are a relatively few predictable ways that volunteers can talk about why they volunteer. In interviews, volunteers from the cultural mainstream carefully avoided sounding self-righteous or "Goody Two shoes." Many could say volunteering felt good to them or simply made sense at the time, without having a ready vocabulary for explaining why other people should do volunteer work instead of other things that also feel good or happen to make sense at the time. Millions of volunteers and a few ways to talk about volunteering: that is a society's shared culture at work.

Civic Culture and Its Different Forms

Culture is a big concept; culture is in play anywhere that people communicate shared meanings. Sociologists often distinguish different spheres of culture, and some study *civic* culture—the cultural patterns that shape the means or ends of civic engagement. Those patterns include group-building customs. When citizens work together, some of what they say and do together is structured by widespread cultural routines—customs—that they are not making up locally from scratch. From this perspective, there is a limited number of sets of customs; this book highlights five sets. The five do not exhaust the customs of American civic culture, but likely there are many American civic groups that share one of those five sets.

Why is it reasonable to think the customs I heard in the Lakeburg groups were not just idiosyncratic, but part of a larger civic culture? Neoinstitutionalist scholars make a parallel argument. They conceive organizational routines as elements of culture shared across large sectors of collective activity—corporations, schools, nonprofit enterprises, the religious arena, or even social movements.[32] In this view, entire organizations and even entire sectors of society act out those routines. I am focusing on the customs of group settings rather than styles of entire organizations. The cases in this book will demonstrate why the difference matters a great deal empirically. Using the same perspective, it is reasonable to think that by studying customs in the Lakeburg groups, I was getting a view of potentially widespread forms of group togetherness, not just the unique subcultures of a few cases.

Evidence from other ethnographic studies strengthens the argument. Chapter 4 recognizes the style of Catherine's Justice Task Force in studies of other activist groups. Chapter 3 recognizes the Humane Response Alliance's volunteer customs in scholarly descriptions of other volunteer groups. I found that some church-sponsored programs for former welfare-receiving families in the American south sounded very similar to upper-midwestern Lakeburg's Adopt-a-Family pictured in chapter 5.

Sociologists are only now noticing civic group customs, but have given a lot of attention to the vocabularies people use in public life to talk about what makes a good person, a good act, or a good society.[33] These vocabularies are important forms of civic culture too, and I paid attention to them in the Lakeburg groups. People spoke from biblically inspired vocabularies of social justice and compassion, and secular vocabularies of citizenly duty; I was hearing civic culture when they did. The words and phrases—literally, the vocabularies—were not just made up on the spot. Even the most cursory knowledge of the Bible, or American culture for that matter, would tell the listener that these were not particular to the groups I studied. Idioms of social justice and compassion have long histories in the Judeo-Christian traditions. They influence—not strictly determine, but influence—what adherents of those traditions can say meaningfully at least some of the time.

Studies of moral vocabularies belong to a larger trend in sociology, a growing focus on public language. Different schools of research on public language all share a fundamental insight, that language constructs and not merely reflects reality. Interests, grievances, or demands come alive only in the words that groups use to articulate them. These researchers pay attention to language itself rather than taking language as a proxy for abstract motivating "values." They have developed a variety of concepts—"collective action frames," "hegemonic discourse," and "narrative," for instance—to put their insight about language into research practice.[34]

While honoring the basic insight in these studies of public language, I found that vocabularies acquire particular meanings and uses in interaction, *through the customs of group life*. Explicit vocabularies and quieter customs both influence how groups communicate, act, and spiral outward. Cultural vocabularies mattered because they gave the Lakeburg groups the words, phrases, story lines for thinking about community service. So I paid attention to vocabularies *in conjunction with* the customs that made those vocabularies mean particular things in group settings, with particular consequences for action. Cases in this book will show that to explain my findings in terms of discourses or vocabularies alone would miss crucial parts of the story.

In the Humane Response Alliance, for instance, a vocabulary of "civic renewal" opened up fascinating puzzles: Wouldn't a community group that explicitly affirms "reconnecting the caring community" be one that is good at talking about its relations with other local groups and agencies and establishing ties with them? HRA's leader, a man with over two decades of community service and administrative experience, ironically did at least as much as anyone else to thwart careful, thoughtful pondering of relations between the fledgling alliance and other groups. He followed customs that actually undercut the vocabulary of civic renewal; he simply was trying to keep the group together as a group in the best way he knew. But the customs kept the HRA from "renewing" civic ties in Lakeburg, no matter how earnestly the director talked about civic renewal. Other research showed, for instance, that the vocabulary of social justice did not *have* to mean self-marginalizing critique, but it did have to mean that in the context of the Justice Task Force's customs.

INSTITUTIONAL STRUCTURE CONDITIONS CUSTOMS TOO

Customs come from the larger civic culture, but groups do not draw on the larger culture randomly. Each of the Lakeburg groups and projects were responding in some way to an institutionalized set of roles that characterize social service agencies. Scenes from the Lakeburg groups will show how that structure rewards some kinds of citizen efforts with resources, and pressures, ignores, or misunderstands other kinds. Many American community service groups, secular and religiously sponsored alike, take for granted today a specialized, task-oriented, time-limited "volunteer" role, the duties of which are defined by social service professionals (Wuthnow 1998, pp. 50–51; see also Schervish et al. 1995; Wuthnow 2004). Professional service organizations elicit, and reinforce, a kind of volunteering parceled out into slots for the indispensable work that nonexperts can do: answering phones, stuffing envelopes, serving a meal, or tutoring a child.

The delimited volunteer role has become *customary:* There are widespread customs of boundary drawing, bonding, and speaking that shape many Americans' volunteering experience. Plug-in style volunteering as many Americans now know it developed as the social structure of paid professional service workers expanded after World War II.[35] The Humane Response Alliance settled into just these customs of loose networking and volunteering.

The institutions that organize community service become prominent reference points on volunteers' social maps. Volunteer groups define their boundaries in relation to those prominent institutions, reproducing the social structure of professional-volunteer roles and relationships. Even groups that contest the routinized forms of service elicited by state social service agencies are in effect making those institutions part of their very understanding of who they are—or are not—as groups. Civic groups that depart from the script of volunteer service face the tensions and cross-pressures of working outside the institutional mold. The Justice Task Force, Adopt-a-Family, and Park Cluster pursued alternatives to the most conventional style of community service. They drew boundaries differently and bonded and spoke differently. Case chapters will portray these differences and show what kinds of tensions the groups endured.

Still, civic groups' customs do not correspond in a perfect, one-to-one way with social-structural contexts. There is more than one possible way to construct a citizen group in response to the state-sponsored structure of social service. As William Sewell Jr. has pointed out (1992), people relate to resources *only* through cultural definitions. Resources matter of course, but they do not exist as self-evident realities; the same is true of opportunities. Groups may define the same material resource or opportunity very differently in different contexts.

That is what I heard in the different Lakeburg groups. County social service workers made opportunities available for the Lakeburg groups, religiously based groups no less, to get involved in community service. And they made resources available too, especially in the form of their own time and expertise. Lakeburg county social workers knew the welfare regulations better than most church volunteers. Sometimes they knew what people in low-income neighborhoods wanted from outside "helpers." They knew how to do the bookkeeping for church-sponsored assistance grants. Different customs made groups more, or less, able to enlist these resources or opportunities for creating civic ties outward. Customs enable and constrain the relationships that citizens have with the state and other institutions as well as with each other. That means civic groups have some leeway to limit, or accede to, social service institutions' influence.

The Layout of the Cases Ahead

The following case chapters work together toward reconstructing the social spiral argument. Each will present a group's or network's larger institutional context and its main vocabulary of community involvement. The chapters lay out the customs in each case, showing how these shaped communication inside the group and contacts with the social world beyond. Cases will show how the customs made cultural vocabularies of social justice, compassion, or civic duty mean specific things in everyday practice; they will show how customs complemented or occasionally challenged or sat uncomfortably with their institutional context. Customs influenced social reflexivity in each case, and reflexivity or its absence in turn influenced bridge-building. Stepping back, I ask whether or not the group in question could be said to have empowered civil society at the local level. The case chapters each try out alternative accounts, strengthening the case that customs matter.

If talk itself is what makes civic groups distinct from other kinds of organizations, as theorist Mark E. Warren (2001) says, it should not be surprising that the following chapters portray a lot of group conversation. Let's listen closely.

Chapter Three

NETWORKERS AND VOLUNTEERS REACHING OUT

"Pray for this city," the executive administrator of Lakeburg County had told a special meeting of Lakeburg religious leaders in 1995. He was worried about what would happen when the county's social welfare programs got cut. Long-time volunteers in the Urban Religious Coalition (URC), along with a few pastors, took up the executive's call—and that, in short, was the origin story of the Humane Response Alliance (HRA). URC director Donald would repeat it many times. He said often, too, that they were going to rebuild the caring structures of Lakeburg, weaving together churches, community service associations, and county agencies into a new social safety net.

It was an ambitious bridging project, and the URC brought to it nearly twenty-five years of experience dreaming up and spinning off community service projects. Fifty-two churches were affiliated with the URC when I began going to HRA meetings. HRA's leading members included the director of Lakeburg's largest homeless shelter; a lawyer and one-time director of the state peace and justice coalition; a former manager of a food service company who worked now as a food pantry coordinator; a longtime pastor and former social worker; a nun liaison from a Catholic hospital; the articulate, globe-trotting leader of the URC's prayer group; the deputy county social services administrator in charge of family support programs; and a volunteer program organizer with experience in another urban religious coalition. They were used to working in organizations, working with people, working with words. Like many of the URC's other members, some had been active in the civil rights movement thirty-five years earlier and had remained involved in public causes ever since. In their late fifties and older—occasionally much older—they were part of what Robert Putnam has called the "civic generation." They were part of the aging cohort that is still active in civic life and even has increased its individual volunteering since the 1970s (Putnam 2000, pp. 128–32). Donald put it wryly if appreciatively: "They've been here forever."

Donald was a civic broker extraordinaire. Dubbed the "charismatic gadfly" of the URC, he managed to make nearly everyone in Lakeburg's religious circles trust him—conservative evangelicals, liberal mainliners, the head pastor of a prominent African American Baptist congregation. He could parry evangelicals' dismissive comments about pagans with a quick, respectful sentence about "the earth religions." He could nudge liberal Protestant HRA members into shame for not having reached out to a band of evangelical churches starting their own service network. He could get theological liberals and conservatives to meet monthly and talk informally over supper about red-button issues: the meaning of family, the value of welfare reform, the experience of sexuality, the nature of God.

But even with experience, resolve, savvy, and a compelling vision of civic renewal, Donald could not help the HRA build any of the bridges it set out to build. He himself put up some of the biggest barriers. At monthly meetings, HRA coordinators' feelings and ideas were renewed and their "hearts enlarged," with dire prognoses on human needs in Lakeburg County. But group process depended on particular customs of networking and volunteering that locked the HRA into narrow horizons and short-term tasks, instead of empowering them to begin reconnecting the caring structures. Between these busy, overwhelmed networkers and the busy, determined volunteers the networkers recruited, no one was left to talk through the bigger picture. Networking and volunteering ended up derailing reflection on who exactly the HRA was, in relation to whom. Donald himself assumed that enough "doing" would add up to new civic bridges, without a clear, agreed-upon picture of what Lakeburg's groups, communities, and institutions looked like. He told me that the HRA effort had been a disappointment.[1] The HRA dissipated a year after the kickoff meeting. This chapter does a double duty, showing how networking and volunteering worked together to undermine Donald's broad vision.

The Alliance's efforts did produce some valuable goods. The HRA spun off several projects, including the Justice Task Force pictured in chapter 4, and a gathering of church volunteers that became the autonomous Park Cluster, explored in chapter 6. It also created new opportunities for short-term volunteer work. Creating short-term, plug-in style volunteer opportunities is a civic enterprise itself, valuable in some ways, but it does not accomplish the more ambitious bridge-building that was the HRA's ultimate goal. It does not build community in any broad or deep way. The HRA's experiences suggest that plug-in style volunteering may not generate the social connections signified in the fuller meaning of the concept of social capital, even though statistics on volunteering are a prominent indicator of social capital in recent research.

At the end of the chapter, with scenes from the field in view, I will explain why it makes sense to say that HRA did not empower civil society in Lakeburg. The county social services agency did not help the HRA create new bridges with itself or other groups, but that alone could not be the reason for HRA's disappointments. County workers' own institutional routines made it hard for the HRA to build relationships that would empower HRA as a partner in a new social contract. But the HRA's customs, which members affirmed in religious terms, had their own, autonomous momentum.

THE VISION OF A CHARISMATIC GADFLY

A Vocabulary of Civic Renewal

The HRA had a noble vision. In the words of a URC newsletter's lead article, it was going to "rebuild the supportive infrastructures in our communities, not just for the sake of the needy but for the sake of us all." Cutbacks in social programs were driving more people to food pantries and homeless shelters, the article observed. Social service workers already were despairing, burning out. Neither the state nor the market was going to solve the problems of poverty. "We need a third, formerly ignored sector. This is the civic sector, made up of nonprofit, neighborhood, and religious communities. These three sectors operating together are essential if we are to rebuild the supportive fabric of our communities for the common good of all our citizens." This was more than the usual call to go out and volunteer; the article emphasized civic ties. It did not say that the needy would need even more from beneficent providers. It was saying we all depended on civic ties; we were all in it together as state-supported welfare transformed—for worse if not better. It was a manifesto of bridge-building between churches, community groups, and state agencies.

Donald was a remarkably consistent spokesperson for this high-minded, vague vision. At HRA meetings, monthly URC board meetings, convocations of volunteers, and in private chats with me, he always called the Alliance an effort to "rebuild the caring structures of our community." In a newsletter article, and at my first HRA meeting, Donald asked, "How do religious and spiritual people fit into this public sector, private sector, civil sector partnership . . . to reconnect the caring systems?" Strikingly, Donald also argued that rebuilding the caring structures would require "shifts in the way faith communities get involved in action." "Presently, we . . . function as isolated institutions which provide volunteers and money to develop or support social service or political action projects. . . . This approach leads to feelings of isolation, frustration, anger and burn out."[2]

Donald was challenging the common sense that many American churchgoers share about both volunteering and social activism. Many churches have committees that perform charitable deeds for their larger locale. They collect food donations, visit sick people in hospitals, cook meals for homeless shelters, or run secondhand clothing shops. And many have "social action" or "church and society" committees that support struggles against economic or racial injustice.[3] Donald was saying that rebuilding the caring structures would be different from either social advocacy or charitable "fixes" that do not attend to fraying social ties.

God in Civic Renewal

There was little explicit religious talk in the HRA. Leaders and some volunteers in Alliance projects did say in private interviews that they had religious motives for their community work, and they kept the specific sources of these motives largely private. Scholars of American religion have debated whether and how religion promotes the civic good, and chapter 7 will revisit this discussion in light of evidence from the different groups and projects. The HRA had a faith connection, but Alliance members did not identify themselves explicitly with a specific religious mandate or a story line from any single tradition. They called the HRA an effort by "people of faith."

General appeals to faith are congenial to, and dependent on, some religious traditions more than others. The Alliance's religious tone resonated with the nonideological "Golden Rule Christianity" that Nancy Ammerman has described (1997b). It is a Christian faith that emphasizes "right living" over "right believing" (p. 197) and upholds a transcendent God, albeit imagined in "fuzzy" (p. 207) terms. In that spirit, it makes sense that Alliance leaders usually referred to Alliance members as people of faith, or members of "faith communities." Though all the Alliance leaders and core participants belonged to churches, the network was officially interfaith—unlike the explicitly and exclusively Christian Adopt-a-Family project I will describe later on. None of the leaders I heard at monthly Alliance meetings ever appealed to specific texts or traditions in support of a project or a new plan of action.

Donald's own definition of the Alliance included an abstract vision of Godliness. His stirring newsletter article on "rebuilding our communities" implied that people cannot create healthy civic connections if they are not connected to the Divine: " . . . God, like the air we breathe, is essential to life. We will die without this connection. And this is more than just a personal relationship. It is the recognition that all structures of our world need to be "in God" if we are to be healthy. Without this relationship, the dysfunction and deterioration will continue."[4]

I never heard HRA members discussing whether or not Lakeburg's civic structures were "in God." But Donald was saying that organizational isolation and frustration would continue unless the Spirit of God suffused civic efforts, like those of the HRA. He sometimes closed monthly Alliance meetings with a benediction in the same spirit, calling on us to discern "the Spirit of God working through us" as we pondered the Alliance's next steps. After one meeting filled with tart exchanges between Alliance leaders, Donald told us, "I would urge with your prayer—or meditation or whatever you call it—we each commit to pray for insight and guidance." Just as Donald tried to include everyone with his benedictory offering, so the Alliance tried to keep its different parties integrated into the alliance. It was not easy.

PROJECTS IN SEARCH OF A GROUP

At the September 1996 kickoff meeting in Lakeburg Presbyterian's basement, churchgoers heard about what they could do to rebuild the caring structures.

Pastor Edward Lindstrom, a URC board member and former social worker from a small evangelical denomination[5] presented his project in less than two minutes. Lindstrom headed up the still-forming congregational clusters project. "Clusters draw people from different faith communities to figure out where faith communities and social service workers can be in conversation together. . . . Is there a way we can get members of faith communities to get together and talk about our shared concerns?"

Then there was Polly, of the Fun Evenings project. Polly worried about Lakeburg too, and told a story meant to agitate her audience with a frightening comparison: Just fifteen years ago, a big city not far away used to have low murder rate. Everyone knew that was not the case now. "We don't want to go the way they did." Inspired by a program launched in that big city, Fun Evenings would organize drug-free, weapons-free evenings of dancing, snacking, basketball, and Ping-Pong for "at-risk" teenagers in school auditoriums and community centers. A program like Fun Evenings might help stop the cycle of violence and drug abuse that pulled in kids from low-income families.

Catherine, of the Justice Task Force, introduced herself as an "angry granny" with a different kind of message. She started the Task Force so that churchgoers could study the bigger, social-structural issues behind the individual pain and suffering that other speakers told us were awaiting families on welfare. "Join us," she called out, half-beseechingly and half-mischievously. "We get so wrapped up pulling people out of the water that we forget to look for the causes upstream."

There was something for everyone—upbeat volunteering, weighty civic deliberation, political education. How would we know what to do? The last item on our agenda sheets was a ritual titled "What am I or my congregation called to do?" Clarisse, a technical educator in her late forties, read us a prayer she had composed. The prayer identified us all as "people from different faith communities" and bid us to meditate on what kinds of service we could offer the community. At the close, Clarisse invited us to walk up to the signup sheets taped to a line of cafeteria-style tables at the front of the basement meeting hall, "while still in a prayerful state," and volunteer ourselves for the church clusters project, the Fun Evenings project for teens, the Justice Task Force, or the Safety Net group. There was silence. For several minutes, we sat in our folding chairs, listening for our inner callings. Slowly, silently, people walked toward the tables and stood in line behind the signup sheets. But for a few whispers, no one spoke until Donald closed the meeting fifteen minutes later. The ritual said that HRA participants were people of faith, moved by private values to act for the public good.

Earnest, private commitments did not keep HRA group leaders from miscommunicating and arguing. Sometimes it was as if they were using completely different maps that drew very different boundaries. Lindstrom, for instance, envisioned the whole Alliance as a union of congregations with civic responsibilities. Churches needed to think of themselves as belonging to neighborhoods, communities. Like Donald, Lindstrom hoped faith-based groups could build civic relationships that state agencies might not be able to initiate on their own. The "parish nurse" idea is a good example. "When you think of faith communities, churches and synagogues and what-not, as little nodes of holistic healing, [then there is a lot they could do.] The nurse can ask what are the needs immediately surrounding a church that a parish nurse can satisfy. . . . You can define a parish as broadly as you want." More than just a collector of donations from churches, the nurse could be a kind of civic go-between, creating a new set of relationships to complement state-sponsored social service.

Polly had a different map. In her view, the Alliance was less a union of congregations, bound by faith-based precepts, and more a collection of potential volunteers for youth, who happened to go to churches. In the winter of 1997, we all heard the depressing statistics and gloomy prognoses: Most food pantry users were poor working people—not the something-for-nothing bogeys of conservative antiwelfare rhetoric. Most pantry patrons now depended on pantries continuously, instead of using them as a stopgap at the end of the month. Homeless shelters were going to fill to capacity quickly, as more former welfare recipients lost their homes. In the middle of the grim proceedings one month, Polly came bounding in, apologized for being late, and assured us we would forgive when we heard the good news that United Way had just decided to fund Fun Evenings with a generous grant.

As she started updating the group on the Fun Evenings project, "angry granny" Catherine bristled. She tried to shift the floor of the conversation right then and there: She passed around a bar graph that illustrated growing economic inequality in the United States since the 1950s. She told us she had become increasingly frustrated. The justice group had been talking about "what to do" for some time, and she was not sure it was making progress. It was putting together a workshop on wealth and poverty in the United States, and hoped that lots of local churches would host the workshop as an adult educational session on Sundays. It wanted to pass a petition against maximum security "Supermax" prisons. It wanted to support the local Campaign for a Living Wage.

Sparks flew when Polly responded to Catherine:

POLLY: Couldn't these all get distilled into a list of things people could do? Like taking clothes to the homeless?
CATHERINE (*cutting in sharply*): Taking clothes doesn't change structures!

Taken aback, Polly started over. She tried to explain herself. If the Alliance created a list of things people could "do," then people who wanted to do something right away would have the information they needed, and others who wanted to address the larger social justice issues that mattered so much to Catherine "could find a group to raise them in." To Catherine, it was Band-Aids versus solutions; to Polly, it was empty talk versus effective action.

On Catherine's social map, the Alliance was not volunteers fighting shadowy social problems with bright confidence. It was truth-speaking social critics poised bravely against dominating social structures. "Social structures" and especially the structure of corporate power loomed over all else; neighborhoods and civic institutions barely showed up on Catherine's map. Alliance members did not need to be people of faith or members of congregations, as far as she was concerned. It was just as good to get the Task Force's educational workshops into workplaces or secular clubs as into churches. Much as she thought the Judeo-Christian heritage scorned greed and injustice, she thought that criticizing welfare reform was everyone's duty, whether or not they identified with congregations. Which map should they use? What kind of member would be a good member of the Alliance?

The Network Solution

Doing Things Together Loosely

The kickoff meeting's closing ritual sacralized a notion of civic involvement that is extremely familiar in American secular as well as religious settings: It is up to each of us, on the basis of our private, individual values, to do what we think is right. Some individuals want to take winter coats to the homeless, while others want to criticize capitalism for making some people too poor to afford homes; all should be free to act on their values. Why not form a network that gives people the freedom to address complex problems in different ways? It is a customary, commonsense organizational solution to the dilemma of competing values.

I dub the HRA a "loosely connected network," after Robert Wuthnow's observations on (1998) Americans' "loose connections" in civic life. Loosely connected networks contrast with an older style of civic organization, the civic clubs that play a famously declining role in American civic life. Loosely connected networks are coalitions of volunteer groups and professional or state-employed social service workers who define tasks for the volunteers, while older-style civic organizations are often self-contained clubs that belong to regional or national club federations, as I mentioned in chapter 1. Loosely connected networks form around a particular issue such as welfare reform, rather than around a strong group identity. Loosely connected networks, like the HRA, prize efficient, task-oriented volunteers and efficient, knowledgeable networkers with lots of social connections. Older-style civic groups prize loyal group enthusiasts, whether or not they have specialized expertise. Loosely connected networks often sponsor the task-oriented, short-term, plug-in style of volunteering that has become nearly synonymous with volunteering in the United States. In spite of its broader goals, the HRA spent much of its time organizing meetings at which potential volunteers could learn about opportunities for plugging in.

Unlike some loosely connected networks that sociologist Wuthnow has described (1998), the HRA drew on a pool of volunteers, many of whom already were volunteering with URC projects and attended churches affiliated with the URC. At least half of the thirty-five to sixty people I saw at each of three HRA quarterly public meetings were people I recognized as core participants in HRA project groups—the Justice Task Force or Safety Net group, for instance—or else were URC members who attended other URC meetings I had attended. Though it did not intend to, the HRA cycled new volunteer opportunities to a lot of people already working in HRA projects.

What kind of social spiral can loosely connected networks empower? Sociologist Wuthnow is ambivalent. Potentially, they are more flexible than long-established, multipurpose civic clubs such as the Kiwanis, but they also must spend more of their time making their short-term volunteers feel good about volunteering, feel as if they really are part of a community (1998, pp. 90, 190). Loosely connected networks can accommodate busy schedules; they ask volunteers to commit to short-term tasks for a couple of hours a week. They do not require indefinite, loyal commitments to a group as a whole. On the other hand, they address social problems that many other organizations and state agencies address, and may have a hard time keeping in regular contact with other groups whose work bears directly on their own (1998, p. 98). I set out to see how exactly the HRA as a loosely connected network would create new bridges between churches and agencies. If community service coalitions made up of church groups are as common as recent research shows (for instance, Chaves, Giesel, and Tsitsos 2002, Ammerman 2002; Warner 1999; see also Wuthnow 2004), then a close look at the HRA network and its customs should teach us something about a wide swath of community service efforts in America.

Networking and Volunteering Customs

Networking customs helped Alliance leaders work *simultaneously* without working *together*. Different members had different understandings of the Humane Response Alliance's relations to other groups—its boundaries. They pictured an Alliance with different kinds of group bonds, too. They carried different assumptions about what was the most appropriate speech for HRA meetings—and clashed over them, as I will show below. To keep working together as a loose network, HRA leaders shared a vaguely defined social map of civic groups, county agencies, and churches, spreading outward indefinitely. As for group bonds, it upheld a baseline of mutual respect between members as individuals of faith—or individuals friendly to the notion that spirituality if not religion had a place in civic effort. And the HRA adopted a business-meeting style of speech that was familiar to all, a speech style that focused speakers on tasks, and narrowed the space for more exploratory kinds of discussion. These customs do not sound remarkable, but they were very different from others I heard in Lakeburg groups, and they had a powerful influence on how HRA carried out its ambitious goal.

The service projects relied on customs of volunteering that I will explore later on. If loosely connected networks exist mainly to assign tasks and accomplish short-term projects, then volunteers are the other half of the equation: Volunteers carry out the tasks—ideally, with heart. In the most common cultural understanding, volunteers are compassionate individuals whose selfless acts make a difference.[6] Volunteers want to help individuals "person to person"—maybe out of a biblically informed sense of compassion, or maybe because it just feels good to help other people. In Donald's view, volunteering by itself would not create the bridges that HRA intended to create. But I watched and listened carefully as an HRA volunteer myself, to see if white, middle-class volunteers who did volunteer stints with kids of color from low-income families or stints in a church homeless shelter project might learn bridge-building skills, even if their job was not to build organizational bridges themselves. The volunteer projects I participated in seemed unlikely to encourage these skills. Volunteers focused on getting things done, trying to keep busy, rather than learning how to relate to other people or groups.

"Interacting Flexibly" or Agreeing to Disagree?

The beauty of loosely connected networks is that they can accommodate differences—networkers do not even have to talk much about them. In the HRA, project groups held their own meetings. Volunteers could join whichever project they pleased. The group coordinators met monthly so that representatives could hear updates from the various projects and plan larger meetings designed to pull more volunteers into the projects. *Group bonds* within the network could stay thin; a more or less respectful coexistence, even at some distance, was enough—and even that seemed difficult. URC volunteers did not have to listen to Catherine's social critique if they did not want to; they could join some other group. Activists did not have to put faith in Polly's can-do volunteerism; they did not need to sign up for Fun Evenings. No one really had to bother trying to figure out how community institutions related to one another, as Edward and Donald would have liked; they could join a congregational cluster if that project seemed compelling. URC participants could choose their niche, assuming that someone else was figuring out the bigger picture, making it all fit together.

Donald as much as anyone else drew HRA's bigger picture, its sense of *boundaries* with other groups. Donald invited hospital administrators, chaplains, and food pantry organizers to HRA meetings along with project leaders, volunteers from URC, and the county social services deputy and his assistant. The HRA got the opportunity to see itself, quite literally, amidst diverse civic and governmental entities. The county social services department was the most prominent of the outside groups on the HRA's social map. The church leaders treated its representative as a consulting expert.

It could have been John Dewey's ideal in action: Donald wanted the Alliance to develop new relationships with other groups in Lakeburg by acting like what he called an "action/reflection" group. Group members would keep talking through how the different groups related to one another and to other Lakeburg organizations, especially the ones that sent representatives to HRA meetings.[7] Inside the network, stopgap, emergency shelter, and food projects[8] would learn from the horizon-broadening social criticism of Catherine's justice group. The justice group would keep its sophisticated social criticism grounded in the daily struggles of pantry patrons and shelter guests it heard about from other volunteers. Or at least that was the vision.

The energy and the tension at meetings went in other directions, though. Alliance networkers were busy figuring out how to get more volunteers networked into the projects. Group members were busy carrying out tasks, offering direct service, or in the case of Catherine's group, decrying social injustice, local and national.

Customs Keep Us on Track: Action, Not Reflection

As it turned out, the service projects rarely communicated with one another except through business reports at Alliance meetings. For all their differences, none of the group coordinators challenged the assumption that talk was a waste of time if it did not lead directly to action. And Donald, more than anyone, enforced the dominant *speech norms,* those of the task-oriented business meeting, even though he said he hoped to generate an action/reflection dynamic. He told us at one early meeting, he hoped we would be able to reconnect the caring community "without a lot of meetings." The point was to organize tasks and go out and *do* them, not talk about doing. Donald's noble vision of civic development coexisted with some very conventional understandings of what meetings should be like, what talk is for, what counts as "doing."

The appeal to "doing" and all that it entails about talking could shut down more exploratory conversation. At my first Alliance meeting, for instance, Donald worried that one pastor's plan to buy old hotels and turn them into low-income housing would become simply "another church-run social service." It might fail to make ordinary volunteers more collectively responsible for their community as a whole. "I don't care if it's churches doing it, I want *the community* [emphasis his] to do it. . . . We've jettisoned our caring community for individualism—organizational individualism." The pastor said that Donald was indulging in mere "verbiage" and retorted that "while the caring community is being mended I want to care for the people who need a place to live. I want to *do,* not talk."

Donald had no argument against the pastor's criticism. The HRA did not end up discussing at that meeting or any other what the difference might be between building the caring community and mobilizing volunteers for a professionalized, church-run social service—even though the difference was central in Donald's published and spoken statements. Donald resolved the conflict with the pastor, network-style: We had different points of view, we could act on them in different groups.

It turned out that Donald also preferred that people do, not talk. He had already assured us at the kickoff meeting that we were going to learn "concrete things we can do" that evening. Of course "doing" did take talk, task-oriented talk. Throughout the year, Donald goaded group leaders into identifying concrete tasks that volunteers could carry out. He did this with all the leaders, not just ones who proposed to talk critically about their relation to Lakeburg.

To take one typical meeting as an example: When Catherine said it was important to name capitalism and social structures as root causes of poverty, Donald interrupted *twice* to ask if she had a "specific action suggestion" to relay to the URC or to volunteers. It's "organizing poor people," Catherine shot back, not missing a beat. When the food pantry expert recited the grim figures on growing pantry patronage, Donald broke in to ask what she would tell people to "do." They could donate food to their local pantries, she answered. And what could the URC prayer fellowship tell people to do? The prayer group leader said she could tell people to include prayers for needy people in their weekly worship. All the project groups could come up with something to "do."

We spent the rest of the meeting drafting "I will" statements for the various project groups, that volunteers could take home with them. "I will sign a petition." "I will schedule the economic justice presentation for my congregation." "I will begin to share my food with community members." Networking customs divided up Donald's big vision of civic solidarity into doable bits. Each of the eight planning meetings I attended proceeded with a similar focus on doable tasks that project groups could carry out with volunteers. We indulged social criticism on occasion—grousing about the media's rosy portrait of welfare reform at one meeting, for instance. At several others we spun out creative ideas for projects, like taking busloads of middle-class church people to see poor neighborhoods firsthand. But always there was the overriding goal of developing doable tasks, ones that project groups like Catherine's, Ed's, or Polly's would publicize at quarterly HRA meetings for Lakeburg's churchgoing public at large.

Ideal versus Custom: The Pantry Project

For a year, Donald kept alive his vision of reconnecting the caring community, hoping that more networking might produce new bridges. The following summer he and his staff assistant had written an ambitious proposal for a new program designed to increase the donations to local food pantries. But it was supposed to do much more than that. It would create a stronger union of local churches, ready to collaborate for other civic-minded ends. The proposal articulated Donald's larger vision of building civic bridges: "Develop systems and relationships among congregations in this food pantry effort which will enable them to work collectively with one another and with secular voluntary, public, and private sector institutions on other issues of community concern."

The pantry project was the first and largest bridge-building project that the HRA proposed. The HRA's Safety Net group leader Paula, a woman who knew the food advocates in Lakeburg, said that no one was doing what the grant proposal proposed; it had an important niche to fill. Donald's assistant had been working many hours a week for the previous several months, trying to establish lines of communication between the URC and its dozens of member churches. She was doing the hard, person-to-person contact work that community organizers do (Wood 2002; Mark R. Warren 2001). She was trying to create new bridges in place of the loosely networked relations, sometimes nearly dormant relations, between the URC and dozens of churches who supported the URC financially or allowed their names to remain on URC letterheads.

Networking customs cut short an urgent invitation to reflect on the pantry project and talk it through. Having heard Donald's assistant tell us how difficult it was to get Lakeburg churches interested in the project, a woman from Community Advocates, a federally supported community service coalition, told her side of the story. Working with congregations was difficult. Church pantry volunteers would complain, "You make us submit these reports about how many people [use the pantry], what more can we do?" She answered the rhetorical question: "You have to take responsibility, establish connections with faith communities. . . . The days of 'gimme' are over! In the early 80s, the late 80s, yes, it was gimme food, gimme housing . . . but it's gone." She concluded, frustration mounting in her voice: "It's wonderful that churches, faith communities want that no one go hungry . . . but you must take *responsibility* [emphasis hers]" Churches were parochial. "It's a matter of turf . . . faith communities must get beyond turfism," she insisted. She described what happened when she suggested that a large, affluent Methodist congregation direct some of its donated food to a poorer neighborhood. "They wouldn't hear of it and nearly laughed me out of the room." She wanted to see things from churchgoers' point of view:

> WOMAN (Community Advocates): I understand the church—it makes them feel good. . . . Who are we to come in and tell you what to do?
> CHARITY LIAISON (Lakeburg Gas and Electric): It makes them feel good to put their little cans in.
> EVAN (Adopt-a-Family): The whole notion of looking at the systems level of need isn't—[what they do]. They just want to "help people."

The Community Advocates staffperson concluded that any countywide pantry support system should remain attached to her organization. Religious congregations did not know how to "care" on the level that a pantry system required. Donald looked dejected.

Donald and the rest could have taken the woman's plea for more "responsibility" as an urgent call to talk self-critically about relations between churches, at that meeting or somewhere else. She was, almost literally, crying out for a new kind of collaboration amongst volunteers and their organizers, and a new sense of connection between distant churches, neighborhoods, populations—a different social map. Wasn't that exactly what Donald had been talking and writing about the past year? The collaboration would not just organize itself, nor would abstract talk about civic renewal in newsletters bring it about. The HRA would have to talk carefully, even painfully, through the details of relationships between groups and communities that apparently did not always want to acknowledge each other.

Instead, the meeting took for granted that church people, in their capacity as church people, would continue to act like volunteers in the commonly understood sense, parochial ones at that. Donald's assistant observed, "Congregations don't identify with community organizations. . . . We go to our churches and we [lifting her head skyward in prayerful pose]—it comes from the spirit. We don't identify—we do in the rest of our lives but not in our congregational lives."

I recalled then the closing ritual at the kickoff meeting. It called us to commit ourselves as individuals with deeply held, private values, not as collaborators in communities. Donald's assistant was observing that individually driven volunteering is, after all, customary. Congregations and secular community organizations would continue to occupy spaces on opposite sides of strong boundaries between them on the HRA's social map. People around the table might have taken that map as an object for critical discussion. They might have talked about how to begin *changing* relations between churches, community groups, and government agencies, in line with the Community Advocates staffperson's criticism and Donald's year-old vision.

Immediately the conversation moved into the genre of tasking, instead; networking customs clicked in. There was staffing and logistics to figure out if the Alliance was going to get churches into relationships with food pantries. Of course it was an absolutely necessary conversation to have at some point, if churches were going to put the big plan in place. The group did not discuss something at least as important, though: how volunteers and churches should create new relationships in the postwelfare environment. That kind of conversation may have seemed more "abstract," less realistic, a luxury in a time when more and more people were going hungry. But Donald's community-building plan was *meant* to challenge routine and "realistic" ideas about what church volunteers and leaders could do for Lakeburg. That was what URC members were signing on to do.

Donald himself translated the issue into one of organizational strategy and interests. As if making an embarrassing disclosure for honesty's sake, he observed sheepishly that "the network around pantries could be used for other issues. So it's also our self-interest too." "Self-interest" is a good way to close down conversation, an appeal to something we take as the lowest common denominator of human nature, not an invitation to *explore* what interests are alive in a group.[9] Donald was trying hard to be a good person, to come clean with less than altruistic motives. His comment conveyed that the HRA was but another network with organizational interests, just like Community Advocates.[10] The pantry proposal had become a vehicle of the "organizational individualism" that Donald decried months earlier. We ended on a note reminiscent of the "I will" statements: Everyone promised to bring to the next meeting three concrete ideas for increasing the flow of food in Lakeburg.

Of course the Alliance was being realistic. They assumed they were not going to change the very ordinary, familiar customs of volunteer involvement. The HRA stuck to a group process that, in spite of itself, suppressed possibilities for creating new or different relationships between churches. There were plenty of barriers—financial, administrative, logistical—to a union of churches and food pantries. What is striking is that the HRA's customary assumptions stopped the effort before it got a chance to run up against those barriers. Changing institutionalized relationships is *not* realistic. But that is just what community development advocates and activists try to do, occasionally with some success.

A year of horizon-broadening, heartfelt conversation had brought the HRA no closer to building bridges than it was at the kickoff. Donald's vision had not changed. Just before the food pantry discussion he told a URC board meeting the same things he had said a year earlier, about the limits of networking and volunteering: "Congregations often view themselves as recruiters of volunteers for projects rather than as institutions or communities with their own goals and objectives, making decisions for the good of the community. . . . How do you deal with the church/state separation and still have congregations working together with the public sector for the common good? That's what Bill Bradley put out there." He could have been right about congregations as networkers of volunteers. Inside the church outreach committees I picture in chapter 7, committee members did learn to think in terms of volunteer pools. No one at this board meeting or in the HRA spoke against Donald's vision or his critique of community-service-as-usual. They had very different ideas, though, about how to create groups around the vision.

Room for Reflexivity?

How would the HRA create new bridges with churches or other groups if it did not communicate about what those bridges should be like? Donald's assistant had spent weeks phoning and visiting church outreach leaders because the food pantry proposal said that churches should coordinate with one another, not act as pools of volunteers loosely networked with one another. Churches were hard to coordinate; clearly, bridges needed to be built, and the HRA existed to do just that. The HRA would not likely get beyond what the Community Advocates woman called "turfism" if it did not first own up to the turfism among its churches, take it as an object of critical discussion.

An insight from social movement studies is crucial: Groups must talk about their collective identities if they are going to change routine relationships in the wider social world. As social movement scholar Alberto Melucci pointed out (1988), collective identity is not a static group characteristic. Rather, groups discover their identities always in relation to a larger field of groups—allies and antagonists among them. Put simply, group identities are relational. The same group usually has more than one way it might identify itself, more than one way to carve out its larger "multi-organizational field" (Klandermans 1992). Similarly, I am arguing that civic groups need to talk self-critically, not only strategically or self-promotingly, about their relationships with their social context if they are going to create new, enduring connections outward.

This is especially the case for groups that would challenge institutionalized definitions, the definitions that hold the most power over people even if the agents of that power are not in the room. The dominant assumptions about community service hold that volunteers usually "plug in" to a bigger picture of relationships that is mostly preplanned. Groups cannot wiggle out from under those routine assumptions if they do not make an issue of them by talking reflectively about how would-be volunteers should relate to other people. The HRA's customs squeezed out that kind of communication.

DID THE COUNTY STUNT THE HRA'S SPIRAL?

There is a popular idea that social welfare agencies are more interested in controlling their clients than cultivating clients' strengths. Some social theorists and activists take a similar view, that state bureaucracies are much better at administering citizens than learning from them or with them. In their view, state agencies overpower citizen groups that try to do their own community-building.[11] So it makes sense to wonder if county agencies in Lakeburg would refuse to take civic groups seriously as partners in social service. Outward-bound social spirals of civic renewal would run up against state-mandated professional expertise.

This viewpoint helps illuminate some of my field notes, but presents two problems. First, in its simplest and hardest form, this colonization thesis would underestimate how uncertain, self-critical, and ambiguous county agency officials were about their own response to welfare policy reform. Their signals to the HRA were much more ambiguous than a simple colonization or domination argument would guess. Second, the thesis conflates two separate questions. I ask whether or not the HRA could spiral outward and create bridges. I also ask if the HRA in some way helped empower people as citizens in relation to the state. Maybe unintentionally, county agents did play a large role in disempowering the HRA from working with them. But that does not necessarily mean those agencies held the HRA back from spiraling outward into civic life, building bridges to and between churches or other civic groups. The HRA's own customs were not simply a mirror of the county agents' ways of doing things. Civic groups have more than one way of responding to governmental agencies, and chapter 6 will show Park Cluster challenging social service workers' routines. Even under the obviously greater power of state agencies, a civic group by definition has *constructed itself as a group*. It has created its form of togetherness, with boundaries, bonds, and speech norms.

A Big but Ambiguous Presence on the Social Map

Ironically, the HRA ceded a lot of direction to county agencies from the start, even as some county social service workers invited groups like the URC to envision new civic roles for churches. URC leaders assumed at early HRA meetings that county agencies could define their niche for them. Edward observed at one meeting, for instance, that he "saw the HRA's sponsor, URC, as one of the players in the larger picture" but that "we have to figure out what that piece is in a program really set by the county." Of course they did—unless they were going to try replacing state-supported services with church-run social programs, and no one in the HRA wanted to do that. Recognizing the state's authority did not necessarily prohibit them from figuring out who *they* were as a civic entity.

As it turned out, the Alliance leaders did not give themselves the conversational space to define new, more proactive roles as community-builders in Lakeburg. Groups poised to take advantage of the "political opportunity" afforded by the new welfare policies might have carved out a strong role for civic groups within the emerging social contract. But the Humane Response Alliance did not take that initiative. Local, faith-based groups may not know how to take more responsibility for a community's well-being, even when given the opportunity.

County social service workers had no such firm ideas about what religious groups could do for the newly emerging social contract, at least not at first. County social services deputy director Steve Lanky and URC director Donald both groused about the time they had wasted with a county-sponsored Welfare Coordinating Council intended to cushion families in free fall after they had used up their welfare benefits. Steve admitted that the county had no plan for dealing with the human fallout of welfare reform, and said at my first HRA meeting that the county should be trying to work with community people from outside the welfare system, "leverage people in who can mobilize resources" as he put it. Steve also asked: "What can you do to trigger the spiritual response? It's not just responding, it's having a spiritual experience that gives them [Lakeburg citizens] ownership of their community. . . . It takes interacting with people who are impacted, on a very personal level." He implied that HRA project groups should bring participants into contact with former welfare recipients, in order to trigger that response. Meanwhile, he reported, whole families had started camping out in the hall outside his office. Donald deduced that the county "was not even asking the questions" yet, and he asked plaintively at this and other meetings, "What niche can the religious community fill?"

Three months later, Steve came up with an answer. The URC could organize dialogues between welfare policy makers, social workers, and welfare recipients. The conversations could happen in neighborhood settings, close to the people affected most by the new policies. As a government employee, Steve could not make these dialogues happen. He hoped the URC could. Steve's vision of dialogues never came to fruition, but it is not exactly what critics of bureaucratic domination would expect: The key liaison from the county was asking the HRA to initiate public dialogues and generate spiritual experiences that could give people a sense of ownership of the community.[12] He was not asking the HRA for more stopgap donations and volunteer time.

The county manager, Inge Olson, similarly signaled that church groups could play new parts in a postwelfare social safety net. She told us at HRA's kickoff meeting that part of the challenge was "how to partner differently and effectively with the faith communities." Though the separation of church and state created some necessary barriers, she observed, her own faith commitments and her eagerness to find new solutions made her think new partnerships were worth trying. She did not articulate any more definite answer to Donald's question of what niche the religious community would fill.

The county's chief executive for welfare services tried to answer that question at a convocation of URC volunteers four months later. Donald had invited her so she could explain how religious communities can get involved. She told us that volunteers can provide "the human dimension" in the transition to a new welfare regime. She had in mind the kind of compassionate one-to-one service that many people associate with church-based volunteering. At the same time she, like the county executive, briefly suggested "new" kinds of partnerships that Donald envisioned for the HRA.

First, the executive took pains to distance herself from the standpoint that lauds "private" church efforts over public, government-sponsored programs. Norma, the executive, told us "as a bureaucrat and a religiously concerned person" how stunned she was by a senator who had told a churchgoing friend of hers, "'If church people did what they were supposed to do, we wouldn't need welfare!' It blew my mind." Groans and shaking heads around the room signaled that many shared Norma's indignation.

What could URC do? It could create personal relationships between caring volunteers and former welfare recipients coping with the new reality. "Congregations can't replace a public safety net, but a public safety net doesn't replace interpersonal ties. . . . Religious people with their values and principles can bring the human element . . . people who share the value of human beings and people who care about other human beings." Observing that many people in her agency did in fact have religious commitments, she said that "what bureaucracies can do is not the same thing as personal commitment to a particular need or a particular person."

Though privatized, personal support figured prominently in her suggestions, Norma left the door open for more institutional kinds of involvement: "Rather than purely political solutions or programmatic solutions—or [pausing slightly] voluntary ones," we need involvement from "different parts of the community.... Private, nonprofit, and civic groups and anyone who's interested [can] create a safety net. The big system says 'You didn't do it (you didn't get a job before your benefits ran out). Goodbye!' Well—" (and her voice trailed off in a tone of disgust). It would be hard to characterize her talk as authoritative. It meandered into a sotto voce commentary. Stopping midsentence, Norma told us, "I don't know what I'm doing up here, I'm used to giving a talk with charts." Her voice faded; the presentation was over. One could reasonably take the administrator's comments as an invitation to create new ties, ones that, as she hinted here, might include something aside from either "voluntary" effort or political advocacy.

Norma was not just putting on a show for liberal churchgoers. She and other social service professionals communicated the same ambivalence about welfare reform, with more ironic bite, at semimonthly meetings of the Welfare Coordinating Council.[13] At these WCC meetings, county administrators and representatives of community service groups devised ways to stretch state welfare funds as far as possible. Representatives from the URC's Humane Response Alliance and the Adopt-a-Family program attended these meetings. Was school going to start soon? Maybe there was money left over in the state's welfare disbursements for pencils and book covers. Were chronically ill people availing themselves of the new welfare policy's subsidies for medications? Maybe the WCC could set up informational tables at the Kwanzaa celebrations downtown and hand out pamphlets about these benefits.

A few sarcastic quips about clients aside, neither Norma nor the social service workers sounded interested in punishing poor people for being poor, as some popular critics of welfare reform would imagine. Like other social service workers across the United States, they worked hard at making welfare reform less painful for clients whose fates really did matter to them (Hays 2003). Neither the administrators nor community group leaders sounded confident about how families would fare:

> WOMAN (Salvation Army): What do you have to offer people even with an $18,000 a year job? One of my employees, $18,000, full health insurance, she can't make it with three kids.
> WOMAN (Interfaith Social Services): Let me ask a silly question. How *do* people do it? How are they surviving?

ASSISTANT DIRECTOR (County Welfare Services): Piecing it together, a little here and there—
PROGRAM MANAGER (county-sponsored Family Friends) (*sotto voce*): Some
are in the underground economy—
NORMA (*drily*): These people don't all have stable middle-class lifestyles.

Norma livened up these meetings with gallows humor and a bit of off-the-cuff
political commentary. About the guidelines for spending the state's welfare
funds, she remarked, "It's so odd—we can pay someone to take care of someone else, not to take care of their own kid."

WOMAN (Salvation Army): *That's* welfare!
NORMA (*ironically*): That's welfare, not work.

Titters of derisive laughter broke out around the table. Norma was grateful for
what support the new welfare program did provide people, for "emergencies,"
for instance: "Thank God they defined labor and delivery as emergencies!" And
she hoped that the larger public would not become complacent, thinking welfare reform had solved the poverty problem. She ended the meeting in characteristically dry humor, encouraging any and all of us to go to a public hearing
on the county budget and "say that money for poor folk of Lakeburg County is
a good idea."

The Power of Institutional Routine

Over several months, county workers settled into the assumption that religious
groups would do just what they had always done. They would fill donation barrels with cans of beans and peas, cook free meals for community celebrations,
or give of their time to visit shut-ins. They would plug into service networks designed and managed by service professionals. Social service people wanted
faith-based groups to collaborate with them in weaving a new safety net, but
they left less and less room for new kinds of collaboration. Not overpowering
ideology or clear-cut interests so much as institutional routine limited the opportunities for collaboration with HRA leaders *who already were narrowing
down their own horizons* with a "do, don't talk" definition of civic action. And so
the WCC's discussions barreled forth on the assumption that faith-based groups
could come up with material resources and volunteers to meet new individual
needs. The few times anyone mentioned faith-based groups, it was in the context of short-term volunteering, not a new safety net partnership to which
Norma alluded in the presentation pictured above.

Service workers mentioned religious groups most in the context of a new referral service. Resourceful administrators had set up the omnibus service, figuring that people newly cut from the welfare rolls would have plenty of reason
to panic—when they needed help fixing a car to get to new, state-mandated

jobs, when their cupboards were bare, when they were about to be evicted from apartments for defaulting on the rent, when they needed daycare for infants while they attended job-training classes. Lakeburg Help Referral would put needy people in touch with other agencies and charitable groups—including churches—that could offer a bag of groceries, a free battery recharge, or an emergency babysitter. Norma made a point of telling me during the next meeting that if I wanted to know about community responses to welfare reform, I should really talk to the referral service director. "He has a show-and-tell, a package he does for churches." While signaling a new openness to religious community groups, county administrators stuck with well-established understandings of what these groups could do.

If Humane Response Alliance volunteers had gone to these county meetings expecting to talk about how they fit into the big picture, they would have met up with off-putting language and narrow assumptions about what religious groups could do. Social workers and community leaders at these meetings fell into a forbidding social service jargon. Steve Lanky, the man who said at HRA that Lakeburgers needed to have a spiritual commitment to help poor people and "take ownership of the community," told the WCC meeting in a different register that "we need to have more at the front-end to engage families." Then he proposed "targeting one of the highest density areas for intensive case management." What we really needed was "to develop these integrated networks of relationships." His *tone* gave the issue more urgency than all the abstract nouns. I finally figured out that "more at the front end" meant brochures that would tell new clients about job-training programs or local charities; "high-density areas" were neighborhoods where lots of people would get shifted to the new, time-limited welfare benefits. "Intensive case management" was what social workers did when they gave their clients wake-up calls in the morning, reminding them to keep appointments with job counselors. When the assistant county director of social services unveiled a new plan to "try to combine out-stationing with outreach," I gathered it meant that social workers should go out looking for people eligible for welfare, instead of expecting them to come to social workers' offices. When he told the group that he did not have to specify which "populations" could benefit from out-stationing, because "we all know, we all work in this business," I figured that busy social workers needed to get their work done without explaining everything for a hypothetical newcomer in the room. If county social service professionals were going to welcome community groups into new partnerships, there would have to be a very different kind of meeting.

No wonder Donald and Edward complained about the WCC meetings when they talked to the rest of the Humane Response Alliance. Donald said that he left these meetings no more sure of the URC's role than when he had arrived. Edward stopped going; the meetings were painful, he said. Strikingly, Steve Lanky *agreed*, at Humane Response Alliance meetings anyway, that early efforts to involve community groups in creating a new safety net were frustratingly void of results. He had hoped to do much more. The effort had progressed by the time of the meetings just pictured above; faith-based groups had gotten a conventional volunteer "slot" in a bigger picture conceived by social service administrators. Churches could do the good things they had always done.

It is not so surprising that county social service workers stuck with long-established understandings of what they and volunteers could do together. In sociology, neoinstitutionalist scholars point out that large, formal organizations adopt routine ways of doing things. The routines keep their participants relating to one another in comfortable or at least predictable ways. Sets of routines may become dominant, taken for granted, within an entire institutional sector like education or medicine, as organizations look for models, ways to style themselves.[14]

These models are something like group-building customs, and neoinstitutionalist thinking influenced my concept of customs laid out in chapter 2, but there are important differences. Neoinstitutionalists tend to talk about the organizational routines of an entire sector or "industry" of social activity. But as I have found, even one organization's participants may follow different customs in different settings. They may clash over which customs ought to be in play, or which "logic" of relationship should be driving the group, as scholars of institutional life Boltanski and Thévenot (1991) would put it. Further, the customs of civic groups are often less formalized than those that organize, say, the state-run social service sector: When people like Catherine, Donald, or Polly are involved in voluntary associations, they must negotiate their groups' place in the wider world, their responsibilities to other members, their definition of a worthwhile agenda. In a government agency, these "group-building" tasks may be less open to question and more explicitly mandated.

The Relative Autonomy of Networker and Volunteer Customs

County welfare chief Norma, along with other county social service workers I listened to at meetings and interviewed,[15] *all* promoted volunteer and networker roles for faith-based groups like the URC's Humane Response Alliance. But these roles did not necessarily prohibit HRA leaders from creating their own bridges. In the longer view, it is possible that HRA leaders' image of a good volunteer was itself influenced by expanding state welfare bureaucracies of either the Progressive or post–World War II eras.[16] It is also reasonable to think that "practical," "efficient" civic action resonates deeply in a shared American tradition, one that Tocqueville already described long before an American welfare state emerged.[17] We need more historical studies of American volunteering to know how much either or both are true.

HRA leaders affirmed loosely connected networking and individual volunteering on their own time, and on their own sometimes religiously articulated terms. That is what Clarisse's ritual did at the kickoff meeting. Donald was the one who called for doable tasks and "I will" statements while county agent Steve Lanky was calling for public forums and spiritual awakening. And at the January meeting, before Norma spoke, a nun read a statement saying that "welfare reform has not worked so far," and that giving out blankets would not solve the problems of people who have jobs but could not afford Lakeburg rents and Lakeburg food prices. She closed with a prayer that the Divine Spirit enlighten the corners of our hearts and give us "perfect charity" and "perfect humility" so that we could each find a way to help people in need: In other words, HRA participants just like county welfare administrators proposed individual caring as a response to social-structural problems. Clarisse's appeal to our inner calling is extremely old and deeply rooted in the religious traditions that HRA participants affirmed. It was hardly an ideological blinder foisted on concerned churchgoers by state agencies trying to squash community-building and keep people atomized. With a much wider historical perspective, one might even argue that state bureaucracies' own definition of volunteering comes ultimately from deep religious sources in Western civilization. It makes sense to see the HRA's customs as somewhat autonomous from the state instead of treating them purely as an effect of it.

The case of the Fun Evenings project reinforces the point. Halfway into my study, the county youth services department brought Fun Evenings under its own umbrella. Previously, Polly had written grant proposals to support expenses she incurred as an intrepid volunteer organizer. For two years Polly continued to serve as the Fun Evenings coordinator, with the county's sponsorship, before she left Lakeburg altogether towards the end of my study. I studied two Fun Evenings before the change, and two after. The volunteer customs of Fun Evenings, as I will picture below, did not change at all over this three-and-a-half year stretch. People learned the customary ropes in Polly's volunteer project, and some of the same volunteers were showing up, doing things the same way once Fun Evenings was a county program. The customs had an autonomous existence.

A skeptic can argue that the state's social service sector created the entire cultural repertoire of volunteer customs to serve its interests, unbeknownst to contemporary volunteers who simply do what is now customary. The trouble is that this supposes state agencies exist outside discourses and customs, manufacturing them as necessary, and it supposes that in real life as well as in our conceptual models, "state" and "the rest of society" are two separate things. Neither supposition stands up well to recent challenges.[18] We do not need to deny the state's own institutional power or autonomy to agree with Mitchell (1999, p. 83) that "the line between state and society is not the perimeter of an intrinsic entity that can be thought of as a freestanding object or actor." It is one thing to say some customs evolve on a terrain marked heavily by the state; it is another to say groups have no agency of their own.

But what about the volunteer half of the loosely connected network? Polly's Fun Evenings project did get several dozen URC volunteers to chaperone the nighttime events for teenagers over the next three years. Other URC-assisted volunteer projects did get under way. Slowly, Edward's congregational clusters effort did get going; the first of the clusters, Park Cluster, did establish new relationships between Lakeburg churches and the low-income Park neighborhood. Let's look more closely now at volunteering: Were volunteers learning, reflecting, spiraling outward, even if networkers did little to help the process along?

WHAT A LOOSELY CONNECTED NETWORK *DID:*
VOLUNTEERING IN THE HRA

Did It Cultivate Social Capital?

Some sociologists criticize volunteering in the same way that Catherine sized up Polly at the HRA meeting. They conceive volunteering at the opposite end from politics on the spectrum of civic action. Volunteering is apolitical and promotes Band-Aids instead of solutions, they say. Volunteers may feel good about volunteering while bracketing the larger social-structural relationships that soup kitchens and shelters cannot address (Poppendieck 1998; Wuthnow 1991; Eliasoph 1998). These are important criticisms, but I want to ask questions we cannot treat if our terms of discussion lock volunteering in a dichotomy with political activism.

Does short-term volunteering in loosely connected networks produce bridges? Does it give volunteers bridge-building skills? Many Americans are used to hearing that volunteering "strengthens the community." It is not only city mayors and television newscasters who credit volunteering with community-building potential. The same idea is implicit in recent research that takes volunteering as an indicator of social capital. The idea in this research is that at least some kinds of volunteering have the potential to thrust volunteers beyond their usual social rounds, bringing different kinds of people together.[19]

Is casual, serial volunteering a good indicator of social capital? That depends on what we want to mean by social capital. Because volunteers do often come in contact with people they might not otherwise meet—the people volunteers serve in the larger community, or service professionals, or perhaps other volunteers—it makes sense to conceive volunteering as social capital. On closer look, though, the indicator may not do full justice to the concept it indicates; alternatively, the concept may be problematic: In the fuller meaning of the term, social capital is comprised of relationships in which people are "doing with" others, rather than "doing for" others. The relationships that constitute social capital sustain a "regular connection among individuals" (Putnam 2000, pp. 51,

116–17). If volunteer relationships are a kind of social capital, by this definition, then saying so implies that volunteers develop regular connections over
time. It also suggests those connections might give volunteers the social assets
they need to create more bridges.

Volunteering did not work that way in the field I studied. Volunteering in a
loosely connected network gave me and other volunteers practice creating brief
interpersonal—sometimes very impersonal—relationships. It did not teach us
how to create more enduring bridges. HRA participants were offered many opportunities to spiral into individual volunteer slots in either the HRA or other
loosely connected networks. Volunteering did not require volunteers to become
part of ongoing, instituted relationships. It did not require them to develop "regular connections" with other volunteers *or* with the people served. Counter to
Putnam's assumption, I found that volunteering, in several different projects,
was not something one would "do with" others, in regular connection with others. For these reasons, I suggest that volunteering may be a poor measure of social capital as neo-Tocquevillians want to understand the concept.

A Short Spiral of Plug-in Volunteer Opportunities

Four months after the September kickoff, the HRA held another public meeting. Just like the September meeting, this one was supposed to feed volunteers
into task groups and solicit reports from task groups for a broader audience than
HRA's steering committee. There were thirty-five people rather than the fifty or
sixty I saw in September, and I recognized many of the same people from the
earlier meeting. In effect, the meeting offered more volunteer opportunities to
a lot of people already volunteering with the URC's projects. The vision, however, had been to entice previously unaffiliated churchgoers into joining one of
the HRA projects.

A nun read her critical statement about welfare reform, with its appeal to perfect charity. Then welfare chief Norma gave her presentation and fielded questions—mostly about which populations would endure which kinds of cuts in
welfare support. In a volunteer-soliciting mode, group leaders then introduced
their projects and said what they would do in breakout workshops for the rest
of this meeting. Polly told us that Fun Evenings were designed to produce a
drug-free, violence-free evening, and that there were lots of opportunities to get
involved; the next Fun Evening was March 7. A woman from the Safety Net
group said that she wanted to "put a face on some of the families that Norma
talked about," and that they would do that in her breakout workshop. Kate from
the Justice Task Force said the group had been "educating ourselves" and coming up with "direct actions" to carry out. A woman from the Prayer Empowerment group said that her praying group started after a former municipal executive said Lakeburg citizens should "pray for the city" in the wake of welfare
reform. Her breakout workshop would talk about how to get the prayers the

group wrote into church services. Later they were praying, off in a far corner of the room.

Project leaders did not say anything about how HRA projects added up to reconnecting the caring community. Closer to Donald's practice than his vision, group leaders focused on discrete, short-term, doable tasks. The Safety Net woman hoped to entice volunteers by putting individual human faces on social problems, not by inviting people to become part of a bridge-building, safety-net-mending project. The food pantry discussion I portrayed before was much more about groups and relationships and coordination than the call for volunteers at this meeting. Given how customary volunteering is, that is not surprising. And that is the point. Interaction at this meeting encouraged people to think of civic involvement as a matter of individually plugging into predefined tasks in predefined groups, not defining new relationships between evolving HRA projects, other civic organizations, or state agencies. One did not need to think or act as a member of any group in particular, HRA or not, in order to get involved. Loosely connected networks offer busy, mobile people that flexibility. Someone else would have to reconnect the caring community somewhere else.

The Prayer Empowerment group worked more at doing this reconnecting than the other groups at the January meeting. They play a curious part in the HRA's story of elusive togetherness.

Imagining Social Relationships, Prayerfully

Prayer Empowerment group members wrote prayers that were printed in the URC's bimonthly newsletter and read at some of the quarterly meetings. I was fascinated by how Prayer Empowerment group members composed these prayers: Members visited "challenged" neighborhoods in Lakeburg—neighborhoods with lots of low-income people—and met with neighbors, community center leaders, anyone willing to talk to them. They asked people "what would you like us to pray for?" Neighborhood residents never had a hard time naming people or places, the prayer group said.

The Prayer Empowerment group hoped that offering their prayers would help prayer givers focus more intently on the particular groups and institutions of diverse neighborhoods in Lakeburg. At the January meeting, the group offered this prayer for the Park neighborhood in its breakout session:

> Today we focus our prayers on the Park neighborhood, a community of crowded apartment buildings and single-family homes, of parks and playgrounds and community gardens ... bounded on two sides by highways. ... African American, Southeast Asian, Euroamerican, and other peoples live here, many of them recent arrivals. ... Pray for the Neighborhood Center—its Board, staff, and volunteers. ... Pray especially for people to envision and bring into being a new Community Center and a revi-

talized Food Pantry. Pray for the Lakeburg County Head Start staff and the teachers, parents and children. . . . Pray for the schools of the Lakeburg district that serve families of the neighborhood, and the large and small retailers located on the periphery of the community. Pray for the elected representatives of the area. . . .

Remarkable to me, these prayers were inviting HRA participants, and churchgoers throughout Lakeburg, to imagine themselves connected to local neighborhoods—to make those neighborhoods part of their own social maps. The prayers invited a meditative, individual form of social reflexivity. So it turned out that reflexivity had its place—way off in a corner, literally as well as figuratively. The communication about *where* we were on the map, in relation to *whom,* which did not take place in other HRA settings, was happening in this silent, prayerful form, separate from the rest of HRA.

My own experiences helped me understand some of the joys as well as limits of volunteering in the HRA. In volunteer settings, I found myself just as concerned with serving individuals as were other volunteers. In the setting, I worried about whether I was being a good volunteer, being useful, making kids happy. I felt the fear of failure and the joy of being wanted. I was not thinking about my role as a participant in a program reaching out to a wider community. Without really thinking about it, I bracketed the bigger picture.

The Customs of Volunteering

Scenes from Fun Evenings

Graffiti-style lettering announces the Downtown Youth Center on the back wall of a warehouse-sized room. Pool tables and brown plaid sofas crowd the floor like a secondhand furniture showroom. Multicolored faces on another wall stare down mischievously at pool players. The scene says "this place should look cool to teenagers." A huge hardwood dance floor sprawls across the space behind the game room. Polly's office is nearly hidden behind a locked door at the end of a narrow hallway behind the dance room. "Oh, the old URC volunteers are coming back!" Polly chimes, finding me perusing a Fun Evenings pamphlet in the waiting area outside her office. She insists on taking my coat and locking it in her office. I wonder why my coat needs to be locked up. She says there is another volunteer she wants me to meet, introduces us, and disappears. Volunteers, and teenagers, are just starting to show up for this evening's fun.

The kids are a rare sight in most Lakeburg neighborhoods: Dozens of black, Latino, Laotian, and a few white teenagers line up, waiting to get into the big front room. They are going to enjoy an evening without drugs or violence. Pool, Ping-Pong, dancing, and a youth leadership training are designed to keep them occupied, and safe. Some of the volunteers are from URC-related churches and have volunteered in other URC projects; I recognize two core people from the Humane Response Alliance. The volunteers are all white. These kids of color, one or two generations younger than most URC volunteers, are very close by, just outside the big picture window. No one remarks on the difference between the volunteers and the kids.

At my first Fun Evening, and each of three succeeding ones, I find out that other volunteers wonder what I also wonder: What am I supposed to do here? I ask Clarisse, whom I recognize from the justice task force and the HRA kickoff meeting, if Polly had told her what to do as a volunteer. She muses that she never really knows what to do when she goes to Fun Evenings. It does not seem to bother her; it seems customary. Other volunteers do not know exactly what to do, either. They wander around, watching the teenagers, looking interested in whatever the teenagers are doing. During my second Fun Evening, in a high school cafeteria, I try to strike up conversation with Sherry, a woman that Polly recruited for this evening from her own Episcopal church. I notice Sherry is circling the cafeteria floor, looking busy and smiling like someone freshly amused by the things kids do these days. A few kids are swaying to the rap over the loudspeaker, others are revving up their bodies to the beat but failing to ignite in dance. I saunter out into the hallway, and Sherry buzzes by us.

PL: Do you know what you're doing?
SHERRY: No, providing an adult—presence, I guess. It's fun to watch, though.

I run into Polly and ask if there is something else I should do; I'm worried about it. "Just walk around and look like adults." I keep walking around and run into Carson, whom I recognize from the Fun Evening at the Downtown Youth Center. Polly assigned him his post by a side door at the end of a long corridor, to make sure no one tries to come in the building with drugs or weapons. Shirtless, sweat beading on his forehead, he is practicing tae kwon do, a martial art. "Don't stop on my account," I urge. He has found a way to keep busy. I think we have met before, at a previous Fun Evening, and he looks as if he may remember it too.

I gather after two Fun Evenings that we are supposed to be genial with other volunteers, but keep our eyes on the scene. Polly encourages us to help ourselves to coffee at the Youth Center; she points out the pizza and pop in the cafeteria at the high school. She makes a point of introducing another volunteer. We are invited to make ourselves comfortable, in other words, yet it looks as if there is a lot of work to keeping one of these events going. I feel guilty for not being somehow busier every time I see Polly, who seems out of breath as she checks and coordinates and double-checks on her periodic rounds. I want to secure some minimal companionship for the evening—which will also make me feel better about being a watchful adult amidst teenagers. But I want to be a good volunteer worker; I want to be invited back.

I am on a list with other people who have placed themselves in Polly's pool of prospective volunteers. Dozens of others have signed up, either at the HRA kick-off meeting or at some other event at which Polly has presented her program. Each time Polly has thanked me profusely for coming, so I assume that a lot of the pool remains inactive a lot of the time, and that I might not see the same volunteers at next Fun Evening. The companionship we strike up is temporary, modular—it never occurs to me that anything I say or do will create a reputation that anyone, except Polly, would remember. I notice that I come home *without* the participant-observer's worries I feel after other URC activities: After HRA meetings, Justice Task Force meetings, Park Cluster meetings, or URC board meetings I worry not infrequently that I may have offended someone inadvertently, talked too much or too little. These are meetings at which I do things *with* other people and have a more regular connection to the same people over time. At Fun Evenings, in contrast, my worries about having looked like a dowdy representative of adult order evaporate as soon as I have left the scene.

There are good grounds for the worries I endure briefly at Fun Evenings. Polly reminds us at each of the four Fun Evenings I attend, in the same language: "The kids aren't supposed to leave the building, and if they do they can't come back." Comings and goings invite the risk that the teens will bring drugs or weapons into the safe space. At the very first Fun Evening, Polly tells us that "if anyone comes in with booze on their breath, kick 'em right out," bouncing her thumb toward the door. Volunteers seem hesitant to project that kind of authority. While helping Mike guard the front door, I watch him interpret Polly's directive loosely. When several boys say they need to "get stuff" for the talent show, Mike pauses a moment, says "Oh, OK" and lets them out. A foursome of girls needs to go outside to direct their friend to the right building. Mike and I hesitate, and I ask if they could just signal with their hands from the window. But we let the girls out. I feel awkward and inadequate as a volunteer policeman. I never see anyone but a muscular youth counselor physically trying to stop kids from using the wrong door. I feel a little better knowing that there are youth counselors around who can play bad cop if necessary.

Clarisse, Carson, and Mike all say at my first two Fun Evenings that these volunteer stints are a good thing because they are something concrete to *do.* Clarisse, who dropped out of the Justice Task Force, says she does not want to go to any more meetings. URC is too focused on "changing systems," she complains, and she would rather "do something, work with people." I appreciate the urge to act, move, relate, beyond talking around a table at a meeting. Yet Clarissa and the other volunteers do not work with the teenagers for any appreciable amount of time, and they, like me, do not know exactly what to do. Carson does not want to go to meetings either, but wants to be given something to do. Mike says that Fun Evenings is a good idea because it comes as a "package"; he implies it is a good program because people can do it without a lot of planning from scratch. A long-time URC volunteer who tried unsuccessfully to cheer up a girl with a Ping-Pong game says she likes the "doing" too, but most of all, someone her age likes to "see the children." Each of these people have volunteered for different community events; none are new to volunteering. The success of efforts like Polly's depends on people like them, and Polly's effusive thanks at the end of every Fun Evening shows that she knows it well.

I have just been picturing what I call volunteer customs in action. They may guide many different kinds of plug-in style volunteering in the American cultural mainstream, because other researchers have made quite similar observations.[20] This style of volunteering has become part of the larger civic culture. It is reasonable to think that churchgoers such as Clarisse, Carson, and Mike know in general what it means to volunteer, especially because they all had volunteered before, though they needed to learn the particular inflection of volunteering here, the idioculture (Fine 1987) of Fun Evenings.[21] As observer and as participant, I learned those customs and their particular inflection in Fun Evenings by watching and listening to other volunteers and Polly at my first two Fun Evenings, and watching the teenagers' responses to us. I felt the pull of volunteer customs just as strongly as the other volunteers.

I learned that volunteering meant carrying out tasks drawn up by volunteer organizers or professionals who define the *group boundaries* of the social map. The most salient groups on the map here were monitorial adults, low-income teens of color, and youth service coordinators, all hemmed into a small space by dangers outside, faceless social problems. Interestingly, the kids themselves constituted a vague presence on the map; social problems were much more specifically designated. Polly's presentations never explained to volunteers exactly who were teens likely to go to Fun Evenings, how they would find out about these events, or how they would get to them.[22] There were simply kids at risk for getting seized by social problems—drugs or violence. It was not clear who would identify these potential victims. Polly never intimated the teens themselves were "bad" kids; she implied rather that they were kids we should worry about. We could guess they were kids from low-income neighborhoods euphemistically designated as "challenged" in local newspapers. But the most important boundary defining these kids was the one they would cross if they stepped outside the safe space of a Fun Evening, into a world of threats.

Volunteers sustained loose, easily detachable *group bonds* with other volunteers. The "group" in these cases was an aggregate of temporary comrades like Clarisse or Carson with whom one might strike up quick conversations and not see again at the next Fun Evening. *Speech norms* were simple because speech was minimal: Volunteers limited conversation to genial chat, in the interest of serving kids and watching kids. To engage in longer conversation would risk appearing callous about our responsibility to keep kids safe while trying to present them a fun evening.

In this particular kids' program, unlike some volunteer programs with kids,

being a good volunteer did not necessarily mean developing even temporary relationships with the kids—or talking to them. Neither Clarisse, Sherry, nor Carson talk to any of the teens during my volunteer stints. On my night at the
Downtown Youth Center, the volunteers stood in a bunch by a table. During my
night at the high school, some volunteers circled busily like Sherry. Sherry's husband played Scrabble with a boy on the far side of the cafeteria; later on, the boy
had gone and Sherry's husband was playing solitaire. Several volunteers played
short games of Ping-Pong with teens who did not want to dance or play basketball. One volunteer told me she tried to comfort a girl who wanted to go
home, tried to get her interested in Ping-Pong, but, she cracked, the girl was
cheerier when left alone. It seemed an unpromising setting for white, middle-
class volunteers like me to learn how to develop relationships with teens of color
from low-income families. Maybe a setting like this teaches that more privately.

Imagining Social Relationships, Privately

It is possible that volunteers' experiences helped them arrive privately at new insights on how teens from poor and minority neighborhoods relate to white authority figures, or parents, or hip twenty-something youth counselors, or volunteers from church social outreach groups. Occasionally, I heard volunteers
expressing furtive curiosity about other groups and group differences, unfinished thoughts. Here is one example, for instance, from my last Fun Evening. By
that time, the program had been established several years and its customs were
familiar to me.

During a Fun Evening with a multicultural theme, at the high school, Sherry
and I marveled at what the volunteer's handout called an "African-American
Caribbean dance troupe." Dancers in goldenrod pants and black, yellow, and
white tops, and a congo drum ensemble transformed the dingy, curtained stage
into a confetti of golden hues and limbs akimbo, all to a gripping conga beat. A
woman in an African cloth wrap told the audience that her dance company accepted people of any race. Sherry called the troupe amazing, and quipped, "I
wonder what they would think of a fifty-year-old white woman!" I wondered
what she meant, and asked if she would like to join. She said she would like
learning dances like these but didn't think she was up to it. I asked if she knew
where the troupe was from, and she did not, but had assumed they were "not
local to our state." She was surprised to hear the emcee announce they were from
a nearby city. The dancers were supposed to be part of this evening's "multicultural fling" theme. No one had told us anything else about them, or how their
presence might relate to the teenagers, or to Lakeburg. We were helpers. It was
perplexing, a teachable moment, had someone been available to instruct us. The
performance was disorienting more than illuminating. The diverse group of
teens were "multicultural," the dance troupe's dances represented "cultures," and
the volunteers were spectators taking in a spectacle.

I remembered that Sherry was not the only one who thought about interracial relations at these events. At my second Fun Evening, early in the program, Clarisse told me in a lowered voice about the time she tried to get some URC volunteers involved in a voter registration project. She said she wanted these "lily-white" volunteers to have "direct contact with people of color." Clarisse, a white woman, belonged to the NAACP, and brought the volunteers with her to a festival the NAACP sponsored at the sports arena. The URC volunteers did not know where to do their voter registration work. They ended up sharing a table with the people running an NAACP membership drive, and "some racial things were going on," Clarisse said cryptically. I just did not get it, and asked several times for her to clarify what she was saying. Wanting to make sure I understood, I asked whether lily-white volunteers behind the table might have scared black people off from signing up to become NAACP members. That was it, Clarisse thought, adding only that the NAACP vowed never to have URC volunteers at another event. Why had Clarisse thought of this experience now, at the Fun Evening? Did she think the other white volunteers were benefiting by their temporary proximity to kids of color?

Volunteers like Clarisse and Sherry imagined things about intergroup relations during their volunteer stints, even though they did not talk much with the teens they chaperoned. Volunteering was not something volunteers would "do with" other volunteers or the people we served. We played solo roles, loosely choreographed by Polly. The volunteer ensemble produced a Fun Evening, an end in itself. Along the way, Sherry learned that unfamiliar-looking black dancers lived in her state, without learning much else about them or what they were supposed to represent at a multicultural fling for teens. Clarisse was reminded of her earlier experience with lily-white volunteers at the NAACP booth. She, like the other volunteers, had little or no contact with the kids. Maybe she was following what she intuited to be the custom.

So what if they don't have much contact—isn't it good enough if a program raises volunteers' individual awareness of diverse people? Many would agree that awareness is a good in itself. Imagination is an important part of bridge-building, too, underappreciated in social capital frameworks that count social contacts but neglect meanings. Chapter 6 will show that imagination empowers bridge-building when members of a group *share* their imaginations aloud and link them directly with plans of action. When people imagine and learn only silently, they make interesting private guesses about other people or other ways of life. They do not always get to find out if their guesses are right. Like Sherry and me at the dance performance, they don't find out why they are seeing what they are seeing, what the context is. If Clarisse thought volunteering taught volunteers like Sherry more about how to relate to people of color, or at least how to think about them, my observations suggest she was mistaken. If, alternatively, Clarisse's experience at Fun Evenings only reminded her how difficult it is for whites and people of color to relate to each other, then she apparently was not learning much about what it takes to build bridges proactively.

I was not learning much about that either. Listening to Polly talk about dangers, and going through the motions of securing doors and monitoring teens, I left thinking more about moats than bridges. Of course not all volunteer experiences map volunteers into a world of drugs and violence. I wanted to see if other volunteer settings might teach some kind of bridge-building skill more readily.

Like Fun Evenings, Summer Fun Camp was supposed to serve young people. It was a two-week day-camp program for elementary schoolers in the low-income Park neighborhood. A county social worker stationed in Park neighborhood oversaw the planning for Summer Fun. The URC-sponsored Park Cluster helped round up volunteers who would serve breakfasts and lunches and do art projects, nature walks, or find other ways to give the kids a good time. Similar to the social map at Fun Evenings, we were adults and kids—mostly kids of color from low-income families, kids who might become problems if they did not have something to do in the summer. Similar to Fun Evenings, I struck up genial, temporary liaisons with other volunteers, none of whom I saw again in URC circles except for those who were members of Park Cluster. Unlike at Fun Evenings, relating directly to kids was very much the norm at Summer Fun. I found myself and other volunteers relating to kids, and to other volunteers, as sincerely caring individuals. While Fun Evenings enervated me, Summer Fun showed me the joys of volunteering. Both programs taught me how to carry off different kinds of temporary relationships with kids and volunteers I might not see again. They were not designed to teach me how to sustain a relationship over time.

The Joys of Busy Caring

I wonder whether I look racist or merely prudent if I am seen locking the doors before leaving my car on Park Street. Lakeburgers know this low-income, mostly minority neighborhood mainly through crime reports on television. I see five white adults sitting at a picnic table outside the neighborhood center while kids are running around in the field beyond. They seem less worried about being busy than the Fun Evenings volunteers were. One volunteer tells me later she is glad this program is relaxed; it "flows with what the kids want to do."

In the neighborhood center basement, a cheery woman from Lakeburg Children's Museum is cutting pieces of white paper and Mylar with two dozen mostly African American kids. The kids are making kaleidoscopes out of paper, Mylar, and a straw. I feel my face freeze into a glaze of cheery, wide-eyed affirmation. I want to be helpful; I need to be busy helping, doing something. The museum staffer says she has run out of scissors and I seize my opportunity: I had just found a bunch of extra scissors at my house. Should I bring them when I come again on Friday? Quietly informative, the staffer tells me she is only there today. Suddenly I realize it is silly to assume she would be back; on another day, another guest will shepherd the kids through a different activity. I ask if there is something else she needs help doing, and she tells me everything seems set. I'm still smiling: at least I can appear to ratify that good fun is happening here, even if I can't contribute much to it. Sauntering outside, I find Kenneth by the picnic table, near the other volunteers, setting out crayons in cardboard box tops, and scratch paper. He invites no one in particular to come and do an art project.

My frozen smile belies a sinking feeling: I'm not helping. I am not *doing*. About a half hour later, Maria walks by with a huge bassett hound. My mood changes dramatically when Maria asks if I will go with her and some kids to walk her dog around the neighborhood. Now I have something to do; maybe I can make it as a volunteer after all.[23] Maria likes to bring this great barrel of a dog to Summer Fun because the dog needs a walk, and walking her is a simple way to amuse kids on a hot day. The kids love the flap-eared hound with her morose face, and they try to ride her like a horse.

Maria volunteers at Summer Fun because the kids like her bassett hound; bringing her is something Maria can do to help out. Maria does not remember how she heard about Summer Fun; maybe it was from a URC newsletter. I tell her I found out about it through Park Cluster, a group of representatives from URC churches that sponsor projects in the neighborhood. Maria has not heard of Park Cluster, though she sat on the URC board several years ago. Similarly, a volunteer who takes the kids on nature walks in the field beyond the picnic tables tells me she just likes doing it for the kids. "I think the idea is to come and share a little of yourself," she says. Another volunteer on another day sounds frustrated because she has not done much constructive for the kids, and the program has not been well organized:

> VOLUNTEER: I asked what I could do to be helpful. They said "come here at ten-thirty." Nothing had happened at ten-thirty.
> PL: So were you helpful?
> VOLUNTEER (*skeptically*): I was a beanbag. Had about four kids sitting on me. I saw you were a beanbag too, over there.

These volunteers thought of Summer Fun as an opportunity to be helpful, to make the program engaging for kids by sharing a bit of themselves. At Park Cluster meetings, in fact, Cluster members said anyone who could lead art projects, play an instrument, tell stories, or share an unusual hobby would be especially welcome. Volunteers were encouraged to be creative and inspire the kids' own creativity, much more than in the Fun Evenings project. Similar to the Fun Evenings project, though, the day camp was not a place for volunteers to learn more about how to relate to people in the neighborhood or to the community groups that led programs there.

Short-term volunteers like Maria and Park Cluster members like Kenneth evaluated Summer Fun as a *service* for kids who matriculated through it. Kenneth said that he thought the program was a success this year, but that it did not enroll as many kids as the previous year's. Ken's assessment was a real departure from his usual way of talking at Cluster meetings: There, in a different setting, that is, Kenneth made the point convincingly that church groups should talk about the good of the neighborhood because that is how it would build ties between churches and neighborhood groups. But neither he nor other Park Cluster members, nor volunteers I heard chatting at Summer Fun, talked about how volunteers or the program as a whole related to people in the Park neighborhood.

And of course they did not. That would not be customary for volunteering. The point of the program was to serve individual families' needs for their kids to have safe, fun things to do during the summer. If it fit into a bigger picture of civic ties in Lakeburg, that would not get figured out during the Mylar projects and dog walks. I would have felt awfully uncomfortable introducing seemingly "abstract" conversation into the day camp's round of morning activities, even if it had occurred to me to do that. Volunteering in this setting produced valuable goods, but it did not put volunteers in sustained contact with one another, doing things together. And it did not by itself teach bridge-building skills beyond the ability to keep a kid happily occupied for an hour or two.

We are there to "share ourselves," and I want to share myself, too. When Maria asks if I would go on the dog walk, a little girl immediately asks if she can ride on my shoulders. I say "sure" in a Daddy-like way. Jenna, the little girl, does not need to know who I am, where I am from, what group I represent. She just figures I can give her a piggyback ride, and that it will be fun. In an instant, mass-mailing clichés run through my mind: Make a child happy. She needs love. They just need attention from a caring adult. I want to shoo these intruders away and just see how it feels. It feels as if I am wanted. This is about me—or about Jenna's feelings as they relate to me, to be exact. I step into Daddy persona as she climbs up my back and I ask jauntily, "Do you want to get halfway up or all the way up?"

I concentrate on her name, trying to remember it—I've met a lot of kids already. I appreciate how Maria remembers all the kids' names. I try to think of things to talk about with Jenna atop my shoulders. She asks me how old I am. Am I as old as her mother? I ask how old she thinks I am. She plays with my hair, the way she must play with a doll's hair. I'm a new pet. Soon other kids want to ride me, too. My new name is "Horsy" and I oblige the kids with a whinny or a neigh now and then as I trot down an empty sidewalk, past brown-and-beige apartment buildings, iron window bars, and foot-worn grass patches under an August sun. Two kids ask if I will be back tomorrow. They know volunteers come and go. I want to come back. I like the kids, and I'm glad they like me. And I'm glad, I have to admit, that even though I'm a white person from outside the neighborhood, I have been able to relate to these kids from low-income, mostly minority families, however briefly.

I knew these kids had distinctive social markers in mostly white, middle-class Lakeburg. But I did not have to say anything or do anything about those markers. Volunteering did not require me to learn anything about how the kids or their families thought about the neighborhood, the schools, or the twenty-two agencies and community groups that sponsored a program in the neighborhood. I wasn't thinking about any of that; I was trying to remember Jenna's name and think up things to keep her happily occupied. The kids did not need to know about my neighborhood, my identities. Relating interpersonally, I could *imagine* what these kids' lives might be like, while relating outwardly to the kids as people *off* of any social map. They could relate to me that way too. And in fact I did not learn much about how to care for these particular kids, any more than I learned about the "at-risk" kids at Fun Evenings. What I knew about these kids was what I could guess from being present—along with what I happened to know about the neighborhood from attending Park Cluster meetings, something that most of the other Summer Fun volunteers I saw had not done.

Aside from giving kids a morning's worth of fun, volunteering for Summer Fun gave me practice at breaking the ice with kids. I sharpened some of my skills in adapting to an awkward, *temporary* interpersonal situation. In a world of loosely connected networks and volunteers, these are civic participation skills. I did not learn how to create a relationship that would last after the ice is broken and the situation is no longer temporary. That was not the point of Summer Fun.

Are Kids' Programs Just Different? Another Comparison

Maybe volunteering in Summer Fun Camp and Fun Evenings was different from volunteer work with adults. But the volunteer customs that I have portrayed are not particular to kids' programs. Temporary, modular liaisons characterized one of the most popular church volunteer programs too. Taking their cue from a nationwide program, Lakeburg church leaders and homeless shelter workers organized a network of church-run homeless shelters for families, called Interfaith Shelter. The shelter network came up several times at HRA meetings, and URC-affiliated churches offered to take turns hosting the shelter in their basements; companion churches would commit volunteers to help serve meals, set out cots, and play with kids before bedtime. Shelter organizers considered the program a great success at attracting volunteers; it had a much harder time keeping its few coordinator positions filled. People wanted to do something, care for other people, not coordinate other people. At a training required of all homeless shelter volunteers, I heard the same customs, articulated more explicitly, that I'd heard in the kids' programs.

The training's purpose, above all, was to teach us how to respect homeless people's personal dignity—an unimpeachable goal. I learned along with other volunteers that it was rude to ask shelter guests about their backgrounds, or why they were at the shelter. A half-hour video reinforced the message. We needed to treat our guests, like guests at a hotel, with circumspection.

Volunteers at my training were keenly interested in the social context of the shelter program, though. A lot of the questions volunteers asked the trainer had to do with who the guests were and how they related to service institutions, churches, and volunteers. What are the guests' backgrounds? Are there enough churches to accommodate all the guests? Have there been any complaints about the network from homeless people? How about if the network tapped into the YMCA with its weekend programming? Is it a problem that homeless people had to be driven from downtown intake offices to churches tucked away in suburban neighborhoods? Do people find jobs while they are in the shelter program?

The shelter etiquette that we were learning, the customs, enjoined volunteers from learning much *from guests* about this bigger picture.[24] The shelter director himself asked whether the training video might make us freeze up in fear of saying the wrong thing to guests. One man asked what we *could* talk about with the guests.

Shelter director: "Food, kids, the church, the locale they're in."

To put limits on shelter conversation may seem simply decent, not surprising. But it was very surprising given the rationale that the director used for volunteering with the shelter to begin with. It was a rationale much like Donald's call to strengthen civic ties and reconnect the caring community. He said shelter volunteering was a way to get closer to people we would not meet otherwise: "You hear about the poor—Meridian, East Broadway, Park [neighborhoods]. You don't see them at the mall. We've separated ourselves. This program tries to reacquaint us of our own flesh." The director's vocabulary of human solidarity suggested that working on a shelter volunteer team would encourage people to spiral outward and build at least temporary new bridges to people they knew otherwise only in the abstract. But the customs, taught by the video and the director, cut short that possibility. We were, in effect, being taught to relate to people in the abstract. Given the opportunity to meet fellow human beings different from most of us, we were not supposed to relate to them as people with any particular social context.

If Robert Putnam and others are right about declining social trust,[25] the training's assumptions may be right on target. Middle-class church volunteers may not share enough common ground with shelter guests to discuss each other's social circumstances in a respectfully inquisitive mode. Meanwhile, volunteering in the shelter program gave people practice treating individuals with dignity—an important civic skill. Given the shelter network's design, the relationship would not likely last longer than one week, the amount of time that any single church hosted the shelter program.

SHORT SPIRALS, NO BRIDGES, AND A FAILURE OF EMPOWERMENT

Summary

This chapter suggests that the "loosely connected" network may accommodate differences of style or interest at the cost of building bridges. It will take more research to find out if this is true for these networks in general or for only certain kinds. Scenes from the HRA at least raise the question of how wise it is for either citizens or scholars to expect that these networks can reweave the fabric of community life. HRA networkers were busy trying to define doable tasks— recall the "I will" statements—and find people to carry them out. There was not time for talking about new civic relationships with agencies or churches, let alone building them. There were hungry people, projections for more and more of them, logistics to figure out.

Meanwhile, volunteers plugged into slots and got practice sustaining easily detachable connections with other volunteers. They were not doing things together in the sense that the social capital concept implies in recent research. Volunteers learned how to carry off short-term liaisons, monitorial or interpersonal, with the people they served. There was not space for talking about new civic relationships with minority or low-income people and their children. There were bored teens, lonely kids, homeless families, names to remember, people's dignity to preserve. HRA director Donald had written that volunteering alone was insufficient for the new civic connections he imagined, and he was right. But the strong pull of customary routines kept him from making the HRA into more of an "action/reflection group" that might have done the collective imagining and communicating that a group must do if it wants to *change* relationships that work by custom.

The social spiral did not unwind very far in HRA. The networkers gave themselves the task of helping volunteers spiral into short-term volunteer opportunities. Volunteers did not need to build relationships that would last more than a couple of hours. Of course a program like Summer Fun, *as an entire program*, could strengthen the bridges that churches or civic groups build with neighborhood centers or social service agencies by boosting the reputation of the churches or groups as decent civic partners. But someone has to initiate that bridge elsewhere. The volunteer experience itself would not teach people how to relate as church members to neighborhood centers or service agencies. They would not learn what it takes to produce a program that residents think is appropriate or that a neighborhood center wants to cosponsor. In short, interaction at HRA meetings and volunteer settings did not complement the broader civic bridge-building agenda that HRA set for itself.

Checking Out Alternative Interpretations

Even if volunteers by themselves do not build bridges, does that mean no kinds of volunteering ever help volunteers cultivate bridge-building skills? We need more research to find out. Tutors and mentors who meet regularly with children over months or years, for instance, may develop very different relationship skills from the ones people learned and practiced at Fun Evenings, Summer Fun, or the church shelter network. Those kinds of volunteering might suit the social capital concept better than any of the kinds of volunteering I observed.

In the meantime, scenes from the HRA should caution against applying the social capital vocabulary uncritically to volunteering. If the act of volunteering by itself produces social ties, then some of those ties are very temporary at best, not the broad, enduring ones that scholars concerned for America's social infrastructure would like to see (Putnam 2000, 1996; see also Fukuyama 1999). We need to identify different kinds of civic relationships much more carefully than the capital metaphor can do. Group-building customs influence the ways people define and create relationships. Scenes of networking and volunteering in Lakeburg suggest that some of those relationships fall far short of neo-Tocquevillian ideals that have prompted some of the research on social capital.

These scenes also suggest that the way people build groups matters even apart from the *discourse* that motivates the groups. Some proponents of community life have argued that American civil society is weakening because Americans talk too much about what is good for themselves or depend too much on the state to solve social problems. Yet civic-minded, communitarian discourse and imagery were not hard to find in HRA circles. Donald spoke and wrote explicitly about the need to fashion new civic ties for the good of the whole community, and liked to invoke communitarian and one-time presidential candidate Bill Bradley to make his case. Pastor Lindstrom asked again and again at HRA meetings how faith groups and social service agencies could work together for the benefit of Lakeburg as a whole. At HRA meetings, social service administrator Steve Lanky spoke too about communal responsibility: Volunteers needed to develop a stronger sense of "ownership of the community," he said. The Prayer Empowerment group created richly detailed portraits of life in Lakeburg neighborhoods, inviting all of us to care about those neighborhoods as our own. And the director of Lakeburg's church shelter network did not scare volunteers away with his broadly community-minded talk of reconnecting with fellow humans we would not otherwise see: So many churchgoers signed up to volunteer that there were not enough weekly slots for everyone.

Customary ways of sustaining civic groups may shrink our broad-minded discourse into small, narrow spirals of civic engagement. Communitarian theorist Amitai Etzioni has asked whether or not more civic groups really create a better civil society (1996, p. 96). By challenging indiscriminate praise of civic engagement, his question sits well with this chapter's observations—much as not all loosely connected networks need have the same strengths and weaknesses as the HRA.

The communitarian answer Etzioni proposes, however, is less useful. Etzioni argues that instead of boosting civic engagement per se, Americans ought to "remoralize" their civil society. They must discover, or rededicate themselves, to core, shared values that can prioritize social goods and identify social evils for all to see.[26] Yet even the most heartfelt, compassionate, and communitarian values remain frustratingly ineffective if people who hold those values also hold onto customs ill-suited to their projects. I have no argument against moral dialogues. Scenes from the HRA suggest to me, though, that even if groups can agree on broad moral values in the abstract, they need to know how to talk in practical and critical terms about their group relations if they are going to institute new civic bridges. The right values are not enough. Knowing how to create reflexive groups is different from knowing how to rank priorities.

The county social service agency did not help HRA figure out how to do new things together. While opening the door to new collaborations with religiously based community groups, the agency settled into well-worn ways of creating relationships, leaving HRA leaders feeling baffled or unwelcome. The HRA did not create new partnerships with the county. It makes sense to say then that HRA did little to empower civil society in relation to the state. The county agency is at least partly responsible, if passively so, for this failure of empowerment.

The (local) state did not necessarily keep HRA from spiraling out into Lakeburg's civic life, though, even if it ended up being an inflexible partner. In contrast with some state-centered interpretations, I have proposed that the HRA bears some of the responsibility, given its own routines. The HRA might have granted itself more autonomy. It was, after all, part of a long-established urban religious association. Other sociologists, too, argue that even suppressed civic groups can carve out "free spaces" for fashioning identities that might challenge powers that be (for instance Polletta 1999; Gamson 1996; Boyte and Evans 1986). They may need that space for social reflexivity too.

A noble project with a persistently elusive mission, the HRA folded after a year. Skeptics might only feel vindicated when they compare Donald's talk of civic bonds with the accomplishments of the Humane Response Alliance. The Alliance struggled to get churches paired with pantries; meanwhile, more people went hungry in Lakeburg County, and only a few people questioned new policies that were swelling the rolls of pantry patrons as welfare rolls shrank. Some scholars wonder whether all the talk about social capital and community ties and bowling leagues does not represent an "escape from politics," an unwillingness to deal with hard issues.[27] Maybe civic groups need the customs that allow them to talk critically, politically, about the powers that have weakened community life to begin with. Catherine of the Justice Task Force would say exactly that. The next chapter investigates the possibility.

Chapter Four

CRYING OUT: SOCIAL CRITICS

No Polite Church Ladies Here

Justice Task Force members were insurgents. In the year before Lakeburg Presbyterian's kickoff meeting, the URC held meetings to plan the Humane Response Alliance. Catherine attended them and challenged the HRA's whole approach, calling it more social-service directed than systematic-change directed. "I got up and did my spiel: 'We've got to change these structures, this whole thing of welfare reform is stupid, it's not fair, it's unjust.' Surprisingly enough, a bunch of people were interested."[1] Those people began to meet as an HRA project, the Justice Task Force.

Every Task Force meeting rang with social criticism. I picked up on the customs early on. At my second meeting, the group was sizzling with righteous anger as they sat in a church classroom studying charts and bar graphs. While pious faces gazed down at us from a print of Norman Rockwell's *Golden Rule,* members were learning what Catherine already knew: There had been a huge shift in the tax burden over the past forty years, from corporations to individuals. "That's why welfare reform sells," Catherine summed up, because "individuals are feeling pinched. We've had a shift in wealth, partly because of a change in tax law, partly because of an increase in payroll tax."

> CHARLENE (*adding sharply*): Don't underestimate the effect on poor people—it's a regressive tax!
> KATE (*crying out indignantly*): *That's not fair!*
> CATHERINE: I love this conversation!
> FRANK: The information in this chart must also address the [mass-mediated] mythology that keeps this all in place; it's extremely powerful.

Donald's voice was the only dissenting one in the chorus of angry criticism. He cautioned that "we damn the wealthy, but we aspire to wealth, too." Other members had tried out the idea that they were responsible for homelessness because of the unused bedrooms in their own homes. Frank thought the emphasis on individual responsibility was a distraction from the real issues. Most members agreed with Frank.

Thanks to the Task Force, churchgoers who worked in the URC heard a perspective they might not have heard otherwise. HRA networkers and volunteers heard Catherine and other members criticize welfare reform and decry America's growing gap between rich and poor at HRA meetings and convocations. Through their educational workshops in churches, the Task Force communicated a social justice perspective that churchgoers should have recognized from their Bibles, Task Force members would say, and yet heard little of in their churches.

Task Force members were very ambivalent bridge-builders. They wanted desperately to communicate their message, but they sometimes scorned would-be audiences of churchgoers who, they assumed, would scorn them for being critical and angry in public. Kate said the Task Force was like a support group for church people with a critical perspective. Members were not content, however, to cloister themselves, and they kept trying to spread the critical message, at their Economic Injustice workshops in churches, at URC meetings, at the URC's monthly public forums, at least once at a State Council of Churches convocation. These were not just self-indulgent political sorties. For Task Force members, speaking out in Lakeburg's church circles was an ongoing exercise in relating to an ideological bloc that they defined in one of two ways: Their audience were victims of systematic manipulation by corporations or victims of a general church culture that silences social criticism or both. Rarely if ever did Task Force members allow themselves to reflect aloud on their *relationship* to this generically defined audience.

Still, it was a relationship, even if Task Force members worked at distancing themselves from the very audience they wanted to reach: That *was* their style of building bridges. I suggest at the end of the chapter that many other political groups in the United States have styled themselves similarly. If political networks and social movements are important reservoirs of "bridging social capital,"[2] then we should learn how would-be agents of consciousness raising try to build bridges. When studies of activists look at that process, often they focus on the discourses that activists use to convince their audiences. Like activists themselves, we want to know which ideologies work on which people. I want to ask, instead, what the consciousness-raising relationship itself means to the people trying to initiate it, not just what their ideology means. By understanding the customs that produced that relationship, we can learn a lot about the potentials for church-based social criticism.

BAND-AIDS OR BRACING SOCIAL CRITICISM: A FRUSTRATING
DICHOTOMY FOR CHURCH ACTIVISTS

Can people communicate social criticism while also talking and acting as if they are part of a larger community to which they are speaking? There is no natural reason why not. With recent studies of religious activists in mind, I had figured that the Justice Task Force would find a way to communicate social critique while identifying with Lakeburg church people, instead of alienating themselves from them.

Yet the Justice Task Force ended up marginalizing itself even as it tried to reach out. They assumed that marginality was the price for speaking truth to power, though members felt at least as frustrated and lonely as ennobled by their stance. They did not like being marginal. When Kate said that people at her Lutheran church walked the other way when they saw her coming, she sounded more hurt than proud. The only alternative, on their social map, was to engage in Christian compassion as they understood it, to focus on individuals and narrow their ideological vision from social critique down to service-oriented "Band-Aids." With choices like these, they were in a difficult bind.

This chapter will show why the Task Force locked its choices within a dichotomy of individual compassion and angry social criticism. They did not choose the dilemma, but their own choices perpetuated it. The Task Force's larger context made it very hard to construct a group and a message outside this ultimately self-defeating dichotomy. Customarily, the group allowed little critical reflection on the dichotomy that made being in the group frustrating even if morally compelling.

The chapter illustrates a more subtle theoretical point, too: To analyze society critically is not the same thing as talking reflexively about how one's group relates to other people or groups. Sometimes scholars equate the two, in the spirit of Tocqueville's vague notion that civic groups would broaden their members' horizons.[3] Scenes from the Task Force suggest that the difference matters greatly for politically progressive groups that want to reach out.

A VOCABULARY OF SOCIAL JUSTICE

Discovering a Bigger Picture

Early on, URC director Donald brought to the Task Force a news item that had people in Lakeburg riled up: Local banks charged homeowners fees for servicing their mortgage loans. A new, obscure state regulation required that a portion of these fees go to homeless shelters. Homeless shelters had already appeared a lot in the news at the end of 1996, partly because a big shelter in a church basement downtown needed expensive repairs if it was going to continue sheltering people safely and withstand the six-month Lakeburg winter. The problem was that the banks had not been sending any proceeds from the loan fees to homeless shelters. Here was a mission for the Task Force, Donald thought.

No one on the Task Force sounded enthusiastic about it. I learned a lot about the Task Force's social justice sensibility when I found out why not. Frank's comment set the tone for the conversation: "What are we trying to get out of it? It's a one-shot thing. . . . It's a beautiful target, but how do you plug it into something bigger?" The problem, the group decided, was not just the banks' negligence. The deeper problem was that, as Kate put it, this new law simply squeezed money out of struggling homeowners to give to homeless people, instead of getting money from the truly wealthy: corporations. Doreen, a new member, said that she would rather banks give the fee money to homeless shelters than not do it. No one disputed her; no one found the new law morally satisfying either. Catherine said people should call their own banks, thank the bank for releasing the fees if the bank eventually did so, and then ask "What about affordable housing?" What was the bank doing to make home loans available to low-income people? Frank stressed that affordable housing should get mentioned on the group's project agenda alongside the bank fees issue so that the matter of the fees would "not just be about giving donations to shelters."

They were not about ministering earnestly to the needy. These people dared to talk about injustice, corporate power, the oppressive weight of mass-mediated common sense. They had taken a seemingly private issue and made it a public one, a matter of justice (Pitkin 1981). They also seemed to understand, as students of social movements have come to see, that talking about social problems has very much to do with remedying them; talk is not "mere talk."[4]

Terms of Faith

Sometimes, and more than other members, Catherine used a biblical justice vocabulary. She quoted the Hebrew prophet Micah in her interview, observing that in his oft-quoted teaching on what God requires of humankind, "doing justly" came even before practicing "mercy" and "walking humbly" with God. At one meeting, she pulled out several social-justice-related passages from Jewish and Christian Scripture. "As people of faith, we need to bring in some of the injustice language from the Hebrew and Christian Bibles: 'He will punish and avenge the wrongs people suffer.' . . . 'Listen to the reapers.' . . . and 'justice, mercy, honesty, these you should follow.' This is judgmental language, but we say we're people of the book, we believe this stuff, but we don't do it."

And occasionally, members spoke in Christian-influenced terms about treating people compassionately. In a scenario below, Task Force members tried out the idea that corporate executives deserved compassion. As one member put it, we needed to see that "morally, people are doing the best they can do." Compassionate caring also meant reaching out to people who were poor and maybe dangerous; "Christianity is a risky proposition," concluded one member. When they did use religious terms or metaphors, though, Task Force members preferred to communicate the imperative of justice, not compassion.

My account may risk sounding like political critique itself, in the same way that my account of charitable volunteers risked sounding uncharitable. I should point out that I often agreed with the Task Force's criticism. I admired their bravery, even if sometimes I tired of the righteous anger. I will not say that the Task Force needed to show more compassion to mellow its criticism, nor that members should have done more volunteering along with social advocacy. It would be better to understand the Task Force beyond the terms of the "activism versus volunteering" dichotomy altogether.

INSURGENTS AMONGST VOLUNTEERS:
CHALLENGING INSTITUTIONAL POWERS

When I began going to Task Force meetings, members were just deciding to create Economic Injustice workshops for churches. It was the group's first major project, and Catherine's favorite. She put on most of the roughly twenty workshops herself. URC board members listened with interest when cochairs Catherine or Frank described the workshops, but the URC board did not end up allotting any staff support for the workshops. The Task Force also ended up endorsing public statements as the "Justice Task Force of the URC," but did not represent the URC directly.

Donald and Catherine disagreed on what Catherine called the Task Force's "confrontational approach." For Catherine, the point of a group like the Task Force was to "be very verbal and up-front about things, and to challenge congregations that belong to URC to face this thing [social injustice] and talk about it and really see it as a structural thing rather than 'oh, we've got to help these poor people.'" The URC had hosted a forum on welfare reform near the start of my study. Two people with different viewpoints had spoken to the 135 people assembled in Hilltop Methodist's meeting hall, after which the audience discussed the issues in small groups. The forum struck Catherine as "too much an exchange of ignorance." One speaker had talked about her own experiences moving off of welfare. "It was too much a touchie-feelie, social services—I just didn't like the process." Catherine wanted forums like these to present the hard facts of social inequality. Donald insisted that the forums be places for sharing and self-expression. Catherine resigned as chair of the Task Force shortly after the big forum, but continued going to meetings.

The confrontational approach characterized much of the Task Force's style both at its own meetings and outside them. They were insurgents not only in the URC but even more so within their own churches. Most of the core Task Force members shared Catherine's experience of feeling marginal within their congregations. "Being a prophet is not a popular thing to do," Catherine observed drily after a meeting. Catherine had done ecumenical work on justice issues and heard how conversation sounded in other Lakeburg churches. "In most religious circles" and not just her own Lutheran ones, she claimed during her interview, people did not welcome critical talk about the gap between rich and poor. Catherine characterized most congregations as being "co-opted" by a polite kind of religion that "doesn't challenge the powers that be, and buys in, and tells people to pull themselves up by their bootstraps."

Kate felt marginal, too. When fellow churchgoers saw her, they walked the other way, she told me. Task Force cochair Frank left his former Catholic congregation for a small Catholic fellowship of people who had felt like outcasts in their own congregations. Interviews only reiterated what already had become clear to me at group meetings: These people felt different from fellow churchgoers. The *only* one of eight core members I interviewed who expressed an unambivalent attachment to a congregation and a denominational tradition was a woman from Lakeburg's Friends meeting. Not surprisingly, the Quaker tradition in America stands out historically for its adherents' active commitment to social justice (K. Hays 1994).

Task Force members' perceptions of their own church milieus were plausibly accurate, according to some recent research.[5] What matters most here is that Task Force members *understood* themselves as insurgents. They were not antireligious. Like Catherine, they affirmed their political stance on biblical grounds. But they distinguished themselves from their church milieus all the same.

> CATHERINE: I have very strong feelings about faith-based groups, and I've had the same experiences in my own congregation. And I've always been a voice in the wilderness. The way I read the Bible, and the way I read what it is we're going to be about, it's to do justice. It's the Micah chapter: "Do justice, love kindness and walk humbly with your God." Those are the requirements—and the first one is do justice!

Bucking the trend in their own churches, and in the URC's church network, too, Task Force members challenged at least two kinds of institutional power. One was a quiet kind. Contesting the bounds of acceptable discussion is a political act, as sociologists Anthony Giddens (1991), Jürgen Habermas (1987), Alberto Melucci (1989), and Nina Eliasoph (1998) have argued. Though we usually think of power as the ability to control material resources or other people, or both, the ability to limit an agenda of public discussion is a kind of power, too (see Lukes 1974). The logic is straightforward: People cannot exercise their power as citizens over topics about which they cannot speak.

The Task Force's social criticism challenged the more obvious power of social service institutions also: As a church-based group in a religiously sponsored social service effort, the HRA, the Task Force identified itself amidst a field of social service outfits, but rejected the "social service approach," as Catherine called it. Lakeburg's social service administrators did not proscribe broader civic roles for URC groups, but they perpetuated the customary definitions of what ordinary citizens, especially church members, could do to promote social welfare. They could plug in to predetermined volunteer slots and help service agencies administer clients in a humane way. By criticizing welfare reform and its root causes, instead of finding ways to "plug in" or serve individuals, the Task Force challenged institutionalized definitions of citizen responsibility that URC leaders shared ambivalently with social service administrators. The task force's very alternative mode of community service represented a different culture of citizenship, one that came from a different institutional field,[6] without the resources and imprimatur of the state.

Task Force members had the difficult task, then, of creating a group around insurgent definitions of civic engagement. They wanted to uphold biblical mandates against injustice—the vocabulary of injustice. But by the *dominant* definitions circulated by county agencies and URC leaders,[7] religious people concerned about social welfare would not raise their voices in social criticism. Concerned religious people would serve their larger communities as volunteers and networkers. Task Force members were religious people who wanted to do something different.

The Customs of Social Critics

The Task Force had difficult work to do. It wanted to reach out to churchgoers while being *itself*, which meant marking itself off from dominant images of religious community groups. In the institutional context I just described, building a group around critical prophecy would have to mean fighting, defending, drawing firm boundaries, not building bridges and blurring distinctions. Activists who publicize new, challenging ideas in unwelcoming milieus must often draw firm boundaries around their own groups.[8] Fighting and defending are what I heard as I listened for the Task Force's group-building customs.

Just as with other Lakeburg groups, the Task Force's customs were easiest to notice when the group had direct contact with new members, when conflicts and misunderstandings arose, or when members repeated statements beyond what an average speaker would need simply for comprehension. Here I want to identify the customs at work, drawing examples from early in my study to show the customs as they were crystalizing. Then, scenarios from later in the group's history show how those same customs cut off possibilities for spiraling outward and building bridges.

Boundaries: Brave Prophets amidst Looming Structures

Catherine's presentation at the HRA's kickoff meeting had already clued in the audience. We get so busy rescuing people, she had said, that we don't step back and see the larger picture of social injustice. Many, many more times at Task Force meetings members drew the same sharp boundaries against corporations and "volunteer" projects. The boundary work was especially easy to hear when new members were attending for the first time.

Catherine often set the tone, and other members contributed or elaborated. Doreen, a new member who came during my first few months, was a leader in the League of Women Voters, and found the Task Force different from other groups. At first, she appreciated the difference she was hearing:

> DOREEN: This is the only group that talks about the structural [issues]—
> well, other groups talk about it on the side but it's not the main thing.
> CATHERINE: Most of us have done other things—direct community ser-
> vice—
> KATE (*acquiescing*): And it needs to be done—
> CATHERINE: And we are the ones who really want to talk about *structure*
> (*emphasis hers*).

The Task Force was going to address the forces that made life so painful for so many.

Most prominent on the Task Force's shared social map was the corporate-dominated economic system that made rich people richer and poor people poorer. Individual corporations acted badly; the corporate system as a whole was the real enemy. The matter of bank loan fees became interesting to the Task Force *after* members realized they could define it as an instance of the corporate banking system pinching money from homeowners for homeless shelters, while keeping homes out of low-income people's reach altogether.

Opposition to corporations was more than a cognitive viewpoint that the group applied to issues. It was a way of identifying the group on a larger map of the world. Even when they were not deliberating a position or responding to local news, members peppered meetings with jokes and stories about corporate excess—the *same* jokes and stories. There had to be a point to telling them repeatedly. They were not just entertaining each other; they were saying something about who the group was and who it was not. That is not to say that the group's analysis itself had no value. My point is that anticorporate sentiment was deeply imbricated in the group's own sense of togetherness as a group.

At several early meetings, for instance, Kate retold her favorite injustice payback scenario: "There are *so* many vacant beds in this city, all the [suburban] fringe hotels with empty beds. They're all set up with sheets and towels and blankets. So why not get buses to take homeless people to them, and pick them up at ten in the morning?" she observed, "You can't blame the Holiday Inn or anything—it's structural." The whole structure of housing relations in a corporate-dominated economy left Lakeburg with empty hotel beds and overflowing homeless shelters.

Kate and Catherine also liked to tell us that the plush, reserved seating areas at the new Lakeburg stadium, the "corporate boxes," should get opened up for homeless people when there is no game going on. Kate would toss in that the parking arcade for the stadium cost so much money to build that each parking space was worth $25,000. Members who did not appreciate the anticorporate esprit de corps did not last long in the group, as I will show later, *even if they agreed with the group's analysis.*

Catherine policed the boundaries with sharp wit. At one of the first meetings in the fall of 1996, for instance, a newcomer wanted to talk about what was going to happen to poor kids from abusive families once welfare reform kicked in. The new person herself had three stepchildren, all victims of sexual abuse in their families of origin. They were lucky; they had a role model, she said. What of children who did not? "The church was the original social support," she told us, "before the other areas kicked in. The church has got to pick up the pieces." But where do you start? She was nearly in tears.

CORA: Bring 'em in out of the cold.

CATHERINE: Oh, I think you start before that—change some tax laws!

Members often got reminded that their mission required them to keep a big, social-structural map at the ready.

Bonds: Progressive Thinkers Stick Together

Task Force members would say that it was hard being a prophet. "How do we support each other?" Catherine asked several times that first fall, as welfare reform was just kicking in. Frank wondered the same thing. He proposed the group spend a weekend together and get used to being the kind of people who carry this kind of viewpoint; "grind body and soul together" as he put it. Kate similarly told us at one meeting that trying to illuminate large, powerful social structures was a daunting task; people in the group would have to "trust" each other. I had figured a shared religious faith would help them trust each other. But the "we" in need of support was a politically defined we, not a religious one. Members all knew each other to be churchgoers, and introduced themselves with church affiliations at the start of each meeting. They did not *represent* churches, however. And local churches represented comfortable complacency to most Task Force members. While the Task Force grew out of the church-based URC, a good, respected member did not need to be a churchgoer, or a person of any religious faith, as long as she did not mind occasional allusions to radical priests, Liberation theology, or Martin Luther.

Outspoken, progressive politics mattered more for good membership than a heartfelt religious identity. In a group of people at least some of whom felt like outsiders in their own churches, that is not so surprising. Group leaders Catherine and Frank always talked of taking their Economic Injustice workshop "to the churches," as if they were not churchgoers themselves. Catherine even suggested the group define the workshops' audience more broadly. After two years and disappointingly few requests from churches for the workshop, Catherine brought up the audience question again: "Churches are still a good place, because in the Judeo-Christian tradition, God is a God of justice. So it makes sense to take it there. But I wonder if we want to get more to human service professionals." Churches were "there"; Catherine sounded as if she came in to them from outside. Frank and other members considered Kiwanis Clubs and other civic groups as potential targets, too. They sounded less like people embedded in church life, more like outsiders who could feel like fellow exiles from church.

During that first autumn, Catherine was already saying that the group ought to welcome people who were not necessarily "church people." The group could welcome even someone who derided religion, like Maggie. Maggie carried on a one-woman campaign to politicize low-income blacks from south Lakeburg, to get them to speak out about life in a tightening economic vise. At one meeting she called religion the "drug of choice" for prisoners. The next meeting, she equated religion with Protestant fundamentalism. She could participate because she shared the group's critical esprit de corps, as well as its social map. She was fighting looming social structures as a singularly motivated prophet.

Speech Norms: Speaking the Truth in Righteous Anger

The jokes about expensive stadium seats, the injustice payback scenarios, the crescendos of indignation: it was not hard to figure out the purpose of speaking in the Task Force. Members valued outspoken talk that revealed the truth, angrily. The privileged genre was not "business meeting," as it was in the HRA. It was a contemporary version of biblical prophecy. The prophets of the Hebrew Bible decried injustice, spoke truth to power. American civil rights leaders such as Martin Luther King Jr. are only some of the most recent exemplars of this genre. As Catherine urged at one of my first meetings, "We need to name the white elephant in the room . . . raise some righteous anger!"

Task Force members hashed out social issues intensely, but the point was not just to figure out their opinions. Sometimes they seemed convinced of their opinions from the start. The point was to open up an angry forum, not a purely deliberative one.[9] From the start, the Task Force members impressed me with their passion for speaking out, their refusal to contain themselves with businesslike procedure. At one of my first meetings, Catherine presented some new project ideas. It started as an administrative exercise, but soon became a forum for discussion and criticism, especially when we came to Welfare Watch, a project to keep track of how changing policies affected people in Lakeburg.

Frank started. He had heard a business leader say that business could not provide the jobs that welfare reform presupposed would be available to former welfare recipients. Yet President Clinton had said that welfare reform would work only if the private sector could provide jobs. "There's a contradiction right there," he summed up. Kate added that "people will say we are jumping the gun" by criticizing the new policies when they haven't had a chance to work yet. But there was evidence already that they were not working. Kate's voice was rising. Now Frank tossed in a tale about a relative of his who had to support a family member who could not get a job, whose childcare subsidy had gotten cut, too. Kate pointed out this was just what she was talking about. Doreen told us that people would approach her at conferences to remark on all the wonderful things her state's governor was doing to change welfare. "They just believed it, the media story," she observed indignantly. It all was supposed to be a conversation about planning for the next meeting; it had turned into a venting session.

It was not enough, then, for members to agree privately with liberal-left opinions. Good members expressed their outrage and invited others to sound off too. One of the first projects that the Task Force considered taking on was to collect "stories" from people newly kicked off of welfare rolls. The group might even post an 800 telephone number so that people might call in while their harrowing experiences were still fresh in mind.

PL: What's good about it—who would listen to the stories we collect?
CATHERINE: The act of doing it is good in itself . . . so the stories don't get swept under the rug. We can bring them to legislators, journalists.

Only later, after spending time with the Adopt-a-Family project, pictured in chapter 5, did I realize what was remarkable about this plan. No one said that learning about *particular individuals'* pain was good in itself, as Adopt-a-Family volunteers believed so deeply. Rather, witnessing to and publicizing injustice was good in itself. The stories would represent the awful truth of welfare cuts in an unequal society. The stories would represent an issue, not individuals. The project had a lot to recommend it; my point is that the Task Force gave the act of public criticism a distinctive value that is easy for progressive social scientists to take for granted, but hardly universal among Americans. Communication was good when it named white elephants, broke through complacency. In Catherine's terms, the group needed to be an "action group, not a study group." So when the group pondered new facts about welfare and inequality, it treated them as fresh coals for a fire of angry solidarity, not simply evidence to weigh against other evidence.

The institutional context explains some of the constraints on the Task Force's customs. Those customs, in turn, constrained the ways that the group could articulate its call for justice without threatening the group itself. Scenes from the Task Force show what the customs concept contributes to how sociologists think about activism.

A VIEW FROM SOCIAL MOVEMENT SCHOLARSHIP:
BEYOND THE QUESTION OF FRAMING

Hearing Catherine and Frank apply their anticorporate discourse to every issue the group considered, regardless of how people responded, I wondered why the group did not seem more interested in "framing" issues strategically for their audience. Sociologists consider framing an important task for movement group leaders (for classic statements, see McAdam, McCarthy, and Zald 1996; Snow and Benford 1988). Part of the reason may be that Catherine and Frank's anti-corporate frame had swayed most of the group. Catherine hinted to me after one meeting that other people in the group needed to have their consciousness raised. "I'm at a different place," she observed, "further down the road." She wanted to make sure other members shared her definitions of root problems and real solutions. Other members agreed a lot of the time, at least outwardly; there were very few "frame disputes" (Benford 1993) between members. But it was much less clear whether or not many audiences outside the group resonated with the frame.

The framing concept does not answer all questions that are worth asking about meaning in social movements, as sociologists have been finding out (Steinberg 1999; Lichterman 1999, 1995b; Hart 1996). It will not cover all the things that culture does in a group like the Task Force. Participants might agree with the group's social analysis, its "diagnostic frame" (Snow and Benford 1988), and yet become frustrated with the group.

Scholars of framing have pointed out that as activists are framing issues, they are simultaneously creating identities for their own group and other groups (Hunt, Benford, and Snow 1994). These scholars rely on a valuable insight from the sociology of interaction: When people communicate in any concrete situation, they have to locate one another in some field of actors (McCall and Simmons 1978; Stone 1962). That means people do not just take up ideologies or "frames" in the abstract. We have to have an identity. We have to *be the kind of person or group* who can think things like that and say them to others (see Downey 1986; Snow 2001; Lichterman 1996; Swidler 2001).

I want to take this insight on interaction further. It helps explain why the Task Force as a whole seemed little concerned with framing issues strategically. Members did not seem to care if they scared off newcomers, if they offended some of the audience at Economic Injustice workshops. Plainly, something besides the frames,[10] the cognitive definitions of issues, mattered greatly.

The framing perspective abstracts the culture, the frames, from the group process in which frames get communicated. My alternative approach highlights the way people build groups, in customary ways, around vocabularies or frames: The words and phrases become meaningful, usable, only in the context of group boundaries, bonds, and speech norms. As they communicated social justice, Task Force members were not just defining issues or identities, though they were doing that, too. They were enforcing the group's customary *form of togetherness*. The vocabulary of social justice, or the "justice frame" if we like, came embedded in a customary form. In everyday life, people cannot separate the two. Communicating, talking social justice in this case, always also means maintaining a setting, even if a virtual or imagined one.[11]

The Task Force *cohered* through its customs, a shared mission to name white elephants, loudly. Some members shared the same definitions of the causes and consequences of inequality, the same definition of corporate responsibility. But they related to these definitions differently. Given the chance, they would have built a group around these definitions in a different way. They would have carried these definitions with different customs.

Agreement on the Terms, Dissent from the Customs

A few dissenters made the existence of dominant customs all the more obvious. The dissenters' experiences also convinced me that customs mattered, and could set barriers, even when the dissenters valued the same vocabularies or frames as other members. A few people said the brochures, fact sheets, and bar graphs forced "correct" answers. They did not disagree with the information; they had trouble with the style of conveying it. At one of my first meetings, Catherine brought in a little test, a multiple-choice quiz named "The Economic Insecurity Rat Race." While spoofing multiple-choice tests and board games, it taught a serious message: Most people have to run very hard just to stay in place economically, while a few get richer with every step. As we filled in our answers to quiz questions, bemused titters broke out around the table.

WOMAN (across from me): I think it's funny!
ANOTHER WOMAN: I like it.
CHARLENE: I found it offensive.

She thought it was leading people to a preferred point of view, telling people how to think.

BABETTE: Well, it's what I call the "garden path" approach.

It led people along. The first woman agreed with her, but was not offended by it. Charlene was unmoved. Most but not all Task Force members took the dominant speech norms, or other customs, for granted.

Charlene did not want to be told what to think, and didn't want to tell other people what to think either. After we took the rat race quiz, Charlene said we "need to talk more about how we should talk about these issues to congregations." No one took her up on the topic. Charlene did not disagree with the group's analysis of welfare reform and poverty. As she told me at a URC event some months later, "I'm a pretty liberal person." She agreed wholeheartedly that Lakeburg was socially divided, and for that reason she made a point of doing voter-registration work every election season. She, like other Task Force members, scoffed at "well-meaning volunteers" who did more harm than good by imposing themselves on less powerful people. She is the one who told me that is just what some white URC volunteers were doing when they tried sharing a table with the NAACP at a local festival. But Charlene thought that the Task

Force ought to do presentations that "let people make up their own minds. We need to learn how to dialogue." Frank disagreed: People had group (class) interests, he said, and needed to confront them.

The meaning of speech itself and group bonds were different for Charlene than for other leading members like Frank or Kate. Kate let on to me in the middle of one meeting that the group existed, among other reasons, to "support" people whose politics made them feel like rejects in their own churches. No one had disagreed. Charlene apparently expected the group to be about something else. She stopped attending the Task Force meetings after the rat race quiz. She told me, later on, that the group was "too politically correct." The group's way of making style into substance annoyed her.

Doreen, too, stopped attending after a few meetings, leaving the dominant customs in place. Doreen had the same criticisms of welfare reform as other members. And on a survey form she ranked her political views at the extreme "liberal" end, giving herself a one on a seven-point scale. Doreen was the new member who had told the group she appreciated it for being the only one that talked about "structural" issues. But Doreen, too, assumed different purposes for talk than the ones most favored in the group as a whole.

I noticed other instances in which clashing speech norms led to misunderstandings even when the speakers held the same viewpoints, as in this exchange:

> Wayne asked rhetorically, "Do the majority of people care about welfare reform? If you get out of Lakeburg, to some place where the typical wage is five dollars an hour, and see how people talk about welfare, they think there are just lazy people" who won't work. Better, Wayne opined, for there to be a guaranteed "living wage."
>
> Later on, Doreen tried to correct Wayne, telling him that some people would never be able to work at a good paying job, and needed to be cared for in a humane way. Wayne explained that he *already* thought the same thing, and was assuming it as background for his own comments.

In other words, Wayne was not representing the opinion about laziness in order to affirm it or to throw another opinion out on the table for thoughtful consideration. He was not trying to say everyone can and should work. He was representing to us a world in which many people do think that way, the *wrong* way. This might be clear enough in a group of people who shared not only the same politics but the same assumptions about the appropriate speech genre and the same assumption about group bonds, that political progressives need to stick together. Wayne's comment was saying there are many of "them," who are not like "us." But his solidarity-building intent would not be clear to someone like Doreen, who figured the group was more an educational forum than a political support group.

Doreen, a leader in the local League of Women Voters chapter, thought the point of talking was more to discuss and learn than to critique and build group solidarity around anger. That is why she misunderstood Wayne's intents. A similar clash of speech norms hit her harder the following month. Catherine had invited a guest, a welfare rights advocate, to announce a "speak-out on poverty" that would happen soon at a local neighborhood center. Doreen disapproved of the new welfare policies, just like everyone else; sitting next to me, she whispered several criticisms that anyone around the table would have affirmed. But she said after the guest's announcement that the new policy included some support for childcare for working mothers—a provision that had not been part of the original bill in the legislature. Her tone said things were not hopeless. It was a different tone from the righteous anger burning through most other members' comments.

WELFARE ADVOCATE (*not missing a beat*): They got daycare changed because it affects middle-class people—
ANOTHER MEMBER: Uh huh!
FRANK: That's right.

Doreen drew back in her seat, her lips thinned, as if making way for the sharp analysis darting by. Doreen agreed with the group's analysis but she valued a different speech genre more. I did not see her at another Task Force meeting during the following two years. When I asked in an interview why she stopped going, she said the group's style annoyed her.

PROPHETS REACHING OUT

Interaction in the Justice Task Force gave members a lot of practice with standing outside of local civic life, even as they tried to spiral into it. They worked themselves *off* of the local social map: A good member was one who would not let civic relationships distract her from the overwhelming reality of corporate domination. Catherine liked to picture the Task Force as an agitator in a crowd. As she said at meetings many times, her favorite idea for a group project was to put on political street theater, in one of Lakeburg's shopping malls, in hopes of energizing one or two appreciative onlookers while shocking the rest. As the street theater example itself implies, Task Force members wanted an audience; they wanted a relationship with a listening public, albeit one they imagined in unflattering terms.

The Task Force's customs emboldened members to talk critically, without helping them create relationships with a broader audience that could participate with them in social criticism. Critical talking and writing were major activities, both inside the Task Force and in its contacts with other groups in Lakeburg. Sometimes consciousness raising took the form of position statements, like the ones the group drafted on welfare reform and prison policy for the URC. Sometimes it took the form of instruction, as in the Economic Injustice work-

shops. Sometimes Task Force members tried to raise other people's consciousness more spontaneously.

A good example of the group's style of reaching out is the "ten chairs" exercise that became the centerpiece of Economic Injustice workshops. A hands-on
demonstration of the distribution of wealth in the United States, it was supposed to open participants' minds and hearts to a new understanding of the gap
between rich and poor. The exercise helped launch a few people into critical
conversation about wealth and poverty in the United States. Task Force members did not see the exercise as an opportunity to critically ponder relationships
with audiences.

Economic Injustice Workshops

Catherine asked mischievously, did we want to try it out? We lined up ten chairs
behind our meeting table. Now we needed some volunteers. Frank agreed to occupy seven of the ten chairs. It was not easy to do, even for hefty Frank. He
sprawled arms, body and feet over the yellow and orange plastic-cushioned
folding chairs, trying to lay claim to them all. Catherine chose someone else to
occupy one chair. Then she counted off eight more people, and asked them to
walk over and claim the two remaining chairs. Amused and a little confused,
they headed toward the chairs. One woman sat down immediately, leaving the
rest to stand around the chair grinning awkwardly. There were so many people
hunkered around the single folding chair, I could not see the chair at all.

Catherine pushed the envelope: "Anyone want to talk about feelings?" Kate
said that the scenario did not match the real-life situation that well. "In reality,
the eight don't know who they are, and who the one with the seven chairs is."
Other onlookers at the meeting agreed, that people did not see their whole social situation—they just knew that they alone were hurting. They did not know
more, Frank instructed, because "corporate power controls the media, and controls the government." A woman from a Presbyterian church agreed that corporations control the government. The conversational exchange was fast, sometimes furious. Lots of the fifteen people in the room nodded and agreed with
the critique of capitalism; no one objected. The exercise had produced the right
response.

Though Charlene and Doreen had dissented from it, the group's dominant
understanding of the workshops was that they were meant to *instruct* participants and give them a shock of moral enlightenment too. They were not forums
for exploring issues as an end in itself. Frank and Catherine's way of talking about
the workshops made that clear: Frank told a URC board meeting how surprised
and pleased he was after one workshop at a Methodist church because he "didn't
get much flak" from the people who attended. Catherine told me on another occasion that "some people get it and some people want to nit-pick the numbers."
She would be happy if a workshop "energized" one or two people into working

for the Living Wage Campaign or some other economic justice issue. The workshops were supposed to confront mistaken perspectives with correct ones.

I asked on three different occasions if the group might like a sympathetic outsider's evaluation. I asked Catherine at least once over the phone. Would members like to know what participants thought of these workshops? I could go ask some participants. Might it be a good idea to figure out how to communicate with potential audiences? I was surprised that Task Force leaders received my very genuine offers with tepid enthusiasm.

Why didn't they want this free consultation? I had made clear that I agreed with the basic social justice message of the workshops, so the group should have had little to fear from me. But they had a different definition of the workshops' purpose. Given the boundaries, bonds, and speech genre, that made sense: *Critically reflecting on the group's relations with participants* in these workshops threatened to distract the group from its customary version of prophecy. Why put a lot of attention into figuring out how to appeal to people if part of the practice, in fact, was to be a brave prophet and hammer away at an awful truth?

One might guess that the group did not really care about how it communicated with a broader public. Maybe enunciating criticism and shocking people was an end in itself, like the expressive youth politics of 1960s.[12] Maybe Task Force members' real goal was to announce their identity (Melucci 1989)—in this case, as marginalized churchgoers shut out from any institutional influence (see M. Bernstein 1997).

But observations told me that members wanted to do more than express themselves for the sake of expressing themselves. Several times Catherine told the group she was frustrated that more churches did not sign up for the Economic Injustice workshops. She was disappointed that the URC had not given the workshops more administrative support and would not let the Task Force speak unconditionally on behalf of the whole URC. That is why she resigned as chair of the Task Force. In bewilderment, Frank characterized the workshops project as marginalized, "off in a corner somewhere." Neither Catherine nor Frank had stopped expressing themselves on welfare policy; it mattered how the project was doing as a part of the Task Force's public mission. Other members wanted the group to contribute in some way to other campaigns. They did not want the group to be a private debating society or a safe haven for radicals and nothing more. Task Force members did not cry out solely for the moral satisfaction of voicing their truths, much as it did seem to give members like Catherine a satisfying moral charge. Yet their customary style might make audiences guess that disruption was itself the sole goal.

Prophets at Large

At larger forums I heard a rug-pulling exercise in play. When the State Council of Churches had its annual convocation in Lakeburg, I watched Frank and

Catherine try to shift the entire floor of discussion about welfare and poverty
with a strident excursus on the growing gap between rich and poor. Another
time, Frank "took over" one meeting of the URC-sponsored Religious Anti-
racism Coalition with a long analysis of the economics of race. This may have
been consciousness-raising on the spot. It was not building relationships with
church groups. At the Coalition meeting, people listened politely, treated
Frank's quietly impassioned lecture as an announcement, and moved on when
he was done. From Frank's point of view, it was a matter of speaking the truth,
raising some righteous anger. The HRA's quarterly convocations were another
venue for speaking out.

At one convocation, Kate tossed out a critical salvo. It may have baffled other
participants more than raising their consciousness. It was the big meeting of
volunteers with the county's "welfare chief" Norma, pictured in chapter 3.
Norma was telling the volunteers that there used to be a "bedrock assumption"
that welfare money was coming in for rent, but that this was no longer the case.

Kate asked from the audience floor if there was not a "new bedrock assumption" now, that "for every welfare recipient there is a high-paying job" to pay the
rent. Norma told Kate she did not understand, and asked her to repeat the question. Kate did, and Norma continued to look perplexed. She offered, finally, that
there was an assumption that in the relatively healthy Lakeburg economy of
1997 there were jobs to be had. Pressing her point, Kate asked again if there was
not an assumption about high-paying jobs, not just jobs. Norma responded that
she did not think there were high-paying jobs for everyone. She looked dissatisfied with her own answer, and with the whole exchange; facilitator Donald
stepped in to say we were out of time.

Kate had taken her question straight from the previous month's Task Force
meeting: Frank had observed that political leaders said welfare reform could
work only if there were high-paying jobs for former welfare recipients. Everyone knew—or at least sharp-thinking people in the Task Force could assume—
that there could not be enough such jobs for former welfare recipients. Frank
had brought up the claim about high-paying jobs in order to criticize political
leaders; he was hoisting them on their own petards. But the big meeting with
Norma was a different context, in which people did not necessarily share the
Task Force's preferred speech genre. They would not necessarily know that Kate
meant her question *itself* as a criticism, the way Frank had meant his observation as a criticism. They would not necessarily know what Kate meant to do with
words. Lakeburg County's head coordinator of volunteers did not know for
sure: Bringing up Kate's question during a conversation with me, she said "we
would *hope* that there would be—but I don't think any of us think that is going
to happen."

> PL: I thought Kate was being critical of people who think that there are
> going to be high-paying jobs for everyone.

COORDINATOR (*sounding uncertain*): Well, Kate is a very bright person. . . .
I think she must have been being facetious.

She repeated the term "facetious" slowly, as if arriving at an interpretation of a
puzzling situation.

Pulling the rug out, instead of offering some conversational common ground,
will not help a group initiate actual relationships.[13] Groups, or representatives
of groups, cannot create ties over time if the parties cannot even communicate
clearly enough to make sense to one another. The confusion that Kate engen-
dered in the volunteer coordinator reminded me of the confused exchanges inside the Task Force between Doreen and Wayne. How would people at this big
meeting know how to relate to the Task Force if, intentionally or otherwise, it
made itself more inscrutable?

SHORT SPIRALS, NO BRIDGES

After three of these quarterly convocations, the core membership of the Task
Force remained the same. A few new participants who became regular core
members later joined the group through their acquaintanceship with Catherine
or the URC director. Many activist groups puzzle over how to enlarge their
membership, especially across class or racial lines. It is not news that personal
connections are some of the most effective conduits of recruitment to activist
groups.[14] Scenes from the Task Force show, as other research has already suggested (Lichterman 1995b; see also Becker 1999), that clashing customs may
make building bridges more difficult, even when potential allies or members
share the same stance on social issues.

Refusing a Bridge

Catherine kicked off some of our meetings with a quote from populist Texas
congressman Jim Hightower: "There's nothing in the middle of the road but yellow lines and dead armadillos." It was a suitable motto for the group's relation
to other groups in the URC, and other Lakeburg entitites.

One night, two years into my study, a man from a local prisoner mentoring
program came to solicit volunteers. He talked a human service worker's argot
that had become familiar to me from listening to county administrators patch
together assistance for former welfare recipients. He told us all about the various mentoring programs for prisoners, many of whom had "significant issues
going on," including "criminal thinking issues." Mentors could teach prisoners
how to identify their own feelings, so that they would respond to everyday frustrations with flexibility instead of with criminal thinking. In all, mentors could
"break down the criminal thinking, help with goal setting . . . and all sorts of

longer term issues. Join us and you will make a real difference in an individual's life."

Predictably by now, the man elicited little interest. Bored, Catherine twisted her pencil in her fingers throughout his presentation. No one said they intended to join up. No one talked about any next steps the Task Force might take with the mentoring program. No one said anything for what seemed like a long moment after the presentation.

Catherine told the mentoring program director, *after* the meeting, that "It's not an either-or, it's both"—this in reference to volunteering versus activism. He replied that when he and his partner had first started the mentoring program, they did want to talk about the root causes of crime. This was just the sort of critical dialogue at which the Task Force excelled. Why, then, couldn't the Task Force have tried creating a relationship with the prisoner mentoring program? It sounded like the mentoring program could have been a partner in consciousness raising.

By now, prison issues were become a major focus of the URC's work. Task Force members had gotten interested in thinking through the place of prisons in an unequal society. As usual, the group wanted to place prisons in a bigger social picture.

Doris said, "The state is not spending as much money as it should on education. . . . All these issues are being bled right now for prisons. . . . The black community has been devastated." Ironically, the state endured revenue caps on spending for schools while prison building continued unabated.

Frank added that he had just heard the governor saying that "if the economy slows down because of the stock market crash, it's going to be hard not to raid schools for building prisons."

Catherine added, "Not just prisons—the whole welfare reform is based on the assumption that jobs will be available."

Doris was the group's leading contact for a new prison issues coalition that "pushed the structural issue. It's not just 'an individual made a bad choice.' There are things funneling people" into the prison system. She asked rhetorically, "In what ways is the criminal justice system forcing people to commit crimes?" And she went on, that if the welfare net is removed, people may be forced to commit crimes to live. If there are no jobs, people may need to commit crimes to get money. The analysis stood; the Task Force found it a sound one.

The Task Force might have tried relating to the mentoring program, fitting it out with an educational component in line with the director's own original plan. But groups like the mentoring program were "volunteer groups." In more open-minded comments after a meeting, Catherine said that the solutions to social problems were not "either volunteering or activism," but both. But while in session, the group worked hard to keep the *group boundaries* strong, *bonds* tight, and the *speech* loud and angry. Group customs cut off the possibility for an ongoing relationship.

The mentoring program director represented, in effect, a distraction from what the group was about. It was a potentially threatening distraction, rather than an opportunity to link up with a popular program. Catherine opined after the director finished his presentation that the group was drifting too far toward a "service" mentality—the volunteering versus activism dichotomy again. The prison issue was popular because it was more about service than about social structures, she thought. Yet the Task Force was perfectly capable of making seemingly personal or service issues into social-structural ones if it wanted to. Recall its response to bank mortgage fees when Donald foisted the issue on the group. Groups representing service issues were on the wrong side of the boundary, the side with complacent volunteers and charity-minded churches, with huge, looming social structures casting a shadow over all from the other side. A volunteer group would not make a meaningful bridge-building partner.

Janet's Story

In a similar way, the Task Force passed up opportunities to make regular members out of new participants who did not already share the group's map of society or adopt it quickly. One night, a woman in her early fifties with pageboy haircut, glasses, and thin gold necklace told a heart-breaking story. Janet had never come to a Task Force meeting, but needed to share her harrowing tale with people who cared about prisoners. I took notes on the story:

A good friend of hers had been threatened physically by her own son. The friend did not know what to do and decided her son needed to be straightened out. She pressed charges, and her son was imprisoned. The son, she explained, was "bipolar" and had a hard time controlling anger. He was on a waiting list for anger-control classes. He became sick in prison and cried out in pain. The guards thought all the noise was just troublemaking and did nothing. A few days later guards apparently relented and believed that he had a problem, but it was too late, and his appendix ruptured on the way to the hospital. Upon his return from the hospital, the man got in a fight in the cafeteria. "I don't know why," Janet said meekly, in a tone saying that it's just one of those things that can happen. For that he got put in a "segregated" cell, and fed what prisoners called "gag loaf": a blender-processed puree of all the leftovers from prison meals. Said to be enough to live on, the man lost 45 pounds. Janet was near breaking down. This man committed suicide after seven months in prison. Now Janet was crying.

No one said anything for several seconds. It felt like the right time for someone to offer a benedictory statement, to recuperate the group. It was hard to hear about the real, human consequences of injustice.

> DORIS: That's why I started here—at least there's a structure to get information out to congregations, as slow as that may be, so some people can become witnesses, take on those roles.

Catherine said that it was important to hear the stories, but all the same she was feeling like the group needed to take some steps beyond that.

> FRANK: How do we bring in churches?
> CATHERINE: Well, it's partly the churches, but also the powers that be. You need the educational piece but you also need the social change piece. . . . "Ain't it awful" isn't enough.

Janet sounded defensive now; she wanted us to understand why she had come to tell this story to begin with. The prisoner's mother was a good friend of hers, and had not expected it all to come to this.

> DORIS (*supportively*): She wanted help.
> JANET: Three meals a day! Aren't they supposed to provide that? Something to look forward to. Isn't that what my tax dollars are for?
> CATHERINE: You would think so.

Still no one came up with something more comforting to say. Catherine offered that "it may sound sort of gross, but it could make a good 'human interest' story." Doris said the mother could try getting a lawyer. Janet said the mother was too angry to think about that now.

Janet's purpose was different from the group's: She wanted comfort, and answers, not critical analysis. She did not speak as if she shared the group's map of the larger world. A mother was hurting, a son was dead; it was a human tragedy, not necessarily a social one. Task Force members did not find ways to bridge her perspective and theirs. Janet did not come to another meeting.

To sum up, Task Force members' customs bid them to keep a critical distance from church groups—except individuals in those groups who similarly felt marginal for their radical outlooks. The group kept wanting to speak to an audience of some sort, to spiral outward somewhere, yet its customs restricted the places members could spiral *toward:* Churches were suspect, and other volunteer groups were not bridge-worthy. Still, there was the world of loosely connected, progressive networks.

Spiraling into Loosely Connected Networks

Task Force members learned about political issues at their meetings. Many times, someone passed around a petition on one or another progressive issue. We signed petitions against the construction of a maximum-security "Supermax" prison in a town several dozen miles away, for instance. We talked a lot about the grim details of the prison, with its seven-by-seven foot cells and withering fluorescent light. Members learned the Supermax probably violated the Geneva Convention. The Supermax prison aroused righteous anger, partly because members thought it violated basic human dignity and partly because it played a grim role in members' analysis of the "prison-industrial system" that cycled poor whites to low-wage jobs and poor blacks to prison. The Task Force held a press conference to denounce the prison; local television news carried the conference.

The Task Force got much more peripherally involved in other issues, too. During the first year, one member brought some literature on election finance reform to a meeting, after hearing a report on the subject. It made sense to support election finance reform. Without it, chances were slim that candidates could emerge who were willing to do without the big money that supported conservative welfare policies—or that is how the group reasoned. After a short discussion at one meeting, they quickly formed a subcommittee on the issue. Many groups in Lakeburg supported a local network of the national Living Wage Campaign. They wanted municipal employers, and hopefully all employers eventually, to commit themselves to paying an hourly wage no less than that required to secure "livable" rental housing and food. The Task Force signed on to the local Living Wage Campaign, too.

Both campaigns were nationwide, with citizen action committees in many cities. Both, as well as the statewide campaign against the Supermax prison, were loosely connected networks, focused on a particular issue, directed by campaigners and supported with money or volunteer publicists in loose congeries of groups like the Justice Task Force that already existed to pursue other issues. Joining the Task Force, a new member would learn at least a little about the issues these networks pursued, and have the chance to be affiliated on paper with them—becoming one of the thousands or millions of "supporters" that a campaign can claim in the case of election finance reform. Loosely connected networks achieve political goals sometimes, at least in a piecemeal way. Networks can be effective vehicles for representing a mass of individual opinions with educational campaigns and lobbying.

Whether or not they are effective, coalitions whose members come together mainly for media events do not represent the ties that neo-Tocquevillians have in mind when they imagine civic groups as workshops of social solidarity. On the one hand, that is one of the limits in neo-Tocquevillian thinking—it underestimates the other contributions civic groups make to a healthy democracy. The Task Force could have played an important local role in the Supermax campaign, at least, by framing it in religious terms for church audiences. They saw their role that way too, and developed a statement for their press conference that emphasized human dignity. On the other hand, neo-Tocquevillians as well as social network scholars would be right to point out that the statement could carry more weight if the messenger had good relationships with the audience. It would take a separate study to find out what Lakeburg churchgoers thought of the Task Force's statement against the Supermax—if they happened to hear it at all. Since the group styled itself as separate from many churchgoers even as it wanted to speak to them, it is a good guess that their role as a *religious* voice against the Supermax was not as powerful as it might have been given different group customs.

Affiliating with loosely connected networks was not the main kind of connection the Task Force *wanted* to create. They wanted to build political bridges, at least within the URC's constellation of churches and projects. They wanted to speak to people directly—in church-sponsored workshops or URC meetings. They aimed to do something other than join the memberships-on-paper of regional or national campaigns.

IMAGINING CONNECTIONS

Occasionally members did talk about their relations to the wider social world. Often, they imagined themselves in a brutal world of economic interests. Less frequently, they imagined charitable, personal relationships on a social map that their own customs stigmatized. There was a place for their audience on both maps, but neither image of their audience became the object of much reflective, searching conversation. That is because group customs made it difficult for members to question their way of understanding themselves in the wider world, even when invited to.

Social Connections as a System of Economic Interests

Task Force members talked a lot about the "interests" of ordinary middle-class people in Lakeburg. While planning Economic Injustice workshops for church audiences, usually they assumed that audiences should be able to identify with the analysis. The message was that most people's interests were closer to those of welfare recipients than those of large corporations. The middle class simply was economically insecure, frightened, and took out its anxieties on welfare recipients. As Catherine put it, "that's why welfare reform sells."

Catherine was not criticizing the middle class. She was criticizing the big economic interests that she thought made middle-class people feel squeezed. Implicitly, Catherine also was picturing a relationship between social critics like Task Force members and the people they wanted to enlighten. Task Force members figured that people who did not identify with their analysis had been duped by ideologies in the mass media. They did not learn enough about other groups in town to see whether their line on putative economic insecurities would help them speak to fellow churchgoers and Lakeburgers. They sustained lively arguments with people who disagreed, or else considered them ignorant, without questioning their definition of the consciousness-raising relationship itself. Workshop audiences rarely if ever were *perplexing* to the group; sometimes audiences were just wrong.

In the Task Force's discourse, the real world of social connections was a world of economic interests. People identified with or rejected other groups on the basis of economic interest or misunderstandings of interest created by countervailing corporate economic interests. When Wayne, for instance, said that people outside of Lakeburg thought people on welfare were just lazy, Kate articulated the rest of the picture thus:

> KATE: People feel like danger is biting at the back door. That's why they're worried a lot about welfare reform [because of their own economic insecurity]. . . . It's not that they have suddenly developed compassion for the poor. (*repeating the analysis*): People are driven by economic insecurity.
> CATHERINE: The middle class and the poor are stuck in the same overall situation. We're in this together.
> KATE: That will be our solidarity—we're in this together.
> CATHERINE: We've got to make common cause with the poor.

It made a lot of sense. Nonaffluent people ought to realize they have a lot of interests in common. But would that analysis alone help people *hear* the critique, assimilate it?

Next month the group applied the same analysis to a new issue: The Supermax prison proposed for a town thirty miles away had been receiving publicity in Lakeburg. The prison would provide jobs in a small rural town; civil libertarians said its tiny cells with no direct sunlight were inhumane and illegal. Two members proposed protesting the prison. They imagined asking local residents, potential employees of the prison, "Would you do that to your child? Would you do that to your dog?" One said we must break down "this barrier between we and they," between "good" people and evil prisoners. Kate saw a larger, social-structural reality that was more basic, and others agreed: "Tie it structurally to how isolated we all are and scared we all feel. . . . It is that biting at the middle-class again." Kate's point was that people were willing to write off other people, throw prisoners into veritable dungeons, because their economic interests made them insecure about stigmatized groups. It certainly was plausible.

Why, however, did the group take this bit of wisdom so much for granted? Why did the group excuse itself from learning more about how outsiders actually felt about the social world? I heard the economically insecure audience being conjured up at many meetings. It was an important if rarely questioned part of the group's own self-understanding, part of the context that shaped its own social identity. Sometimes, political groups want to scope out their skeptics' viewpoints carefully. Community organizers, for instance, spend a lot of time getting to know about the particular people whose consciousness they would like ultimately to "raise." There are good reasons the Task Force, with its focus on critiquing welfare reform, would not adopt the methods of community organizers who often pursue different kinds of issues with different kinds of constituencies.[15] Still it is hard to see why the Task Force could not have reflected more on the characteristics of the audience it wanted to reach, and its relationship to that audience, particularly since they belonged to the URC circle of churches they hoped to reach first.

Not only Catherine and Kate, but Frank and others relied on the same assumptions about their audience. When Frank disagreed with Charlene about whether or not Economic Injustice workshops should invite people to make up their own minds instead of telling them what is right, he based his opinion on the notion that everyone has group interests and acts on them: It is wrong-headed to presume people have individual minds to make up when, in his words, "everyone comes from somewhere." Better for people to confront the assumptions they have as occupants of a rung in the social structure.

What, then, were the Task Force's interests? Were they not middle-class people too?[16] Why were they not implicated in the system of interest-driven, fear-driven relationships? Maybe they escaped their own condemnation because they heeded the Bible's social justice message more attentively than other churchgoers who did not rank "justice" first in the prophet Micah's trio of divine requirements. My point is *not* that powerful economic interests don't exist. It is that "interests" stood as a ready-made answer that the group, apart from dissenters like Charlene, accepted without elaboration—perhaps at its own peril.

When Donald invited the group to reflect on its own motives, at one of the first meetings, I saw that the Task Force was in a terrible bind. The answer to his invitation easily might threaten the group's existence.

Social Connections as Compassion

Donald put it bluntly at one meeting: "We all aspire to be wealthy—we damn the wealthy but we aspire to wealth, too." He sounded as if he were cautioning us to be more humble. In the context of a religiously based social action group, it was an unremarkable, Christian thing to say. He had just been criticizing the "good versus bad" tone of the ten chairs exercise and the rat-race quiz. He was saying that we were not above the sins we criticized. No one responded.

A couple of months later, this theme of individual culpability came up again. This single set of exchanges is worth following closely because it shows that Task Force members were not just self-righteous scolds. They did not just think other people were bad. They wanted to acknowledge other people's worth, without sinking into an apolitical understanding of compassion. But they confronted a cultural dilemma that forced them to choose between being people of faith with an individualizing perspective instead of a critical social one or else prophets with an elusive connection to an audience. Most chose the latter.

It was December 1996, and debates about welfare and poverty were animating Lakeburg's religious circles. At the monthly Task Force meeting, members were deciding what they should do as a group: promote the Economic Injustice workshops? collect horror stories from people thrown off of state assistance? One new member, Beatrice, sounded a theme I had heard only Donald articulating in the previous months. "The people in power are not necessarily malicious as persons." Catherine's husband responded that some of the people "at the top" are indeed malicious. Beatrice held her ground: "I *know* some of them personally, that's why I know they're not." The two disagreed over what "at the top" meant; Beatrice had in mind the social service workers who were doing the best they could under trying circumstances. Kate wondered, then, if some of these social workers might be persuaded to refuse compliance with the new welfare policies. They were just people "caught in the system," after all. Catherine's husband, Rick, was dubious: "How many would quit their jobs?" Beatrice suggested that the group "invite some corporate people to go serve the meals" at All Saints homeless shelter. Catherine loved the idea; it was wickedly political, like street theater. Beatrice cautioned that she didn't mean to punish corporate executives. "I don't want to pose an enemy."

That is exactly what the group had been doing. If corporations and their handmaidens in media and government were not the enemy after all, then the Task Force would need a different map, different group bonds, and a different sense of what talk was for. An alternative was available: It charts a world of sinful *individuals,* some with more worldly power than others, all with human hopes and faults, all worthy of love. The map makes a lot of sense for a group bound by shared Christian faith, rather than shared social critique, and it invites other kinds of speech than righteous anger alone.

The group switched maps; the conversation became an impromptu exploration of personal responsibility. Rather than assail the economic system and the elites who benefited most from it, Task Force members mulled over the morality of their own participation in it. One observed that people at the top, and those caught in the system too, might still have some personal goodness. "You have to see that people are doing, morally, the best they can do. Even the governor is doing the best he can do." The discussion had changed Rick's mind, at least temporarily. "When someone dies, he doesn't want to be remembered for being able to see twenty-five patients in one hour" (Rick was a doctor). In other words, people want to be known as good persons who did something besides amassing power or wealth. And what if we all worked on the homeless problem by putting up homeless people in our homes?

RICK: We have two—no, three bedrooms not being used. The problem is us too.

CATHERINE: That's right, but—
KATE (*cutting in*): But we don't have the seven chairs, and we want to get to the ones that do, and they're the Holiday Inn [*allusion to the "hotels for the homeless" injustice payback scenario*].

Neither Kate nor Catherine were ready to switch customs altogether. Some people around the table were implying that social change would not happen unless they themselves made personal sacrifices. They acknowledged that they were not ready for that; in the Christian imagery Donald had used at the previous month's meeting, they all had their dark side, all had their sinfulness. Good Christians had to agree. Besides, as one member put it, "letting people into the house could be scary." Kate remarked now on how she locked her doors when driving through a black neighborhood; it made her feel awful to do it. Another summarized, "Christianity is a risky proposition." Still, Catherine held out for the part of the Christian heritage that she preferred: "Letting them in [the homeless] doesn't change the structure." Others agreed. "It's a Band-Aid."

Christianity was a risky proposition in more ways than one. Brave prophets could stand alone, criticizing the system of economic interests and its doleful consequences, and scaring off potential compatriots. Or they could draw on other, familiar Christian themes, and imagine themselves in a world of sinful individuals all of whom deserved compassion—even corporate executives. But the Task Force associated compassion[17] and appeals to individual culpability with their own churches, people and groups on the wrong side of the boundary, people who literally ran the other way when they saw Kate coming, the people who made Catherine feel unpopular.

It would be hard for Task Force members to speak as critical, *church-based* people and also imagine themselves embedded in churches. It would be hard for them to voice social critique and express a sense of collective responsibility at the same time—because in the context of church groups, responsibility so easily implied *individual* moral responsibility, not collective responsibility. In the dominant view, reinforced by the institutional structure of social service, church-based people were compassionate volunteers with little need for a social-structural imagination. They could continue to be lonely and judgmental or they could let down the barriers and surrender the moral high ground of social critique. Seeing themselves as activists surrounded by social service agencies and charity groups, there seemed to be no other map to point the way out of a very small, uncomfortable space.

Opting out of the Dilemma: Trying to Disconnect

Task Force members could not make up their response to the dilemma of church-based prophecy from scratch, any more than people ever respond to larger institutional and cultural contexts with pure, free will. In caricature, the

Task Force propounded the "political correctness" that political conservatives misread and lampooned throughout the 1990s. More sober observers would see that the group's customs have a noble history.[18] These are the customs of many American social activists, especially American radicals since the 1960s, for whom morality and good politics are inseparable (Lasch 1966; Lichterman 1996). These customs are themselves a tradition, one that bids people to rely on a deeply individualized sense of social obligation, rather than identifying very closely with existing institutions, in an endless quest to change society for the better. This deeply individualized sense of social mission is what I have called personalized politics (Lichterman 1996). It is a sensibility that made Jane Addams commit herself to a deeper connection with her social surroundings; it leads others to try disconnecting from society altogether.

Some Task Force members wanted to disconnect, at least symbolically. A few identified strongly with other societies or with groups that opposed "America" in general. Some talked about the Central America solidarity movement with a kind of reverence; it represented not simply a political stance but a kind of critical identity, a way of being in the world that other American activists have shared.[19] Several times, Frank said that his experiences witnessing poverty in Brazil had awakened him and given him an enduring sense of distance from what he had taken for granted about the United States. I admired people who took their principles so much to heart and changed their own lives as a result. I wondered at the same time how many other people could have cross-cultural consciousness raising experiences. Kate and her husband told me that they did not like the fact of being American at all. American culture was materialistic. They, in turn, practiced simple living, refused a bigger house, managed without a second car. Detachment from the image of American society in toto is of course a lesson from Thoreau, a tradition in itself, part of the individualism that many Americans honor.

AVOIDING REFLEXIVITY

Catherine and Frank complained that members did not want to sign up to lead Economic Injustice workshops, and that it was hard getting churches to host them. Catherine had led roughly twenty herself, which was no mean feat. But in a city of 375 churches, over 50 of whom affiliated in some way with the URC, her frustration was understandable. If other Task Force members believed in the message, why were they not more enthusiastic about promoting it? Why did not more churches in politically liberal Lakeburg sign up for these workshops? Why did the URC not give more support to one of its sponsored projects?

These could have been perplexing puzzles that might have spurred the group on to reflect critically about who it was in relation to churches, the URC, the political left. The Task Force never reflected on these relationships at any length during the two years of meetings I attended. They made declarations that stood without further comment: About the workshops, Kate and Catherine said simply that they threatened people's economic interests.

At least once, URC leaders asked the Task Force directly about its relationship to its social context, hoping to figure out more clearly how the group could relate to the URC. Nearly a year after the Task Force began planning Economic Injustice workshops, a URC board member asked Frank, the group's liaison to the board, how the Task Force's work related to Lakeburg congregations. Frank offered sheepishly, "How our work relates to congregations is a tough one." The group had not worked that out yet, he said. During that year, I had not heard the subject discussed at meetings.

The group seemed to pass up other invitations to social reflexivity too. A well-known African American host of a radical program on a local community radio station visited the group, late in my study. His own outspokenness matched the group's. His grass-roots progressive politics and his self-consciously radical persona should have found warm fellowship in the group. But this comrade-in-arms was frustrated by the group. Bewildered after two hours of lecture by Catherine and Frank on corporate neoliberalism, the radio announcer looked barely able to contain himself: Voice rising, he told us that "I represent a race that doesn't live as long. . . . There are lots of blacks who don't care a lot about ideology." He insisted that the group ought to be able to "act on our faith underpinnings." Rising to the theme, he intoned that "We know who the number one activist is, the one who risked everything: Jesus!" Quickly, he qualified himself: "That's my belief anyway." Some others may have shared the radio announcer's belief; some did not. No one else spoke up for Jesus, or religious faith of any sort, even though the others there were churchgoers.

The customs held. The radio announcer did not attend another meeting during my time with the group. The group seemed not to wonder why he did not return. Neither did the group take up my offers, also later in the study, to investigate how church audiences thought about the workshops.

I am suggesting that the group passed up these opportunities for reflexivity because they did not make much sense given the customs that already had taken hold in the group. The point was to be brave in the face of looming social threats, stick together, and reach out by announcing the truth bravely, not by inviting people to religious common ground. The group had easily at hand a language of individual, Christian reflexivity if not social reflexivity: When Donald heard a "preaching to the choir" tone that he did not like in the group, he invited them to ponder their personal responsibility, their individual sinfulness. But that individualizing moral thrust was just what they were trying to escape, in a group that could support them for a critical, social morality.

Maybe the Task Force lacked the right vocabulary or maybe they rejected the civic renewal discourse that Donald promoted tirelessly. It was striking, though, that the anticorporate literature that Frank liked to bring to monthly meetings described the value of "civil society" explicitly. An annual State Council of Churches conference in Lakeburg was dedicated to the theme of promoting civic engagement; Frank, Catherine, and other Task Force members attended, and heard lots of talk about civil society, in addition to what they had already heard about "reconnecting" the community and doing what Bill Bradley would do, from Donald. In an interview, Catherine referred explicitly to civil society, the social "third leg" between the market and the state as she put it. She said that was the leg that supported all the "creative" answers to social problems, the one she depended on most. The civil society vocabulary was available. But invoking it was not meaningful in a group whose customs valorized angry, boundary-enforcing conversation over figuring out civic connections.

Would it have made a difference if the group had been more reflexive about its place in Lakeburg? I did not find another interchurch social justice education group in Lakeburg with which I could compare the Justice Task Force to make the case directly. For a society in which churches sponsor a lot of civic life, the question needs more research: What makes church-based political education campaigns more successful?

It does make sense to think reflexivity could have made a difference, partly for theoretical reasons. As I discussed in chapter 2, recent writings on social ties imply that people would be little able to create ties if they cannot *talk* readily about those ties. Task Force members had an easier time separating themselves symbolically from the churchgoers whose consciousness they wanted to raise than imagining and talking about ongoing relationships with them. The group's own experiences make it reasonable to think more reflexivity could have boosted its ability to communicate social criticism *to its own satisfaction*, in churches. But it would have had to relinquish some of its sense of separateness.

Must Church-Based Social Criticism be Marginal?
A Deep Cultural Gap for Liberal Protestants

The institutional context sketched earlier boxed the Task Force in and limited its choices. Religious social critics do not always marginalize themselves, though. If they did, then prospects for broad-based social advocacy would be very dim in a country in which church membership is the most common kind of participation in civic life (Verba, Schlozman, and Brady 1995). It would be a cruel irony, too, if Americans' notions of social justice, so strongly informed by biblical traditions, were applied to everyday life only rarely in church settings. Catherine thought that irony was simply a fact of church life. Why was articulating social criticism incompatible with a sense of connection to a church community?

The two are not always incompatible. In his studies of church-based community activists, Richard Wood heard churchgoers invoking biblical justice language to support local struggles against corporations and foot-dragging city officials. Activists pursued these fights *with* an ongoing sense of embeddedness in and responsibility to a church and a local community (Wood 2002, 1994; see also Hart 2001). It may be no coincidence that Wood's religious activists were often Catholic or black Protestants.

Most of the core Task Force members except Frank were mainline Protestants. While white mainline Protestants can draw on a Social Gospel heritage that values collective well-being and not only personal piety, some observers have pointed out that it is not *customary* in mainline Protestant circles to use a lot of explicitly biblical language in public. In these circles, "Bible thumping" is not polite. I will develop the point much further in chapter 7. For now I observe that it may be much harder in the American context for liberal or mainline Protestants to signal their church basis, their religious roots, in a way that would invite other mainline Protestants into social criticism with them.

The social coordinates of mainline Protestantism in the United States are part of the story. Arguably, at least some Americans of color understand and live religious identities differently from the way white and middle-class mainline Protestants do. Many African American Christians, for instance, understand political struggle on behalf of the (black) community as struggle on behalf of a religious community too (see for instance Lincoln and Mamiya 1990). These religious traditions may help their adherents cultivate different kinds of relations to a wider community. For white and middle-class mainline Protestants like most Task Force members, it may be very difficult to promote social criticism and create wider ties with church or community at the same time. Task Force members built their group in dissenting relation to institutionalized social service, and in dissenting relation to their own churches. If members were not "ordinary" churchgoers, not churchgoing volunteers supporting social service professionals, and not a secular group either, than who would it make sense to *be* if they were going to voice their critique of conventional approaches to welfare and poverty? They seemed to lack for a social identity they could share broadly with fellow churchgoers and civically involved Lakeburgers.

Maybe these people wore their Christianity very lightly, ready to shed it at any moment, yet in interviews, none of the Task Force members had the slightest trouble tying their advocacy directly to biblical precepts. They could relate their group efforts much more tightly to specific biblical teachings than did churchgoers we will meet in Chapter 6. American liberal Protestantism has held the torch high for social reform, for decades (Marty 1981; Michaelsen and Roof 1986; Wuthnow and Evans 2002). And Lakeburg was a politically liberal city, to boot. Yet, given the institutional and cultural context, it was hard for these church-based people to build group togetherness around a vocabulary of social justice without creating distance and marginalizing themselves or else surrendering themselves as a distinctive group.

As if the barriers were not high enough, it does not help that a lot of Americans, including churchgoers, assume that public religion is rancorous, culture-warring religion. Lakeburgers might easily associate public, *Christian-based* advocacy with abrasive fundamentalism (Besecke 2002), especially when the advocates are white. Few secular people take offense when an African American gospel choir sings praise to Jesus Christ at a political rally. "That is just part of their culture," progressive whites say. "Their" religion gave them strength to endure the worst kind of social subordination. But what comes to mind if someone asks us to picture white, middle-class people who are propounding a public message *as Christians?* We probably do not imagine critics of capitalism. Local, religiously based social justice advocacy may be very difficult to pull off for people who cannot readily claim that their religion itself is a form of resistance to economic or racial subordination. For them, the culture gap may be very hard to close.

Despite the best intentions, national church offices may have done relatively little to close the gap. Like Catherine and other Task Force members, I learned that denominational headquarters in New York and Washington had often written position statements on social issues. They framed those issues consistently to the left of mainstream political discourse. Not only the much publicized Catholic bishops, but Presbyterian, Lutheran, and other denominational leaders wrote statements on economic equality and social responsibility (Steensland 2002). Denominational leaders have wondered why these statements do not influence the "people in the pews" more strongly (Wuthnow and Evans 2002). National church leaders may need to rethink some of their assumptions about the power of framing. They, like some sociologists and some activists too, may assume too simple a notion of how new ideas promote social change.

Many activists, secular and religious, believe some version of the old biblical promise that the truth will set one free. In secular language: If we get our analysis right, and repeat it constantly, people will come around.[20] The popular idea of "consciousness raising" depends on that assumption. Scholars of activism, and some activists, may put it this way: If you frame the issue in terms that appeal to the target constituency, then people will come around. The case of the Task Force suggests that the facts of group interaction matter as much as the facts of social injustice on paper. Social criticism on paper does not create new collective wills. Even the most logical and biblically consonant arguments for equalizing wealth and promoting social welfare will fail to appeal widely to church audiences if churchgoers do not find it meaningful to *communicate* the arguments *in church settings.* People must do more than agree privately with the discourse. People must be able to sustain forms of group togetherness in which criticizing social relations is a meaningful thing to do with words. Participating in this kind of discussion, in church settings, will not be a meaningful thing to do if there is no identity that people can *be* as they talk the talk. Activists who promote the talk must welcome churchgoers into relationships with them, find common ground, share not only ideas but group customs too. Scenes from the

Task Force suggest the circle of social critics will not widen if activists cannot reflect critically on how they relate to other people.

Of course social critics will not always want to create forums for free discussion, or any kind of forum for that matter. Sticking by what is right, publicizing it at the risk of being unpopular, may take just the sort of group customs that the Task Force sustained. The survival of critical ideas is a good. While the Task Force did not live up to the expectations of the social spiral argument, it would be very wrong to read my analysis as a condemnation. The scenarios here do suggest that it would take somewhat different customs for the Task Force to meet some of its own goals.

Some Lakeburg churchgoers dissatisfied with institutionalized volunteering went in a different direction. They tried deep compassion.

Chapter Five

CHRIST-LIKE CARE: SOCIAL SERVANTS

PLANTING A LITTLE LOVE DYNAMITE

"This is a great day for your churches, and for the city of Lakeburg," Evan announced. For weeks leading up to this hot July evening, Evan had been working with county social service people, identifying families that were losing their welfare benefits. Evan's Adopt-a-Family program would match up these families with local church groups of six or eight volunteers each. Volunteers would learn how to support the family while the breadwinner cast about for paid work. This evening, fifty churchgoers, most from theologically conservative, evangelical Protestant churches and all white, had come to Adopt-a-Family's orientation meeting in an airy church sanctuary. Evan explained how Adopt-a-Family sprang forth from a vision that came to a woman in his prayer group, months before: "People were going around planting love dynamite, to blow up the barriers of isolation, indifference, hopelessness." The answer to a prayer, the project was also the answer to Evan's own question of what Christians could do about welfare reform.

Now Evan introduced the keynote speaker, Teri, an African American educator and poet in her mid-forties. Her metaphors of Christian love sounded much gentler than dynamite. Teri proceeded to walk down each row of pews, shaking each volunteer's hand. She wanted to greet us as brothers and sisters in Christ, she said after her quiet tour of greetings. A square sticker on Teri's yellow tunic proclaimed "I'm special." Teri told us her name was short for terrific. She had learned a lot from children, she said. She taught in a Christian after-school program in a mostly African American, low-income neighborhood. "How I relate to children and how they relate to me helps me understand how I relate to the Lord," Teri said. Adults are God's children too. We could see each adult in these families as a unique child of God, a gift, not a burden. "We only have to ask for spiritual eyes to see."

The title of Teri's handout sheet read "Christ-like Care." That is what Teri had modeled for us on her opening round of greetings. Each individual was a gift to behold. To remark on the adopted families' social backgrounds, to note that the families were mostly black, that they lived in poor neighborhoods, would only bring up "cultural barriers." That would be negative. Teri knew about cultural differences, she assured us, and had spoken about them to other audiences, but that was not why she was here tonight. "I'm not going to do a cultural thing. I'm

going to speak from what I know from God." What she knew with quiet certainty was that each individual was special, and deserved to be served as one
would serve God.

Project leaders and volunteers agreed that "Christ-like care" was the best way
to word what the project did. Christ-like care, Teri pointed out, meant being not
just a friend but someone who served the Lord by serving others, someone who
practiced compassion in light of biblical teachings. Christ-like care was not
about proselytizing people, as Evan would explain several different times. It
would model Christian goodness in action, do what Jesus would do.

Bridging, Evangelical Style

Adopt-a-Family's plan for Christ-like care was very ambitious: Like Catherine's
social critics, Adopt-a-Family represented an alternative to the conventional
script of volunteering. Very unlike the social critics, these volunteers were going
to create personal relationships. As Evan liked to put it, church groups were
going to move out of their "comfort zones" and dare to get involved in their families' lives. Evan told the orientation the same thing in the same words that
county social services director Norma used to address her audience of skeptical
URC volunteers earlier in the year: Church people could offer the "relationships," the "human element," that social workers could not give clients entering
the new world of limited welfare benefits. But relationships in Adopt-a-Family
meant something different from relationships in the URC's world of networkers and volunteers. Unlike the URC volunteers, Adopt-a-Family volunteers in
this church sanctuary were excited and a little anxious about their new role.
They felt like they were signing on to something much bigger than a monthly
stint at a homeless shelter—and they were. One woman marveled at the end of
the orientation, "This is what things must have been like in 100 A.D.," when followers of Jesus were fashioning a new way of life.

Christ-like caring depended partly on the helping hand of social service agencies, though Adopt-a-Family volunteers learned to think of their project as very
different from anything government might do. When Bryan, a white county
housing services employee in his thirties, spoke at the orientation, he offered
homey, practical advice, and none of the facts and figures and social service jargon I'd heard at county social workers' Safety Net meetings. He titled his presentation, "Building the Ark." Laying out a time-line for building a protective
ark of relationships with the families, Bryan told volunteers to "listen to needs,
assess needs, initiate creative ways to meet needs." But he assured us he did not
mean assessing needs "in a complicated social work way," but more in the lov-
ing way that Teri would.

Behind the scenes, careful administrative work by Lakeburg's county welfare agency had turned up eight willing families for the project's first run. Twenty-five churches had showed some interest in the project, but by the orientation in July 1997, a total of seven had organized volunteer groups to serve the families.[1] Over the next half year, six[2] mostly white church groups served their mostly African American adopted families. Church group volunteers accompanied family members to appointments with doctors and social workers, put on picnics, took kids to McDonald's, threw a baby shower, bought telephone service for a family, took moms shopping at secondhand stores and grocery stores, and invited families to go Christmas caroling. They prayed for their families, privately and in church group meetings. They took risks that no other volunteers in this study took. Reaching out stretched their comfort zones painfully.

What exactly did Adopt-a-Family accomplish for its families? The church groups did not set out to teach family breadwinners employable skills or help place them in jobs, the way some church-based welfare-to-work programs began to do under new federal welfare policies.[3] Helping the families in small, practical ways, their main form of support was moral. It would be very hard to measure the program's success by tangible outcomes. Evan and the church group members agreed that the program's overriding goal was for volunteers and families to create enduring connections, to become part of each other's lives. That was Christ-like care, and that was the way to make real change happen.

Six months later, Christ-like care had become extremely perplexing for the volunteers. Staying connected with the families at all had been a challenge. Church groups puzzled over why three of the families left Lakeburg suddenly. One group had discovered that the mother of its family was not in the welfare reform program at all; she was certified disabled and did not need to worry that her benefits would end if she did not find work. Bridge-building proved an elusive goal. At a workshop for group leaders, pastor Nick from one of the groups I studied looked back on the past half-year: "How quickly idealism goes away in the face of need. The long-term thing the welfare system was doing—and to think we could come in and—the idealistic side of me [hoped it was possible.] It's one thing to go to the grocery store, but . . . I hoped it was different. I find that I'm very tired. Long-term care is what's needed, and how to deal with it. I'd like to think I could, but I have a way to go." The next month, this pastor's group dropped out of Adopt-a-Family. Several other church groups joined up over the next year. Three years after the initial orientation, the Adopt-a-Family program was no longer being mentioned in fund-raising letters written by Adopt-a-Family's parent organization, Tumbling Walls. By the time American voters were hearing about the virtues of faith-based social service during the 2000 presidential election, Adopt-a-Family's experiences already showed that even Pastor Nick's steadfast faith was not enough to create supportive relationships across social divides.

SPIRALING OFF OF THE MAP

By participating in Adopt-a-Family, the volunteers spiraled briefly into the larger community. Their orientation session introduced them to social service providers who told them all about the world of emergency services. Some of the volunteers visited food pantries with their family members. A woman in one church group talked to social workers at a county housing agency several times, trying to find out whether her adopted family could qualify for subsidized rent. Pastor Nick learned about the Salvation Army while hunting down baby shower presents for his adopted family's mom. Evan kept in regular contact with Lakeburg social service personnel. He liked to describe the project as an opportunity for volunteers to "get to know our neighbors again." Adopt-a-Family church groups could have gotten volunteers into new, ongoing connections with neighbors, social service workers, or other community groups in Lakeburg. The church groups did not build these bridges, at least partly because their own customs did not let them.

Was it all just misguided from the start? There are good reasons the project could have created satisfying relationships *from the church groups' viewpoint,* if not necessarily the families'. At the outset, Adopt-a-Family had both expertise and local knowledge. Four leading participants had social work experience: Before becoming an evangelical Christian, Evan had worked in the state's department of social services. He knew the value of social networks. In the church group I followed most intensively, pastor Nick had been a state-employed social worker, too. Another member, Keith, made his living as codirector of a religiously sponsored social service organization in a nearby town. Jerry, in another church group, was a high-level social service administrator who had spent two years learning about community development. Participants like Jerry and Keith were in regular contact with many other social workers and administrators as part of their jobs, and they had experience with recipients of support too, of course. They had the kind of social capital that could have eased the way for Adopt-a-Family to establish a niche in the social service world. But as researchers Bartkowski and Regis (2003) point out in their own study of faith-based social service groups, it is not enough for a church group to have access to social capital. The group has to "activate" those connections. Adopt-a-Family encouraged volunteers to build connections from scratch, more than mobilizing social connections and know-how.

Adopt-a-Family cannot stand in for all evangelical Protestant volunteer groups, much less for evangelical-led social justice efforts.[4] Still, it represents the style of civic engagement that many evangelicals might honor when they are acting with their religious "hats" on. The social spiral argument does not help us understand this group style or its consequences for relationships beyond the group. The church groups tried to move out into the wider community *without* deepening their connection to the wider community; figuratively, they tried to float above it. On the one hand, volunteers were sensitive to the families' social context, especially their racial backgrounds. They worried that their minority families might not appreciate white volunteers' help. On the other hand, they *worked* at conceiving their families, and themselves, apart from social contexts altogether. Volunteers talked as if racial differences, and differences in privilege, were not truly real and should not matter. Thoughtfully sensitive to *differences* between their families and themselves, the volunteers did not move from sensitivity to active, reflective curiosity about a bigger social world that made "differences" into inequalities, as well as barriers to communication. They worked hard to imagine themselves and their families without social coordinates at all, as compassionate servants and special people in need.

Focusing intently on individuals, the volunteers were trying hard to avoid racism. They meant to take individuals each as infinitely valuable persons. These were not the smug bigots that secular or religious liberals sometimes imagine Christian conservatives to be (see C. Smith 2000). When purely interpersonal relating became frustrating, members did reach for quick racial or "cultural" explanations of their perplexities. Their way of not being racist, ironically, led them to trade on some pat racial characterizations instead of learning more about the people they worked so hard to serve.

Jane Addams had wanted would-be "helpers" of the poor to face perplexing contacts in everyday life with reflexivity rather than certainty. She bid them to change their own sense of who they were, to become citizens all over again *in relation to* the people they formerly saw as the served. Adopt-a-Family volunteers met plenty of perplexity as they tried earnestly to serve former welfare-receiving families. They remained certain of the servant's humble mission; the social relations of their servanthood went unexamined. I am suggesting that the project would have been less frustrating for the church groups had they practiced more reflexivity, though that might have made them change the terms of the project too. A very brief comparison case amplifies my claim.

STUDYING AN EVANGELICAL PROTESTANT GROUP

Adopt-a-Family was exclusively Christian, while the HRA, the Justice Task Force, and Park Cluster were not. Evan administered Adopt-a-Family and several other projects, including a campaign to distribute free videos about Jesus, as the executive director of an umbrella organization, Tumbling Walls. The organization's advisory board included local pastors, a construction company executive, and a black Christian women's group leader. How could I carve out a role in the project? When a mailing in December 1996 informed me that Tumbling Walls was planning a program to serve former welfare recipients, I had just

started following the Urban Religious Coalition. Excited at the chance to compare efforts across theological lines, I sounded out my idea for writing about
Adopt-a-Family with Evan the following spring. Evan welcomed me to observe
the project. He was not sure whether or not non-Christians should do any of
the volunteer work of Adopt-a-Family. The point, after all, was for Christians to
model Christian unity for the "Church in Lakeburg,"[5] which Evan criticized as
too complacent and too focused on its denominational differences. I wondered
if Evan took me as a supporter of welfare reform—eager to see ordinary citizens make the new policies work—or a religious person eager to see other people of faith move into community life or a disaffected Jew opening himself to
conversion under the cover of research. Evan invited me to attend Adopt-a-
Family's meetings and distributed a short description of my project to the
board.

At the orientation, I figured out that I would learn a lot more about Adopt-
a-Family if I could participate alongside one of the church groups. I had taken
a seat near some people listening to a woman's story about driving a car into a
lake, twice, each time by accident. The woman seemed to relive her bemused bewilderment as she told the tale; everyone laughed in disbelief. I was happy to
have found people with a sense of humor. When Evan asked the groups to talk
over their first plans, I realized I had been sitting amidst a church volunteer
group, and made sure Evan would not mind if I introduced myself to the jovial
group with the unlucky lakeside driver. The group's informal leader, associate
pastor Nick of Community in Christ church, invited me to become a part of the
group and "get a real insider's perspective." "We don't feel like guinea pigs," he
assured me—not that I had asked. I felt lucky, and still a little queasy at the
thought of being proselytized, but determined to carry on. I accepted his gracious offer to join the group, and attended the Community in Christ group's
monthly meetings until the group withdrew from the program.

I listened carefully and participated lightly. I enjoyed the group's dry humor;
I enjoyed the group members in a way they would honor—as individuals each
with special talents and dreams. I brooked pastor Nick's subtle and not-so-subtle
forms of Christian testifying to me with curiosity and forbearance. Communicating his faith might be part of a civic relationship in his eyes. The group in
turn was wonderfully hospitable. When I told them at the first meeting that "you
should feel free to ask me to leave if you ever want me to," Angie responded that
"you should feel free to leave if you ever want to." A gently ironic twist on my
sober researcher's etiquette was just what I needed to feel more comfortable.

Was this group different from the other ones at the orientation? Had I been
drawn to it because its members laughed a lot, because they were somehow
more like me than the other groups? Over the next two years I acquainted myself with one of the other church groups from Lakeside Reformed Church.
Community in Christ and Lakeside Reformed were both almost entirely white.
Community in Christ's group was younger on average; its ten regular members

ranged from mid-thirties to seventies, while the majority of members in the Lakeside Reformed group were in their sixties or seventies.

The two groups ended up being good choices: They were the two most active groups in Adopt-a-Family. They also represented very different traditions within the constellation of conservative Protestant theology. Community in Christ's pastor Nick explained that his nondenominational church was "part charismatic, part evangelical." Lakeside Reformed was affiliated with a denomination, the Reformed Church in America, one of the conservative heirs of the centuries-old reformed Protestant tradition. While their worship styles and theological vocabulary differed, their Adopt-a-Family church groups practiced very similar group-building customs. Pastors of both churches identified with evangelicals at URC-convened meetings of church leaders, and used a Jesus-centered language to describe their place in Lakeburg; for these reasons I tag them "evangelical," mindful that the tag works better as a rough social identity than a specific theological one. The Lakeside Reformed group stayed in the program longer than Community in Christ's, but both enjoyed similar satisfactions and endured similar challenges trying to relate to low-income African American families from one of Lakeburg's minority neighborhoods.

Institutional Context: "Can Anyone Get Us Connected to Families on Welfare?"

We've professionalized care. It used to be that my parents would care for people who lived down the street, in the neighborhood, but we let that go. I don't know the exact history of it—there was the New Deal . . . and then government got more involved, and then government said "we're the best."

This is what Evan told me during our first conversation. He said people had to learn to care about their neighbors all over again. Evan insisted at an Adopt-a-Family board meeting, "professionals are not the only ones that can care. Neighbors can care. . . . We've got to be willing to care for people as good neighbors." It sounded as if Evan was saying that ordinary people needed to take more responsibility for society—as citizens, not only as Christians motivated by Jesus' example. Evan sometimes sounded like Donald, who had urged the URC's Humane Response Alliance to "reconnect the caring community" in response to welfare reform. Evan and Donald would have agreed heartily that Christians had a biblical mandate to care for poor people. Christian compassion can take different forms, though, and Adopt-a-Family prized the compassion of deep interpersonal relationships over the compassion of service networks and plug-in volunteering.

Evan worked hard to make connections and find families. He visited community centers, talked with public health nurses, conferred with county social

workers. Dealing with these contacts and connections seemed more of a necessary chore than something worth teaching to Adopt-a-Family volunteers. Evan
complained a lot about the administrative work. "It takes so much work, just for
neighbors to be neighbors!" He repeated three times at the first steering committee meeting in spring 1997 that he wanted to hear from anyone, "even you,
Paul," who could "get us connected to families on welfare." From the start, families on welfare were distant neighbors.

County social service workers offered the initial opportunity for Evan's project to receive families, and they offered resources the project needed in order to
keep going. Evan was always careful to say that the volunteers needed to "honor
the systems already in place" for dealing with welfare recipients. At a steering
board meeting, Evan asked, "What if an emotional, psychiatric crisis comes up?
The church [group] feels responsible now. What should the volunteer do?"
Pauline, the psychologist on the board, answered without hesitation: "You need
a resource." She said the family would have to be referred somewhere.

Human service professionals, especially state-employed ones, would be a
moral last resort. Recall Brian telling volunteers at the orientation that they
could "assess needs" of their families, but "not in a social work way, but more
like Teri." Church group leader Nick emphasized that donating clothes to the
group's adopted family did not constitute "a new kind of welfare," and one
member affirmed several times that "we're not just another government program." Still, Adopt-a-Family depended on social service agencies, even more
than did the HRA. The HRA generated a variety of projects that were supposed
to strengthen civic caring in Lakeburg apart from responding to the consequences of welfare reform. Adopt-a-Family in contrast defined itself very specifically in the terms of welfare policy reform by developing a volunteer program
especially for former welfare recipients. But Adopt-a-Family's relationship to
governmental agencies was hard for the church groups to discuss at any length
within their customary limits. Government agencies were an "other" against
which the project drew its own boundaries. County employee Bryan, described
above, had cued in the volunteers already: He told them at the opening orientation that the policy changes were complicated and that even he did not understand them. They were disorienting. He dramatized the point with a little exercise. He invited volunteers to try writing their names on paper sheets held to
their foreheads: Most people who took the challenge wrote their names backward. Bryan did not invite people to feel a sense of ownership of public policy,
in other words. The message was more that these complicated matters were not
worth trying to master. A protective ark of caring relationships would ride out
the sea change in policy.

To build and populate the ark, someone needed to identify welfare-receiving
families that would be good candidates for Adopt-a-Family; Lakeburg County
Social Services identified candidates for Evan. Someone needed to check potential volunteers' legal records for any signs that a volunteer might be too risky

to welcome as a servant; the state Department of Records offered the service for a low fee. Someone needed to give volunteers at least a little information about family members' circumstances so that volunteers would know why a family was in the program, why a mother needed a ride to a doctor. A public health nurse and a work-preparedness trainer passed that kind of information along to the church groups that I studied. These were necessary connections but not the heart of Christ-like care. Evan kept up these connections, so volunteers could do the real work of caring.

Like the HRA, Adopt-a-Family used state-sponsored opportunities to carve out a niche in the new social contract. County social service people seemed ready, even eager, to let Adopt-a-Family become part of the social service world. Social service people were showing a "remarkable openness" to religious groups, Evan said. Adopt-a-Family defined the opportunities very differently from HRA. How exactly did evangelical Protestantism influence the project's response to the county's new openness?

The Faith Connection

Evangelicals in Civic Life: Beyond Received Wisdom

Evangelical Christians constitute an increasingly large presence in American life.[6] There are compelling reasons to find out how evangelical church groups create civic connections. Yet earlier scholarship may have dissuaded sociologists from investigating closely *how* evangelicals reach out apart from proselytizing. Scholars often have argued that in the last century, mainline Protestant churches like the ones in the HRA were public-oriented or "worldly," while evangelical or fundamentalist churches were more otherworldly, focusing on personal piety inside demanding churches that channeled much of their congregants' volunteer work to the church itself.[7] Recent studies are reconsidering the received wisdom that evangelical Protestants do not get very involved in the community beyond their own churches. Sociologists Regnerus and Smith (1998), for instance, find that evangelicals participate in religiously based community groups *more* than mainline Protestants or Catholics, and are often more active in lobbying and voting than other Christians. Studies by Mark Chaves, Helen Giesel, and William Tsitsos (2002) and Robert Wuthnow (1999c), on the other hand, maintain that evangelicals are less likely than mainline Protestants to volunteer in civic efforts beyond their own churches.

Is there is a distinctive style of volunteering among evangelicals who do reach out? If so, then the growing evangelical presence may be changing the shape of American civic life profoundly. But we cannot find out if we stick only with the received terms of debate about whether or not conservative Protestants are less civically engaged than other Christians. The "actual connections" between faith and civic engagement are not so well understood yet (Wuthnow 1999c, p. 23). Chaves, Giesel, and Tsitsos (2002) have found that mainline and nonmainline Protestant traditions follow different patterns of civic activity even apart from the (significant) influence of theology; they argue convincingly that none of the currently prominent explanations for these differences are completely adequate. The case of Adopt-a-Family suggests that group customs matter apart from theological belief systems if we want to understand how evangelicals both move out into and recede from the wider world.

Adopt-a-Family sounded different from the URC-sponsored groups in this book. Contrast Teri's vocabulary of Christ-like care with URC director Donald's talk of civic ties. No participant in Adopt-a-Family ever equivocated about the object of one's spiritual devotion, as Donald did at the end of a Humane Response Alliance meeting, asking us to keep the Alliance in our own "prayer—or meditation or whatever you call it." Evangelicals would not identify much with the sentiment of "right living over right believing" that motivated the Alliance's "Golden Rule Christianity" (Ammerman 1997b). Certainty as well as centrality of belief defines the core of modern evangelicalism: Salvation comes from accepting Jesus Christ as one's Lord and Savior, and living life in a personal relationship with Christ. This "sense of possessing the Ultimate Truth" (C. Smith 1998, p. 126) obviates any need to finesse religious references for a prospectively interfaith audience: Adopt-a-Family volunteers were always "Christians," not "people of faith," and they belonged to "churches," not "faith communities." Evangelicals, unlike many fundamentalists, court relationships with the surrounding, nonevangelical world. These are opportunities to spread the Gospel.

Yet the groups did not proselytize the families. When members of Adopt-a-Family church groups asked whether or not they should be inviting their families into the Kingdom of the saved, Evan made clear that groups were "there to help," not to elicit new commitments to Christian faith. I never heard church group members testify about their Christian faith to family members—the way pastor Nick did to *me* frequently. Even the most outspokenly evangelistic church volunteer I met agreed with the dictum that intentional proselytizing was beyond the bounds, though she observed that in ordinary conversation, one's Christian faith may simply "come out naturally, as you talk." Adopt-a-Family intended to reach out to people who might not be Christians at all, and might never become so. To get beyond the received wisdom on evangelical Protestants, we need to listen carefully to what they say, where.

Vocabularies of Relationship

Adopt-a-Family's emphasis on personal relationships distinguished the project from nonevangelical Christian efforts. Sociologist Christian Smith has summarized helpfully one of the core characteristics of American evangelicalism: its commitment to what Smith calls the "personal influence strategy" (1998; see also 2000). Evangelical theology insists that one's salvation depends on a *personal relationship* with Jesus Christ. For evangelicals, Christ becomes like a close friend, a confidant, a patient teacher, a cosufferer, to whom one prays and with whom one rejoices on one's daily rounds. The self-transforming, heart-changing relationship with Jesus Christ becomes a model for all relationships. As Smith observes:

> [E]vangelicals see mainline and liberal Protestants as different because evangelicals think they place too much faith in "social activism" and political reform as the way to change society. . . . By contrast, evangelicals see themselves as uniquely possessing a distinctively effective means of social change: working through personal relationships to allow God to transform human hearts from the inside-out, so that all ensuing social change will be thorough and long-lasting. (1998, p. 188)

Seeing each of us through God's eyes, Teri modeled this evangelical ideal of relationship as she carried out her opening round of personal greetings. From the beginning, the church groups talked about their mission as one of creating personal relationships. They would "dare to get into the families' lives." They would "stretch their comfort zones."

Volunteers used other vocabularies for their relationships with the families, too. Sometimes Evan characterized the church groups as "good neighbors" or "friends" of the families, or as "citizens." When church groups could help former welfare-receiving families without needing social service agencies, then it would be "citizens helping other citizens." At the end of my time with the project, when one church group leader asked if it was okay to keep her church group going even if Adopt-a-Family folded, Evan smiled warmly and asked rhetorically why he would keep citizens from helping other citizens. Later I will show how volunteers relied increasingly on a vocabulary of "cultural differences" to make sense of their frustrations.

Though Adopt-a-Family volunteers heard and used a variety of idioms of relationship, their personal style of creating those relationships was remarkably consistent. It sounds like Smith's "personal influence strategy," so why not rest content with that? Why bother peering closer into group life? We have to look and listen more closely to understand *how* that strategy works and what makes it difficult to change.

Zeroing in on Evangelical Culture in Interaction

There is no reason to question that evangelicals privilege the reality of the personal, but there are quite different ways to conceptualize that fact, and the differences matter. We can conceptualize it as a personal influence strategy (C. Smith 1998), a cognitive grid (see Emerson and Smith 2000), or a set of beliefs (C. Smith 2000, p. 37) that groups use to answer the question of "what should we do." The concept of customs gets us further with my questions about Adopt-a-Family than concepts of belief, interpretive grid, or strategy; the choice of culture concepts matters here for good empirical reasons.

First, the volunteers had more than one interpretive framework. Fieldwork taught me that the volunteers knew a lot more about the social world than we imply if we say that their interaction was guided by a personal influence strategy or a belief system. The volunteers kept *struggling* to fit their volunteering into a worldview that makes personal relationships the royal route to all meaningful change. The church volunteers were not ideological dupes blind to social reality; I will show later that they were not self-conscious proponents of a single ideology at all. It is more accurate to say that group customs encouraged members to discount or silence their other ways of viewing the world, rather than to say they had one interpretive strategy. We need a culture concept that is sensitive to the ambivalence, that illuminates how the back-and-forth of discussion in Adopt-a-Family groups hit up against quiet barriers.

Second, notions of a personal influence strategy or belief system do not help us understand why the evangelical emphasis on personal responsibility and personal power *endures*, even when it creates frustrations for people like Adopt-a-Family volunteers. Having explored evangelicals' emphasis on personal relationships with a great deal of insight, Smith arrives at an interesting puzzle: American evangelical leaders failed to develop "a theology and a strategy for social influence that is distinctive, cogent, realistic, and effective. Instead what we often find are one-dimensional social change assumptions and practices which promise only limited effectiveness" (1998, p. 192 n. 3). Smith is criticizing the reductionism—in effect, the lack of a sociological imagination—in a relationship-centered strategy which holds that changing hearts, one by one, will add up to social change. The criticism is fair enough on sociological grounds. It implies, though, that evangelical leaders simply made a strategic mistake. They picked the wrong strategy, the wrong beliefs, and ought to drop them now for others that work better.

I suggest an alternative: Personal influence is not just a framework of beliefs that astute evangelicals might drop for a more effective way of viewing the world. It is also is a style of evangelical *group life*. Built into the customs of groups like those within the Adopt-a-Family project, personal influence constrains what evangelical groups can do together, who they can be together. It is a way of creating settings for interaction. Adopt-a-Family volunteers' combination of insight and awkwardness regarding racial difference suggests to me that the personal influence strategy was a customary means for keeping their own groups afloat. Changing it would threaten the togetherness of groups constructed around evangelical Protestantism. It is worth the time to explore Adopt-a-Family's group customs and see how they shaped the volunteers' way of reaching out.

Building an Ark: The Customs of Servants

A variety of settings constituted Adopt-a-Family.[8] The customs of the church group which had "adopted" me were similar to those of the other church group I studied more briefly. As in my other groups, I listened closely for *group boundaries, group bonds,* and the preferred *speech norms.* I listened for evidence of customs jelling in early Adopt-a-Family meetings, especially in contacts with new or potential participants, at awkward moments of silence, and in enduring group routines.

Boundaries: Trying to Build Relationships off the Social Map

From the orientation onward, Adopt-a-Family volunteers got practice imagining the families outside of a social context. Volunteers talked very little about extended families, neighborhoods, other churches, local institutions, or county agencies as they pondered how best to serve their families. The orientation meeting set the tone: Bryan, the county social worker, invited the volunteers to acknowledge their own confusions, without inviting them to become more familiar with the world of social service. Did we even know whether welfare reforms had gone into effect or not? A show of hands confirmed that some people in the room thought the new laws had taken effect, others thought they had not. "See? We really don't know. It's confusing. It confuses me. . . . This is how confusing the system is to be part of." Affirmed in our confusion, we were told that Adopt-a-Family staff would provide all the "technical information" that volunteers needed so they would not need to get tangled up in the complexity. The message was that something else mattered far more than the institutional backdrop.

Bryan might have made the audience's confession of partial ignorance into a teachable moment. In his capacity as a public employee, he might have explained who the relevant agencies and players were. Bryan was speaking as a Christian servant, not a public one, and he located himself and the project on a map that highlighted individual helpers and needy families. In the Community in Christ church group I studied most intensively, I never heard a more elaborate discussion of social welfare services or charities than the sketchy picture Bryan offered at the orientation.

Early in the Community in Christ group's seven-month stretch, I did hear volunteers ask for more information about new policies. One volunteer, Kara, found out that Bryan did not know how the new policies might affect Quenora, the mother of the group's adopted family. Two months into the program, another volunteer, Angie, asked whether she would get some information on paper about welfare reform, because she wanted to know how Quenora would be affected. The group leader, pastor Nick, did not know when, or if, her benefits would end. It did not get clearer than that.

Members of the Community in Christ group went ahead and tried to relate to their adopted family off of any detailed social map. Kara's early responses to Quenora and the group's response to Kara illustrate this style of relating: After her first sortie, driving Quenora to a doctor's appointment, Kara offered to take her out for a Sno-Cone. Kara figured that meant going to an ice cream shop. But instead, Quenora led the two of them down the block to a cart set up right on the street, ice and all.

> PAT (*lightly ironic*): Entrepreneurial!
> KARA (*visibly reliving her discomfort, said this gave her a real sense of the neighborhood*): This is where she lives! This is what she's about! . . . My immediate reaction was "I want to move her out of there!" That's my long-term prayer.

Kara spoke slowly, as if trying to comprehend something utterly new, disorienting.

> There were bad spirits there. . . . We build on land, but we don't think of it spiritually. I saw oppression. . . . I saw depression all around.
> PASTOR NICK: It sounds like you had some culture shock.
> KARA: It was a culture shock for me.

Kara did not want to learn more about Quenora's neighborhood or neighborhoods like Quenora's where an informal economy exists alongside conventional marketplaces. Having now found out that such a neighborhood existed, Kara wanted to get Quenora out of there. No one had a different response.

Kara was anything but callous. Quenora had a lot of doctor's appointments because she was expecting a baby soon. Kara recounted how during a phone conversation one day, Quenora said she was having abdominal pains. Kara had insisted on driving right over to take Quenora to the doctor's office. Kara interrupted her own story and pondered: "What must it feel like when you're there [having a baby] all by yourself?" Kara wanted to get into Quenora's life, really feel what she must be feeling. Quenora had told Kara she would have had an abortion if she could have afforded one. Kara said nothing about abortion to Quenora. Theresa, another church group member, said she would simply give her phone number to Quenora on a slip of paper and say, "Call this when you're having your baby." Kara and other church group members wanted not to be judgmental, even on the signal issue of abortion. It was just that getting into a family's lives did not have to mean getting into their social milieu.

Early on, Keith of the Community in Christ group suggested doing just that. He asked twice at the group's first meeting in August 1997 whether or not Quenora had a social network. "I don't want to assume that she has nothing," he cautioned. Maybe she had friends that she would like to invite to events with the church group. Quenora, it turned out, had a sister just down the street from her—one who was an "adoptee" herself of another church volunteer group. The group was surprised to discover Quenora's sister, sitting with her own church group, a few tables away, at Adopt-a-Family's first potluck. But neither Keith nor the Community in Christ group ever followed up on the insight about networks. I gathered that was not what the group was about.

Adopt-a-Family did map *itself*, if not its families, into a larger world of groups and agencies. It was a simple map, with church groups on one side and social service agencies on the other. At the orientation session, for instance, Bryan had assured the volunteers they could "assess needs" in a compassionate, Christ-like way, not a "social work way." Pastor Nick of the Community in Christ group made similar comments when the group was deciding to give Quenora clothes for her newborn. "We want to do it as a friendship thing, not 'here's a new kind of welfare.'" In his opening prayer that evening, pastor Nick offered thanks to God for the opportunity to be simple servants. "Thank you—that we do not have to have all the answers." Throughout that meeting, Nick was contrasting the group's humble efforts from the heart with "welfare" and bureaucratic expertise. Anyone should be able to tune in to other people's needs. Other members picked up on the boundaries. Kara affirmed at two other meetings that "we're not just another government program. We're really here to build relationships." Evan, the group leaders, and group members alike agreed that their church groups were different from social service personnel because church groups could create warm, personal relationships with families.

Bonds: "Whatever We Do, We Do in Faith"

Unlike the networkers of HRA, the volunteers in the Adopt-a-Family program were explicit about Christian teachings. Teri's presentation on Christ-like care at the orientation would have made little sense without the assumption that group members shared a commitment to Christ. A volunteer group would not be able to look with God's eyes on former welfare families if not all members shared the same evangelical Christian understanding of God. A good volunteer group member, above all, was one who acted with forbearance and faith in Jesus Christ. When Community in Christ was about to give up on serving its family after seven frustrating months of trying, the group's facilitating pastor consoled the group that at least it had tried to act in faith.

Unlike the Park Cluster group in chapter 6, a good Adopt-a-Family volunteer did not necessarily act *as a member of a congregation*. In Adopt-a-Family, a good, responsible member of the project was one who could practice Christ-like care *as an individual*, driven by individually nurtured faith. A good member, one who would command the most respect, was one who stepped out of his comfort zone to pursue relationships, the way Jesus did when he ministered to poor people and outcasts.

For instance, during our very first conversation, Evan beamed as he told me that one Sherry Peterson was on the board. Why was that good news? Sherry, a street preacher, was someone outspoken about her faith, and someone with enough Christ-like patience and prayerful resolve to have talked a woman off of crack cocaine and gotten the woman started on a new life. Sherry talked openly about how God interceded in her day-to-day plans, once telling her she ought to go to an Adopt-a-Family steering committee meeting instead of staying home. Like Jesus, Sherry could take risks for others. When Evan brought up the risks of working with families from low-income, high-crime neighborhoods at the first steering board meeting in June, he told us that some pastors refused to involve their churches in Adopt-a-Family at all, for fear that volunteers "would just get in with drugs." But taking risks like that was part of the project, Evan said. Pauline, a psychologist and steering committee member, agreed. "Jesus didn't put himself among *those* people!" she mused ironically. Carla, another favorite volunteer, similarly excelled at Christian forbearance in the face of risk. Evan told me he wished he "had ten volunteers" like Carla, who talked at length about how the Lord was working in her adopted mother's life and who refused to get discouraged when the mother unexpectedly left the state.

The volunteers were supposed to relate to each other as Christ-like servants, too, with respect for an individual volunteer's gifts. If the motive for compassion came from within, then the volunteers needed to respect each others' individual limits, which only the volunteers could divine with the help of prayer. Volunteers listened to each other respectfully, trying to draw out each other's contributions. No one, not even Pastor Nick, posed as a general authority on how to serve a church group's adopted family. Theresa's off-the-cuff idea to throw Quenora a baby shower, for instance, became a full-blown plan and produced a most interesting and awkward evening that I will describe below. Angie hoped that her skills as a lawyer might make her useful in the group; the group and Angie decided together that Angie would be the best person to help Quenora navigate the social service bureaucracy.

Each volunteer would contribute something "from the heart." Groups that highlight individual contributions can promote a deeply personalized, enduring commitment to a cause (Lichterman 1996), or they can foster a looser connection of personal convenience that individuals unhitch when they feel like it (Wuthnow 1994; Bellah et al. 1985). Community in Christ's group bonds felt closer to the latter. Volunteers were not compelled to attend meetings regularly. They came when they wanted to, when they felt the call. As Teri told volunteers at the first orientation, the energy for volunteering with Adopt-a-Family had to come from "overflow." It came from whatever compassionate goodness people had left over after caring for their own families. These volunteers did not have to court burnout to be valuable members of the group. The contrast with the familiar workaholic ethic of (underpaid) social service workers was not lost on the woman from Catholic Social Services, who had come to give the church groups a little savvy advice. After telling them that the families should make sure to use up their quota of food pantry and shelter visits before requesting emergency cash, she cracked, "Overflow! Got to get me some of that!"

Speech Norms: Discernment

What did Quenora's family need? What does God want us to do? These questions motivated much of the conversation in the Community in Christ group. Having found my two church groups very similar, I will focus on Community in Christ. Their meetings were not like the HRA's task-oriented business meetings or the Justice Task Force's sounding-off sessions, but more like contemplation aloud. Every month, the group met to ponder what it could possibly do to help the family. The topics changed but the theme was always the same. Maybe Quenora needed clothes for her newborn. Maybe her teenage son Phillipe needed a job: Getting a job would be easier with a driver's license. Karl offered to ask Phillipe if he would like rides to the Department of Motor Vehicles. Amusing and horrifying Kara and Theresa, Karl considered offering to teach Phillipe how to drive. How come Quenora did not ride buses? Maybe, the group reasoned, Quenora had never learned how to read and could not master a bus schedule. Angie said she would ask Quenora whether she knew how to read or would like to learn. And so the conversations went.

Discernment meant imagining an individual's needs in a special way. No one asked if Phillipe was in high school, if his school had a driver's training program, if he knew how to enroll in the program, if he had been barred from doing so for some reason. No one asked if Quenora had health insurance for her baby, if she knew how to apply for the state's health plan for low-income people. Might the nearest community center have job-placement programs for the son or adult education programs for Quenora? If needs were individual, unique, then talking about the social context of individual needs would be a disrespectful distraction, the conversational equivalent of telling jokes in the middle of courtroom testimony.

At the end of the group's second monthly meeting, Pastor Nick inadvertently threatened the speech norms that had jelled pretty well by now. He asked the group to take an educational quiz on welfare and poverty—something like the "rat race" quiz in the Justice Task Force, but without the bitter irony. A state agency had sent Evan the quizzes with other information, and Evan dutifully passed them on. The quiz scenario suggested several interesting things about the group, and I will return to them later. For now, the odd silence during and after the quiz, in this very voluble group, said that we had entered uncustomary territory. Contrast the Justice Task Force, where an educational quiz was *intended* to produce conversation, and had them crying out in righteous anger. Customarily in the Community in Christ group, the point of conversation was to figure out how to serve individual needs, and thereby discern God's will for the group—not to decry the social relations of poverty.

TRYING TO SPIRAL OUTWARD

Quenora's Baby Shower

It was a bold, comfort-zone-stretching idea. Some volunteers might not put themselves out so far. Some might have figured that a mother who had wanted to abort her baby did not qualify for a shower. But this was what real, nonjudgmental Christ-like care was all about. As Theresa put it: "The church should be having birthday parties for prostitutes!"[9] The group's idea for a baby shower stretched way beyond the call of conventional volunteer duty. Community in Christ was going to act on commitments that members had made at the orientation. They were going to create a relationship.

The spartan basement meeting space achieved cordial friendliness if not festiveness the night of the shower. The church building had been converted from an insurance office, and the insurance agents' desks had left little square craters and gulleys in the beige indoor-outdoor carpeting. Huge, blue "male" and "female" signs on the restroom doors lent this small church's common space an incongruously institutional feel. Descending into the uninviting meeting space with lots of anticipation and a homemade salad, I was happy to see friendly faces. There were long tables with white plastic table coverings and small centerpieces with autumn themes, a side table featuring the Jell-o, macaroni, and meat-with-thick-gravy dishes that had become familiar to me from other church potlucks.

Quenora sat quietly at one table, baby asleep in a car seat next to her. The baby, Adonarius Victor, had soon become the focus of awkward attention from people who were used to talking about babies and clearly needed something to talk about. Does he sleep well? How old is he? Where did his name come from? I heard people ask about the name at least five times. Quenora responded in quiet, short answers to them all. Kara and Angie seemed absolutely right when they said Quenora was difficult to talk to. Some members of the group had met Quenora several times now, but the conversation still did not come easily. Nick the pastor had been right, too: From now on, the group would be stepping "outside its comfort zone" all the time.

Opening baby presents did little to loosen up either Quenora or the church group. Quenora did not initiate conversation, and the questions volleyed her way got tossed back quickly.

DAVE: Adonarius—where is that name from?
QUENORA: His father gave him the name.
DAVE: What does it mean? Maybe he had an uncle—?

QUENORA: I don't know—I had another name—
TRACY: So I take it you wanted to call him something else.
QUENORA: No, I didn't know what to call him, hadn't thought about it.
KARA and TRACY: Oh.

Everyone smiled politely, and that was the end of it. The gift umbrella stroller was a conversational goldmine—for the church group. Where is the CD player? Does it have power brakes? Want to go for a drive? To Indigo, one of Quenora's sons: "You want a ride in it?!" It was much easier talking about the stroller than talking to Quenora.

Open-ended relationship-building was hard work. Quenora said little more two months later, during Christmas caroling or during the Adopt-a-Family program potluck, than she had at the shower. And yet the group tried to pursue the relationship in good faith. They thanked the Lord in one of their monthly meeting prayers for having sent the group someone who at least had obvious needs to meet.

"Relationships Take Two"

Six months after beginning the relationship with Quenora, Nick told the group it was time to talk about next steps. They had done different things with Quenora's family in the previous month: Kenneth had met with Quenora's son Pierre a couple of times, but each man had gotten the date of a job-training workshop wrong and missed their planned connection. Kara had toured food pantries with Quenora until they found out that people could not just go to any pantry they chose. Nick went with Quenora to a toy giveaway at the Lakeburg Sports Arena. Quenora had told Nick she wanted to attend Christmas Eve services at Community in Christ; he thought the communication had been clear, unambiguous. It was her own idea. Nick had told us several times already that Quenora should not go to services if she thought she was supposed to in order to stay in Adopt-a-Family. Quenora was not home, though, when Nick came to pick her up. He smiled sheepishly: it was just another of those missed connections.

Nick reported something new about Quenora, too. "It turns out that Quenora is not on welfare. She is on SSI [disability income]. So she's not being told she has to get a job. Her motivation is different." Kara agreed that her motivation would be different: "Why would someone want to get off of SSI?" Nick invited the group to share its experiences over the past six months and discern God's will for the group's relationship with Quenora. It is worth following the conversation closely for what it tells us about the group's challenge in building a bridge to Quenora's family:

Always voluble, Kara started in forthrightly: "The need is not as great as it would be for someone with childcare issues." Quenora was needy, Kara admitted, but catering to Quenora's needs might only make the group into an "enabler."

Kenneth thought that all the group could do now was to give Quenora some options and wait for Quenora to take the initiative to contact the group.

Kara agreed, and some frustration started to show. "When I start a relationship with someone different from me, what I'm really doing is building a friendship—or something deeper. . . . But it's been difficult." She enumerated the frustrations. Quenora was not always home when she said she would be. Quenora lived on the other side of town. Quenora was hard to contact.

> KARA: In our community, we're already doing this [trying to help needy people]. I don't know if I can fit in any more. . . . Do we have to have Adopt-a-Family to do this? What our family is already doing and will keep doing? We finish one and the Lord brings us another [needy person].
>
> My first response when we started this was "get her out of that neighborhood and over to West Lakeburg where people are who can help her."

Kara was already stretched for time, and Quenora took so much energy just to communicate with that it hardly seemed worth it. What's more, Kara found out something dumbfounding from Quenora's public health nurse. "She told me that Quenora will not take a bus!" Surprised indignation spread around our meeting circle, as if we had just been told of a child who refused to eat birthday cake. "And I thought, 'Now—that's—an—interesting—concept!'" Kara reasoned that "part of what Adopt-a-Family *is* is to help people overcome what really are fears—that's what they are."

Nick added, "It is all about relationship-building. Relationships take two." If one side puts out the effort and the other does not, the relationship will not work. Nick mentioned that someone had taken up Theresa's housecleaning idea and phoned the church with an offer to pay Quenora to clean house.

Kara almost scolded: "Clean house? Well, noooo—you have to—Theresa wants—I disagree with her on it, you have to take care of the kids, there are taxes to do at the end of the year."

Angie sounded more sympathetic to the job idea. "Her SSI is going to go down because of welfare reform." Kara tried to be more gracious, but wondered "How will Quenora get there [to a cleaning job] if she doesn't take a bus? Theresa the creative thinker!" She playacted a dialogue on the topic: "'Well, she can take a bus.' 'Ok, and what if her baby starts to crawl?' 'We'll get her a playpen!'" Kara was not convinced.

I said, "I have a naïve question. Maybe I don't understand something about Adopt-a-Family, but if her SSI is being cut, then she is in need in the way that people are who have been on welfare." Nick and Kara said they were not sure whether or not Quenora's rent would go down too when her SSI was cut. They did not know how much her SSI would be cut, and had not asked.

"Like Paul, I thought 'here's a person in need. So let's help her,'" Angie said.

"What does the Lord want to have happen?" Nick asked. "The way we're constituted as a group, it takes as much time to talk about it as to simply—just do it." Nick was not sure that more "contrived events" would help Quenora in the long run either. "There have been some good things about being involved. It's definitely a different neighborhood, and it's stretched us. I've learned some things." Nick did not say what he had learned.

And so the conversation continued. What did Quenora need that the group realistically could provide? Maybe she would like to learn how to read. No one was sure if she knew how; they had not gotten far enough to ask questions like that. Joking that Angie, the lawyer, was good at asking hard questions, the group nominated Angie to ask Quenora if she knew how to read. Months of awkwardness and frustration were taking their toll on the conversation, and the humor darkened. Angie playacted a drill of questions, satirizing both lawyerly inquisitiveness and Quenora's reticence to articulate any needs: "'Do you want more money? You don't? Ok, just asking. How much money do you make? Do you want to learn how to read?'"

Nick quipped that it was best to go to Quenora's apartment with a cell phone because that way you could phone up someone inside to let you in. Otherwise you might never get an answer at the door.

"Yeah, bring a brick. Press your nose up against the window." Angie garbled words as if her nose was smooshed into the glass: "Hello?? Hellowthph?" After six months, it was still hard getting in the door.

Quenora's needs were not so obvious after all. Adopt-a-Family's version of Christ-like care required family members to be good at defining needs in private, individual terms that a volunteer group could meet. As feminist scholars point out (for instance, Fraser 1989), people or institutions that define what counts as a need can exercise a kind of power over the people with needs. Little of Quenora's life depended on the church group, so it makes little sense to say the group held a great deal of power over Quenora or her family. Still, Adopt-a-Family's framework positioned the families as subordinates in the relationship—though families had the power to end the relationship, and several did, by leaving town. Volunteers tried to act like servants, not superiors, and clearly were not feeling very powerful in the relationship. Because Quenora's family turned out not to be very good at being helped, the subtle, potential power in the church group's position became more obvious.

Had Quenora been receiving welfare support, the group would have had the logic of welfare reform on its side. Even individuals not good at being helped might feel compelled to accept help as the state-sponsored social safety net was being yanked away. Once pastor Nick learned that Quenora's support from the government was not going to end if she did not find a job, he figured her "motivation was different." The group would not be able to lean on the "push" of welfare reform if its own "pull" proved less than compelling.

It would be very wrong to conclude that Adopt-a-Family groups were nothing but a gloved hand of state domination, easing people into a harsher welfare regime. Families did not need to keep dates with their church groups, accept their support, or even stay in contact with them. But the church groups did have the privilege of designing the protective "ark" for their families. Families could enter or exit at will but could not collaborate with volunteers in redesigning Adopt-a-Family. Having defined themselves as selfless, caring servants, volunteers did not ponder other ways to build relationships besides starting from scratch with sociable events. What might cement relations between strangers from such different social locations? The two church groups I studied rarely gave themselves the space to mull over the challenge.

SHUTTING DOWN SOCIAL REFLEXIVITY

Keeping the Servant's Map in Place

People with experience in social work, like pastor Nick and Evan himself, kept their social worker's map of the world at bay when they participated in Adopt-a-Family. Their know-how might have helped volunteers reflect on their relationship with their families, but that would challenge the customary group boundaries, as in this example: Jerry, a member of the group sponsored by a large, evangelical church in the suburbs, had helped draft some of the provisions of the state's welfare policy reforms. Just like Keith of the Community in Christ group, Jerry challenged Adopt-a-Family's pristinely interpersonal focus by suggesting that families might have social connections worth knowing about. Jerry's comments, like Keith's, got dropped from consideration at a meeting of volunteer group leaders.

Jerry felt ambivalent about Adopt-a-Family's version of relationship-building. He told us sheepishly that his church group had been very slow to contact its adopted family. Another group leader asked if it was difficult for this (white) group to make personal contact with African Americans. Jerry said that that might have played a part in the group's hesitation, but he seemed unsatisfied with this explanation. He added, in a much softer voice, that he had "spent two years learning about community development."

"Coming in as a suburban west side church . . . I have gotten so sensitive to coming in and overpowering her [the mother's] sense of neighborhood." Jerry felt as if he needed to adjust, in other words, to a style of relationship-building that paid little attention to the adopted families' own social map. Kara had felt "culture shock" when she first encountered Quenora's neighborhood; Jerry felt culture shock upon encountering Adopt-a-Family's way of mapping Lakeburg's local world. The program's map needed to stay in place. Evan nodded sympathetically and smiled a tight smile, but seemed little concerned that the church groups were missing something about the families' social worlds. He said nothing about whether or not the families' "sense of neighborhood" mattered to his program. No one else took up Jerry's bid to reflect on who they were in relation to the families and who the families were in relation to them. Neither Jerry's group nor the other church groups represented at the meeting challenged the program's image of relationship-building between isolated families and individual agents of Christ-like care. Teri had said at the initial orientation that she was not "going to do a cultural thing." The proscription held. Members tried hard to create relations from scratch, without drawing on the expertise that project volunteers might have summoned while wearing other "hats."

Trying to Make Race Disappear, and Failing

I kept hearing volunteers mention social differences they ascribed to race. Sometimes they called them "cultural." Their customs gave them little opportunity to *talk through* the perplexing group differences they kept noticing between themselves and their adopted families. Building a personal, compassionate relationship meant focusing on the family and its needs, without imagining the church group in that relationship. This was selfless service. Good servants focused on the served, not themselves.

The group from Lakeburg Reformed Church enjoyed a picnic with its adopted family. One of its leaders, Jane, described the picnic at a project leaders' meeting. At first it seemed as if she tried to follow the dictum Teri had laid out at the orientation: Social differences were to be respected silently, not dwelled upon and discussed. Jane did not tell the rest of us where the group's adopted family lived, what the mother, Lakisha, did for a living, or where the children went to school. After telling us quickly that Lakisha's first need was for a driver's license, Jane launched into a description of the picnic, an event that she took as a test of interracial cooperation: "It was a great experience. Nine white people , and she's a very dark black. And you say you don't notice color— you sure do! . . . It was very relaxed. We all helped set up the table."

Jane told us that the kids, the church group members' and the family's, all wanted to swim together. Kids and food always helped break the ice, she said. And then she observed some more about color, how striking it was to see a lily-white kid and a very dark black kid in the sandbox playing. "Lighter skin is a status issue in the black community," Jane noted in an authoritative voice, and then commented, "I don't know why I brought that up." No one else seemed to know either. No one took her up on the topic. Jane was brimming with observations about contacts across racial lines, but found little place for them within the conversational confines of servanthood.

Evan originally thought Adopt-a-Family would help Christians cross social barriers rather than transcend them altogether, to get to know our neighbors again. He too, though, expressed a lot of ambivalence about differences. Neighbors should be able to be neighbors, without a lot of complicated thinking about their social backgrounds. Sherry, the white street preacher who was such good news for Adopt-a-Family, remarked to Evan and me shortly after the orientation that she wanted to learn more about "racial differences [that] got glossed over." Little gestures like putting one's hand on another's back, she observed, may make an African American "feel like it's a master-slave relation." Sherry sounded like she wanted to learn how to create relationships across differences in social power, not only personal style. Her master-slave metaphor implied that race was an inescapable relationship, one that defined both parties—not that there were two parties that happened to have different race-based styles. Evan appreciated Sherry's point because without knowing how to treat each other properly, making friends with the families would be harder. But he felt impatient with it all:

"Race is [*pausing, grasping for words*]—the dominant—way of talking, and it's not just race. It's not just racial. It's how to be with each other. If I put my hand, [*gesturing patting someone's head*] an innocent gesture, it gets so complicated!" Evan's off-the-cuff plaint says something important about the status of social differences in Adopt-a-Family. They were a bother, not an open invitation to understand a wider world. Why couldn't neighbors just be neighbors?

The volunteers did not end up getting more information on how to build relationships across differences in power and culture, though I heard several ask for it. Repeatedly, I heard volunteers worrying about violating cultural boundaries, or puzzling over differences between themselves and the families, or simply observing, like Jane, that the families were different from them. It seemed impossible for the groups to live out Teri's color-blind, Christ-like care.

At one meeting, for instance, Nick told how he and Kenneth had trooped over to Quenora's apartment, but got no answer at the door. A man who turned out to be her brother said that she was not home. Then they tried phoning, but the telephone had been disconnected. He imagined what Quenora's neighbors must have been thinking as he and Nick waited outside the apartment. "What were those white guys doing there??" He repeated it several times that evening. Later on, he said that Quenora's baby shower would come off better at the church than at someone's own home; the church would be more comfortable for Quenora's boys than a private space. Kenneth said, "The guys would be more at ease, instead of going off with old white guys." Nick repeated "white guys."

The Community in Christ group defies the assumption, popular among some liberal religious and secular people, that evangelicals must be prejudiced, self-satisfied whites because their faith is conservative. Keenly they felt the frustrations as they tried to build compassionate relationships from scratch. They hit on a way to make sense of it all. Quenora was an exotic other.

IMAGINING CONNECTIONS: "CULTURAL DIFFERENCES"

Adopt-a-Family put volunteers in close orbit around other people's social worlds without helping volunteers make those worlds less perplexing. In theory, the program's experiences could have helped church group members learn to relate to people different from themselves. That is the social spiral argument. The program guidebook for volunteers that Evan wrote explained that Adopt-a-Family would give the church groups the opportunity to "Learn about cultural differences i.e. what may be normal for an African- American, Hispanic, or Asian Family, that would not seem normal to a Euro-American and vice versa." It is hard to learn about differences if people cannot talk about them. Volunteers were learning not to entertain that kind of discussion. In the first two or three months, the Community in Christ group tried hard to discern its family in color-blind terms. But the frustrations with Quenora kept mounting.

Leaders of both church groups I studied developed a shorthand for dealing with perplexing differences that Christ-like care was not bridging. They were "cultural differences." Appealing to cultural differences was like appealing to "interest" in the Justice Task Force. It was a device for satisfying curiosity. It *ended* the conversation.

Pastor Nick introduced the cultural difference trope first. When Kara described her first, harrowing trip to Quenora's neighborhood, pastor Nick had suggested that Kara was experiencing culture shock. Kara agreed, though the cultural difference theme was not yet a regular way of characterizing the relationship. The group was trying hard to discern Quenora as an individual, seeing her through God's eyes as Teri had taught. No one had said anything more about what Kara might learn from the shocking experience, what she might learn about lives like Quenora's. In the next four months, Nick more and more frequently described their difficulties with Quenora as cross-cultural challenges.

Families like Quenora's were from a "different culture." Other cultures were like separate worlds, though Nick implied that "other" cultures could be similar to one another. Nick had spent seven years as a missionary in Guatemala. The experience became a major reference point for understanding social differences in general, and other group members were happy to lean on his wisdom. The baby shower struck Nick as a good idea for Quenora, for instance, because "I know from Latin America, other cultures, they like to have events, they know how to party." In fact, "maybe we can do something [at the shower] that crosses both our cultures," he offered. "It's not easy to do when we're so different."

Kenneth suggested that they should just try doing some different things. Nick replied that banging on a piñata, in Latin America, "is an excuse for just being together. In our culture, we don't have anything like that."

As long as Quenora was from "another culture," the group would have an easier time interpreting the frustrations, even if her culture was not Guatemalan. If Quenora seemed uncommunicative, it was because she was from another culture:

THERESA: She's shy.
KARA: The interesting thing is, I can communicate with her.
ANGIE (*sounding dubious*): Did you understand her?
NICK: I had trouble too, but being in another culture, I could deal with it.

Six months into the program, building a relationship with Quenora proved to be even more difficult than the group had expected. It was because she was from another culture. Building relationships took two, and sometimes each side put in different kinds of effort.

NICK: That's where cultural differences really come in.
KENNETH: I could try asking Pierre what his needs are, but that would be me asking questions and he giving short answers.
NICK: That's different cultures again.

It was hard enough talking about needs to people "in the same culture," but "talking across cultures" would be much more difficult.

If the group ever sounded mean-spirited about Quenora, it might be because building relationships in a social vacuum must be enough to try anyone's compassion level. For all its sincere effort, the Community in Christ group was teaching members to see beyond the world of differences and inequality, rather than to embrace it. If Guatemalans and African Americans were interchangeable "others" on the group's social map, then participation in the group was not helping members build bridges to anyone in particular.

Over a year later, Jane's Lakeside Reformed group was having the same experience as members tried building a relationship across social divides. The Lakeside Reformed group sounded more overtly judgmental about the differences, though, than the Community in Christ group. Jane tried putting her group's relations with Lakisha's family into racial—often meaning "cultural"—terms. Others let Jane's pronouncements stand.

A summer picnic produced a veritable culture clash. Only one of Lakisha's kids was home when Jane came by to pick them up and drive them to the park. Lakisha and her other kids had gone to see their grandmother at Lakeburg hospital, the daughter at home had said. Jane told the rest of us around the picnic table that she thought she was getting a story. The daughter had cautioned, "You better not go there because they won't let in people who aren't family." Jane told us she had never heard of not letting people in who aren't family, and figured the daughter did not want her to find out that the family was not really there. So Jane called from the gas station and found there was no one of Lakisha's family name on the hospital roster. Jane sounded annoyed as she retold the tale: "It's a cultural difference. . . . Black people do not have the sense of time." One has to learn to be on time, Jane observed, for school or a job. But black churches, she observed, work the same way: "You go to a service that is supposed to start at nine, and maybe it starts at ten. And then it lasts all day."

"Oh, they do that in church *too?*" Joan remarked. It was all a matter of cultural differences, she summarized. And those differences come up "when the church community gets involved with the non-church community, and then when you add different races—" No one elaborated on the unfinished sentence.

Like the Community in Christ group, Jane's group let the notion of cultural differences do a lot of work. But Jane's group sounded more sure that some cultural habits were better than others. Jane did not say black people have a different sense of time—itself a huge generalization. Her wording implied instead that blacks *lack* a sense of time, that they lack what normal people need in order to go to school and hold down jobs. The long church service sounded like a big inconvenience, not an interesting immersion in different worship habits. You "add" different races in; normal life starts without them. Deep compassion had not made the church group feel much more like a co-dweller with African Americans in the same society.

A year later, Jane's group was still in contact occasionally with Lakisha's family. The group had taken Lakisha's kids to a Christian-themed puppet show at Lakeside Reformed Church one summer morning, and had them over for a barbecue lunch afterward at two members' home. Relating was still difficult. Chatting alone with Jane, I asked if it would be a good idea for Lakisha to be the host next time. Jane thought Lakisha's apartment was too small and dark, but then told me "If Lakisha came over to my house she would see that our social backgrounds are different. I wouldn't want that to become a factor in the relationship."

It struck me afterward that this was the first time I had heard an Adopt-a-Family volunteer refer so clearly to differences as being intrinsic to the character of the relationship *between* volunteer and family. Jane was implying she had things Lakisha lacked. If Jane opened her own life more to Lakisha, the relationship would be threatened, not deepened: "I think economic differences are the biggest ones. I wouldn't want Lakisha coming over to my house and seeing— we're really different." Adopt-a-Family volunteers were in a difficult position. The program was predicated on a server-served relationship, in which the two sides ultimately may be moral equals but were clearly not social equals. So to keep the relationships from being threatened, volunteers would try to "know another person's world" as the program guide had put it, while avoiding encounters that confirmed the difference in privilege.

Confronting social inequality directly would violate taboos that many Americans, not just evangelical Christian service groups, honor. In a society that fancies itself one of equal opportunity, it is not polite to subject people to situations that only confirm their social inferiority. It is a noble American sentiment: People should be able to relate to other people as equals, shorn of their social markers.[10] The difference between evangelicals and other Americans here is that most other Americans have less of a *religious* impetus for trying to develop deeply interpersonal relationships across racial and class lines from scratch. As social servants, Adopt-a-Family volunteers tried to overcome the awkwardness with even stronger, more faithful, Christ-like compassion that would move them outside their comfort zones without moving the served closer to them.

CUSTOMS OR IDEOLOGICAL CRUSADE?

What if Adopt-a-Family volunteers were just trying to coax welfare recipients into a Protestant work ethic? There would be less reason to focus on group-building customs if we could just as easily explain the project as the outgrowth of a Christian-inspired, individualist ideology that made volunteers think compassion and will power could overcome poverty. Common sense among some political progressives, and some scholarly analysis (Diamond 1989) has it that conservative Christians promote politically conservative agendas under the guise of religious commitment. Maybe Adopt-a-Family was a just failed crusade to enlist church people as agents of tough love.

Calling Adopt-a-Family "ideological" implies that it was driven by ideas that complement or promote powerful interests. The ideas might be that people on welfare are lazy and undeserving or that anyone who works hard can succeed in America. The powerful interests would be those behind the legislators' moves to end welfare and shrink the federal government, the big corporate interests that Catherine's social Justice Task Force spent so much time criticizing. In more sophisticated treatments of ideology, people's ideas may be conflicted; people may hold contradictory ideas about welfare reform, the roots of poverty, the need to care. But ideologies, simple or complex, explicit or implicit, end up supporting dominant interests. The reasonable assumption behind studies of ideology is that some ways of seeing the social world are far more congenial to economic and political elites than are others, and the congenial viewpoints circulate more widely and are easier to put into simple language than more threatening viewpoints.[11]

If church members joined the project mainly to promote conservative welfare policies that burden poor and unemployed people, then focusing on customs only obscures a more basic conflict of interests between the church groups and the families. But the Community in Christ group's fascinating response to an educational quiz at one of their earliest meetings showed that they hardly were invested in welfare reform. They did not sound strongly committed to ei-

ther conservative or liberal beliefs about poverty and welfare. Since Adopt-a-
Family defined its outreach completely in terms of welfare reform, it is fair to
say the church groups did not question commonsense ideologies of individual
opportunity in the United States. That by itself does not explain how the church
groups constituted themselves as groups, or why the groups elicited a lot of discussion on some topics but so little on others.

Evan had received some "poverty quizzes" from a research center and passed
them on to Nick. The educational quiz was intended to correct common misperceptions of people in poverty—that they lack ambition or have many children. We took the quiz, and went through each question as a group; some of us
called out our own answers and checked them against the answers printed on
the back of the sheet. On many of the ten questions, at least one member greeted
the correct answer with surprise, and willingness to correct misperceptions:
One found she had "overestimated the compassion of the government" for assuming that welfare payments could support more than two people; two were
surprised that the average number of children in a welfare-receiving family was
only 1.9; several lightly surprised, polite "uhs" greeted the information that
earnings, not welfare payments, food stamps or help from relatives, constituted
the biggest source of income for families with poor children.

It was a remarkably quiet exercise. No one argued with any of the correct answers. No one sounded invested in the commonsense notions that welfare families have lots of children because welfare supports them or that poor people are
lazy and depend on handouts. Only one of the ten answers elicited dialogue at
all; members had greeted a few of the other answers with quick, single-sentence
commentaries on their own misperceptions. To the one conversation starter
about the causes of poverty (correct answer: "unemployment/underemploye-
ment"), Sonya said she had heard someone on the radio say that there would be
no poverty if everyone simply followed two principles: "don't quit a job until
you have another one," and "don't spend more money than you have coming
in." Sonya found the principles puzzling. "That's it? I thought it would be something deeper." Nick said he had heard that sometimes a person who is working
gets told that he can make more money on welfare. So the person quits. Nick
did not say whether or not he thought the story represented many people, or
was a comment on working people or government policy, or whether he
thought the story was a pernicious myth or a cautionary tale. Kenneth chimed
in, that he could imagine someone like that "who is not going to take a job . . .
and to some extent understandably so." A person like that "is going to stay home,
especially if you have kids to put in daycare. . . . It is going to take someone who
is committed to it [a job]."

Kenneth's comment could be read as a judgmental stance on people who do
not hold jobs. Still, it does not sound like an ideological commitment to welfare
reform. This was the longest exchange about poverty, welfare policy, and employment that I heard during my entire seven months with the group. The ex-

change was striking mostly for its ambivalence, the lack of clarity on where—if anywhere—people stood on welfare and poverty issues, the seeming lack of a *need* to form political opinions. Of course, political conversation would have stretched if not violated the customary speech genre. It would be mere talk, philosophizing, not caring and discerning. In one of very few explicitly political judgments I had ever heard in the group, the speaker criticized the local school district for denying a boy his need for special attention: The boy suffered the school district's gross failure of *discernment,* in other words.[12]

Interviews with group members confirmed what I had already gleaned from group meetings: Volunteers were not motivated by strong opinions about welfare reform. No one said that supporting the new welfare policies or shrinking the government were reasons for being in Community in Christ's group. Of all the people in Adopt-a-Family, only Evan made welfare reform sound like an unambiguously positive thing. Only Evan voiced some ideological investment in the new policies. As he said at a potluck for the church groups and families, "We've wanted welfare reform, now we have it. So what can churches do?" He never defined the "we," and speaking for some undefined constituency, he remarked several other times during my time with the project, "We don't want to go back to the old system." No one else ever commented so forthrightly, or positively, about the new welfare policies. No one, including Evan, ever said "get those lazy people working." No one said "the taxpayers have supported them long enough."

It would be hard to explain all the project's frustrations simply as the inevitable friction of conflicting group interests mystified by ideology. Given the option by county social service workers, the adopted families had all chosen to participate in Adopt-a-Family. None joined against their wishes. By participating in Adopt-a-Family, church group members perpetuated some common-sense notions about paid work: Supporting former welfare recipients' transition to employment presupposed that the transition was worth supporting, that worthwhile jobs awaited family breadwinners, that the main task was to ease the transition, not to question the terms of welfare or employment. These notions are "ideological" because they are easy to challenge and they complement powerful political interests. By themselves, though, they would not tell church group members how to organize groups and build relationships with the families.

Empowering Civil Society?

Experts Are Hard to Validate and Indispensable Too

Sometimes the volunteers thought they needed a professional's assistance after all, even when the customs made professionals or state agencies hard to validate. Outside help seemed appealing, for instance, when volunteers in both church groups I studied needed to talk to the families about making money and learning practical skills. It was awfully awkward otherwise. Community in Christ had been surprised to find out that Quenora was not being supported by welfare payments. They did not know whether or not she could read. Asking would take some gumption, and they had to "nominate" Angie to pop the question. Jane of Lakeside Reformed expressed the same ordinary sense of civility. She told me, unprompted, during a phone chat, "I've never felt comfortable asking people things—you feel like you are prying." She said it was difficult knowing whether the family was really in the state's new time-limited welfare program or not. Fortunately, she observed, Adopt-a-Family had hired Teri, who was not only a deeply religious woman but a professional educator, who "can deal with the families in a different way" and find out more about them.

Jane should have been in an especially good position to find out things about Lakisha. Lakisha happened to attend a work-preparedness class in the same office building where Jane worked. Jane would see Lakisha now and then and had at least brief opportunities to catch up with her. She reported to me on the phone, "Lakisha is working now, and that's kind of good." But she wasn't sure whether it was work that delivered a paycheck, or "training" that did not. "Gee, I should know better than this. I ought to ask Teri about it." It was easier talking to Teri about it than raising the topic with Lakisha herself even though she was close by.

Much as it aimed for compassionate care, neighbor to neighbor, the Adopt-a-Family program ended up getting the church groups into situations that would be easier for a state agency or some other third party to handle. Neither Christian compassion nor neighborly concern were giving church group members the sense of social legitimacy that social service workers usually have when they ask personal questions. That put the volunteers in a terrible cultural bind, since social workers represented the coolly bureaucratic alternative to warm, Christ-like care.

Rediscovering Conventional Volunteering

Called to evaluate Adopt-a-Family after six months, volunteers from different church groups now had an explicit opportunity to reflect on their families, their families' social conditions, their relationships with the families. What they talked about mainly were the frustrating logistics and uncertain prospects of the relationships. They did not investigate the server-served relationship itself. It turned out other groups shared Community in Christ's and Lakeside Reformed's experiences. The volunteers converged on the idea that the church groups' relations with families needed more guideposts, more driving goals, and an outside institution to provide them. They needed to latch themselves more tightly to state-sponsored social services. The volunteers converged on this new understanding as they responded to Evan's question about whether the church groups should be required to make long-term commitments to their families:

"I walk with women who have major problems . . . ever since I became a Christian," Kara said. But working with Quenora had been frustrating. "I first went into this as a relationship person—and it's been the hardest for me! She's far away. I'm in West Lakeburg, she's on Cannery Lane, it's fifteen minutes away." Her tension was rising. "She has three kids and her—it was the most amazing concept, them in my car! . . . Maybe we have to get realistic about what we can do—take on specific tasks."

"Without a clear sense of boundaries there's too many needs," Nick added. "We had ten people for our group without a clear understanding of what we're supposed to do. . . . Maybe a year's commitment [and no more] is OK!"

Kara was still fascinated with the logistical difficulties: "My kids go to Hilltop AWANAs [evangelical Christian youth groups]. I'd have to go twenty minutes, leave at five-thirty." It was a daunting scheduling problem to fit Quenora's family into her rounds. "I need to balance my desire to build a relationship with my time."

Evan introduced the possibility of an "action plan," a specific plan that the group and family would share. The plan would be saying "we can work this way to move you further or care for you," and it would be "deliberate" in "moving" the head of the family toward employment. "The group knows why it's there and how it fits . . . and the people in the [social service] system know." Nick, putting Evan's thoughts together, deduced that "the action plan *is* the group's plan. The group knows it's OK to talk about it—so the action plan needs to be both for the group and the person—sit down and talk, maybe with a social worker." The action plan would codify, from the state's point of view, who the church groups and families were in relation to each other and in relation to the social service system.

No longer relying on prayerful discernment alone, the groups would talk like administrators, not only like servants. They would be empowered as adjuncts to government-sponsored social services, rather than as autonomous civic actors. The action plan would give Adopt-a-Family groups a new legitimacy. They would be able to talk through relationships that they did not feel right to talk about before. They would get that legitimacy through a close alliance with the county, not on their own reputation as caring servants or community advocates.

Evan now introduced the metaphor of "handing off." Social workers would hand off a person or family to some other group outside the social service system. "The case worker has to get involved with us—with the family's permission—and explain to Adopt-a-Family" what the family's circumstances are. A case worker has sixty days, Evan continued, and then leaves the picture. "We can be a continuation of a real relationship . . . with everyone clearheaded about where we can go." Closing the meeting, Evan told us that he had applied to the county for money to fund a half-time person to administer Adopt-a-Family.

Suddenly the group was recasting social servanthood as a "continuation" of a county social service program, not open-ended caring that comes from a warm place beyond the state and touches hearts. The group was jettisoning its own boundaries, bonds, and speech norms: Social service agencies would no longer be distant, morally unsavory entities on the social map. The church groups would spend more time monitoring plans and evaluating, rather than discerning needs with God's eyes. It might even matter less for good members to do what they do "in faith"; a good member might be one who could help make the action plan work. Adopt-a-Family would borrow much more from the conventional script of volunteering and social work. It would all feel a lot less like A.D. 100.

Intensely interpersonal relating frustrated Adopt-a-Family volunteers, even as they upheld its value, and the pain prompted the volunteers to start recasting the program at this meeting. But as Kara pointed out earlier, the volunteers could practice compassion individually, as good Christians, without Adopt-a-Family at all. Evan and the volunteers were barreling toward a new vision of the project that would be much less "Christ-like" in their understanding. No wonder the Community in Christ group folded a couple of months later. It may be no surprise either that Adopt-a-Family, too, closed up after three years of working against the conventional grain of volunteering, even though county workers had supported it, even made it possible. The project's own customs did not allow it to receive that support in a meaningful way.

Adopt-a-Family's protective ark had never really left the safe harbor of the social welfare system. Group members had learned to see their work as completely separate from the state. Transcending bureaucratic care had not done anything to lessen the social service bureaucracy's importance to Adopt-a-Family, even while church groups tried hard to do something different from "a new kind of welfare." In this case at least, Christ-like care did not threaten the state's freedom from religion, as some critics of faith-based social service would fear. Instead, the customs of Christ-like care made it hard for caring servants to discover why their form of care was less independent than they imagined, and much more frustrating than they would have guessed.

Servanthood Meets Social Reflexivity: A Brief Comparison

John Dewey and Jane Addams thought that community life in a genuine, modern democracy required social reflexivity. Park Cluster's experiences, in the next chapter, add a great deal to a positive, sociological case for social reflexivity. Scenes from the Humane Response Alliance and the Justice Task Force offered negative cases. Portraying their frustrations with different kinds of bridge-building, I suggested that a lack of reflexivity might have hindered them. Constrained by their own customs, HRA and Task Force members kept reaching out in self-defeating ways.

Adopt-a-Family's experiences offer a different kind of negative case. Church group members expressed frustrations colorfully, directly, even bitterly. At the start of the venture, Keith and Jerry in their own ways had invited volunteers to consider their families' social circumstances; they had invited social reflexivity. We cannot know whether or not Adopt-a-Family's experiences would have been more positive had members taken up the two men's ways of thinking about the families, but the men's approaches made good sense in light of research on low-income families and community development.[13]

Very briefly I observed another bridging project which brought evangelical churchgoers and a few Park Cluster members into contact with residents of the low-income, mostly minority Park neighborhood for free dinners twice a month. The two organizers of the free meals project felt some of the same frustrations that dogged Adopt-a-Family groups. The project kept running for awhile *after* its two leaders sat down to reflect with Park residents on the project's relationship to the neighborhood. Run by two women from outside Park neighborhood, the free meals project meets my definition of a "bridge" in chapter 2 since the women clearly saw themselves as reaching way beyond their routine circles, though the twice-monthly free meals constituted an extremely modest sharing of resources at best. During my brief research stint, the women said they might hand the project over to Park women—itself a telling conclusion.

While observing and participating alongside Park Cluster, I kept hearing about "two moms" who cooked a free meal every other Tuesday and served it to several dozen people at the Park neighborhood center. When a neighborhood center staffer first described the two moms' meals to Cluster members, it was as if the meals appeared out of nowhere. Who cooked them? Were they part of some larger project? To what church did the moms belong? I wanted to know why they were such a puzzle. One Tuesday, I helped serve, sat, and ate with diners, and interviewed the two moms afterward. They were members of an evangelical Catholic[14] church some miles from the neighborhood. Their style, I learned, was like Adopt-a-Family volunteers' in a lot of ways. It invested great religious meaning in self-sacrificing, compassionate acts.

The moms told me they felt called, as Christians, to serve people in the Park neighborhood in some way. They resolved that since they knew how to cook, they could serve dinners. As one of the moms, Theresa, put it: "I had been praying a lot. . . . It's a big part of our Christian faith that we're supposed to love our brothers and sisters and serve one another. . . . *here* is where I needed to serve. I was overwhelmed with excitement." Theresa had known that Park was a low-income neighborhood; she did not know much else about it. She opened the phone book and made calls to find out how she might serve this neighborhood that she had not spent time in before. She asked if the owner of an abandoned restaurant near the neighborhood wanted to donate the building so that she could serve meals there. A city official told her there was a neighborhood center in Park. It had not occurred to her to ask. The official directed her to the center's director. Theresa told Charmaine, the director, her idea for serving meals and Charmaine asked if she and her meal-making partner Karla would like to serve them at the center.

Theresa and Karla's free meals project, like Adopt-a-Family, started with prayerful discernment. The two women were planting their own kind of "love dynamite." The women did not mention their church, though they were active in it and Theresa's husband led a Bible study group there. In their own understanding, the moms were not coming from a group or an institution so much as from their own prayerful hearts. Like Adopt-a-Family volunteers, the two women cared and discerned and acted from the heart.

They discovered, though, that they had to develop a more self-conscious relationship to the Park neighborhood if they were going to continue serving individuals at all. After some months of serving biweekly hot meals, the two moms "got told ever so politely that while people appreciated our presence, the food was too bland," recounted Karla. Meanwhile, members reported at a Park Cluster meeting that Park residents had criticized this meals project as yet another case of well-meaning white people disempowering African Americans in the guise of serving them. For their own part, Karla and Theresa said that they continued to feel like outsiders for months after they had started serving their meals. They said they did not feel trusted.

The moms said both they and neighborhood residents felt much more comfortable about the meal effort after they *talked about their relation to the neighborhood* at an open community forum. For the first time, they explained to residents who they were, what they were doing, why they were there. Theresa recounted that one Park woman had told her, "You need us too, don't you?" Theresa was touched. The woman was right. She had not thought about it quite that way before. Until they had this discussion, the two moms had no social standing in the neighborhood. They were quizzical if well-intended strangers from outside. Their heartfelt individual motives by themselves could not identify them meaningfully to Park residents who saw them as powerful outsiders rather than sincere servants.

Why did the two moms dare this discussion, while Adopt-a-Family volunteers mostly did not? The main difference between the two projects, other than the obvious, big difference in scale, was that the two women did not define their meals project in relation to governmental policy, the way Adopt-a-Family groups did. Their social map was different from Adopt-a-Family's. They did not need to fear looking like "a new kind of welfare" or an un-Christ-like adjunct to a bureaucracy. They understood themselves in terms of Christian motives, but did not counterpose Christian servanthood to governmental bureaucracy. Some honest, risky, back-and-forth conversation helped make the two women more welcome to the neighborhood, and made them *feel* more welcome.

Once the women stopped defining the relationship exclusively in their own, albeit well-meaning, terms, the relationship was on its way to vanishing: Theresa and Karla told me that, having talked with some Park women about the project, they realized the Park women could plan the meals themselves and season them to local tastes. Neighbors could help serve them, and even take over the whole project. Advocates of community empowerment might only cheer this denouement. Charity imposed from outside may count as a kind of bridge relationship if the charity is accepted and endures over time, but it hardly empowers social self-organization the way neo-Tocquevillians would hope.

There is no reason to assume that social reflexivity must always evaporate the bridges that servant-style groups try to build. Adopt-a-Family volunteers might have found a way to honor Keith's or Jerry's thinking about former welfare-receiving families, and create bridges that would help the families in some small way to take more control of their lives, on their own terms. It is an open question. Being more reflexive would mean changing the customs of social servanthood, but not necessarily as drastically as Adopt-a-Family groups would have by becoming partners to "action plans" generated by social workers.

What We Learn about Evangelicals, and Americans

Maybe Adopt-a-Family did not need to exist. Some proponents of community empowerment see little good in a service project like Adopt-a-Family, on the notion that local autonomy is good and service directed toward a locale from outside it is bad (McKnight 1995). It is hard to imagine Justice Task Force members finding much value in the enterprise either. From the social critics' point of view, Adopt-a-Family offered only to ease victims of injustice into harsher conditions, instead of criticizing the conditions and their hidden perpetrators. Why reflect on charitable relationships that are little but a distraction from the real issues?

If there are reasons for dismissing the project, there also are reasons for being more open-minded. As sociologist Robert Sampson points out (1999), local autonomy and empowerment run up against serious limits in low-income locales. For better or worse, public agencies and other organizations outside low-income neighborhoods have resources that neighbors need. In an era when evangelical Protestants have become prominent in American life, it is important to find out what contributions they may make to the civic ties that distribute resources to people who want them.

Were they really even trying to create civic ties? Were church group volunteers doing things together with the families, not just with each other? I argue they were, though cultural blinders may make it hard to interpret the volunteers that way. Though the church groups assumed their relationships with the families would unfold largely on the church groups' terms, these relationships still were a kind of collaboration. The "adopted" families needed to be good at enunciating needs and receiving help from strangers. Or as the Community in Christ pastor Nick put it, relationships take two. That is true whether or not relationships are egalitarian. Restricting "doing things together" to egalitarian relationships only obscures the variety of ways people create togetherness. It may substitute liberal-progressive biases for a more complete understanding of what civic relationships mean to different people. Researchers are learning that civic life around the world often does not resemble the egalitarian, individual-affirming model prized by intellectuals in the West, and real civic relationships in the United States do not necessarily mirror this normative case either. Dismissing the Adopt-a-Family volunteers as ideological enterpreneurs does not help us understand what they were doing.

They tried to do what Jane Addams's charity visitor tried doing. Rather than reflect deeply on their perplexities, though, they opted to bring in powerful outside help. In the process they greatly diminished what made Adopt-a-Family meaningful and compelling to them to begin with. It will take more research to find out what the limits and potentials of servant-style bridging are. It is clear, though, that some of our existing terms of discussion do not clarify this distinctive style of civic engagement.

Adopt-a-Family volunteers were brave to embark on such a demanding version of community service. Some sociological portraits depict volunteers who are unself-consciously condescending toward the people they serve (Liebow 1993; Ostrander 1984). Adopt-a-Family volunteers in contrast, especially the ones from Community in Christ, tried hard to respect their families. Some studies portray volunteers who are clueless about the power that courses through service relationships across class or race divides (Daniels 1988). Adopt-a-Family volunteers, in contrast, took clues but could not do anything with them. If volunteers had a difficult time connecting with their families, the problem was not simply that they scorned the families from the start for being lazy or morally deficient. Neither was it that the volunteers had access only to a single cognitive, theological grid. They were not blind altogether to social differences between the families and themselves. Neither ideologies nor belief systems in the abstract but group-building customs made the difference. The church groups' customs bid the volunteers to establish interpersonal relationships from scratch; doing otherwise threatened not just their beliefs but their own constitution as groups. Mutual friendliness proved to be an undependable bridge for relationships across social gaps that volunteers recognized dimly but could not discuss.

Adopt-a-Family's experiences highlight the limits of the social capital concept. Did the church groups have "bridging" social capital? On the one hand, their faith gave them the norms and initial sense of trust to go out and create relationships with people utterly unlike themselves. On the other hand, their style of relating made it hard to build these bridges. After the fact, we could say that Adopt-a-Family groups lacked bridging social capital. That makes it hard to distinguish them from Humane Response Alliance volunteers who also, in hindsight, lacked bridging social capital. The difference in style between the evangelical and mostly mainline Protestant efforts is at least as interesting as the ultimately similar outcomes.

We get farther when we unpack the social capital concept and discover the different customs that help or hinder different kinds of relationships across social divides. The customs of social servanthood encouraged Evan's volunteers to take brave risks that conventional volunteers or networkers would not have considered. In Adopt-a-Family, real connecting, real compassion, *meant* interpersonal, one-to-one relating, and the groups built themselves around this definition. This is not an exhaustive study of Adopt-a-Family's successes and failures. But the scenarios here make clear that one of its most active groups, Community in Christ, folded because it could not succeed meaningfully with its form of togetherness. Keith's initial suggestions and other secular, social-service knowledge may have helped sustain the group longer, but this kind of knowledge could not have worked *meaningfully* in a group that constituted itself as servants.

Adopt-a-Family's version of compassion may seem extreme or peculiar to a regional evangelical church culture. Other researchers (Bartkowski and Regis 2003) have found a very similar model of church-based social support, though, in Mississippi. Adopt-a-Family's deep compassion takes to brave limits an ideal that many Americans affirm, an ideal of social solidarity through personal relationships.[15] Many Americans learn in churches, synagogues, schools, or workplaces that a multicultural America becomes more cohesive when members of the majority culture "make friends" with people from minority groups. Adopt-a-Family volunteers tried doing, albeit in distinctively Christian terms, what many Americans would find ideal to try if they had the time and commitment: Many Americans think that deep interpersonal relationships are more "real" than the complex world of social services. They say the personal touch is better than the bureaucratic handshake.[16] Adopt-a-Family's experiences might show what an ideal style of relationship-building would look like in practice.

This is no argument against cultivating friendships across social divides. But experiences like Kara's, Nick's, and Jane's show that a more solidary civic community will not arise from interpersonal goodwill alone. If anything, intense interpersonal relating heightened these volunteers' sense of their separation from some of their fellow citizens.

Adopt-a-Family represents yet another style of civic engagement that frustrates the social spiral argument. So what if Tocqueville and Tocquevillians have implied that civic groups spiral people outward? Maybe I am holding Adopt-a-Family to the wrong standard. But neither the Justice Task Force nor the Humane Response Alliance made good on the argument either. These projects produced valuable goods. They failed, however, to institute enduring bridges. The next chapter pictures a church-based effort that instituted new relationships across social divides and new public goods. They could do so in part because they dared to talk thoughtfully and self-critically about those relationships.

Chapter Six

A SOCIAL SPIRAL WINDS OUTWARD: PARTNERS

Fools Driving In?

On the second Wednesday of every month, the deceptively quiet street outside of Park Neighborhood Center becomes busier, parking space becomes tighter, and white faces become more common than usual. It is Park Cluster's monthly meeting. A dozen church people, mostly in their sixties and seventies, meander into the small neighborhood center packed into a former apartment building. A food pantry inhabits a former bedroom; loaves of white balloon bread huddle together on wooden shelves crafted by a Cluster member. Upstairs, the new public health nurse shares a former bedroom with the office of the Moving Girls teen club. Cluster members head for a living-room-sized space for their meeting. The once-cozy apartment is a cramped neighborhood center, but there are few other places to meet in the neighborhood. Park has no school, no library, no recreation center.

For many Americans, "low-income neighborhood" conjures up rows of crumbling, half-vacant brick apartment buildings in a Bronx slum or sagging bungalows with iron window-bars, baking in the Los Angeles sun. The Park neighborhood looks different. The main route into the neighborhood weaves between blocks of shopping-center parking lots on one side and a six-lane highway on the other. City planners must have assumed people would drive to and from the neighborhood; few pedestrians would find the corridor inviting, with its wide vista of parking lots, superstores, and cars whizzing by. The route dead-ends into the street for which the neighborhood is named. Park Street runs down a gauntlet of two-story, motel-style apartment buildings standing on square plots of grass worn down to dirt around the edges. Park is the street I trotted down while giving piggyback rides to kids in the Summer Fun day camp. Cluster members observe that there is little reason to drive down Park Street unless the driver is going to the neighborhood on purpose. There are more direct routes to the shopping malls up the street or to the park that anchors the neighborhood's opposite end. Like other low-income, minority neighborhoods in America (Wacquant and Wilson 1989), Park is relatively isolated for anyone without a car.

What are white middle-class Park Cluster members doing driving in a low-income, black, Hmong,[1] and Spanish-speaking neighborhood? Are they naïve if compassionate volunteers trying to "help the underprivileged"? This chapter argues that they are doing something else. They are trying to build bridges, just like the other Lakeburg groups, and slowly, fitfully, they are succeeding. Reaching out, for them, is very different from Adopt-a-Family's Christ-like care, the Task Force's consciousness-raising, or the HRA's volunteering and networking.

Over a year's time the dominant style of interaction in the Cluster transformed, and the Cluster instituted new connections with other people and groups. Distinctive customs helped the Cluster take itself more and more seriously as an empowered civic actor. New ties ratified the group's evolving customs, its evolving sense of itself, leading to further new connections. Critical, sometimes embarrassing reflection on its relationships powered an outward-bound social spiral. I want to show in this chapter how the social spiral uncoiled for the Cluster, despite the resistance of at least one vocal Cluster member who customarily defined the role of church-based volunteers differently.

Park Cluster is an alliance of volunteers from different congregations: Episcopalian, Lutheran, United Methodist, Presbyterian, and a Friends meeting. Several of these volunteers, almost entirely laypeople, tutored kids, visited sick people, or accompanied after-school programs on field trips—a few for nearly a decade. They and other volunteers initiated Park Cluster in 1996, as one of the "congregational cluster" projects of the URC's Humane Response Alliance. Recall that Pastor Edward Lindstrom of the HRA had proposed that congregations unite in clusters to care for their surrounding neighborhoods. The Urban Religious Coalition had hoped that alliances like Park Cluster could strengthen local safety nets, catching at least a few of the people that URC leaders imagined would be left to fall freely once their welfare benefits ended. The URC sent its director or a staffer to help the Cluster administer its projects. The URC liaison's role changed during my study, as the Cluster accumulated and then actively embraced more responsibility.

WHAT THE CLUSTER DID

Volunteering and Community Development Projects

In its first two years, Park Cluster members did direct-service volunteering, similar to HRA volunteers. As one member put it, the Cluster began as "a conduit for volunteers"; the HRA could have been described the same way. Lakeburg County's social service agency, Family Friends, sponsored a Southeast Asian Festival, a Christmas party, and other celebrations throughout the year. Volunteers from Cluster churches plugged in and carried out tasks—setting up party tables, picking up food donations from grocery stores, collecting donated Christmas presents and Thanksgiving food baskets from churches, serving meals, cleaning up afterward. Some also tutored Park kids after school, led nature walks for them, or taught sewing classes to adults. A loose aggregate of individual volunteers or donors from different churches found valuable ways to serve individual needs in the Park neighborhood and assist social workers. There was a lot to do.

Increasingly, Park Cluster adopted a different group style that at least some members, I learned in retrospect, were capable of engaging even at my earlier meetings. The Cluster mounted modest community development projects. Community development builds shared public assets that "improve the quality of life among residents of low- to moderate-income" neighborhoods or communities" (Ferguson and Dickenson 1999, p. 5; see also Sirianni and Friedland 2001). Community development potentially involves very different kinds of organizations—formal and informal, professional and volunteer, entrepreneurial and nonprofit, organizations with big budgets and ones with nearly no budget (Ferguson and Stoutland 1999).

As incipient, grass-roots promoters of community development, the Cluster tried to sponsor public resources for the neighborhood, in consultation with neighborhood leaders, residents, and Family Friends county services staff. Cluster churches cosponsored a public health nurse for the neighborhood. They organized annual payments to a central "eviction prevention fund" that Park residents could tap if they were in danger of losing their apartments. Repeatedly, anxiously, Cluster members discussed how to get Park residents involved in the eviction fund and the nurse project as agenda-setting partners rather than subordinates. The Cluster also began to do some advocacy and organizing work in the neighborhood, toward the end of my study. It pushed for a public forum with school board members, held in the neighborhood center basement, so that residents could speak directly to board members about busing, discipline and "social promotion" of failing students.

Direct-service volunteering and community development both are valuable ways of serving a locale. The difference between them matters if we want to understand how the social spiral works when it works. By the end of my time with the group, Cluster members still were volunteering to supervise kids at the Summer Fun Camp, clean up after the annual multicultural festival, or prepare Thanksgiving food baskets. What made them proud of the Cluster, or worried about the Cluster, though, were its community development projects. They considered the Cluster successful when they established new relationships with other groups, and when those relationships produced goods for the neighborhood.

BRIDGE-BUILDING IN THE CLUSTER

Toward the end of the study, neighborhood residents began attending Cluster meetings, and one became the group's facilitator. The neighborhood center director attended Cluster meetings, and Cluster members, in turn, got to sit on two of the neighborhood center's steering committees. Relationships with a Lutheran retirement home and the Family Friends service agency resulted in the public health nurse and the eviction prevention fund. In all, the Cluster built bridging relationships with the neighborhood center and its director, other nonprofit groups, and city and county agencies.

The Cluster had a sense of accomplishment, hard-won, ambivalent accomplishment, which the Task Force, Adopt-a-Family, and the Humane Response Alliance mostly lacked. I pictured more disappointment and a sense of isolation in these other groups because there was more to hear and see. Cluster members often were frustrated, sometimes exasperated. But they also were the only group in this study that *celebrated* one of their efforts coming to fruition, the parish nurse project.[2]

Customs, reflexivity, and institutional resources all empowered the Cluster's spiral outward. I revisit alternative arguments about the social spiral at the end of the chapter, in light of scenes from the Cluster and the other Lakeburg groups and projects. Customs I will call "partnership" let the Cluster practice more social reflexivity than other groups did and create new ties. Acting more and more like responsible civic actors, the Cluster took on projects that reinforced partner customs. A broad-minded partnership with the Park neighborhood slowly developed; the social spiral uncoiled.

Partnership also limited the Cluster's ability to think in complex terms about the neighborhood. Partnership limited the Cluster's ability to criticize its own projects and their effects on the neighborhood. All customs involve trade-offs; partnership is no exception. Partnership customs did help the Cluster begin realizing its ambitious, long-term bridging goals. They did not keep it from enduring frustrations.

I emphasize how fraught and tenuous bridge-building was. Critics of neo-Tocquevillian thinking like to say that too much of the writing about social capital and civic engagement conjures up broad-minded citizens who work happily together for the common good and welcome everyone as equals.[3] Cluster members were not saints or heroes. Sometimes they tripped over their own parochialism. Sometimes they treated a multiracial neighborhood as if it were an African American one only. Their new relationships and projects were modest at best, less than their churches could have afforded. Sometimes they hit up against limits imposed by their would-be partners in the Park neighborhood. Bridge-building takes two. Just as Jane Addams discovered in her many years at Hull House, social reflexivity did not necessarily promote consensus or "build community" in the way Americans often mean the phrase. Practicing reflexivity does not guarantee by itself that new ties will result, either. It involved a trade-off of goods, but one ultimately worthwhile to Cluster members.

A Varied Vocabulary

Cluster members described relationships they wanted to create with a mix of idioms. Park Cluster's brochure tapped most of them and is worth exploring in detail. First, on the front cover was the motto "faith in action." An older version of the back cover included a single biblical passage, from Isaiah (1:17): "Devote yourselves to justice, aid the wronged. Uphold the rights of the orphan; defend the cause of the widow." A newer version replaced Isaiah with Margaret Mead: "Never doubt that a small group of thoughtful committed citizens can change the world. Indeed, it's the only thing that ever has." I will say more in the next chapter about religious discourse in the group. For now, the language implies that the group is ultimately about social-structural change. And at least one founding member told me in an interview that she thought the group should be about social justice, among other things.

More vocabularies emerge inside the brochure: "Park Cluster are people of faith, committed to service, who join together with a common goal; to assist our neighbors in the Park area." A different paragraph explains why the group does its work: "By working together we believe we can help our neighbors build community in their neighborhood." And further, "As people of faith we believe we are called to act in solidarity with our neighbors as they work to rebuild and renew their neighborhood, and to improve the overall spiritual, physical, and mental health of residents. We also recognize that this partnership provides the opportunity to strengthen race, class and cultural relationships in the Park area." It is a remarkable statement of purpose. It folds in community-building and service, both somewhat different from the social justice message of Isaiah and Margaret Mead. The first, particularly ambiguous sentence may imply a certain paternalism, too: It is not clear whether the Cluster or the residents themselves are improving the spiritual, physical, and mental health of residents. Clearly different vocabularies of relationship coexisted in the Cluster.

Cluster members used the term "partner" to describe their relationship with the neighborhood. I have borrowed it to name the customs that became predominant in the group. But I do not mean to equate the vocabulary with the customs, any more than I would with any other vocabulary. A vocabulary of social justice, for instance, did not *have* to convey self-marginalizing criticism, but it acquired that meaning in the setting of the Justice Task Force. Partnership could mean different things too. Cluster members all willingly used the word *partner* to describe the Cluster, but they did not all mean the same thing. One member, Ned, used the phrase "helpin' out" to describe the Cluster's mission during several tense discussions. The Cluster, in his view, would be a partner by helping out the neighborhood and the social service workers. Helping implied that someone else had already drawn up the bigger picture and decided on the tasks. Some people—Park residents—needed "help." That was not how many other Cluster members saw it, though. From the mixed vocabularies of relationship in the Cluster, it would be hard to guess what the Cluster's priorities were or how they changed. Different customs could turn partnership into different kinds of relationships.

VOLUNTEER CUSTOMS IN THE CLUSTER

The World According to Volunteers

Earlier in its three year history, Cluster members defined themselves similarly to volunteers in the Humane Response Alliance. Their map of the local world featured individual servers and an aggregate of individuals served, with a professional agency as orchestrator. They wanted to help professional experts carry out tasks. They asked the director of Park's neighborhood center and the head social worker from Family Friends what they could do. The social worker, Kendra, described to me how she would "give" the Cluster ideas for projects their first year. For Kendra, the Cluster was a handy means to securing volunteer assistance: "I've used Ned and Elizabeth Coulter [husband and wife members of the Cluster] to get out and help individual families." Elizabeth Coulter got into a relationship with a Park woman with diabetes, tended to the woman like a nurse, ran errands for her. Kendra told me it would not matter much if there was simply a list of potential volunteers from churches instead of a civic entity called Park Cluster. She would get the person power she needed either way. She said she thought that the Cluster organization did matter to the volunteers. It helped them feel connected and support each other.[4]

Throughout my time with the Cluster, Ned and Elizabeth—Kendra's favorite volunteer contacts—continued to use the social map that complemented Kendra's approach, even as the predominant understanding of the Cluster's boundaries seemed to be changing. Ned and Elizabeth defined themselves as charitable helpers, representing an aggregate of potential charitable helpers at their church. To them, the Cluster was itself an aggregate of aggregates, helping out Family Friends. And on that map, Park neighborhood was an aggregate of individual and family needs. Ned said the Cluster should be able to get people from member churches to donate goods quickly whenever Kendra called up— a thousand diapers, if that was what she needed for her clients. Ned liked to help out with his handyman skills. He is the one who made the wooden shelves for the food pantry at the neighborhood center.

Like Ned and Elizabeth, Nancy liked to help people. Nancy warmed to the parish nurse idea because she herself was a retired nurse. She could appreciate one-to-one caring. She let the group draft her as liaison to the nurse. It turned out that being the liaison would involve a different kind of caring—caring about institutional relationships—less familiar to Nancy. Nancy attended meetings of her Methodist church's outreach committee that decided how much money to give to Cluster programs; I picture the committee in the next chapter. Nancy missed the committee meeting at which she was supposed to report on the new public health nurse. I told her at the next meeting that I was impressed at how many projects the church outreach was sponsoring now. Nancy looked confused: "Oh—? I didn't go? I guess I didn't go." She didn't sound worried about missing the meeting, and I wondered why not. She only sounded surprised. "Were they—expecting me?"

Then I remembered that Nancy had told me that she liked the nurse project because it was a way to help people. She continued on, telling me she felt badly for single mothers, people who had to live at the YMCA downtown, and people who did not have enough blankets. She did not say anything about the nurse's contribution to the Park neighborhood as a whole. When other Cluster members asked the nurse to say more about her goals for *the neighborhood,* and for churches, Nancy did not join in. For Nancy, the nurse program and the Cluster itself were opportunities to serve needy individuals compassionately. Needy individuals in YMCAs were not distinct from needy Park neighborhood residents on Nancy's social map. All were needy.

I did not run into any Cluster members more often than Ned and Elizabeth when I made my fieldworker's visits to the neighborhood. The pantry needed shelves; the woman with diabetes needed someone to run errands for her. Ned and Elizabeth met these needs. Their caring was greater than the terms of volunteering imply. One morning at Summer Fun Camp, a Family Friends social worker was leading a crayon-drawing project with kids at a picnic table. Ned was one of the volunteer counselors that morning. Urgently, Ned pushed a note into the social worker's hand. It said that the woman with diabetes might get kicked out of her apartment because her daughter's crack habit had gotten her in trouble. Ned had taken the initiative to check on the woman. He cared when he didn't have to.

Talking Like a Volunteer: Speech Norms

At the start of my fieldwork, most Cluster members spoke mainly to *report* on tasks accomplished or to ask simple questions. The main speech genre was "business meeting," with leaders in control of the agenda. Members did not often initiate new topics or discuss the group's overall direction. They waited for task leaders, the liaison from the URC, or Kendra the social worker to issue reports. During my first year, meetings almost always ended on time, sometimes early. At my first meeting, the URC liaison was shepherding the group along. She introduced three of the six major items on the agenda. Three months later she led on three of five major items, and reported from the subcommittee charged with writing a brochure about Park Cluster, even though the subcommittee's own chair was right at the table.

I learned even more about the speech norms when I got a ride home from Nancy after one of my first Cluster meetings. To my surprise, she had noticed that, during a long, bewildering discussion about federal restrictions on food pantries, someone mentioned in passing "the Minnesota interpretation of the federal program." Nancy told me she wondered if local pantries could fight for the Minnesota interpretation and keep the federal benefits they were about to lose. It was a very astute point, yet Nancy had said nothing whatsoever during the discussion. Cluster members, I discovered, were alert at meetings, but they did not feel empowered enough yet to voice the questions they harbored in private.

Stretching, Then Straining, the Volunteer Mode

Going to Cluster meetings during the first nine months could be like watching a movie occasionally interrupted by another movie with the same characters but a different plot and scene. For a lot of the time, members signed up for tasks, learned about volunteer opportunities to publicize in their own churches, found out what donations the pantry needed this month. They looked to the URC liaison or Kendra the social worker for direction. They covered agenda items expeditiously. They divided up tasks easily. Occasionally, though, their social horizons would broaden, and they would ponder or complain rather than report and decide. I gathered this was a rather flexible group that could do different kinds of things together.

At a particularly tense meeting I will picture below, I heard members castigating their own group structure and disagreeing with the small minority that continued to want an informal, ad hoc, can-do group. I went back to my previous months of field notes. I realized the "interruptions" I just mentioned may have been early signs that there were limits to the volunteer mode's flexibility. The group never appeared close to dissipating. With hindsight, it made more sense to say that volunteering was in conflict with a different set of customs that became more recognizable when, feeling under pressure, Cluster members criticized some of their own group style. Let me sketch the group's halting transition from the volunteer style toward partnership.

Sometimes Cluster members sounded as if they thought their churches should be something besides resource banks and aggregates of volunteer time. They complained, and the complaining could be telling. At one meeting, for instance, Dora sounded frustrated at her own congregation's engagement with the Cluster, even though hers was one of the core congregations. "I'm still here, still motivated by that original vision [of building the community], even if my church—(pause), well, they give presents at Christmas, but." At another meeting, members quipped bitterly about their own relations with their congregations:

STEVEN (*warily*): Maybe we want to bounce these [proposals] off our faith communities.

MARTHA (*sardonically*): Some of us *don't* bounce with our faith-based communities!

BETTY: We bounce but we don't meld!

They complained that the pastors of their congregations, involved at the very beginning, had dropped out. At one meeting, Betty sheepishly admitted "I have not given up that local pastors might come," as if the idea were hopelessly naïve. Martha retorted, "I *have* given up." Others chimed in that "not one pastor" was there. Why would that matter? What was the complaining about?

Cluster members *never* said that pastors could give them more clout or bring them more volunteers. And judging from the Cluster's success at getting church-goers to staff the Southeast Asian Festival, the Christmas party, or the Summer Fun Camp, they did not need more volunteers. Volunteering at these events, I sometimes found myself with little to do. I learned the problem was more that Cluster members saw their congregations, *sometimes,* as collectivities united behind a civic project. That was different from seeing congregations as pools of individual volunteers and donors who clean up after neighborhood events and give presents at Christmastime.

At meetings, members sometimes imagined the Cluster on a social map that included much more than Family Friends and the neighborhood center director. I marveled at how members seemed to carry detailed mental maps of Lakeburg's different neighborhoods. Ned, for instance, knew all about the different thrift shops. He told us which Salvation Army store had the best bread (wheat, not white). He told us how to pick the right St. Vincent's shop when hunting down used jackets and shoes for Park residents (go to the ones with Cadillacs parked outside).[5] Sometimes Kendra broadened members' horizons too, with her reports on the state's welfare policies or an occasional tidbit about city politics. At one meeting, Cluster members had hoped Kendra might give them a list of local elementary schools so that they could think about neighborhood-based academic support programs. Kendra hadn't brought the list, but Mary already knew the territory: Mary knew which churches and synagogues were close to which elementary schools, and thus convenient for congregation-sponsored tutoring programs. She led a fifteen minute discussion on topic and continued it with me in her car afterward.

In some conversations, then, Cluster members brought into play a larger map of the civic world than the one they placed themselves on most of the time during my first nine months. Conversations about the public health nurse, for instance, elicited a larger map, even at my first meeting. Members might carry on a twenty-minute conversation about which kinds of canned vegetables the pantry needed most or which sandwich combinations worked best at Summer Fun Camp.

And jam: Paula took the time on a busy agenda to point out that the pantry really needed jam to go with the jars of peanut butter they were giving out to neighborhood families. It interested me that discussions of peanut butter and discussions of the public health nurse's goals and working conditions could be equally
long. Then members would bring up the other organizations that were going to
cosponsor the nurse. What did Lutheran Home have to say this month? What was
the name of that black Baptist church's community development organization—
was it Genesis or Exodus? Would the nurse be culturally sensitive to the different
neighborhood constituencies? Would there be more government grant money
for the nurse if she promised to do alcohol and drug abuse intake work with her
clients? Members would ask about how their churches would support the nurse's
salary. And who was going to pay her health benefits—the Cluster, Genesis, or
Lutheran Home? The answers were never definitive. That seemed not to matter,
at least for a number of months, while members assumed the URC liaison would
figure it all out. They did keep asking, but they did not insist on knowing.

I kept wondering why Cluster members did not press harder for answers to
their questions about the nurse they had committed their churches to supporting. I learned that volunteer speech norms kept the group within the volunteer mode. Cluster members asked the same questions about the salary and
the benefits at each of my first three meetings, and got no firm answer from the
URC liaison, who then was coordinating the whole effort to bring the nurse to
Park. After one of these meetings Martha revealed her own confusion to Nancy,
without any prompting from me. She said, "I got real disappointed about the
parish nurse. It's taken so long! . . . I don't understand it—Lutheran Home [a co-
sponsor] and Godwin Hospital [another co-sponsor] have both been ready."
Martha did not understand why the arrangements were not finalized yet. I deduced they did not feel right probing more aggressively. Neither I nor Cluster
members quite put it together, until later, that the Cluster had been accumulating responsibilities that strained the volunteer mode.

Recreating the Group: A Crisis Meeting

Heavier Group Bonds for a Group with Weightier Responsibility

The Cluster never discussed formally whether it should switch from being
mainly a volunteer group to a community development group. So it was not a
matter of setting an overriding goal and then meeting the goal. But over time
the group had committed itself to the parish nurse project, without the formal
structure or the informal understandings that a big salaried project might need.
Having wandered into this commitment, with the nurse about to start her work
in the neighborhood, Cluster members suddenly started to sound, nine months
into my study, very unsettled about the group.

One month before the nurse started her neighborhood rounds, the Cluster appointed a subcommittee to start figuring out a new organizational structure. At the very next general meeting, Cluster members complained as never before. They sounded like people with a lot of pent-up frustrations. Their criticisms of the group seemed too specific, too formed, to have been thought up de novo. Putting together the previous month's call for a new structure with the earlier instances of stretching horizons and sharpening tongues, I gathered that members were torn between two different styles of togetherness. Groups may sustain subordinate sets of customs, not just one consensually shared set (Eliasoph and Lichterman 2003). What had seemed like organizational flexibility now seemed like a clash between the volunteer style and another one, which I call "partnership." Volunteer-style group bonds now came in for intense criticism.

Martha was pushing for a new finance committee. Betty agreed. Mary liked the idea, too: "We've taken on the financial responsibility [of the parish nurse] and need the structure to carry it out," she reasoned. All meeting long, Connie kept asking how many months of the nurse's salary were covered already. Dora quipped that if the parish nurse kept hours, there would be no one in the Cluster to give them to. No one said the Cluster needed a formal hierarchy of committees and positions on the assumption that bureaucratic looks better or more powerful. For three years the Cluster had gotten along with rotating chairs whose authority was simply that of discussion leader for one meeting. They relied on the URC liaison to take up the slack and take care of administrative details between meetings. Now they were crying out for more formality.

The Cluster's evolving relations with the outside world required a new sense of commitment in the group. For a lot of members, it was no longer enough to be a handy volunteer who could rely on the URC liaison or the Family Friends professional to keep track of things. Members were saying in effect that a good group was one that met its increasing outside obligations in a predictable way. Loose, informal ties would not let them be good members anymore.

This interpretation helped me understand why the Cluster kept combining conversations about its relations to other groups and conversations about its own structure: Mary had asked the Cluster to "consider [our] relations to URC, to our congregations, to the neighborhood center, to JFF—*and maybe something about our structure, our identity*" (emphasis mine). Next month, Dora blurted out "We're such a loose organization that we're not sure who's doing what!" External relations and internal structure were related closely for Betty, too. She asked, "What kind of structure should we have," but then immediately launched into a memorable declaration on partnership, which I will picture momentarily. A more formal structure would not only make Cluster members feel more comfortable about their risky responsibilities, but would signal to others on its map that it meant to be a trustworthy partner in the neighborhood.

Favoring formality is not universal common sense, not an unambiguous sign of a group that means business. In some grass-roots groups, being serious means relying on deep, individual commitments to the cause rather than formal structure (Lichterman 1996; Epstein 1991; Breines 1982); formal structure represents a failure of real commitment. In Park Cluster, members needed to depend on each other in a new way, and symbolized the new interdependence with a newly formalized structure, with a presiding director, a secretary, and a treasurer. Practically speaking, these positions did not require of their occupants many new tasks beyond ones Cluster members had already been sharing, or doing in an ad hoc way. Ned always kept the books; now he was the treasurer. Someone always took notes at meetings; now there was a secretary. The presiding director was responsible for approving a meeting agenda and communicating with the URC and other outside groups. The URC liaison originally had these responsibilities. The new structure, in other words, mattered most by symbolizing a changed sense of commitment and by making the Cluster more autonomous from the URC.

Installing a Map of Partnership

At this same, critical meeting, Betty addressed the Cluster's purpose with her characteristic combination of eloquence and self-deprecating irony:

> BETTY: Up to the [former] director leaving, we worked as a conduit for volunteers, to go back to churches. Amidst that, we took on the parish nurse and eviction prevention—
> (*From around the table*): Yes, yes—
> BETTY: —without a Center director. "Fools walk in where angels fear to tread!" . . . We took on things without the structure to carry out . . .

Betty turned now to a sheet listing the precepts of "social ministry," and while eyeing it continued speaking to us in an instructive tone:

> Those of you doing hands-on work—with kids, the after school program . . . in the perception of the people you're working with, we are not givers and receivers but partners. We become *not* [*emphasis hers*] givers of the community but partners of the community—that we be perceived not as directors but partners.

Evidently the point mattered enough for Betty to say it three times in the last sentence. Even when doing "hands on" or "direct" service, Cluster members needed to keep in mind that these one-to-one volunteer stints should be meaningful on a different map. They should be part of a broader effort at community-building. Cluster members needed to avoid casting residents as "receivers" of the Cluster's compassionate "gifts" of service. I had heard this different social map of "partnership with the community" emerge now and then at earlier meetings, when members would broaden their horizons beyond the immediacies of server-served relationships.

On the map of partnership, the Cluster was no longer an adjunct to Family Friends. It would relate more self-consciously to Park as a neighborhood with its own history, its own mix of ethnic groups. It would no longer take Park as a locus of needy people in general, served by the family services agency. Most but not all Cluster members agreed heartily with Betty.

Speech Norms: From Reporting to Discussing

The speech norms of volunteering, already strained by quick but repeated episodes of complaining and questioning, changed very noticeably in the months *after* the crisis meeting. Ten months into my time with the Cluster, most of the dozen core members were taking a greater ownership of the group. Martha was not asking but insisting that the Cluster initiate a finance committee to oversee fund-raising for the parish nurse, whose terms of employment were still unclear. Members asked more questions, more routinely, more pointedly. In the next months they would ask the new neighborhood nurse why she was seeing mainly African Americans, not Laotians or Spanish speakers. They would ask to see their own budget figures more often. Aside from issuing reports, they *discussed*. They were demonstrating a greater sense of authorization to speak, and speaking more proactively.

Signs of the new group routine are easy to identify: Discussions after the crisis meeting regularly produced items that needed to be saved for the following month's agenda. Meetings started running over time, every time. Members had to lengthen the monthly meeting officially by a half-hour, and it still was not enough time. Cluster members formulated most of their own meeting agenda items rather than waiting for the URC liaison to do it. Members called for subcommittees to handle large issues that they could no longer discuss to their satisfaction in two hours. Relatively less time got taken with volunteer signups and peanut butter.

Partnership in Action

Dignity, Bland Chicken, Cleanliness, and Godliness

As partners, Cluster members referred more and more explicitly to Park as a low-income, African American, southeast Asian, and Spanish-speaking neighborhood, rather than a place where needy people lived. After the crisis meeting, they talked more and more about how Park's African American children were treated as troublemakers at the largely white schools they attended outside the neighborhood. Watching a local African American pastor talk to some Park residents after a Cluster meeting one day, Martha told me, unsolicited, that she was very glad he had started going regularly to Cluster meetings because he would probably be closer to black Park residents' perspectives than other (white) Cluster members.

Unlike Adopt-a-Family volunteers, Cluster members acknowledged explicitly and frequently that Park residents were socially subordinated and had fewer opportunities than Cluster members—who had the luxury of time for meetings. At four different meetings during the study they tried out ideas on how to make Cluster meetings more accessible to people who worked two or more jobs just to survive. They discussed how changing federal policies regarding food pantries would affect neighborhoods like Park. They observed ironically that a municipal tax proposal could pay for an elementary school in a new upscale housing development nearby, while Park neighborhood had to get by with no local school.

They tried to make this awareness of inequality a part of partnership. They tried not to assume that they always knew better than their partners. They did not want to affect a false equality with Park residents, either. Cluster members had skills valued in the wider society, and access to money and powerful people that few Park residents would have. As a whole, the Cluster tried to relate in a solidary yet not unreflectively supportive way to the neighborhood and its county service agency. Cluster members tiptoed awkwardly around social chasms. Sometimes they tripped. The interesting thing is that these mostly middle-class white people were trying to honor the reality of social divisions, and learn from them.

While exquisitely sensitive to racial differences some of the time, Adopt-a-Family volunteers did not work with such a complicated social map. Volunteers in well-known studies do not either. The upper-class women volunteers in Ostrander's account assumed that inequalities were simply the way of the world. To recognize them was to naturalize them. Ostrander summarizes that noblesse oblige motivated these women to "help some individuals improve their own lives," on the assumption that one does not "rock the boat" by trying to reform institutions (1984, p. 115). Contrast Betty's statement of the Cluster's purpose quoted above—to meet neighborhood residents as "partners," not as beneficent agents of improvement on outsiders' terms. Sorties across race and class lines earned the volunteers in Daniels's account a badge of honor, and gave them the thrill of making contacts in exotic netherworlds. Daniels's volunteers were proud to tell each other about people they met on volunteer rounds: minority group leaders, political activists, mental patients. They made a point of affirming that these people were worth knowing (1988, p. 181). Perceptively, Daniels describes one of her volunteers affirming differences in status even while recounting a tale of boundary-crossing: The woman says that a black community activist, "an utter gentleman," she assures, wants her participation on a board of directors. The volunteer is happy to help this man, referring to him by nickname though he addresses her more formally. She concludes with pride, "That is where I stand with the blacks" (1988, p. 182). Cluster members, in contrast, never sounded self-satisfied about their standing in Park neighborhood. They talked often, anxiously, about how to pursue a partnership across differences and inequalities.

With these other accounts of volunteers, and a healthy sociological skepticism, critical observers might assume Cluster members were stumbling do-gooders, blinded by their own whiteness. They were not radicals trying to disown their own privileges. It is worth exploring how the Cluster's quiet, unassuming, solicitous bridge-building efforts trod a narrow path between facile identification and condescension.

The Cluster's sense of partnership came out in the way members talked about other people's unreflective efforts to "help" or "serve" the neighborhood. My first day at the neighborhood center, low-key Ken disparaged people who came to Park neighborhood with their own ideas about what Park needed. I took it as a friendly warning to an outside researcher. The Cluster's sincere if sometimes awkward attempts to meet Park residents on residents' own terms became especially clear during a spontaneous conversation about chicken dinners. The free meals cooked and served by the "two moms" I introduced in the last chapter were getting poor reviews, and the Cluster heard about them. Reverend Michael let the group in on what Park neighbors said about the meals. He told us, slowly, that "about the meals, there has been—talk." He sounded as if he did not want to criticize the well-meaning moms' efforts, and paused awhile longer before continuing in uncharacteristically stilted language, that "the seasoning is not satisfying to those who are eating." The busy moms' meals did not compare well with the dinners of spaghetti, cole slaw, bread, and cake that Salvation Shelter served to homeless guests. Ned also found that "what we present is not what people like. But we could never find out what they like. . . . Now we'd get breaded chicken, with salt and pepper, so you've got some yummy chicken. So what would we add?"

Kendra's student intern blurted out: "Hot sauce!"

Reverend Michael pointed to the student: "You've got it. That's it. . . . The seasoning may not be great but hot sauce will smother anything." Could the busy moms learn anything about seasoning for next time? Ned wanted to know. Reverend Michael answered somewhat sheepishly that "I refrain from doing that because I don't like to offend cooks. If I taste it I can tell. This *is* a barrier." Practical-minded Ned pressed on, asking Reverend Michael about what to tell the moms to put in the pot with the chicken.

Did it really affect race relations in south Lakeburg if a Cluster volunteer and two busy moms from the suburbs served bland chicken to Park residents? A fifteen-minute conversation about cuisine, amidst other pressing topics, suggests that Park neighbors' tastes in chicken mattered to the Cluster. Reverend Michael was a busy man; he rarely stayed for an entire Cluster meeting. If he thought it worthwhile, if awkward, to comment on the dinners, then it makes sense to take seriously his remark that the food was "a barrier" to relationships between black Park residents and outsiders. Even seemingly trivial matters of taste mattered within the Cluster's effort to take Park residents as partners.

Though members like Betty and Martha spiced the Cluster's meetings with saucy wit, members *never* joked disparagingly about Park neighbors—something that could not be said for the Adopt-a-Family volunteers. Cluster members did sound lightly judgmental once in a while. Once, a member suggested that children who ran around making noise during the busy mom meal at the neighborhood center had "behavior problems" that "parents can't control." Another time, Mary muttered in a judgmental sotto voce that careful, long-range planning was "not how things are done here" at the center. Ned was less precious about partnership. More than once he commented wryly that if people needed help carrying donated computers and furniture into the center, they might go up to the street corner and "ask one of the drug dealers to do something for his community."

But apart from Ned's penchant for tart remarks, a more formal respect, sometimes awkward respect, was common when Cluster members were imagining or actually having contact with people in the neighborhood. At the end of one meeting, for instance, Steven announced: "There is a person who volunteers regularly at the center, who [*pausing uncomfortably*] is in great—need—of some—personal items, great financial need. . . . It's causing some mental health problems at this time, and—may—develop into mental health issues if the needs aren't met this month."

Someone from the table asked, "You said someone who volunteers here?"

Steven answered yes, and told us he didn't want to say anything more about "who this individual is" but that money donated for this "individual" "will be appropriated for the needed items."

Steven had no trouble saying things stridently and liked tossing bawdy comments out now and then to keep people from getting pretentious. Upon hearing someone else suggest that Park residents were too shy to meet with Lakeburg's mayor, he quipped, "Why? The mayor wears pants just like everyone else!" But now, straining to preserve the anonymous man's dignity, he froze into a bureaucratic register of passive verbs and generic nouns quite unlike his usual delivery. Talking across differences in taste or personal comportment was no easier for Steven than for Reverend Michael. But he was trying.

In a similar vein, Dora commented earnestly and stiltedly on "differences of lifestyle and perception" between Cluster members and Park residents. In another example, a neighborhood center employee, a Park resident hired through a job-training program, had just been arrested for alleged domestic violence. The URC liaison strained for the right words to convey her opinion that sometimes people in trouble need to work with social welfare workers even at the risk of being labeled by an agency: "When we invite people from the community—or all walks of life, how do you handle [*speaking more quickly and softly now*]—

well, low-income people treat these things differently. . . . They need to make [social] services less of a stigma."

And during the planning for Park's annual Southeast Asian Festival, Steven wondered whether it was appropriate, rather than presumptuous, to ask if a local Asian foods market might be willing to donate something for the party table. He sounded sincerely afraid of offending anyone.

A skeptical reader might take these verbal workouts as attempts to cover over impolite racial biases. But in a culture that encourages most white Americans to think talking about racial inequality at all is impolite (Eliasoph 1999; Lamont 1992), it is just as reasonable to read the stilted locutions and hesitant pauses as efforts to build verbal bridges toward more egalitarian relations with Park residents. That does not mean verbal self-consciousness reduces racial tensions by itself. It means that as partners, Cluster members gave themselves work that did not seem necessary to the volunteer in Daniels's study who was proud of "where I stand with the blacks."

Ned was less circumspect than most of the other members about passing judgment. He too used the word "partner," but the *customs* of volunteering, not partnership, were much more comfortable for him. For Ned, working in the neighborhood was still a matter of regular folks "helpin' out." And regular folks might take their regular definitions of propriety for granted—they might apply them to locales unlike their own, instead of getting precious about different people and groups on a wide social map. A yearly argument about trash at the center illustrates the difference between Ned's relation to the Park neighborhood and the more typical vision in the Cluster.

I learned that every spring, Ned would complain that the neighborhood center was messy. My first spring, Ned told us that a group of residents said they wanted more garbage cans. Patricia responded that she did not know of any such group, but did recall a tutor (someone from outside the neighborhood) at the center telling her that the center was too messy. The issue mattered to Ned, because "We're teaching: That's the way it looks—that's the way it *should* look. The center needs to be a haven of goodliness and Godliness." Paula laughed, recalling that they "got in trouble for bringing this up last year"; Ned frowned. After a short exchange about city trash pickup schedules, Betty tossed in that she wondered if some kids who committed themselves to doing one hundred hours of community service couldn't do some trash pickup. But Ned didn't like the spirit of the idea. "Taking care of yourself and your community shouldn't be punishment." Betty disagreed, saying it would not be punishment.

Ned meant that it shouldn't be community service. "They should do it because they want to, he said."

Betty agreed. "That would be nice but that's not how things are."

Ned said, "I just wish it came more from *within*."

Betty, in a sarcastic riposte, replied, "They *are* within." She was referring to kids within the neighborhood.

The meeting ended but the discussion wasn't over. Patricia kept talking to Betty about it, saying that the approach to the center should be along these lines: "How can we assist you?" I flagged down Ned—who had brought a hammer to the meeting and was walking over to adjust the hinges on the new pantry door— and asked what he was going to do next. He told me plainly that he would talk to the neighborhood center director. I was confused, since Patricia already volunteered to do that. "So, is it 'the more the merrier,' and you both talk to her?" Ned sounded disgruntled: "Yeah, sure." I was recorder for this month; I needed to record followup actions for the meeting minutes. This matter of cleanliness and Godliness intrigued me, too. I caught up with Patricia on her way out the door.

> PL: I talked to Ned; he says you're both going to talk to the center direc-
> tor—about the center grounds.
> PATRICIA (*looking frustrated*): Then I should talk to Ned. We shouldn't
> both do it, that would be redundant. . . . He's associated with last year's
> effort to bring it up.
> PL: What's the issue?

Patricia peered back over her shoulder, lowered her voice a bit, and told me that "it's one thing if it's a topic already at a [center] board meeting, but otherwise it looks like imposing this outside standard." She did not like that.

Patricia stated the Cluster's sense of partnership well: She could be happy to support local residents' sense of standards, but would not want to impose outsiders' customs, especially in the absence of any discussion with neighborhood people. She tried to respect local ways of doing things, rather than presume that outside standards apply universally, with a divine imprimatur.

Differences in tastes or behavior may look like purely interpersonal issues when the differences emerge in face-to-face interaction over a meal or beside an overflowing trash bin. I am arguing, though, that the Cluster tried to approach interpersonal relations with the sense that they were one group, an outsider group, in a diverse and socially subordinated neighborhood—not helpers who were sure about who needed helping and why. Patricia did not say she was worried about offending the neighborhood center director as a person. She was afraid of dishonoring the neighborhood.

BRIDGING AND SOCIAL REFLEXIVITY

If we think of people in civic groups creating ties and building social capital, we might picture a person who joins a club and makes a new friend of whom she can ask a favor in three weeks. That kind of tie is easy to see. But not all social ties are so concrete. Bridging ties that the Cluster wanted to create required *imagination.* Members had to imagine, talk about, how they related to the world beyond the group. Who exactly was out there? What were they like? To which groups should we relate, and how? The Cluster had to allow itself space for imagining aloud.

Partnership as I have pictured it already became the dominant, routine mode of the Cluster soon after the crisis meeting, at the time the parish nurse was making her rounds. Partnership made customary a sense of place on a dense social map, a sense of group responsibility for the sake of outside groups, and a speech style that valued discussion apart from reporting. These customs welcomed, or at least did not short-circuit, some kinds of social reflexivity. Reflexivity could turn the Cluster's service projects into relationships *with* the neighborhood, instead of administration *of* the neighborhood by outsiders. The Cluster's customs also limited some kinds of social reflexivity, as I will picture later.

One way the Cluster created ties to the neighborhood was by supporting public goods from which the whole neighborhood could benefit. Sponsoring a public good requires imagining a tie to a neighborhood of people who benefit from the good. That does not mean the tie was not real; real people benefited from the services of a nurse supported by the Cluster, for instance. But there are different ways to define a public good; they are not self-evident. Park Cluster reflected a great deal on how these goods represented relations between the Cluster and Park as a diverse, low-income neighborhood.

The Parish Nurse: Imagining Relationships

The parish nurse program was the public good I heard the Cluster planning most. There are different ways the Cluster could have related to the nurse. They could have sought out heartwarming stories of interpersonal relating: sick people of little means responding to a caring nurse's ministrations. Stories of privation and gratitude were what church congregations heard when the Cluster sent teams to promote its programs to potential church sponsors. Cluster members and church audiences alike found those stories powerful, compelling. Or they could have left all the planning to others, and worked hard on fund-raisers for her salary. Funding the nurse was an ongoing worry for the Cluster. But they defined her in different terms.

Once the nurse was hired, the Cluster talked a lot on her accessibility, the breadth of her outreach, the character of her clients. In other words, the Cluster tried to imagine the diverse neighborhood she was serving, inferring needs from what she told them. In their imagination, the nurse was another tie to the neighborhood as a whole. The first time the nurse offered figures on her visits, for instance, Connie asked whether there was not a large Asian population in the neighborhood; were the Hmong neighbors getting attention along with the African American contacts the nurse had made so far? Another member wanted to know what all the professional acronyms stood for in the nurse's report. Cluster members did not talk about individual clients, even pseudonymously. Questions aside, the Cluster was happy to sponsor a nurse who was "community" based, responsible to a local community, rather than an instrument of a particular church's outreach program.

> STEVEN (*affirmingly*): The typical nurse program would be referrals by clergy. There are none here [*peering over the nurse's report*]. That shows this is a different effort.
>
> BETTY: Well, not many people here are represented by clergy.
>
> STEVEN (*agreeing*): No. And that shows this is a *community* program.

Cluster members also wanted the nurse program to make imagined ties more concrete for individuals. The vision would be slow to materialize. Two Cluster members asked if the nurse had initiated "care teams" of church volunteers. Care teams might drive the nurse's clients to a hospital; they might take care of kids during parents' appointments; they might help the nurse get a file cabinet for her bedroom-sized office or a cell phone for her car. But the nurse needed to put the care team idea in perspective: "Let me explain. I've been a parish nurse for two years at New Jerusalem Baptist, and I still don't have a team. . . . You determine needs first. Then you get a team." Connie responded, tying the Cluster's eagerness for care teams back to its larger goals: "One of the issues since I've been here is how to get people in our congregations involved in the community." Care teams got initiated just at the end of my time with the Cluster.

The Eviction Prevention Fund: Imagining Relationships

The eviction prevention fund is another example of a public good, a limited one, that the Cluster shared with the Park neighborhood as a whole. Kendra told me that the eviction prevention fund was her idea, that she got from talking to Park residents.[6] They had said "people move too much" for a stable sense of community to develop in the neighborhood. From her perspective the fund was a service administered to individuals more than a means to building bridges.

Other Cluster members, including two black pastors, saw the fund differently. Both Kendra and Cluster members took the two pastors as representatives of the neighborhood's point of view.[7] The differences between their viewpoint and Kendra's made sparks fly when, several months after the crisis meeting, the Cluster considered whether or not people who received money from the fund should be asked to give something back. Given the number of items already on the agenda that day, the lengthy discussion showed that this touched on basic issues.

It is worth following the debate, to hear how the Cluster's desire to relate to the neighborhood on its own terms at least sometimes could override the administrative language of a governmental agency. Kendra was skeptical about the payback. It was unrealistic. She pictured what it might be like to require that beneficiaries give something back. She described some of her clients in the neighborhood. "They're dealing with drug addiction. They're working every day, they're raising kids. I think these are real issues—"

Reverend Brice cut in: "I'm very interested in the core issues that perpetuate people being in a cycle of eviction. I think you have to look at it as a total cycle. In many places God has put me in the place of putting myself out of a job. We want whole people. . . . What are the core issues keeping people [in the cycle]?" At the same time he insisted that the beneficiaries do something in return, however seemingly small. And he pictured himself asking a beneficiary to "give something back" by talking about his experiences being evicted, or by giving back *something, anything:* "'Talk to me.' Now Nancy will tell you I'm a little crazy—"

Nancy grinned and shook her head: "You can say that again!"

"—'So [*back to the imaginary conversation with a beneficiary*] give me a dime. Give me a quarter.' Do I need the dime? No, but just *something.*" Or, he suggested, ask the person to talk about the near-eviction experience with other neighbors. And he closed with his larger concern: "We *have* to look at the core issues, around the mulberry bush; what are the issues keeping people in this cycle."

Kendra still wasn't convinced it was a good thing to ask beneficiaries to give something back. She gave us more glimpses of hard living. "One woman we've helped has volunteered a lot in this community. She volunteered at the Christmas party. Is this someone I'm going to ask—I mean, this isn't, 'Kendra, I got in a fight with the boss and lost my job.' This is domestic violence, this is crack addiction. . . . Another woman, huge legal fines, from age sixteen, she has two kids. . . . she's very involved in her kids' lives. Would *we* have time [to give something back]? No! A letter for her would make her feel good about herself [though]. . . . I see people going to parenting enhancement [classes] as building community." People living hard lives and managing to make do were taking responsibility enough.

Reverend Michael asked, "Can you mention, 'these are some of the people who we have helped, and have done some of these things in return'? So to say you gave them an opportunity to give back. So we've opened the door, welcomed them to give."

Kendra responded that she thought this would be "formalizing a lot of what happens already," but she wasn't against the idea.

Reverend Michael continued on the reciprocation theme. "That in itself makes a statement of helping empower people. Otherwise they become dependent. And it's just a handout. Now, I agree with Reverend Brice that we need to look at the cycle that's causing this."

Seeing the group unpersuaded by Kendra's appeal, Kendra's student intern mounted one last defense. She was impressed at "how Kendra puts an enormous amount of time into the work. And she puts the individual at the helm." The

Cluster needed to be respectful of Kendra's training, she urged. And more, "We need to respect the privacy of people's lives." The Cluster might send a letter inviting beneficiaries to "give back," but the initiative to do so would have to "come from inside themselves." The intern gave a testimonial to professional expertise and personal privacy—guiding values of state-sponsored social service. Cluster members' response highlighted their relation with Park residents; they wanted to keep alive their *imagination* of that relationship. The URC liaison said that beneficiaries could get a letter naming the supporting congregations, because "it's important for individuals to know that they have the backing—that faith communities care about them."

The imagined tie was very real to Cluster members, and real in its consequences for action. The Cluster talked about the fund as an opportunity to institute a connection between the congregations and the neighborhood, rather than as a program to serve as many (anonymous) individuals as efficiently as possible. Cluster members hoped Park residents could share in administering the fund, so that it would be an instrument of community empowerment rather than administration from outside. The eviction prevention fund and the parish nurse program both illustrate how social reflexivity made the difference between the Cluster's notion of bridge-building and a different kind of relationship defined by individual service.

Reflexivity Reveals, and Creates, Group Conflict

Social reflexivity was a means to building the bridges that most Cluster members envisioned, but that did not make it a *harmonious* experience for them. The Cluster had gotten off to a bad start with the new neighborhood center director, Charmaine, during her first year. Discussing the Cluster's expanding sense of mission, Dora pointed out a pink elephant in the room:

"When we bring Charmaine in here, I think there are some prejudices—and there needs to be healing. Charmaine said [at the last meeting] that she didn't understand us, and we don't understand her. And I think there needs to be healing."

Ned came forth bravely: "I admit I've been the major bad guy—"

Dora protested, "No, no—"

Ned continued: "—No, no listen. I tend to say things a certain way, that's how I am. And I'll make a studious effort to avoid that in the future." Everyone paid rapt attention to the duo.

When people give themselves the license to talk about about relationships, they may give expression to conflicts or embarrassing prejudices. In contrast, when members of Adopt-a-Family pointed toward frustrations that they could not explore at length in racial terms, they did not consider aloud that they might be bringing their own prejudices to the relationship.

Practicing reflexivity could also create tensions that would not have arisen if members' role was to take direction from social service professionals. Family

Friends social worker Kendra's opinion about the eviction prevention fund was not just different from the Cluster's and the pastor's; she *disagreed*. The Cluster stuck to its own opinion, emboldened by the black pastor who spoke for the neighborhood. The conversation was long and tense; several other items on the agenda needed to wait until the next month's meeting. If the Cluster had been less concerned with defining the fund as a vehicle for relating to Park, and more focused on raising money for the fund, they would not have collided with Kendra.

Conversations with the parish nurse could be tense, too. "Let me explain," she tried to tell the Cluster authoritatively: "You determine needs first." Experts determine needs; Cluster members were not healthcare experts. Connie had responded with her vision of churches working with the Park neighborhood. It was a clash of visions, unnecessary if the point were to support expertise with efficiency. Practicing social reflexivity may build bridges in the long run, but it does not necessarily build consensus in the short term. It did not make everyone happy inside the Cluster either.

AVOIDING AND CHALLENGING SOCIAL REFLEXIVITY: VOLUNTEERS WOULD RATHER GET THINGS DONE

Cluster members worried that the nurse might neglect part of the diverse Park neighborhood. So when the nurse told the Cluster that she would use "culturally appropriate" techniques, Cluster members asked the nurse, an African American woman, how she would increase the number of Laotian or Spanish-speaking residents in her consultations. Serving as many individuals as possible was not the sole vision. They needed to *talk* it through: how would the nurse's culturally appropriate techniques advance a partnership with a multiracial neighborhood?

Nancy, the nurse's official liaison to the Cluster, did not join in these group conversations about the nurse. I noticed her absence from the discussions because she *was* the liaison. I recalled Nancy telling me earlier that the nurse project appealed to her because she herself had been a nurse and could appreciate one-to-one caring. Nancy herself assisted the nurse selflessly. She made the nurse a large loan out of her own pocket so the nurse could attend a training workshop on breast cancer. Nancy, like Ned, interpreted the nurse's role with the help of a different social map than the one now dominant in the Cluster. A nurse could care for people; what was there so much to talk about?

Ned was more actively antagonistic to all the pondering of relationships and constituencies. He saw the whole parish nurse project as the latest big distraction from the group's proper role as church-based volunteers. He offered his own view during monthly discussions of the new nurse program, disagreeing openly with Betty:

Ned excused himself for talking bluntly, and said, "My vision in the early days was a couple of people coming and meeting and helpin' out." He wanted a plain-folks, "helpin' out" approach, not a complicated picture of the Cluster's mission in the civic arena. "And for me it's become way too mechanical. I don't think the [Park neighborhood] center had a vision back then, it just existed. . . . Now I find ourselves at counterpurposes with the center. And that's OK. . . . At this point, I'd just as soon step back and let the center tell me what it needs. I question the need for this group [the Cluster]."

Betty responded, "Well, it's *not* ok with me if we're working at cross-purposes with the center." For Ned, the extensive talking only made the group "mechanical." Why could it not go out and do things? All the complicated talk about organizing the nurse program in accord with the neighborhood's own standards and preferences violated the can-do customs of individual, charitable volunteering. To Ned, it should not have *mattered* that the neighborhood center had a new director with an Afrocentric vision. There were tasks to carry out, people to care for. Not for the last time, Ned suggested that the group itself shut down entirely. Had the group done so, individual members might have continued volunteering, doing good works in the neighborhood, without all the talk, but there would have been no vehicle for community development.

Ned challenged the partnership approach again, four months after the crisis meeting. A member cautioned at one meeting that the Cluster should distinguish between "the vision of Family Friends [county social service agency]" and "the vision of the neighborhood center." While the Cluster welcomed, depended on, the county social worker's updates and suggestions, it was unwilling to let Family Friends simply represent neighborhood people. The ensuing exchange between Ned and Steven is very telling on this point:

Steven said that the Cluster should be clear on whether a Cluster project involves being "a partner to Family Friends or to the neighborhood center."

NED: Supporting Family Friends *is* supporting the neighborhood. I can't imagine it being otherwise—
STEVEN (*carefully insistent*): Well, there have been issues—
NED: *Oh* (*dismissive*), I'm a trouble-maker, and I don't—that's not—
STEVEN (*cautioning, rising tone*): There have been questions raised—
NED (*declarative*): That's not what we're here about.

"What we're here about," for Ned, was not to think through, ask questions about complicated relationships beyond the group. The point of a church-based volunteer alliance was to serve individuals, in ways defined by authorities-that-be. There were more pressing things to do than worry about whether good works promote one agenda at the expense of others.

Several months later still, the Cluster had become deeply involved in another long-brewing project, a planning and fund-raising campaign to support a new neighborhood center. Unprompted, Ned asked me why Park Cluster was spending so much time on the community center and getting tied up with other groups when there were more concrete needs. Some kids often missed the morning school bus, for instance, because their parents neglected to wake them up in time. He thought Cluster volunteers should go knocking on doors in the morning, to make sure those households were getting the kids ready. Pooling church and community resources to sponsor public goods like a community center made less sense to Ned than addressing the needs of separate individuals and families.

Ned's annoyance with the continuous mechanical talk about relationships came not from any animus toward hard work, but from a different set of customary understandings that were more dominant earlier in the Cluster's history. They made social reflexivity seem like a wasteful luxury. For Ned, the question was much less about how a church group could imagine relationships with a neighborhood as a whole, and much more about what charitable volunteers from churches could do to meet needs. The needs were obvious. Ned brought a hammer to Cluster meetings so that he could fix the broken door to the new kitchen he had helped build in the neighborhood center. That did not require a lot of reflexive imagination. He had built the wooden shelves for the food pantry there, too. A pantry needed shelves; it was obvious. Ned was not excited about a larger community center, but most other Cluster members were. The Cluster was spending more and more meeting time discussing where the center might get built, who might fund it. A new woman with real estate experience and ties to potential funders began going to meetings; members received her warmly. Ned was skeptical. He said he would probably quit the Cluster soon and sign up to volunteer directly with Family Friends—an effective social service agency that knew what it was doing, as he put it. Other Cluster members could not have contemplated such a move without threatening their definition of what it meant to be a church-based alliance.

How the Spiral Kept Uncoiling

The Cluster's vision depended not only on imagining partnerships aloud, but on having potential partners. Without them, Ned's skepticism about the entire enterprise would make only more sense. Repeatedly, members said at meetings how much they wanted to bridge their distance from Park neighbors. Some members continued tutoring Park children or volunteering at the center, and some had casual, chatting relationships with center staffers. They kept alive a broader bridge-building vision at the same time. On the map of partnership, the Cluster's position was more and more troubling. They seemed to be barreling on ahead without a clear mandate from neighborhood leaders; that would make them interlopers, people from white, mostly middle-class churches dictating to the neighborhood—which they very much did not want. For instance, Steven admitted he felt queasy about the Cluster because its meetings did not pull in regular attendees from the neighborhood. Typical was the following exchange:

> STEVEN: I would like to see more people that we work with, around the table. . . . We need to make sure we include them in the discussion process.
>
> BETTY (*agreeing*): I don't think there's a meeting gone by that we haven't said our mission is not met until we have people from the neighborhood around the table.

She added pointedly that we should also "talk about 'our neighbors in the community' rather than our 'clients.'" Others nodded and murmured agreement. In other words no one assumed, the way the "two moms" had, that individual good intentions were enough to make outsiders legitimate in the neighborhood.

The Cluster had made its way for several years without any clear leadership from the neighborhood center that hosted its meetings and without any forums for opinion in the neighborhood. Taking on more responsibility made them more and more uneasy about the politics of their presence. As Martha said: "We can talk and talk about what we are, but we need to know what *they* think." The Cluster's very existence as a partner, rather than a "conduit for volunteers," would make a lot less sense without other partners: Its definition of its own group bonds—cohesion for the sake of outside responsibilities—would seem pointless, far more work and talk than necessary. Neither would there be much reason to take verbal ownership of a group that did not need to exist in its present form. And there would be little reason for the Cluster to distinguish between Park neighborhood entities on its social map, instead of helping out people in general.

Without the other partner, partnership risked becoming paternalism. A few months after the crisis meeting, the Cluster's raison d'être received formal affirmation: Ken passed along a letter of welcome from the neighborhood center director. It invited the Cluster to send representatives to the neighborhood's Resident Forum and the center's steering committee—two new kinds of ties outward. Now the Cluster could have official relationships with neighborhood collectivities besides the Family Friends agency. If the Cluster had stuck with carrying out predefined tasks, helping out the Family Friends agency as Ned preferred, it would have had little reason to care if the neighborhood center recognized the Cluster or not as long as Family Friends did. But this was good news for everyone. For Ned, it meant some direction, finally. For others, the official welcome made partnership legitimate, reinforcing the group's new sense of itself.

The Cluster had come to regard itself as a group that created new civic relationships, and it was getting a public reputation for that too. It had not started out that way three years earlier, and would not stay that way without the kind of communication that annoyed Ned. Toward the end of my time in the field, the Cluster got involved in local school politics on behalf of the Park neighborhood. It also joined other civic groups and businesses in the project to build a new community center that could host more after-school programs than the cramped, former apartment that served as Park's meeting place until then. The spiral kept uncoiling, and the Cluster developed new relationships with people and groups—the Lutheran Home, the local school board, a school district administrator, and others—whom Cluster members had not originally imagined relating to when the Cluster was more a loose, ad hoc gathering of volunteers.

The Tradeoffs of Partnership

John Dewey suggested that reflexivity itself might become customary. His vision of a densely connected, democratic public depends on citizens who make critical discovery habitual. But if social reflexivity is a group experience, it has to happen in some group setting. As long as people are in groups, they practice social reflexivity through customs that keep the group going as they are talking. All customs set limits, or else groups cannot be groups. And much as the boundaries, bonds, and speech norms of partnership were congenial to some remarkably self-critical discussion, they also ruled certain kinds of social relationships outside the bounds of critical reflection altogether.

Trading on Essentialism

Partnership sometimes came at the expense of sensitivity to differences inside partnering groups. Sometimes the Cluster imagined Park in monochrome terms, even when it knew better other times. Discussions showed that the Cluster members knew Park was home to Hmong, Vietnamese, Spanish-speaking Central Americans, African Americans, and a few Euro-Americans. But the neighborhood center director and local church pastors defined "the community" for the Cluster in authoritative terms, and these leaders spoke for a community they designated as African American. They spoke as African Americans themselves, too. It would have made at least as much sense, theoretically, for them to speak on behalf of a "low-income community," or a "people of color" community, or an "oppressed community." But African American identity defined the contours of pride, and prejudice, in the Cluster-neighborhood relationship. As a group committed to partnership, the Cluster was not in a good place to question the identity of the partner.

For instance, Cluster members were happy when an African American pastor, Reverend Brice, took charge of organizing a goals-defining workshop for the group. Reverend Brice did not live or work in the neighborhood. He pastored a largely white Methodist congregation in a middle-class neighborhood across town. Yet his black identity made him, to Cluster members, a valuable representative of "the community," even as they tried to learn more about the Park neighborhood on the neighbors' own terms. Cluster members were assuming that African Americans shared the same sense of the world when it came to issues that might concern the Cluster. And black identity would give one privileged entrée to the neighborhood's needs and aspirations, whether or not one had much experience in the neighborhood. Another African American pastor snapped at a *white* Park resident who asked, at one meeting, if he lived in the neighborhood. He did not, but he said he knew the neighborhood well.

The Cluster hastened to credit the new parish nurse with the same intuition, even as members wondered aloud about the welfare of nonblack people in the neighborhood. At one meeting, Cluster members found out that almost all the nurse's consultations the month before had been with African Americans. When Connie asked whether there were not Asians as well as African Americans in Park neighborhood, the liaison from the URC told the recorder to put in the meeting minutes, "looking forward to more racial diversity." The liaison quickly added, "Of course, she has a *special* facility with African Americans." Martha agreed. No one else took up the issue. Racial identity could stop conversation as quickly as claims about "interest" or "different cultures" in other Lakeburg groups. And several months later, the Cluster's parish nurse coordinator Nancy reported that the neighborhood center director "is very pleased with Rebecca's [the nurse] work here. Rebecca fills a niche that hasn't been filled before. She's relating to people really well." I glanced at Nancy's neatly handwritten notes and noticed that the top line read, "crucial to have African American," though Nancy did not broach the race topic when she spoke to us. Rebecca had no such reticence and told us, "I know that the director wants an African American parish nurse." Even if the Park population identified predominantly as African Americans, it is realistic to ask if southeast Asian immigrants would enjoy the same degree of rapport with an African American nurse.

It would be unfair to criticize the Cluster for conjuring up a black Park neighborhood out of nothing. They knew better. But group customs did not always let Cluster members say everything they knew, any more than could Adopt-a-Family volunteers or people in the other Lakeburg groups. The Cluster took its cue from African American pastors and neighborhood center staff who attended Cluster meetings and spoke as representatives of black opinion. Reverend Michael, for instance, had relayed the collective (black) opinion about the busy mom meals. Reverend Brice offered to help the Cluster find out what Park residents really wanted from the Cluster, by hanging out on street corners and talking to people. He assumed, and the Cluster granted the assumption, that he would have a ready rapport with (black) residents, and told me in an interview that black Park neighbors did open up to him about their lives.[8]

The neighborhood center director, Charmaine, made her race-based rapport with the neighborhood even more explicit. She declared that her black identity gave her a more appropriate perspective on Park than Cluster members could have. During one of the Cluster's long-range planning meetings, members invited Charmaine to share her own view of the Cluster's mission. What did she think the Cluster *was* doing, and *should* be doing, in Park neighborhood?

> CHARMAINE: I had the perception of a lot of people who wanted to do a lot of good things. . . . I felt that as an African American, I feel there were things that could be done differently that could expand significantly— to include residents—so that whatever you do would enhance what is here, rather than mold it. . . . I feel the Cluster came in with an idea of how things ought to be here, and I didn't feel comfortable about that.
>
> DORA (*with quiet satisfaction*): Thank you. That's the tension that I thought was there.

Members listened respectfully; they wanted to know how they could define goals that would complement rather than compete with Charmaine's. In that spirit, Betty offered that Charmaine had "a real connection" to the people of Park.

> CHARMAINE (*responding matter-of-factly*): I have a unique connection to the people here.
>
> BETTY (*solicitously*): You do—I can see that. This is something you can do that we can't. Now, is there something we can do that you can't?
>
> CHARMAINE: You can involve people when we need to help residents support the community.

Charmaine was essentializing her black identity, along with the identity of the multiracial Park neighborhood. Doing so, she cut short any open-ended conversation about different groups in the neighborhood and how they related to each other. She was African American, and therefore knew best; white volunteers could help out. The Cluster was in an extremely difficult bind, of the sort that social servants or volunteers were freer to sidestep. Opinion circulated in the neighborhood that Charmaine could be arbitrary, dictatorial, in some ways willfully aloof from the everyday flow of the neighborhood center. Not only (white) Family Friends social workers and school district personnel but some African American Park residents thought so, too. Yet Cluster members could hardly claim that a neighborhood center director who spoke as an African American was *less* in tune with the residents of a multiracial neighborhood than white "church people" from a different part of town. If the Cluster had long-established relations with Park neighborhood groups, it might have tried encouraging Park residents to sort through their multiple identifications—as people of color, as low-income people, as Christians, as Lakeburgers—so they could have more open-minded conversations about the collective good (Lichterman 1999). It would take a great deal of legitimacy and trust to make such a move. The Cluster's presence was provocative enough. Still, partnership by itself did not give the Cluster grounds for questioning essentialism; African Americans were valued partners.

Narrowing Critical Vision

The Cluster had an ambivalent relation to political issues. Partnership did not keep the group from having political conversations. But as *partners,* rather than social critics, they created relationships on a social map that distinguished civic groups, state agencies, and an occasional business enterprise, without casting any as "them" opposed to "us." That made the Cluster open to relationships that would have threatened group solidarity in the Justice Task Force. On the other hand, it kept the Cluster from acknowledging the limits of their own projects.

Political discussion was by no means out of bounds. At one meeting, the food pantry liaison told us that new federal legislation would reduce from thirty-three to five the number of pantries distributing federally subsidized food in the county. Indignant "tsks" sputtered around the table. The group treated this news as a springboard to commentary, criticism, and some on-the-spot learning.

> Paula noted somewhat wryly that having a variety of local food pantries was "the best way to get indicators of stress on families in the county, especially with the [end of] AFDC." Food pantries were one of the only ways to document family needs.
>
> "What is the political meaning of this change?" Judy asked. "Are they just doing what they want to do?"
>
> Paula described the "political motives" as part of an overall plan to cut food stamps and save the government $26 billion. She said the impetus was "we'll get rid of people who abuse the system, and when they *need* [*emphasis hers*] help, they can go to the local pantry." She mused ironically on policy makers' reliance on pantries as a source of information about how welfare reform was working. "When they instituted welfare reform, they were coming to the pantries and saying 'What do you see?' . . . So they can report the reduction in numbers [now] without seeing the other side."

At another meeting, a report on a fund-raising event quickly became grist for political commentary at the same time that Cluster members were speaking up for Park neighborhood's well-being. The event was supposed to raise money for a neighborhood community center, and members were disappointed that few "neighborhood people" went.

> KENDRA: The mayor said, to my face, "Eh, they don't vote, so why should I put money there?"
> BETTY (*dripping irony*): *That's* an interesting statement.

Paula agreed with Ken that it looked bad if the neighborhood residents did not go to a fund raiser arranged on their behalf.

BETTY: Isn't it a threat to go to these—with the mayor?
STEVEN: Why? The mayor wears pants, just like everyone else!
MARTHA: That's not what I meant. A threat for people who weren't there, that the mayor was there.

Martha thought it would be intimidating, in other words, but others were not convinced, and Paula said the problem was more "the way the event was organized."

MARY: I was the only "community person" there. And it was a command performance! I was told to be there.

Some members occasionally criticized big business, too. Before one meeting began, conversation broke out about three referendums that local voters had weighed in on the day before. Each concerned tax increases for public schools, including a new school that might serve Park children. Steven said that some people voted for two but not all three. I puzzled over people who would vote that way: "A neighbor of mine said she voted against the third referendum— that's the spending cap?—because she didn't like that kind of [suburban, high-end] residential development in that area."

Steven laughed sardonically and said that then she should have opposed the county plans that made development possible to begin with. "Once you have the neighborhood, you're going to have kids who need to get educated."

"Her thinking was that the developers should get the money some other way, maybe have a special tax for people living there," I said

Betty replied wryly. "When in the world has that ever happened?" She thought people in upscale suburban developments get to benefit from new public schools that everyone has to pay for through taxes.

I said I thought it was similar to when developers promise to provide utilities and services for a newly built subdivision, as a condition of getting approval to develop land.

Steven noted ironically: "They *say* they are going to pay."

Their customs did not require the tunnel vision that some researchers have found in volunteer groups (Bellah et al. 1985; Eliasoph 1998; Wuthnow 1991; Ostrander 1984).

At the same time, I did not hear Cluster members discussing how larger social forces limited their own civic projects. This would have been talk about relationships beyond the group—social reflexivity—too. Entertaining that kind of conversation seemed beyond the bounds in the Cluster. One of the black pastors attending the group told me in an interview that the Cluster should have been able to put together far more money for an eviction prevention fund if it was serious about helping residents stabilize themselves. He never ventured the criticism in the group. Cluster members talked appreciatively about all its churches' contributions no matter the size. It was the same kind of appreciation people express for anyone who gives time or money freely. A more critical view might have intimidated some members or their churches, threatening the group bonds. It might have turned partnership into something more like partisanship—with the stronger sense of sacrifice for the cause that the word implies. This observation does not invalidate the ties that the Cluster spiraled outward. It is to note that these ties had customary meanings and were circumscribed by those meanings just like all the other ties.

Did group customs squeeze out this kind of criticism, or was it that members just had not thought of it, or were too busy with other things? A black pastor's angry words at one meeting support my view on the limits in the customs. Speaking as a representative of Park residents in general, the pastor pointed out that their apartments were not necessarily worth keeping.[9] The implication was clear: An eviction prevention fund, at very best, helped several families every month to retain apartments that, in the pastor's description, had extremely high rents, rotted carpeting, broken appliances, doors that would not close, and smelled bad to boot. Neighborhood center director Charmaine nodded her head knowingly. I heard Dora *whisper,* to no one in particular, that the real answer would take a "political" group. She said something similar to me in an interview, while honoring the parish nurse and other projects as worthwhile.

The pastor's comments could have been a remarkable invitation to reflect on the Cluster's mission. Cluster members listened closely, but did not take them that way. They did not argue with the pastor. At least some may have agreed wholeheartedly; one cannot know from the meeting because people took his comments as an interesting or even valuable perspective, a chastening exercise in sharing. People did not discuss them further at that meeting, nor at the three other monthly meetings I attended before saying goodbye to the group.

Seeing Cluster members at other URC-sponsored groups, I knew that at least some thought Lakeburg needed more affordable housing, not just more doleouts. Dora and Mary supported affordable housing at the URC's annual social issues convocation nearly a year earlier. Partnership did not *require* them to express a social-structural critique of housing opportunities in order to be respectable members of the Cluster. They did not have to fear looking like mere meliorists as they would have in the Justice Task Force. But partnership did not give them much of a place to raise those criticisms at length and relate them back to the Cluster's projects, either. Partnership did not mean closing down a critical stance toward local politics or federal policy. It did not mean defining allies and adversaries of the group, either. Partnership customs, like the others we have heard and watched, produced particular goods, the tangible and symbolic goods that very modest community development projects offer, while other goods remained off the map.

The relationships and the civic presence that the Cluster created slowly, painfully, through partnership also enabled it to pursue a contentious political issue on behalf of the neighborhood. The Cluster's experience strengthens my argument that if we want to understand the social spiral, we must focus on communication, not only on the connections that we tally up as social capital.

WHY BOTHER WITH TALK WHEN THERE IS A CAMPAIGN TO WIN?

"Speaking For" or "Standing With"?

Toward the end of my study the Cluster got involved in school politics. Park had over three hundred elementary-school-aged kids and no elementary school within walking distance. Park children took buses to three elementary schools. Some neighborhood leaders and some Park parents thought the school board should build a new elementary school in the neighborhood. They said that busing Park kids to three different schools weakened any potential for neighborhood cohesion, making it difficult for Park kids to develop friendships. Some parents complained that with their kids bused to schools so far away, it was difficult to make appointments with teachers or pick up sick kids from school. Not all Park neighbors agreed. Some Park parents had said they would feel better knowing that while they were at work, their kids were outside a neighborhood the parents considered unhealthy, maybe dangerous.

The following scenarios from the Cluster's sortie into school politics illustrate the difference between open, reflective talk about relationships outside the group and strategic advocacy that assumes that those relationships are obvious and do not need discussing. A URC leader affiliated with the Cluster tried, with the best intentions, to make the Cluster advocate for the Park neighborhood, assuming the neighborhood's interests were obvious. As a result, the Cluster risked marginalizing itself in the Park neighborhood and losing what confidence Charmaine put in the Cluster. Reflexivity is not just a distraction from effective advocacy; sometimes it may be a necessity.

The Cluster wanted to address the schooling issue in a way that might advance the good of the neighborhood. Looking out for a diverse neighborhood as a whole would be no easy thing. Betty's response to the URC liaison's call for action illustrates the quandaries:

> "This school issue is a beautiful example of how it's nice to say we want what the neighbors want. But if you've always lived in an apartment house, and someone else has always controlled where your kids go to school, you would not have the vision to know what it's like for your kids to all go to the same school. We can say we want what the neighborhood wants, but can people [have the vision]?"

It was a daring thing to say. Most Cluster members had made clear by now that they did not want to be like the volunteers that ethnographers love to hate.[10] They did not want to tell the neighborhood what to do for its own good. But

Betty wanted to figure out how the Cluster might act responsibly. It was a beautiful example of the difficulty in imagining respectful partnering, let alone carrying it out.

Instead of pushing a specific policy, the Cluster advocated that neighborhood residents should have more of a voice in the school district's planning. It organized a forum with school board officials so that residents could get a hearing. It also instituted an agreement that school board members would meet periodically in the neighborhood.

The URC leader who went to Cluster meetings saw the school issue in much more conclusive terms. She was convinced that a new school in the Park neighborhood was the best option. Her well-intended strategizing antagonized neighborhood center director Charmaine and threatened to strain newly emerging relations between the Cluster and the center. During one meeting, the URC leader remarked casually that "we had hoped the students would all be united into one school." Charmaine wanted to know who the "we" was, and pointed out that the URC leader was assuming she knew what Park neighbors wanted. The URC leader pointed out in turn that some Park residents had signed a petition against the three schools arrangement. Charmaine retorted crisply,

> "You keep saying you want residents' input. . . . You must stand with them or stand behind them." Frustration in her voice, the director charged that the URC director—and by implication, the Cluster—was still trying to speak for the residents. As for the petition, "that was last August, that was back then. . . . We have to hear them [the residents] now."

Charmaine charged the liaison with *speaking for* the neighborhood instead of *standing with* it—even though the director was advocating the most far-reaching, most politically radical change on the neighborhood's behalf, the option that could easily appear to be the most empowering for the neighborhood.

Cluster members went up and down the streets of the Park neighborhood, urging residents to attend the forum school board members had agreed to hold. At last, I thought, the school board might hear from residents themselves that busing children from the same apartment building to three different schools would only fragment any chance for cooperative ties between parents in the neighborhood. I was surprised at what people said at the forum.

Exactly one person spoke up, indirectly at that, for building a new school in the neighborhood. When two Cluster members asked people at a month's worth of weekly Resident Forums to share their experiences with Lakeburg schools, they found that "some want a school located in the Park area, and others, especially Asians, do not."[11] Yet the URC leader assumed she spoke for the neighborhood's best interests by advocating for a new Park school, not just more decent transportation to other schools. So it was not hard to understand Charmaine's perspective: The URC leader was speaking for residents and filling in their opinions for them.

Advocacy without Reflexivity

It was not hard to understand the URC leader's perspective, either—one seasoned with years of experience as a school board member. The board was poised to take up the busing plan. There would not be enough time to talk about how the Cluster should interpret neighborhood opinion. Should the neighborhood risk more years of fragmentation? The URC leader took another set of risks instead: She assumed the Cluster could speak for an unambiguous neighborhood interest. Yet, as long as Park residents were known to disagree on a political issue, any advocate from outside the neighborhood, no matter how well-meaning, could appear to misappropriate legitimacy, to speak for residents instead of standing behind them. The conduits for communicating opinion about neighborhood issues were just coming into being during this study, with the new Resident Forum. The URC director in effect had bypassed the Park neighborhood's newly developing public forum.

Outspoken people in the neighborhood did not agree on how to define the issues. Charmaine thought race relations were inescapably part of Park children's experiences with schooling. In stark contrast, Xena, a vocal resident active at the neighborhood center, told the school board to stop seeing school issues in "black and white" (racial) terms. In their own ways, both Charmaine and Xena wanted to be listened to by outsiders, not second-guessed. Both wanted outside people to engage with their neighborhood as a collectivity, even if they pictured that collectivity differently. Both wanted outsiders to put time and attentiveness into their relationships with the neighborhood. Both found fault with well-meaning advocates.

Xena told me during an interview that she thought the Cluster was still trying to do things for Park, even when it meant to be helpful.[12] "We need the people. We need the expertise. We need the money. But they need to *listen* to us. . . . We're so used to people coming in and saying 'we want to help you'. . . . It's about money, but it's about time. . . . I feel like we can do things if we have people who come and really want to help, and be here until the end." Xena brought up on her own, at least six different times during our conversation, that the Cluster and any other group that wanted to work for Park neighborhood needed to have an enduring presence, to keep coming back, to "be here until the end."

"Stay. Don't disappear." And further, Xena told me, "I think the Cluster should not just meet with themselves. They should go to all the meetings [of the groups at the Center], bring back what other committees are doing." The message could not be clearer. White volunteers would be very welcome when they got to know the civic goings-on of the neighborhood, the different groups in the neighborhood, over a long haul. That would happen only if they were keeping track of who was who and who was where in the neighborhood. They would have to talk carefully about relationships, not make assumptions. Had the URC leader spent more time sorting through the relationships, she might have been more wary of organizing a campaign based on a year-old petition in a very transient neighborhood.[13]

The URC leader cared about Park's children. Her genuine sadness, her quiet anger, were hard to miss when she described how children from the same city block got bused far away to three different schools. How would the kids ever be able to support each other? Her righteous anger inspired me. Community organizing campaigns depend on articulate, dedicated people like her. It is also the case that she spoke as if she were *outside* the conflicted, messy, everyday world of group relationships in the neighborhood, instead of engaging deeply with them.[14]

Social Capital or a Spiral of Misapprehension?

The URC leader moved quickly into organizing mode. She helped to make Park neighborhood's school situation into an issue for local political progressives. Not only did she attend Cluster meetings and many other URC-sponsored groups, but she was well known in the Lakeburg Progressive Coalition (LPC), a political organization that elected several members to the Lakeburg city council. School board members knew her too, as a former board member herself. Participating in these different civic networks, she enriched the URC and Park Cluster with the overlapping ties that construct a vibrant, effective civic arena according to the neo-Tocquevillians (Putnam 2000, 1996). She lent Park Cluster "bridging social capital"; she was the sort of civic broker who can make things happen, make otherwise distant groups work together (Mische 2003). That Park's school issue became LPC's issue could have been a boon to the Park neighborhood, a sign of social capital at work. The school campaign illustrates how important it is to listen to people creating relationships and not rest content with counting connections.

The school board had already tabled its own discussion of school assignments in Park. The URC leader wielded her connections wisely, and got them to reopen the issue. Meantime, she had little trouble getting the LPC to endorse the idea that Park children should all get to attend a neighborhood school. I attended two meetings at which the LPC considered the issue. The URC leader conveyed urgency, sincerity, and an unspoken sense that the Park neighborhood, Park Cluster, and any left-liberals worth their salt could unite behind the *same* interest in changing the present busing policy. Things were obvious, and it was time for action.

LPC members at a monthly coalition meeting passed a resolution condemning the current three-school enrollment plan. They called on the school board to include Park children in one new school. Neither the resolution nor the brief discussion around it mentioned the possibility that the Park neighborhood would harbor diverse opinions on the subject. The resolution echoed the URC leader's reasoning, almost word for word: "Children in the same [apartment] building may attend different schools, [and] this situation and the distances in-volved make it difficult for parents to attend teacher conferences and school functions, retrieve sick children, etc." As one LPC member said to general ap-proval, this was a chance to do some "community-building," along with helping the children of Park.

The LPC's schooling committee took up the issue for action. The committee chair, a soft-spoken teacher, talked to me for an hour at the committee meeting about low-income, disenfranchised kids. She had told the general meeting that the resolution was the committee's way of finding something that LPC could "do." She had an eager college student to help figure out the action: The com-mittee could leaflet the neighborhoods near to Park. It could do outreach to "multicultural student groups," including black student groups at the nearby college, getting them to sign a petition against the current three-school plan and speak out at the next school board meeting. All of these contacts could help build the LPC, he observed.

Was it a perfect case of civic action propelled by Tocqueville's "self-interest properly understood" or was it building bridges on misunderstandings? The committee assumed that black or "multicultural" students naturally would want to speak up for the school policy that LPC assumed was in the best interest of the (partially) African American Park neighborhood. No one suggested that the education committee should spend time in the Park neighborhood learning about what Park was like, what residents wanted. LPC imagined itself repre-senting a single Park neighborhood interest. And it planned to communicate that interest even more broadly, folding other people in Lakeburg into a new community of interest, all of which took relations between the neighborhood, the Cluster, and the LPC, and progressive Lakeburg citizens for granted instead of being critically reflexive and talking them through.

Ten months after the coalition's resolution, the school board tested the core assumption: Its survey of Park households found that 64 percent wanted to keep the current three-school arrangement unchanged. Seventy percent claimed to be "very satisfied" with their children's elementary school. It is possible that some Park residents feared any change would only be a change for the worse. Some may have feared reprisals had they criticized their children's schooling. No one would know for sure without establishing relationships, over the long haul, with Park residents, their neighborhood center, their local groups—all very distant socially from the white and mostly middle-class, progressive citi-zens of the LPC. Those relationships would take thinking and talking through, risky pondering of who could speak for whom exactly, where.

This is a cautionary tale about the meaning of ties, and the ways both schol-ars and citizens talk about ties. The URC leader used connections to help the LPC do some "community-building" that *in this particular case* was based on an only partial understanding of the Park neighborhood. A seasoned political ob-server could say that this time, someone did not do her homework; of course hindsight is easy. The school issue was not resolved during my time with Park. The sloppy coalition-building did not wreck the Cluster's ongoing relationships with the Park neighborhood in the longer run, but it did not strengthen them either. It did create more friction, not trust, between the neighborhood center director and the Cluster.

In no way am I suggesting that overlapping ties are a bad thing, or that political coalitions should not act strategically to promote their interests and others' when these coincide. The point, rather, is that our sociological terms of discussion about social ties need to help us hear how people try building them. As John Dewey put it, community is a moral fact, not merely a physical one. Civic community requires communication and not only copresence. Counting connections without listening to customs and conversation gives us a partial view of civic community.

In a racially diverse, unequal society, in which people try to define common interests across enormous social chasms, it is likely that people often will try to build bridges on the basis of partial understandings—even with the best intentions. That does not mean they should stop strategizing for fear of offending people. Sometimes there will not be a lot of time to survey the terrain. Still, these scenarios suggest that social reflexivity may be one of the most strategic activities for a bridge-building coalition.

How Did the Cluster Change?

Changing Customs, Changing Talk about Relationships

The Cluster was developing a sense of civic responsibility lauded in civic republican, pragmatist, and communitarian traditions of thought about civic life,[15] but relatively rare in the Lakeburg groups. Observers of social togetherness in America (Bellah et al. 1985; Taylor 1995; Putnam 2000) want to keep alive the conditions that create that sensibility. How did the Cluster change in this direction?

Scenes from meetings suggest that at least some Cluster members knew both volunteer and partnership customs. In retrospect we can say that the parish nurse project tipped the scales away from volunteering, toward partnership. The nurse project ratified that the Cluster related to a larger set of reference points on its "map" than Family Friends. Having surprised themselves with their own agency—"fools walk in where angels fear to tread," Betty said—Cluster members rooted themselves more deeply on a different map. With a different sense of what their group was all about, in relation to whom, members reflected increasingly, self-critically, on relations beyond the group.

The Cluster talked its way toward new responsibilities, like the nurse project, and new civic ties, instead of putting someone else's bigger picture in place. New projects generated more reflective discussion, hastening and ratifying the transition in customs. By the end of my time with the group, a URC liaison could say at a meeting that Park Cluster had a "reputation" for being involved with Park's community affairs—and use that perception to encourage the Cluster to stay involved with school politics. It would have made little sense to characterize the Cluster that way at the start of my study, when it was a conduit for volunteers.

The Cluster had entered a *cycle* of partnership, reflexivity, and bridging relationships that ratified partnership as the group's customary mode. External resources, opportunities and institutional constraints play important roles in the social spiral. As I will diagram below, customs and reflexivity have far more particular, more variable roles in the process than one would guess from Tocqueville's optimistic sketch or from neo-Tocquevillians' inventories of social capital, so I focus mainly on them.

Resources and Opportunities Are Good but Not Enough

Sociologists often argue that public groups need resources and opportunities if they are going to put their visions into practice, no matter how compelling those visions are.[16] Resources and opportunities are part of the cycle that led Park Cluster toward civic development and away from more conventional volunteering. We can say the parish nurse program was a *resource* for acting on the Cluster's growing customs of partnership. It was a resource made possible in part by a retirement home that helped to underwrite the nurse and her health insurance.

While church volunteers and pastors had ventured into the neighborhood for years before the Cluster took shape, the Family Friends agency strengthened the *opportunity* for a faith-based coalition to get involved in neighborhood. Kendra told me the church/state divide was simply not an issue if people from churches were willing to make food, serve food, coach teams in the summer school program, or teach arts and crafts.[17] The Cluster depended on Kendra to tell them how many families had received money from the eviction prevention fund, to tell them when to organize volunteers for the Kids for Peace celebration, or the Walk against Violence, or the Southeast Asian Festival. Having long argued that state agencies typically squash or colonize grass-roots efforts to build community life,[18] sociologists are just starting to see how the state might also *complement* local civic life (Schudson 1994; Skocpol and Fiorina 1999) or collaborate with and even underwrite civic groups (Fung and Wright 2003; Goldberg 2001). On a social service worker's terms, Kendra welcomed the church-based Cluster into the neighborhood; Family Friends always needed volunteers.

What is striking is the way most Cluster members *defined* the "resource" of the nurse program or the "opportunity" to work on a Family Friends project. As William Sewell Jr. has pointed out (1992), people relate to resources only

through cultural definitions; resources do not simply exist as self-evident realities. The same material resource may get defined—realized as a resource—differently in different cultural contexts. The cultural context that matters here is
the Cluster's own customs. These enabled members to define resources like the
parish nurse or the eviction prevention fund as matériel for bridging relationships. With the parish nurse and the ongoing support from Family Friends, the
Cluster could act on its dominant vision of partnership, sever it from "helpin'
out," and create new precedents for further relationship-building. Resources
and opportunities reinforced the Cluster's vision and made Family Friends, the
retirement home, and the school district all the more real as reference points on
the group's social map, as Sewell's analysis might predict.[19]

Resources and opportunities embodied the Cluster's vision of partnership,
but they did not produce the vision nor the customs that helped members talk
about it. The Cluster could have turned itself into a fund-raising auxiliary to the
Lutheran retirement home that administered the nurse and paid half her salary.
For many volunteer careers, the next step after direct-service volunteering is
fund-raising (Ostrander 1984; Daniels 1988). Yet Cluster members defined the
nurse program as an opportunity to "get our congregations involved in the community," as Connie put it. When the mounting responsibility of overseeing the
nurse seemed to fray the Cluster's loose organizational fabric, the Cluster instituted a new structure, symbolizing a shift toward partnership, away from customary volunteering.

Opportunities can get defined in different ways, too. Administered by Kendra, the eviction prevention fund could have been defined by the group as another focus for task-oriented volunteering. That is how Ned, the fund's book-
keeper, saw it. The fund did not have enough money to satisfy Cluster members
or Kendra, let alone Park neighbors who might benefit from it. The Cluster
could have held bake sales and raffles to support the program, to help Family
Friends administer the fund as efficiently as possible. But Ned was in a small minority of those who defined the Cluster as an adjunct taking directions from the
county. Cluster members' talk of building social bonds predominated over
Ned's vision of helping out and Kendra's individual client-centered vision, too.
Customs of partnership enabled Cluster members to communicate a vision in
contrast with Ned's suggestion that the seemingly overextended group disband.

Partnership in a Society of Loose Connections

Going against the administrative grain of Family Friends, the case of the Cluster challenges the notion that the contemporary institutional arrangements
necessarily squeeze social concern into a relationship between a social service
professional and a helpful volunteer. Like the Justice Task Force, Adopt-a-Family,
and the HRA projects, Park Cluster developed at least partly in response to social service institutions that Robert Wuthnow (1998) finds characteristic of a

"loosely connected" society. In a society full of loosely connected networks like HRA, it makes sense that many people would express their care for others in loose, sporadic, limited-term engagements.

My account refines our understanding of how volunteering relates to large institutional arrangements: Volunteers apprehend surrounding institutions through their own customs, rather than simply plugging into the institutions' own routines. Sometimes, a volunteer group's customs mirror those of the professional institution, but not always. Their customs, and the kind of talk they make possible, may enable volunteers like Cluster members to initiate new civic bridges, instead of foreswearing such ambitions as entirely someone else's business. The difference in customs makes the difference between social self-organization and civic disempowerment. By recognizing the role of customs, we see how people maintain institutional arrangements in everyday life, while also seeing openings for alternatives.

There is a lot of good sense to the "loose connections" account of community service volunteering. Park Cluster members did encourage other members of their churches to plug in and serve meals, clean up after the annual Christmas party, or supervise arts and crafts projects in the summer camp. Plug-in volunteering closely complements institutional arrangements but is not the only set of customs for community service work.

What About the Role of Organizational Structure?

Community organizers, or sociologists who study them, might say that another term needs to be part of the cycle I am sketching: organizational structure. The contrast between Park Cluster and the HRA is suggestive. Both tried to pursue community development. But people joined the HRA, both its core group and its volunteer projects, as individuals. Practically all attended churches, but they joined as individual "people of faith," in Donald's words. The HRA was not a loose association of churches the way Park Cluster was. When a Park Cluster member and one former member, Paula and Pastor Lindstrom, participated in HRA, they referred to themselves as "people of faith," or members of "faith communities" in general, not representatives of specific churches. A community organizer might point out that it is hard for a group to create ties outward if the group has no mandate from anyone in particular and is accountable to no one in particular beyond the group itself. That is what a community organizer told the HRA's director at URC board meetings, and some sociological work supports the claim.[20]

It makes good sense that organizational form would matter, but group-building customs help constitute the form. Ned's pastor counted on him and Elizabeth to be the conduits who would communicate with the Cluster, just as other churches counted on individuals to represent them to the Cluster. Representing a church, for Ned and Elizabeth, meant representing a collection of donors and resources. The meaning of congregational membership did not help Ned participate in the Cluster's increasingly ambitious partnership projects; he chafed at them. Had the HRA expected all its core members to represent churches, the way Cluster members did, some may have understood "coming from my church" as representing an aggregate of private donors and charitable interests, rather than a group will. There is no question that organizational form can be a valuable part of a causal story for many interesting group outcomes.[21] In a study of how groups constitute themselves and reach outward, it helps more to see the different customs that might embody the "same" organizational form on paper. Organizational form, as neoinstitutionalists have pointed out, is enacted in scripts—in customary ways of drawing boundaries, bonding, and affirming speech.

Looking back on scenes from the different Lakeburg groups and projects, we now can sketch some patterns and contrast them with earlier claims about the social spiral.

Reconstructing the Tocquevillian Social Spiral

Tocqueville famously proposed that interaction in civic groups would "enlarge the heart" and empower citizens as responsible actors in the implicit social contract. Many have reiterated these claims. Scholars skeptical about recent appropriations of Tocqueville point out that *Democracy in America* identified America's structure of governance and not just its plethora of civic groups as a guarantor of civic health (Edwards and Foley 1997). In less polemical terms, Goldberg (2001) points out that Tocqueville was not nearly as anti state as some conservative appropriations of his work (e.g., Berger and Neuhaus 1977) might make it seem. Still, Tocqueville claimed (1969 [1835]) that habits and mores contributed even more to civic health than laws or governing structures. He found those habits and mores cultivated in civic groups.

Tocqueville was not simply wrong. Patterns of interaction inside the Lakeburg groups did influence the groups' ways of reaching out. My focus on customs resonates with Tocqueville's emphasis on "mores." Building on these Tocquevillian starting points, I propose to reconstruct his theory first with the claim that there is more than one set of civic customs in the socially unequal, culturally and religiously diverse, complex American society today. Civic groups are not simply either civic-minded or narrowly self-interested, as Tocqueville's formulation would have it. The Lakeburg groups had different styles of reaching out and cultivated different kinds of civic goods. We need a better vocabulary to make sense of these differences.

Tocquevillian theory implies that civic groups, in general, empower civil society in relation to the state. Here, too, the Lakeburg groups' experiences compel me to reconstruct Tocquevillian theory in light of contemporary, "postwelfare" social conditions in the United States: At least sometimes, perhaps often, civic groups may do little to empower civil society. The networkers and volunteers of the Humane Response Alliance could not do much to empower the civic sector in Lakeburg, even though they got explicit opportunities to collaborate with county agencies and could share county workers' expertise. The servants of the Adopt-a-Family program got a warm welcome from county social service workers and benefited from county agencies' expertise as they tried to create caring relationships. But they did not empower a long-standing role for church groups in the emerging social contract. As civic groups, they failed to empower civil society. Starting out as a project of Humane Response Alliance, Park Cluster did take an increasingly active, ongoing responsibility for relationships with other groups in Lakeburg, rather than leaving the bigger picture mostly to someone else or assuming that no one could or should have the bigger picture. In its own very modest way, it was contributing to the empowerment of civil society.

Partnership and very modest civic empowerment came at the cost of other goods that volunteering, networking, social criticism, and deep compassion offer. If the Cluster's projects continued to multiply, it is possible the Cluster would become more of a loose networking enterprise like the HRA. It might trade some goods for others. Still the Cluster did spiral outward in ways members themselves did not expect. It created bridges that mattered to residents of the Park neighborhood like Xena, who wanted Cluster members to stay around and get to know the neighborhood, not dart in for charitable sorties. They mattered to the Park residents who originally told Kendra the social worker that they wanted a more stable neighborhood; the Cluster offered the resources to make an eviction prevention fund, modest as it was, possible at all.

Toward Tentative Generalizations about Bridging

Robert Putnam's expansive study of American civic engagement 165 years later built on Tocquevillian themes. Where Tocqueville wrote vaguely, arguing for the larger, cohesion-building consequences of civic groups, Putnam contributed a fundamental social-science insight (2000, 1996): civic life is empowered by ties between people and groups. Putnam conceived those ties in terms of his version of "social capital." He associated social capital with "civic virtue," a concept much closer to Tocqueville's genre of writing. As Putnam put it, "civic virtue is most powerful when embedded in a dense network of reciprocal social relations. A society of many virtuous but isolated individuals is not necessarily rich in social capital" (2000, p. 19). Social capital is the medium through which people develop trust, trustworthiness, a sense of interdependence, and other traits that are good for society (p. 288). Those habits and traits would propel people toward more social connections.

Putnam's framework has insights too. It encouraged me to consider ties between groups ("bridging social capital") as a potential consequence of social reflexivity. The problem is that ties mean different things. Those meanings become effective through talk. The capital metaphor by itself does not help us investigate the meanings. The distinction between bonding social capital (ties within groups) and bridging social capital (ties between groups) is a start. But the Lakeburg groups represent attempts at very different kinds of bridges, powered by different customs. In some ways, social capital is a conceptual step backward from Tocqueville's implicit understanding that ties could have different meanings.

In Park Cluster, Ned and Ken both had a lot of bridging social capital. Both were well connected with their own churches—"point men" for the Cluster. Both had lived in Lakeburg for over two decades. Both developed close, routine contact with the Park neighborhood even though both lived outside the neighborhood. Both also had backgrounds in college-level teaching and were roughly the same age.

But the two men had different assumptions about how to create and sustain a group. They had different ideas about what counts as "doing something." Ned wanted to help out. He could summon aggregates of individual donors to help Family Friends and individual clients. Ken, and other Cluster members, wanted to create relationships between collectivities. They envisioned churches collectively supporting the neighborhood on the neighborhood's own terms, apart from helping social service workers administer their own definitions of local well-being. "Bridging social capital" by itself does not grasp these differences. The case of Park Cluster shows just how important words and imagination are for bridging. The capital metaphor offers a bird's-eye view of trends in group membership, but it will not help us zero in on the ways people imagine their relations beyond the group.

Beyond reconstructing Tocqueville's social spiral argument, I use the Lakeburg groups' experiences to sketch up close two processes through which civic groups create different kinds of ties outward. These sketches highlight interaction rather than invoking the social capital concept. Only one of the two processes sketched below creates bridges as I have conceived them. The sketches are *tentative*, "grounded" generalizations I offer for future research.[22] Money, expertise, time, and an official welcome from county agencies all were important parts of the story. But here I highlight customs and reflexivity because alternative accounts have failed to appreciate their power. I propose that Tocque-

Figure 6–1
Customs and reflexivity in the social spiral

Customary interaction↔practice social ↔bridging relationships
in civic groups   reflexivity

Customary interaction↔eschew social ↔short-term interpersonal
in civic groups   reflexivity   relations and/or loose
                                                  networking relations

ville's virtuous social spiral, one that creates bridges, depends on customs that invite social reflexivity.

Park Cluster was religiously based, just like the other Lakeburg groups. And yet members very, very rarely expressed religious commitments aloud in the group. How, if at all, did religion work in the Cluster?

Chapter Seven

DOING THINGS WITH RELIGION IN LOCAL CIVIC LIFE

What Is Religious Here?

When I started going to Park Cluster meetings, I thought the volunteers would talk about their civic duties in Christian terms, at least once in a while. Park Cluster was trying to build a relationship with a neighborhood whose most vocal leader promoted black separatism and scorned white outsiders. Wouldn't they invoke religious symbolism at some point, if for no other reason than to steel their own commitment to a difficult cause? Cluster brochures called the group "faith in action." I assumed that I would hear about that faith if I waited long enough.

I listened and waited. I imagined being asked to give the opening prayer, and I pondered what kind of prayer I would settle on. In fact there never was an opening prayer until, at the start of a meeting near the very end of my time in the field, an African American pastor offered one. After eighteen months of Cluster meetings, I counted a total of five instances in which Cluster members affirmed their own religious convictions out loud, either directly or more often indirectly, apart from the pastor's prayer. One instance was Betty's quip that the Cluster needed to act on the "Christianity which comes out of our mouths." She must have meant this figuratively, as self-deprecating criticism of well-meaning volunteers, since Christian expression very rarely came out of anyone's mouth. Another instance was Ned's comment that the Park neighborhood center ought to be a "haven of Godliness"; all at the table knew Ned was affiliated with Immanuel Lutheran, so this comment is safely interpreted as an implicit affirmation of the Christian notion of God. Another time, a fundraising professional and new member of the Cluster said half-facetiously that the Cluster ought to do for the neighborhood what "Jesus would do"; in the meantime, she suggested, the Cluster could do some fund-raising. There was one Methodist pastor's remark that God had put him in the place of working himself out of a job: If his efforts to strengthen the Park neighborhood succeeded, he would happily find some other line of work. And Dora proposed at a committee meeting that the Cluster should take a "servant" role, among others. For Christians and Jews, servanthood is a common metaphor for one who carries out God's will. In an interview Dora associated the word with the biblical heritage.

These comments would have sounded "churchy," if not simply a non sequitur, in secular groups. But they were not exactly impassioned expressions of religious faith. The Cluster puzzled me in light of studies that show church-based activists and volunteers using religious language to charge themselves up and stir others to the cause. In this chapter I ask how, if at all, the Cluster was acting as a religious group, and I develop an enlarged understanding of how religion may work in civic groups.

WHAT QUESTIONS CAN WE ASK ABOUT RELIGION?

All of the Lakeburg groups *understood themselves* as religiously based groups, even if being "religiously based" could mean different things. HRA members identified collectively as "people of faith." Task Force members occasionally called themselves "prophets" and followed time-honored speech norms of prophetic criticism. Members, especially Catherine, occasionally referred to biblical teachings about justice when they criticized welfare reform. Adopt-a-Family group members identified themselves as Christ-like servants in relation to a larger, often non-Christian world of uncaring bureaucracies. Their goals reflected the evangelical emphasis on interpersonal relationships, even if they agreed not to proselytize. Prayerful discernment was their privileged style of speech. And Park Cluster members identified as members of churches, though they did not talk explicitly about religious precepts very often. So even the very shallowest "thick description" (Geertz 1973) could hardly avoid the way group members identified themselves in religious terms.

Often we care about a group's religious character because we want to know why groups do what they do or why they do them well or poorly. We expect that religion has influenced the group's goals, or its success in meeting them, especially if the goals seem admirable, or repellent, or just unusual. But I chose to study only religiously based groups, for reasons I discussed in chapter 1. I did not plot any causal role for religion in the social spiral. Without closely matched, secular comparison groups, I will not say whether or not any Lakeburg groups' goals, or successes and failures, were caused by members' religious orientations alone.[1] I ask other questions about religion.

My goal was to learn more about what a religious influence could be to begin with. There were other questions to ask before asking what effect religion had on a group's goals or its ability to build bridges. Questions of *how* and *where* people express religious meanings are beginning to resonate loudly in recent studies, and the puzzles of Park Cluster made them especially compelling in this study. Because they may be more counterintuitive than other questions people would ask about religion in community service groups, they deserve a bit more discussion before I introduce my own answers.

"How" and "Where" before "Why"

I aimed to find out *how* the Lakeburg groups would wear their religious "hats" as churchgoers. The question matters for several reasons. First, some accounts say that the American public square either is hostile to religion or is made a hostile place by religion. It makes sense to wonder how religious groups would act in local community life *as* religious groups. Sociologists have hotly debated the "culture wars" thesis, that American public life is deeply divided between progressive humanists and religious traditionalists who verbally attack or else speak past one another. Even though local religious groups are much more civil, and public opinion on social or moral issues less polarized than a simple "culture wars" thesis would suggest, one of the striking findings to emerge from this academic debate is that many Americans *think* that polarization exists (DiMaggio, Bryson and Evans 1996). I heard the same sensibility early in my study. URC leaders and some group members assumed that deep divisions separated religious conservatives and religious liberals in Lakeburg. The public atmosphere might seem poisoned for or by religious expression of any sort. So how would people in religiously based community service groups manifest their religious commitments, if at all?

The question is compelling also because people may express the same religious commitments in different ways, in different places. It is not so obvious how religious as distinct from secular expression would look or sound. It is wrong to expect that "religious people" must be people who talk a lot of religious talk wherever they are. Close-up, ethnographic research is not the most efficient means of identifying a potential causal role for religion—the "why"— but it may be one of the best means of discerning how religion works in everyday group life.

More briefly, I also ask "where." I compare Park Cluster meetings with meetings of outreach committees that Cluster members attended at their own churches. I heard members of the same church, and even the same people, expressing religious identity differently in different settings. My findings challenge common ways of understanding religion.

It is common sense that religion gives people a stable, ultimate, core identity, a major character trait that defines the person in all social settings whether we see and hear the trait or not (Ammerman 2003, 1997b). From a social-science point of view I am saying, in contrast, that group setting matters for religious identity. That does not invalidate people's own perception of having a religious, core self. It means that social scientists can learn new things when we take a person's or group's religion as a collection of potentially different kinds of cultural expression in different places, instead of taking for granted the common view that religion is a silent, static body of culture that is ever-present for people whom our studies have designated "religious people."

To ask how and where is to broaden sociologists' definition of religion itself. Religion scholars are starting to say that "religion" includes not only the theologies or formal teachings we often imagine with that word, but also *everyday practices and identities* (Ammerman 2003, 1997b; Becker and Eiesland 1997; Wuthnow 1999c). From a social-science point of view, public groups cannot be or act "religious" except through these practices and identities—through lived religion.[2] Courtney Bender's study (2003) of religious expression in an officially nonreligious AIDS food service puts the point powerfully. Her comment on the commonsense understanding of religion is worth quoting at length:

> [It] suggests that "religion" or "religiousness" is a stable quality or characteristic that individuals carry and translate in the same way into various social settings. It implies that religion is a set of values, presumably learned in a religious community or through self-guided seeking and then carried by individual egos into their daily surroundings. . . . [S]uch a measure of individual religiousness begs the questions we need to answer, including where and how religion is learned, expressed, and recognized as such throughout social life. In short, it closes off the path to understanding how people interpret, understand, and enact religion in social settings (2003, ix).

This chapter takes that path.

How Americans Bring Religion into Local Civic Life

Toward the end of my time in the field, relatively few scholars had investigated closely the question of *how* people bring religion into local civic life.[3] The question has become newly pressing, though, as policy-makers are pondering the potentials and dangers of the "faith-based" social services that state policies have welcomed into a new social contract. Some researchers have developed broad ways to categorize religious influence in the social service organizations they study.[4] Others, taking a closer, ethnographic perspective, are listening to religious communication in the community service and activist groups they study (C. Bender 2003; Wood 2002; Hart 2001). In all, existing research suggests it is helpful to distinguish three ways that people bring religion into local civic life:

First, some studies examine the relation between denominational identity or religiosity, and volunteering or community service (for instance, Park and Smith 2000; J. Wilson and Janoski 1995; C. Smith 1998; see the review in Wuthnow 2004). By tapping individual attitudes in surveys, they assume a default position in line with the privatization thesis—the idea that religion is a private affair for most Americans, and that when they pursue public causes on the basis of religious motives, they keep their religious motives private.[5] One may argue whether or not acting publicly on *private* religious motives really counts as bringing religion into civic life; it depends partly on how much significance we grant the spoken word. In any event, it is reasonable to say that some people act on a completely "silent" religion in public.

Second, some studies show groups *publicly articulating* goals in religious terms. Employing what I will call the "religious articulation perspective," they show how compelling religious language can move people to action, winning new rights and building new political coalitions. Rhys Williams (1995) and Aldon Morris (1984) have argued, for instance, that biblical languages of justice and the public good gave the civil rights movement strength and broad appeal at the grass roots. Bellah and his research team (1985) argued that religious language sustains a sense of connection to society as a whole, while more secular languages of free choice and free personal expression threaten that sensibility.

When students of American social movements listen, they hear a lot of religious discourse. Mark R. Warren (2001) observed community organizers defining their causes with the help of theological traditions—Catholic social thought, African American interpretations of the Exodus story, and the liberal Protestant social gospel of worldly reform. In the most elaborate version of the religious articulation argument, Wood's comparative research (2002, 1999) shows that religious discourse can empower collective action when it helps activists deal with the ambiguity in their political environments, and confront and compromise with elites.

Finally, some ethnographic studies have observed a different, quieter way that religion goes public: People create religiously identified groups, even if they do not expound much on their religious beliefs. They identify as a religious group, relating *as* a religious group to the other people, groups, or institutions they see on their social map. Religious culture contributes to a group's *social identity,* apart from influencing group members' choice of *goals* or rationales for goals. "Social identity" is a simple way to name the act of drawing group boundaries— one of the customs discussed throughout this book—so it is the term I will use here.[6] Creating a social identity and defining goals are two different if related kinds of cultural work. Both have their own effects on collective action.[7]

The mere fact of having a religious group identity in public, apart from what particular beliefs go with that identity, sends meaningful signals. A person or group known to be religious may enjoy others' respect or trust because of the meanings others associate with being religious. The fact of having a congregational identity at all helps local religious leaders trust one another enough to unite in risky community organizing campaigns (M. R. Warren 2001; Wood 2002). Municipal officials pay attention to local religious leaders by virtue of these leaders' social identities *as* religious people, apart from their particular beliefs (Demerath and Williams 1992).

The religious identity sends signals to group members themselves, too: Religion scholar Ram Cnaan argues recently (2002) that many American religious congregations share a "norm of community involvement," regardless of their faith tradition. Americans learn, in other words, that being a member of a religious congregation *means* being someone who does, or should, get involved in community service beyond the congregation.

A Focus on Social Identity: Four Findings to Explore

The case of Park Cluster made clear that congregational membership itself is meaningful. Even inside Park Cluster, being from a congregation could mean different things—and the different meanings complemented different preferences for collective action. I will focus on religious social identity; my study is a warrant for much more research on how people signal religious identity in everyday life.

Four findings emerged from the field. One is that religious social identity may be nearly silent yet still exist. Park Cluster members shared a religious identity *as* Cluster members, even though members talked extremely little in religious terms at monthly meetings. Second is that religious social identity can vary by setting, even for the same individuals. It is good to ask "where" as well as "how"; I did so by comparing Park Cluster meetings with outreach committee meetings inside two churches that Cluster members attended.

A third, broader finding emerged from comparing field notes on the four main Lakeburg groups: Cluster members had at least one simple religious term they used to talk about their relationship with the Park neighborhood. Other Lakeburg groups did not find consistently satisfactory religious terms for the bridges they wanted to build. While I cannot say religion *caused* the Cluster's success at bridging, I can suggest that religious identity *complemented* it. What results, very tentatively, is a new picture of religion at work in community-building: Tocqueville (1969 [1835]) thought religious identity could help Americans spiral outward because most religions in general made people more other regarding in general. Yet all the Lakeburg groups could be called other regarding, so Tocqueville's pronouncements are not sensitive enough to be useful. Some scholars would guess that religious identity gave the Cluster a symbolically rich, emotionally powerful discourse that promoted bridge-building. That was not the case either. I am saying instead that religion worked in a more ordinary, profane way. In the Cluster, religious identity gave members a bit of concrete language and shared imagery to use in everyday interaction as they did their bridging work.

The fourth finding is that differing religious identities can promote divisiveness, even apart from group members' beliefs about issues or goals. To make that case, I introduce the Religious Anti-racism Coalition (RARC), the Lakeburg affiliate of the national Call to Renewal network. Composed mainly of pastors and church leaders from mainline and evangelical Protestant churches, the RARC wanted to publicize a religious stance against racism in Lakeburg. The RARC sponsored two large celebrations timed to coincide with Ku Klux Klan marches in town. In the RARC, mainline and evangelical Protestants clashed over their differing social identities even though they *agreed* on religious rationales for opposing racism.

A group's identity is not always easy to distinguish from its discourse about its goals; the researcher has to be looking and listening for it. Groups with religious identities may often use explicitly religious language to talk about goals; this is true particularly of evangelical Protestant, African American, or hispanic Catholic groups. Park Cluster's experience made it easier for me to zero in on religious social identity since the Cluster members expounded very little on any religious rationales for their group goals during meetings. Religion scholars such as Cuddihy (1978), Davie (1995), and Wuthnow and Evans (2002) have pointed out that mainline Protestants are not as comfortable with explicit Christian talk in public outside church settings as other Christians might be. While I am especially interested in mainline Protestants' reputation for being "quiet" about their religion, this focus on social identity ought to illuminate non-Protestant groups as well. The concluding section discusses the payoff of my approach for theory and future research.

CASE ONE: PARK CLUSTER

Loose Articulation in Interviews and Written Statements

Hearing little religious talk at Cluster meetings, I listened carefully to what Park Cluster members might do with religion in private interviews. I read brochures and project prospectuses closely. In open-ended interviews I asked how, if at all, members saw their Cluster work in religious terms. Religion influences the stories people tell in interviews about why they get involved in community work. Interview stories may be a window on how people make civic acts meaningful with the cultural materials at hand (K. Hays 1994; Tipton 1982; Wuthnow 1991; Bellah et al. 1985; see also Taylor 1989). Cluster members did not converge on any single religious frame that would promote a distinctive kind of collective action over others.

Cluster members related their work to Judeo-Christian themes very *loosely.* They used different metaphors that might support equally a variety of projects. None said in an unambiguous way that it felt incumbent on them as Christians or as members of particular denominations to engage in community development—though by the time I began interviewing, all Cluster members would have agreed that the Cluster was about community development, whether they liked that or not. Paula said it was good to have a church-based rather than secular cluster because "it seems like it's part of the reason that we have religion, and caring for other people and caring for our neighbors. . . . I don't know of any religion that there isn't some calling for us to care about other people." When I asked Dora if she came to her work at the Cluster with religious precepts, she said that she used the biblical notion of a "servant" to describe the Cluster, and added that the Cluster should be an "advocate," too. Servanthood sounds different from advocacy; it meant something different in Adopt-a-Family. It implies direct service at least as easily as community development. Advocacy, Dora implied, meant working for justice. Advocacy emerged as her priority:

> DORA: "As much as you have done to them, you've done unto me," that kind of thing. . . . "Feed the hungry." There's also the Old Testament prophets, you know, like—you "do justice"—that's probably my banner.
> PL: You like Micah?
> DORA: I like that one at lot. Something about "your solemn assemblies"—from Jeremiah. Anyway, that kind of thing—and let justice rule. Justice is important to me.

Today, "advocacy" and "justice" imply political organizing, struggling over issues with governments or corporations, at least as easily as community development work. One may see community development as part of a broader vision to bring justice to a low-income community, but neither advocacy nor justice are *close-fitting* frames for the Cluster's community development projects.

Another member, a former Presbyterian associate pastor, answered my question by saying that "'Love your neighbor' would be number one, and 'go out into the world,' yeah." And one new member thought churches could be "visionary," and "see things from the Christian point of view or whatever." When asked for the "Christian point of view" on Park neighborhood, she hesitated, pondered a bit, and said it was "the perspective of always being an open ear and doing things that he could do to help, you know, his brother, the hurting person or the downtrodden or I don't know—just be a nurturing person, I think . . . I think a focus on relationships is what's key to me."

Only Mary wanted to make religious faith a more explicit part of the Cluster's own culture. She had hoped Cluster members would meet outside monthly meetings "to consider who we were, as Christian people who were over [in the neighborhood] doing this work"; she thought the Cluster's proceedings themselves should remain secular. Mary was the only Cluster interviewee who made a direct religious reference—a teaching she attributed to the Hebrew prophet Jeremiah—that might articulate closely the Cluster's distinctive mission of community development: "The exiles [in Jeremiah] are being advised to work among the people, and attempt to work for the good of that community, and so on."

In all, interviewees related their Cluster work to a wide range of Judeo-Christian themes: "caring for our neighbors," "servanthood," "do justice," "love thy neighbor," "be a nurturing person." *Each* of the interviewees quoted here had contributed actively to the community development thrust of the Cluster; none favored direct-service volunteering over community development. Yet it is striking that, with the exception of "work for the good of the community," interviewees' phrases and symbols could articulate one-to-one service volunteering, or political organizing, at least as readily as efforts at community development. It is striking too that a single interviewee might use terms as different as "servant" and "justice" to articulate her work in the Cluster.

Closer, religiously based articulations of the Cluster's work were available: Many core Cluster members were affiliated with the URC, and along with other URC members participated in an annual state council of churches meeting in town. The year before I started attending Cluster meetings, the council's meeting theme was about the civic duty of religious people. Speakers and discussion groups considered "civic" obligations between people and groups in the community at large beyond direct-service volunteering; handouts supported the theme with biblical quotes. These terms would have articulated the Cluster's community development projects at least as closely as "servanthood," "justice," "go out into the world," or "be a nurturing person." The point is *not* that Cluster members' interview vocabularies were meaningless or random. But it would be hard to argue on the basis of the interview discourse that the interviewees shared a religious frame that could drive a particular kind of collective action.

It is possible that Cluster members were influenced by sermons or other kinds of religious expression *during church worship* that communicated the value of community development, even if these did not emerge in interviews. That would be evidence of religious culture working privately, not publicly, beyond church. In other studies, members of religious social action groups articulated their cause in religious terms both during church worship and during community organizing events (Hart 2001; M. R. Warren 2001; Wood 2002).

Park Cluster's brochures and statements of purpose also contained an interesting mix of discourses and metaphors, as we saw in the previous chapter. The biblical and other obviously religious references, again, had but a very loose relationship to the group's projects.

One of the brochures said, "Park Cluster are people of faith, committed to service, who join together with a common goal; to assist our neighbors in the Park area." The statement invokes the same "people of faith" social identity that HRA frequently gave itself. As an offshoot of the HRA project, the group may have borrowed HRA's language for the officially public purpose of a brochure. In the group itself, as chapter 6 showed, members understood themselves and other members as people from *churches*, not individual "people of faith" as they were in the HRA. When I joined the Cluster as a participant-observer, members asked at my first meeting if I might be able to get my congregation involved. "People of faith" politely signals openness to non-Christians; it says little one way or the other about congregational affiliation. Again, the language is not a close guide to the lived understandings in the group.

The brochure explained why the group does its work. As we saw earlier, it said "we can help our neighbors build community in their neighborhood. . . . We also recognize . . . the opportunity to strengthen race, class and cultural relationships in the Park area." The secular descriptions, then, offer a vague discourse of both community-building and service, somewhat different from the brochure's social justice messages from the prophet Isaiah and Margaret Mead. Different metaphors and languages coexisted in the Cluster's self-representation, and these had a loose relationship to the Cluster's priorities.

Had Cluster members been seasoned community organizers or worked with them, or had they been part of a formally established outfit, they might have articulated their goals in more theologically focused terms. Professional community organizers *work* at framing issues in religious terms for churchgoers (Wood 2002; M. R. Warren 2001). In Habitat for Humanity, a religiously based but less political, national outfit that builds houses for low-income people, the organization develops explicitly religious symbols and rituals. Through these, volunteers articulate the meaning of their charitable service to others (Baggett 2000). But Lakeburg groups were all grassroots and nonprofessional. Their members may be similar to participants in the many hundreds of local, church-based service alliances throughout the U.S. (Ammerman 2002). The religious articulation perspective may illuminate formally organized outfits or mobilization campaigns better than less formally organized kinds of civic engagement.

Creating a Religious Social Identity

The Dominant Map

Most though not all Cluster members identified the Cluster in relation to the Park neighborhood *as a collectivity.* Two explicitly religious terms contributed to the Cluster's dominant social map. One was the notion of a parish: Early Cluster members, already volunteers in the Park neighborhood, became part of the HRA's project to create congregational clusters. Clusters would be groups of churches that worked with low-income neighborhoods; HRA leaders spoke of a cluster's shared neighborhood as its "parish." Cluster members used the term, too. A Park Cluster brochure referred to Park neighborhood as part of a "common parish" for Cluster churches. The churches were as much as three miles from the Park neighborhood, but with this religiously based notion of local responsibility, they drew a boundary around their shared neighborhood that included Park. The public health nurse that the Cluster cosponsored for the neighborhood always was called a "parish nurse."

I puzzled at first that, on the one hand, Cluster members said they did not want to recruit people to their churches, but on the other hand identified themselves with a parish. "Parish" signaled that they were *church-based* people, socially responsible to a neighborhood, not that they expected others in the neighborhood to take up their religion. Speaking *from* a particular group identity is not the same as promoting that identity to an audience (Lichterman 1999). Cluster members never expounded upon the neighborhood as a "parish" at meetings. They did not articulate a theology of the parish. But their brochures and their regular references to the "parish nurse" at meetings signaled quietly that the Cluster had a religious source for its identification with a neighborhood.

The other religious term, heard much less frequently, was "social ministry." Nearly two years before this study began, some Cluster members had met with staff from the state council of churches. The staff people were not political organizers but people who distributed educational material and consulted with local church groups. They presented a "social ministries grid," a set of questions meant to help church volunteers think about their role in the wake of the 1996 welfare policy reforms. The idea of social ministry, derived from the social gospel of early twentieth-century mainline Protestantism, was that Christians are called to bring about God's kingdom on earth by creating a more just social order. In this early meeting with the council of churches staff, Cluster members had developed specific questions to ask themselves about how they *presented themselves* in the Park neighborhood: Were they and the neighborhood "partners," or "givers and receivers"? Did they relate to existing neighborhood groups? Did the Cluster's agenda setters include representatives of the community?

During this study, members did not use this grid to discuss which issues the group should pursue with which goals. The grid was not a theological frame for interpreting issues and devising strategies to meet end-goals so much as a checklist for drawing boundaries around an identity on a larger social map. The questions said more about who to be than what exactly to do in the neighborhood. Nearly two years elapsed between the meeting with the church council staff and the crisis meeting that represented a transition in customs; during this time, the group carried out a lot of direct-service volunteer projects, different from the community development projects they took on later. In my eighteen months of meetings, Cluster members never elaborated upon the *theology* of social ministry. They were very unlike Mark R. Warren's community activists (2001), for instance, who said they drew explicitly on the Bible and said they wanted to create a "theology of housing." Rather, like the notion of the common parish, "social ministry" was a tag of religious identity that could help them map themselves into the Park neighborhood, whether they carried out direct service, community development, or other projects. During heated discussion at the crisis meeting, Betty referred to "the social ministry grid" to support her argument that the Cluster should relate respectfully to the neighborhood, as "partners" *no matter whether they did direct-service volunteering or other kinds of projects.* She instructed, to general approval, "we are not 'givers and receivers.'"

Disagreement over the Map: Who Is the Group in Relation to the Neighborhood?

Ned was on the committee that helped write the group's brochure. He affirmed the Margaret Mead quote, the vague language of community development, the appeal to strengthen "relationships" across race, class, and cultural differences. The Park neighborhood was part of his "common parish," but his social map positioned volunteers in that parish differently.

Ned and his wife, Elizabeth, thought of church volunteers as charitably minded individuals who could use their church as a source of individual donations and volunteer time. "What else is a church for?" Ned asked rhetorically at one meeting. Ned said that he envisioned the Cluster as a group of people who could get their churches to donate goods quickly when the neighborhood social worker requested them—a thousand diapers, for instance, if that's what was needed. Ned and Elizabeth said in an interview that they were their church's only active conduit to Park Cluster. Dora and Martha of the Cluster had said just the same thing. But unlike Dora and Martha, Ned and Elizabeth *never* complained at meetings that other church members were not more involved or that their pastor didn't attend Cluster meetings. The collective will of the church as a whole was not as central to their definition of church-based work. They did not say they hoped or expected other church members to join them. As Ned told me, "I do my 'good deeds' on my own." In fact, that was not exactly true about Ned and Elizabeth; they initiated some of their good deeds when their pastor or the Park social worker alerted them to new volunteer opportunities. But the *meaning* of being from a church was more individual-centered for Ned than for Dora or Martha.

"Being from a church" was no less *religiously* significant for Ned and Elizabeth than for other members. In an interview, unprompted, Elizabeth and Ned referred to volunteering as "good works"; the phrase is widely recognized in the Christian tradition. Interestingly, they did not use any religious terms to characterize the community development projects that the Cluster spent most of its time on, such as the parish nurse. Ned described the parish nurse project only in terms of money (it took too much of it) and organization (it was too complicated). The issue was not that Ned lacked the ability to be well organized or keep track of money. In fact, he was the Cluster's treasurer, and everyone appreciated his skills. Rather, it was that in Ned's definition, being part of a church-based effort meant being a servant of individual needs, a charitable helper.

Maybe the Cluster was really a secular group for all practical purposes; it simply happened to have begun with church volunteers. Then we would have to ask why brochures bothered to call the group "faith in action"; several editions of the brochures retained that motto. It would be unclear why the group used religious tags such as "parish nurse," or "good works." We might wonder why they consulted with a state religious council instead of a community organizing outfit. And why did no one but self-identified members and representatives of churches ever join the Cluster? It would have been easy enough to avoid religious terms altogether if they were not important to the group's identity. The Fun Evenings project, pictured in chapter 3, started as a church volunteer-based project, but *never* used religious terms to describe its purpose at all. Project director Polly told me that it made no difference whether or not her volunteers happened to come from churches. The religious basis of the Cluster mattered to members.

Groups may identify themselves as religious groups whether or not they use a lot of religious language to discuss their goals. And religious social identity can vary even within a group whose core members are overwhelmingly mainline Protestant. Table 7–1 presents findings relevant to these points from the four large Lakeburg projects that I followed extensively. How if at all did religious identity work differently in the Cluster from the other groups?

TABLE 7–1
The Presence of Religious Culture in Selected Lakeburg Groups

Group	Religious Social Identity	Character of Religious Discourse about Group Goals
Humane Response Alliance	people of faith	*little* religious discourse about the goal of building civic ties
Justice Task Force	prophets	*close* relation between group's religious discourse and the goal of denouncing welfare injustice
Adopt-a-Family	Christian servants	religious discourse *is main source* of the goal of deep interpersonal relationships with ex-welfare families
Park Cluster	majority: representatives of religious collectivities minority: representatives of aggregates of individual volunteers from churches	*very loose* relation between religious discourse and the goal of "assisting the Park neighborhood"

How Religious Identity Complements Bridge-Building

Among the Lakeburg groups, only Park Cluster had a religiously significant term for bridge-building, a term it found satisfactory throughout its difficult project: It identified its connection to a "parish." That said something about the Cluster itself at the same time that it defined the Cluster's social map.

Humane Response Alliance members called themselves "people of faith" but did not use religious terms to imagine "reconnecting the caring community." Task Force members rarely if ever characterized their consciousness-raising goal in religious terms. While Catherine called the group's criticism "prophetic" on occasion, Task Force members did not use the term "prophet" to talk about their relation to the audiences for their economic injustice workshops. The Task Force would *switch* to a more obviously religious language of compassion when they talked about reaching out to welfare recipients or about welfare administrators stuck with enforcing a policy that they themselves did not support. The group never dwelled upon compassionate caring though, because they thought that would distract them from more crucial, social-structural relationships. Finally, when Adopt-a-Family volunteers became frustrated with their own bridge-building project, I noticed that repeatedly, the volunteers *switched* from a specifically Christian language of servanthood to a much more secular-sounding language of "cultural differences." The families, it turned out, were not so eager to be served. Table 7–2 summarizes these findings.

A pattern emerges: If religious groups are trying to create relationships *as re-*

TABLE 7–2
Everyday Terms of Connection in Selected Lakeburg Groups

Group	Religious Social Identity	Terms for Reaching Out
Humane Response Alliance	people of faith	• "reconnect the caring community"
Task Force	prophets	• raise consciousness subordinate terms: • Christian compassion for victims of the social system
Adopt-a-Family	Christian servants	• Christ-like compassion • crossing "cultural differences" subordinate terms: • "neighbors being neighbors" • "making friends"
Park Cluster	majority: representatives of religious collectivities minority: representatives of aggregates of individual volunteers from churches	• partnership with a "parish" • respect for neighborhood • "helping out"

ligious groups, they may be more successful if they have religious terms for picturing the relationship. That interpretation makes sense in light of recent writing about identity. As sociologist Margaret Somers has argued (1994; see also Wood 1999), identities are part of collective action. Through symbols and stories, groups communicate to themselves identities that make some kinds of action meaningful and other kinds hard for a group to imagine at all.[8] So it might be harder for a *religiously identified* group to stick with a project of creating new ties if it cannot communicate the project in religious terms. If a church-based group such as the Cluster could imagine itself obligated to a "parish" rather than a needy population in general, it might make more sense to them as churchgoing people to stick out all the frustrations they met along the way. I do not want to overinvest meaning in the single word "parish." Still, the Cluster used the term from its very beginning, and became, increasingly, a bridge-building partner with Park neighborhood. Contrasting the Cluster with the other groups suggests that Cluster members could make their project meaningful inside a kind of religious story, though not an especially dramatic or richly textured one.

The other Lakeburg groups either did not use religious terms to talk about valuable relationships beyond the group or else had a religious story about relationships that did not require a group to build. Adopt-a-Family volunteers met people on their daily rounds willing to be served with Christ-like care, whether or not the volunteers were part of Adopt-a-Family. Recall how Cara pointed out in frustration, during one of her group's last meetings before disbanding, that she did not need to endure the complicated logistics of an "adopted" family on the other side of town in order to be a good Christian. The story of Christ-like, compassionate connections did not require a project like Adopt-a-Family at all. The Task Force associated a Christian language of connection with the kind of ties they disparaged or else considered secondary to their main goals. And the Humane Response Alliance's story of civic renewal did not connect in any practical way to their religious identity as "people of faith." People who were not "of faith" might carry out the same project, while it would be odder for people with no religious identity to talk about partnership with a "parish."

In short, to know *how* religious identity complements the bridging work so important to scholars of civic engagement it is not enough to say that (some subset of) religion makes people feel more obligated to others. Neither should we assume religious community groups talk in deeply theological terms about what they do. We also should find out whether or not the group has a simple religious "story" about building civic ties.

WHERE PEOPLE EXPRESS RELIGIOUS IDENTITY: CHURCH-SPECIFIC OR SETTING-SPECIFIC IDENTITIES?

What if Cluster members happened to come from civic-minded churches? Maybe they were transferring a church culture to the Cluster. Different churches have different styles of involvement in or withdrawal from the world beyond church, and some are civic-oriented churches (Roozen, McKinney, and Carroll 1984; Becker 1999). I found, though, that the meaning of being a "church person" can change from setting to setting even for the same individuals. The same people can create religious social identities in different ways. Religious commitment is not simply a uniform characteristic that is always switched "on" for religious people. It matters *where* as well as how people bring religious identity into the civic arena.

I made field visits to the outreach committees of a Methodist and a Presbyterian church in the Cluster, and also observed a "road show" about the eviction prevention fund that the Cluster used to boost contributions to the fund.[9] The committees were Cluster members' links to their churches. Together, the two committees I observed sent a good variety of old and new Cluster members, including several oriented to a conventional volunteer style as well as others oriented to partnership.

The Methodist and Presbyterian church committees both promoted good volunteering, even though some members talked very differently at Cluster meetings. Inside these committees, working on behalf of the group, and the church, customarily meant boosting volunteer levels and increasing donations. It meant matching resources (human or financial) to needs efficiently. Inside church committees, volunteers—including Cluster members—sounded like Ned. They spoke as managers of resources or representatives of individual interests in the aggregate. Reverend Brice in the Methodist committee was a remarkable exception.

The Methodist committee got things done efficiently. It valued conversations that moved the agenda along and got tasks accomplished; it valued members who showed their responsibility to the group and the church by carrying out tasks. It talked relatively little about other groups, communities, or institutions in Lakeburg. It was a group of six hardworking people who, amazingly, kept six different community service projects going. Reverend Brice, an associate pastor of the church who had just started going to Cluster meetings, wanted to change the group's self-understanding.

Reverend Brice passionately wanted the group to reflect on a bigger picture of Lakeburg. He wanted it to consider the "communal infrastructure" of Park neighborhood when it apportioned time and money for Park, instead of finding individual volunteers to serve individuals in the neighborhood. He led months of discussion sessions about the committee's vision and its goals. He kicked off the first session with a New Testament passage from James (1:19–25). He wanted to convey that Christians must be "doers of the word, and not hearers only." Reverend Brice assumed that "doing" the word meant addressing the Park neighborhood's collective needs, its institutional relationships.

"Doing" meant something different to committee members. They were skeptical of the whole discussion at first. During the first session, one member remarked, "So what, we don't look at the bigger picture. We get things done." Another worded her way politely through an evaluation of the committee's first session: "I think we all knew what we were about, but I think it was helpful to articulate it. So this was a helpful exercise. Thank you." The committee listened attentively, but did not talk much about its relations with Park neighborhood at any of the three monthly meetings I attended over a year's time.

At one meeting, several members did make impromptu comments on what kind of neighborhood Park was. Their comments stood without further exploration: One said it was a cheap place to live and another called it a convenient part of town, especially for people with kids. Most Cluster members would have been surprised to hear either statement, since they had learned that Park residents paid comparatively high rents for shabby apartments, that Park kids got bused to schools that made them and their parents feel unwelcome, and that cuts in bus service would make the relatively isolated neighborhood even more inconvenient for residents without a car. Cluster member Nancy was at the meeting and did not remark on committee members' evaluation of the neighborhood. Nancy's style was much closer to Ned's than most other Cluster members.

By my last visit to the committee a year later, the committee explicitly affirmed what it had assumed a year earlier: It needed to pursue projects that would elicit sufficient interest in the congregation. The committee set itself up to satisfy a demand; the congregation was an aggregate of individual consumers of charitable and social action opportunities. I admired members for wanting to take on tough issues like global warming and relations with lesbian and gay congregants. Park Cluster was one more opportunity for volunteer involvement. As the committee chair remarked: "Park Cluster is a huge undertaking, and Nancy is our liaison, and she's only supposed to be the liaison, but she's the only one who's been really involved in it so if we have questions we ask her." Nancy's own remarks affirmed the committee's view of her as a solicitor of volunteer help rather than a catalyst for projects to build ties between the church and Park neighborhood. She told the meeting that "there wasn't much shaking" to report from the Cluster. In the last month, a well-publicized fire had gutted an apartment building across from the Park neighborhood center, Lakeburg School District's first neighborhood-based learning center had just been established in another apartment building across from the center, and the Lakeburg school board held a contentious meeting in the neighborhood center's basement. Nancy was right that there wasn't much shaking, if committee members got shaken mainly by calls for volunteer help. This month there were no neighborhood celebrations in need of meal servers or kids' programs in need of chaperones.

Reverend Brice was frustrated. Why did an affluent church like his donate a mere five hundred dollar a year to the eviction prevention fund, when there were an average of fourteen evictions a month in the Park neighborhood? He thought the church needed to change its whole way of thinking about outreach and the meaning of acting as a church: "We had our Bible study Sunday morning . . . and the question became, as a follower of Christ, who is the church supposed to go out to? And we did the grid [quiz questionnaire]. How good are we in fellowshipping with, just being around, being with people who our society deems as misfits or outcasts? We got a 'one' on that one [out of ten]. How good are we at servicing, providing services? We got a 'five'. . . . Parts of our church are beginning to look at that outreach as not just something we do on the side. It's a major part of who we are." In our interview and in his presentations to the committee, Reverend Brice kept appealing to the bigger picture, to "making it comprehensive"—subsidized housing instead of eviction prevention funds, for instance. He envisioned a church-supported computer center in the neighborhood and church-funded scholarships for job-training. It would be hard to explain his committee's relative lack of enthusiasm for the "bigger picture" as a product of political conservatism: The same committee members spoke in favor of a national health insurance plan and took other politically progressive positions. But Reverend Brice's appeal would seem irrelevant, or overly ambitious, for people defining themselves as good volunteers carrying out tasks. Brice envisioned a different understanding of "who we are" when going out into local civic life.

One could not say the group simply failed to live up to a religious sense of mission that Reverend Brice was promoting. The committee had a Christian understanding of its identity, contained in a vision statement that it had worked on for hours: "As disciples of Christ, our vision is to create an environment within Lakeburg Methodist church which enables this community of faith to be a leavening agent to eliminate the systemic forces that prevent all of God's children from living up to their potential." To pursue Reverend Brice's vision, again, the committee's understanding of being from a church, reaching out from a community of faith, would have to change.

It would be hard to fault the committee for trying to get tasks accomplished and keep its congregation interested in its work. The committee needed to stay afloat; it needed to keep securing volunteers to paint houses with Habitat for Humanity and serve dinners at the men's shelter downtown. The point is that the committee set itself up to create volunteer opportunities that appealed to congregants' individual charitable interests. It would be hard, perhaps even illegitimate, to reserve the amount of discussion space necessary for planning that would build bonds between the church and a neighborhood as a whole. The meaning of church-based action at Cluster meetings was often different from the meaning of church-based action at outreach committee meetings inside church.

The Presbyterian church outreach committee defined its work similarly. This committee included Cluster members Paula and Martha, both of whom promoted public goods for Park as a whole when they attended Cluster meetings. The Cluster had made a point of seeking out Park residents' own visions and definitions rather than assuming them; both Paula and Martha were active in this project of "listening to our neighbors." In the committee setting, both assumed a different relationship between church and neighborhood; their job was to funnel volunteers and money toward aggregates of individual needs.

The church's pastor observed at one meeting that the committee took "the buckshot approach," scattering its money in the direction of many different projects. A member of the Methodist committee had used the same "buckshot" metaphor to describe his committee's relation to service projects. Other members assumed the committee had to attract church members with a smorgasbord of issues; again, the Methodist committee thought similarly. Paula concurred, without commenting on whether this approach was the best if the goal was to establish enduring ties to a neighborhood. At a committee meeting, one member asked, "Do we have a specific goal with this giving [of church money]? A certain, p.c., thing—a political thing?"

Paula replied, "I don't think it has to do with politics at all. We have this pot of money to give out each year and we need to give it out." Paula did not portray the church's involvement in Park Cluster as long-term project to support a neighborhood or build a relationship between the church and the neighborhood. She characterized "local" projects in general as efforts to assist "needy persons, people who are poor, children . . . for individual organizations in Lakeburg that work with that population."

Hearing Paula talk about this generic, disadvantaged "population" of people with "needs," it would be hard to predict how she had related to the Park neighborhood while at Cluster meetings. For she was the one who had carefully pointed out, at a Cluster meeting, that people who used the Park food pantry were not the lazy poor featured in the political conservatives' stereotype, but working poor. She had described in great detail a plan for Park residents to take over unused plots of land and grow the vegetables that they wanted to eat. And these weren't ones such as arugula that white, middle-class people like her wanted to eat, she tossed in self-deprecatingly. Paula's social map was much simpler, more vague too, when she was referring to "needy people" in the committee than when she was relating to the neighborhood at Cluster meetings. Speaking and acting as a church member did not mean the same thing at outreach committee meetings as it did in the Cluster.

Cluster members who gave a panel presentation about the eviction prevention fund at a Unitarian church drew on the same customary understandings as the two committees. Surprisingly, given the conversation at Cluster meetings, the panelists did not characterize the fund as a means to creating relationships in the larger community. Along with Cluster members had come a few beneficiaries of the fund who testified to how the fund had helped them. The stories made us feel for the Spanish-speaking mother and young daughter who told them.

There is no natural or logical reason why committee members could not do more critical reflecting on relationships at committee meetings. Doing so would not necessarily detract from getting tasks accomplished or resources managed, depending on the tasks and the resources. A division of conversational labor between church committees and Cluster meetings may have resulted from customary assumptions about the different meanings of belonging to different kinds of groups. But there is little reason to think such a division is immutable or naturally more rational.

I do not advocate that church committees ignore the varied interests in their congregations. The Methodist and Presbyterian committees contributed to unimpeachably worthy causes, from homeless shelters to Bread for the World, to a hospital for the blind in South Korea. The committees' churches are probably like many others in the United States that adopt a variety of good causes in a marketlike environment of needs in the wider world and volunteer interests in the congregation (Wuthnow 2004, p. 62). In a time when many people wonder about the civic contribution of religious groups, though, it helps to distinguish between different kinds of volunteering. Church-based groups can offer goods other than the one-to-one, compassionate service that has become synonymous with religious volunteering in many Americans' minds. The Presbyterian minister and Reverend Brice did not sound enthusiastic about the "buckshot approach"; they sounded resigned to it.

Churches that aim to create relationships with entire neighborhoods, the way the Presbyterian and Methodist ones in the Cluster did, need not take the buckshot approach for granted. Reflecting more on their community service choices might help them anchor projects of partnership more sturdily inside their own churches. Maybe there will always be congregants like Paula or Martha who know how to do partnership outside their congregations. Martha, the church's retired associated pastor, was in her mid-seventies. Another outreach committee member wondered aloud to me after a meeting what the group would do once Martha was no longer the resident expert for some of the group's projects. It stands to reason that a partnership role in the wider community is more sustainable over the long haul if congregations make space for the identity and the communication that partnership requires, instead of assuming that hardworking, compassionate volunteers will grow into these naturally.

CASE TWO: THE RELIGIOUS
ANTI-RACISM COALITION

Park Cluster members knew that they were Lutherans, Episcopalians, and Presbyterians, not just "mainline Protestants." But they also identified themselves as sharing the same religious territory; that fact became explicit only when they puzzled over the evangelical-sponsored free-meals project in the neighborhood or when they encouraged the Jewish sociologist to get his synagogue involved in the Cluster. When mainline and evangelical Protestants tried to work together in the Religious Anti-racism Coalition (RARC), differences in social identity could create rancorous divisions inside the coalition. Faith traditions influenced different ways of drawing group boundaries, in other words, apart from what the traditions might say about the issue that the RARC took on:

Unhappy that the Christian Coalition had equated conservative Protestant religion with conservative politics in many Americans' minds, some national evangelical leaders had invited mainline Protestant, black Protestant, evangelical, and Catholic leaders to sign a national Cry for Renewal (1995). One Renewal spokesperson came to Lakeburg in 1997 to inspire Lakeburg's religious leaders to form a local chapter. The Renewal manifesto declared that "Christian faith must not become another casualty of the culture wars." It called poverty the most urgent issue facing the country. The month after the Renewal spokesperson's visit, mainline Protestant clergy in Lakeburg along with some evangelical pastors and a Catholic church leader initiated the RARC. Irrepressible Donald of the URC became director of the RARC. He said he wanted the coalition to bridge "the split between the Christian right and left, with the message that God is calling people of religious diversity to leave our differences at the door and address poverty."

But the coalition was dealt a different issue first, by the Ku Klux Klan. Word got around that Klan members from a distant county had applied for a permit to march in Lakeburg that spring. Many RARC pastors thought the RARC should speak up in a religious voice against the Klan, against racism. Divided on whether or not speaking up would only lend the Klan undeserved attention, the RARC finally decided to plan an event that would be a multicultural alternative to the march.

The race issue, at least on paper, could have united the coalition on ecumenical grounds. Mainline denominational leaders have long spoken out for racial integration, civil rights, and universal human dignity.[10] And in the past decade, white evangelicals have become avid spokespersons for racial reconciliation—writing books and study guides, organizing conferences, leading rituals of repentance, and integrating some of their nationwide organizations (Emerson and Smith 2000, pp. 63–66). Prominent evangelical pastors and leaders in Lakeburg participated in a "Service of Racial Reconciliation" with mainliners and Catholics in 1996, shortly after highly publicized bombings of black churches in the South. Yet the RARC endured painful tensions.

Sociologists have debated whether or not a kind of symbolic warfare polarizes Americans into religious traditionalist and humanist camps on social issues (Hunter 1994, 1991; see also Marty 1997; Etzioni 1996).[11] Disagreements among RARC members sounded like these "culture wars" in some ways, but not others. To understand these disagreements better, I needed to distinguish carefully between different culture concepts.

Attending the RARC's meetings and public events over fifteen months, I heard religious liberals and conservatives produce agreements that defy simpler versions of a culture wars thesis: In that way my evidence from the field supports critics of the thesis.[12] Mainline and evangelical Protestants, along with a few Catholics and others, all agreed on the religious grounds for opposing racism. What's more, they agreed that not only interpersonal prejudice but subtle and powerful "structural racism" are sinful. As sociologist James Hunter has argued (1994), ordinary liberal and evangelical Protestants' opinions on social issues may display much more similarity than do mass-mediated statements of professional publicists on each side.

Yet, cultural differences *did* divide religious liberals and conservatives in Lakeburg. Mainline and evangelical Protestants tended to have different assumptions about how to create a civic group around antiracist beliefs. They conflicted over differences in social identity, in other words—differences in customs—even as they agreed on religious reasons for opposing racism. The combination of convergence and divergence is difficult to grasp with current terms of scholarly debate.

To conceptualize cultural polarization in the United States, researchers have named belief systems, worldviews, cultural tool kits, or powerful organizations' discourses as the cultural realities of interest.[13] Those realities *are* important. By themselves, though, these concepts do not help us grasp patterns of group interaction. We need a different specific concept for that. Social identity is part of the customs I've discussed throughout this book, and it does the conceptual work.

Apart from highlighting the power of social identity, the RARC's experience suggests a diversity within evangelical culture that deserves more study. Evangelical leaders in Lakeburg did not always talk about social issues in deeply personal terms, the way one might expect evangelicals to talk. As sociologist Christian Smith argues (2000), evangelicalism is no unitary religious block when it comes to either theology or politics. His interview research shows evangelicals have a varied repertoire of "moral building blocks" (2000, p. 11) they can use to construct social opinion in a variety of ways. His interviews reveal, too, that the great majority of evangelicals talk of American society and social change in terms of personal responsibility, the primacy of personal change for social change, and the power of personal faith and personal example. This is the "personal influence strategy" I discussed in chapter 5. Lakeburg evangelical leaders departed sometimes from the personal influence strategy.

AGREEMENTS

The Sin of Personal Racism

Twice canceled at the last minute before Klansmen finally accomplished their mission, the Klan march took over the bulk of RARC monthly discussions for a year. Discerning shared principles was the easy part.

At one early meeting, the RARC began planning a religious response to the Klan march, a cultural diversity celebration. A subcommittee went off to a separate table to draft a proclamation to accompany the celebration. The small group included an evangelical pastor with a charismatic bent, a lesbian Unitarian minister, and an administrator from a regional synod of the mainline Lutheran (ELCA) church. A big part of planning a public event is choosing the terms within which to frame it, and that can be divisive.[14] This mixed group of pastors, however, sounded as if it was having a good time.

Twenty minutes later, the proclamation group had finished a preamble and reported back to the meeting. It said: "We want to unite as people of religious faith united in believing [sic] that all people are created in the image of God." The phrase "all in the image of God" became the title and theme for the whole celebration several months later. It was hard to believe this group could write a preamble so easily. Yet, when I asked the Unitarian minister if the group had argued about the preamble, she insisted they had not, and that members consented to it wholeheartedly.

Mainliners and evangelicals also united around the notion that any public response to the Ku Klux Klan should include personal confessions of racism. As the Unitarian minister put it: "I want this to be about more than the Klan. . . . I want it to acknowledge the complexities of racism that exist in this community. And one of the words that come to me is confession."

The Lutheran synod administrator chimed in: "We are all at various times racists, as we continue to be sinners." A United Church of Christ minister said that "I can tell myself I'm not racist at all, but then housing—the schools—then I look where I live. . . . we need to affirm that fact that we're all racist, there's no way off the hook." The director of the evangelical-based Adopt-a-Family program voiced similar concerns: "I'm racist in so many ways I don't even know."

The RARC committed an entire monthly meeting to personal sharing: Members took turns recounting their own experiences with cultural diversity. A Lutheran pastor told us what he learned from his one-time Jewish roommate after offering the man a ham sandwich. Another Lutheran pastor learned in the Marine Corps that "blacks from the big city" could be "natural-born leaders." A nun described her experience as the only white person in a small town in Alaska, where native people's style of speech sounded aggressive to her but not to other Alaskans. The pastor of an Evangelical Covenant church told us he spent two years at a Swedish seminary, with people from forty nations, and felt what it was like to be vulnerable as a foreigner. Minority people in the United States must feel like that all the time, he concluded. Across the theological spectrum, RARC members could talk easily about race and cultural diversity in personal terms.

Upping the Ante: "Structural Racism"

A half year into the RARC's work, Donald boldly enlarged the terms of discussion—and everyone went along with it. He introduced "structural racism," instructing us that "structural racism is power and prejudices of the dominant class, affecting institutions and disabl[ing] people who are not part of these." It is "not about whether we individually are prejudiced, but if we are members of the dominant class that benefits systematically." The director's opening prayer intoned urgently that "this group is feeling called by God to deal with structural racism and structural prejudice in our community." Personal confession was not enough. The director asked everyone to picture examples of structural racism, to make sure they understood it. Members pitched in without hesitating:

The incoming RARC director, an ELCA Lutheran, said, "Going into a bank or grocery store and finding trust from the employee because they find me familiar and similar to them, willing to accept my check. A conservative Lutheran (LCMS) congregational president added, "I have a very good job in public relations in government—and there are no black males. I assume this is not a coincidence." A Friends Meeting board chair stated grimly: "When it was announced to teachers at Woodside Elementary that kids from [low-income, minority] Park neighborhood would be transferred, the teachers cheered." RARC members of both theologically liberal and conservative bents seemed to be getting it. Their examples all pictured people in institutional relationships, not purely interpersonal ones.

The director now asked how many people in the room thought their congregations were being called to work on structural racism. *All present* named their congregations; these included Evangelical Reformed, Unitarian, conservative Lutheran (LCMS), American Baptist, ELCA Lutheran, Catholic, Evangelical Covenant, Evangelical nondenominational, Vineyard (evangelical), and Friends congregations. RARC members seemed to be embracing the notion of social-structural racism, including members whose interpretive "tool kit" should have made this notion hard to apprehend. But they had different styles of building a group around it.

DISPUTES OVER SOCIAL IDENTITY

"We Work Together Except When We Can't"

There was one more big decision to make. Would the RARC be officially interfaith? The group compiled a list of activities that they agreed *not* to do together if the RARC was to be officially an interfaith (Christian and non-Christian) group. The list included congregational worship in common, developing new congregations, holding religious classes, and writing new theological credos on racism. Members *agreed* not to attempt activities on that list in an interfaith setting. *After* that agreement, the RARC director asked, "Which congregations can't participate if it is interfaith, even if the group rules out those projects that could be problematic?"

A conservative Lutheran (LCMS) man stated angrily: "I don't like the way the question is worded. Having said that, Savior Lutheran [church]! Our mission is to follow our Savior." A Vineyard man added meekly: "Lakeburg Vineyard. It's nothing about social issues [though]—" Community in Christ representative Keith said, "Community in Christ." He added in a recitative voice, as if embarrassed to be trotting out his church's mission statement: "To build the unity of the Church and see the Word of Jesus Christ proclaimed." Ed of Evangelical Covenant questioned, "Why now? Why have you gone with us this far, but then say no?" Keith answered, "We have not had these questions about interfaith basis in the foreground before. Now they are." The Evangelical Reformed representative stated, "It's going to be difficult for Lakeburg Reformed, especially if you're going to rule out issues we've never talked about, never voted on, like abortion, euthanasia."

And then Donald asked which congregations could not participate if the RARC was only ecumenical Christian, not interfaith. Short responses came from representatives of the Baha'I fellowship, the Unitarian fellowship, a liberal Baptist (American Baptist) congregation, and the liberal Lutheran church that hosted RARC meetings.

At the next meeting the Unitarian pastor proposed that the RARC create spaces for both Christian initiatives and interfaith initiatives. Now, Matthew of Evangelical Reformed took a big step: "If we could do what we said at the outset we were going to do—racism for instance, or one of the other issues—if we can keep that the issue, and this is a big change in opinion from previous meetings, then—[the proposal is ok]. We're not here to promote our faith perspective, we're here to [work against] racism. . . . As long as we can keep the focus on the topic of racism, I can see my way clear."

The coalition's director summarized the proposal: The RARC would agree to think through each of their different strategies of antiracist work and decide whether these would best be interfaith or Christian only. For evangelicals in the room, this was a major breakthrough. The pastor from the liberal Baptist church looked bored. He had parked his eyes in the direction of a bookshelf behind me for much of the meeting. Now he offered his dry summary of the big breakthrough: "We work together except when we can't."

Members all agreed that God called them to address the sin of social-structural racism. But they could not agree on how to present themselves in civic life. They could not agree on social identity; they drew their boundaries differently. As

evangelical Keith himself said when challenged by Ed from Evangelical Covenant, working together became harder when the group placed religious identity
in the "foreground." His earlier statement about seeing the word of Jesus Christ
proclaimed did not mean that the RARC should proselytize, something no
member ever suggested doing; Keith was saying rather that he needed to draw
a line between himself and others who were not committed to the Word of
Christ even if they wanted to fight racism. Matthew was willing to see his way
clear to a "sometimes-interfaith" group only if the coalition could identify itself
as a *race-focused* group, and *make its religious identity less salient.*

The (theologically influenced) act of creating a social identity mattered apart
from religious beliefs about structural racism. It would be wrong to assume, as
liberal observers sometimes do, that conservative Christians are the only ones
who draw boundaries, while theologically liberal Christians are open-minded
and perhaps just as happy not speaking as religious people at all. Mainliners as
well as evangelicals wanted the RARC to speak with a religious identity. Mainliners as well as evangelicals drew boundaries.

The Wiccan Factor: Everyone Draws Boundaries

Though she does not know it, an anonymous follower of earth spirituality became a major symbol for the RARC its first year. This follower of wicca religion
had participated in a URC-sponsored prayer luncheon several years earlier. She
had offered a prayer, holding out in front of her a small, sculpted figure of a
deity. As Ed of Evangelical Covenant recounted, "A wiccan got up and invited us
to pray along, and that's when the shit hit the proverbial fan. It's one thing to
talk about prayer. It's another thing to—watch her dangling this thing [in front
of us] and inviting us to pray to the one-eyed Goddess!" Never had I heard Ed
sound the least bit disparaging of anyone associated with what he always called
"faith communities." The wiccan had breached a fundamental boundary for him. He brought up the incident many more times. The point caught on
with other evangelicals, but did not seem to move the nonevangelical members.

Figuratively speaking, wiccans became a presence at many RARC meetings—
a big presence on the coalition's social map. The evangelical Protestant and
nonevangelical members of the RARC gravitated toward different visions of a
response to the Klan at least partly because they drew boundaries with religious
others—like wiccans—differently. Early on, the evangelicals wanted an anti-
Klan event to include a worship service. Mainline Protestants hoped to have a
worship component too. The director of the evangelical outfit Adopt-a-Family
told us his heart was in an event that would build Christian unity, not an event
that was about race per se as an "issue." *"We want this to be an event that brings
people together. We want this—on a* Sunday*—not to be issue-oriented. I'd be open
to that issue on a Saturday, but—it's a celebration of Jesus."* Matthew of Evangelical Reformed advocated for worship, too, a chance to confess the sin of racism.

Keith of nondenominational, evangelical Community in Christ agreed. *None* advocated for an evangelicals-only event. Rather, the evangelicals felt best about presenting a specifically *Christian* social identity; the way to do that, as they saw it, was through worship.

But should it be Christian worship or interfaith? RARC director Donald pointed out wiccans were just a red herring; realistically speaking, none were going to come to the event. But that did not stop Ed and other evangelical clergy from bringing up wiccans, Buddhists, Satanic cult members, and other potent symbols of non–Judeo Christian identity. Even though the RARC never talked about inviting any non-Christian other than one "representative of the Jewish community," evangelical members' identity as evangelicals was at stake. Wiccans made for a conveniently distant symbol of the taboo that also marked traditions of belief closer to home.

Mainline Protestant RARC members along with the other nonevangelicals also wanted the Klan-alternative event to be a religiously identified event. They too, at least at first, thought a worship component was a good idea. When the RARC voted on the issue, mainline and other nonevangelical members voted for an interfaith service; the evangelicals who did vote (several conspicuously abstained) favored a Christian service. For mainliners, inclusivity trumped Christian specificity. Upon seeing how much evangelicals and others disagreed on the contours of the worship service, a retired Episcopalian pastor spoke up sharply: "Drop the worship. As Christian people, and I'm just addressing the Christian community here, we would all want to say we are against racism. . . . But if we do something that isn't worship, that frees you up to come . . . from our faith traditions. We could talk from our hearts about what needs to be done."

The Episcopalian pastor identified himself among "Christian people" just as Keith and Evan did. He did not imagine dropping his religious identity in order to enter a "naked public square" (Neuhaus 1984; see also Carter 1993). Rather he was drawing boundaries differently *as* a Christian. His mapping was quieter than that of evangelicals who worried aloud about wiccans. An ELCA Lutheran pastor asked us at one meeting to consider what the RARC might lose if it was *not* interfaith, and the liberal Baptist pastor asked how the whole conversation felt to non-Christians. They envisioned a religious identity we might call inclusive—but it would end up excluding evangelicals. Mainliners' and evangelicals' different ways of drawing boundaries around their identities provoked tensions that shared religious principles could not smooth.

WHAT WE LEARN FROM ASKING HOW RELIGION GOES PUBLIC

Expanding Cultural Approaches to Religion

Studying how people bring religious commitments into public, I learned that a great deal depends on the culture concepts we use. Some concepts draw our attention immediately to beliefs and worldviews. Yet people do other things with religion than using religious discourses or private beliefs to define goals for action. It is good to distinguish between different ways that culture works if the goal is to understand what people do with religion in civic life.

This study's approach to religious culture borrows insights from classic pragmatist writings and new scholarship on institutions. From the standpoint of Dewey or Addams, it would not be surprising if religious groups build civic bridges more readily when they have practical terms for communicating the project. Dewey's public, his "Great Community," depended on ordinary, reflective, ongoing communication; public actors must communicate reflectively not only about *issues* but about who they are in relation to others in the civic world.

It is worth mentioning an older, quintessentially sociological source for my approach to religious culture: Emile Durkheim. Classic statements from the Durkheimian tradition hold that religious culture works by way of collective representations (Durkheim 1995 [1915]), commanding values (Parsons 1967a, 1951), or moral vocabularies (Wuthnow 1992, 1991; Bellah et al. 1985). The religious articulation perspective discussed in this chapter is an example of the currently prominent, "late-Durkheimian" approach to cultural analysis in general (Alexander 1988b). This approach focuses on collective representations and ritualized vocabularies that members of society use to describe a good person, a good citizen, or a good society. Some studies probe the deeply internalized, binary "cultural codes" that structure debates about who should be included or excluded in civic life.[15] Others listen for the traditional "vocabularies" or "languages" that a culture offers for envisioning what is good to do as a person, a group, or a society.[16] Either way, the late-Durkheimian approach turns our attention to the explicit, loud, sometimes contentious force of religion that undeniably exists.

Durkheim thought religion worked in a different way, too. Put simply, different religions cultivate different styles of group life. In *Suicide*, Durkheim (1951 [1897]) famously pointed out that different religions promote tighter or looser forms of integration into the religious collectivity. Protestantism allowed looser, more individuated relations of believers to the body of the faithful; Catholicism and Judaism allowed less room for believers' individual interpretations, Durkheim wrote, and achieved tighter collectivities. Of course Durkheim's terms of religious comparison cannot directly inform this study. Neither is my focus on civic ties the same as Durkheim's interest in the ties that bind a religious community. Still, Durkheim was implying that religions cultivate different forms of boundary drawing and bonding, as well as different collective representations—much as these work together in real life. As religion scholars continue to broaden our grasp of religious culture, this basic insight of an "earlier" Durkheim may prove only more valuable for new inquiries.

Rethinking Our Understandings of Public and Private Religion

If religion influences the customs of group life, then we need to revisit some modern arguments about the privatization of religion. As Talcott Parsons stated it (1977, 1967a), Protestant Christianity gave American society fundamental definitions of citizenship and personhood. Originally Protestant concepts became abstract and generalized enough, though, that they could integrate a modern society in which people might no longer identify with the original, religious roots of those concepts. They would no longer be specifically Protestant so much as simply American: Some Americans might affirm the religious roots in private, but public life, on this argument, would be largely secular.

In addition to this historical, now largely desacralized role, religious culture can have a more active public, if quiet, presence. We need a different kind of analysis to hear religious meanings at work in this way. A group may seem secular because its members do not talk much about their religious convictions. Still, members may understand themselves as "being from a church" so that their group has religious meaning for them.

In a similar way the scenes from Park Cluster and the RARC challenge the blanket thesis that the contemporary American public square is religiously "naked" (Neuhaus 1984) or that public life in general silences religious believers (Carter 1993). The RARC's public multicultural celebration, "All in the Image of God," is an easy counterexample. Held in the Lakeburg Sports Arena, it included two Christian prayers of repentance, a gospel choir, and a dance troupe performing a stylized *baile del fuego,* a celebration of the Aztec sun deity—which provoked another argument between evangelical and mainline RARC members over the proper religious boundaries of the RARC.

Whether or not official American institutions, courts or schools for instance, silence religion as Stephen Carter has argued, few close observers doubt that religion is present in local American public life outside houses of worship. But the case of Park Cluster makes a more subtle and theoretically interesting counterexample. County social service people in the Park neighborhood told me that the Cluster's religious basis was not a problem from their point of view because Cluster members knew they were not supposed to proselytize. Cluster members' own unsolicited statements to me about not proselytizing show they and social service personnel shared the same understanding. Nothing from group meetings or interview discussions ever gave me the idea that this was self-censorship under duress, but more that proselytizing was irrelevant to Cluster members' sense of what was religious about the Cluster. It is not clear whether or not Cluster members ever would have liked expressing religious commitments more forthrightly. It is clear, though, that they understood the Cluster as a group with a religious identity, not a group worn down into a secularism of the lowest common denominator. Again, we need to think in more nuanced terms about religion's forms of public presence.

Religion in general does not promote or threaten bridge-building. Scenes from the field suggest that *some* of the religious meanings that mainline Protestants carry into civic life are more compatible with bridge-building than meanings central to American evangelical Protestantism. Listening closely to how people make religious meanings public teaches things we cannot learn if we ask only which religious traditions influence which kinds of action, on the assumption that we already know how and where people express those traditions.

Rethinking the Mainline Protestant Culture

Mainline Protestants would not be surprised to read that Cluster members invoked very little God talk at meetings. The specific cultures of mainline Protestantism may be less scrutinized sociologically than those of other religious groups that have enjoyed less power and influence in the mainstream. Studies of religious discourse in civic life often have portrayed non-Protestant or non-mainline Protestant discourse. When scholars use African Americans' struggle for civil rights as an example of religiously motivated activism, often they are tapping the discourse of historically black Christianity (Morris 1984; Bellah et al. 1985; Williams 1995). Though the discourse resonates with mainline Protestant social gospel traditions, it has strong roots elsewhere—in the black church, an institution with distinctive cultural forms (Patillo-McCoy 1998). Activists who use religious discourse to organize inner city residents against powerful foes are drawing heavily on Catholic traditions (Wood 2002, 1994; M. R. Warren 2001; Bellah et al. 1985) or a theological mix strongly flavored by Catholic and black Protestant traditions (Hart 2001, p. 42; M. R. Warren 2001), more than mainline Protestant ones.[17]

Mainline Protestant culture may work differently in public: Compared with other U.S. Protestant groups during the mid- and later-twentieth century, mainline Protestants have been less inclined to express Christian convictions publicly outside church settings (Cuddihy 1978; Davie 1995). For them, "Bible-thumping" is not polite. Anthropologist Jody Davie argues (1995) that inside church settings, the middle-class, mainline Protestant style of communicating faith is quiet and circumspect; it privileges individual privacy. It is practically the opposite of trumpeting praise or thundering prophecy that calls a community to action. More research can clarify how appropriate it is to use explicit religious language as a sign of mainline Protestant cultural influence. Davie's observations along with those here show in the meantime that mainline Protestant religion has a very quiet kind of influence on groups beyond church (see also Bass 1998; Wuthnow and Evans 2002).

A close look at this quiet influence may solve part of an enduring puzzle regarding mainline Protestants' place in American civic life. Mainline Protestant churches continue to be more likely than other Protestant, or Catholic, congregations to carry out projects that connect their churches to the surrounding community (Chaves, Giesel, and Tsitsos 2002; Wuthnow 2004). Sociologist Mark Chaves and colleagues summarize aptly that these churches appear more likely than others "to act as stewards of civil society rather than as one component of civil society." They played that role for many decades of the twentieth century (Wuthnow and Evans 2002). The researchers note that this difference between mainline Protestant and other congregations holds in the face of multiple controls—*including ideology and theology.* Not all mainline Protestants build religiously based groups in the same way in all settings. Still, customs of partnership and volunteering may have special affinities with mainline Protestant traditions. These customs might make up a big part of what it *is* to be a mainline Protestant. They remain opaque to studies that focus on theologies or formal beliefs alone.

Tocqueville's germinal comments on religion prefigure my investigation. Christian religion, in Tocqueville's argument, was a salutary constraint on the imagination, a source of mores that could keep Americans civil and temperate. What mattered was "not that all citizens should profess the true religion but that they should profess religion" (1969 [1835] p. 290). A shared religious identity, in other words, would help Americans trust one anothers' motives. Translated into currently popular terms, religious identity can be a source of social capital. Religion translates into social capital in very different ways.

Chapter Eight

DOING THINGS TOGETHER: LESSONS FROM
RELIGIOUS COMMUNITY SERVICE GROUPS

First Lesson: Ask a Different Question

By the time I started studying the Lakeburg groups, the URC's Donald and Adopt-a-Family's Evan already had heard about the decline in Americans' civic involvement. But both wanted to do more than get people to join groups. Donald talked about reconnecting the caring community. Evan talked about getting to know our neighbors again. Each set out to do something Americans talk a lot about doing: strengthening community, bridging diversity. Three years later I had discovered how hard it was for most of the Lakeburg groups to create new bridging relationships. What do the Lakeburg groups teach us about the conditions of possibility for a vibrant civic life in America? What are the next research steps? And what practical difference does it make whether or not local civic groups build bridges?

Many theorists and researchers care about civic groups because they think that by being involved in community life, people learn how to broaden the circle of togetherness. People work through the frustrations and cross-talk, instead of pushing perplexity to the corners of their minds the way Jane Addams's charity visitor did. Citizenship comes to mean collaborative community-building instead of carefully measured helping. As citizens strengthen the social fabric, in this viewpoint, they also empower themselves as participants in a social contract that otherwise would give more power to state agencies or the market.

Few scholars hope that civic participation teaches people to resign themselves to their (limited) place, to accept that society is too complex to understand. Even fewer imagine that involved citizens should learn to write off the jumble of local voluntary associations as nothing but a distraction or haven from the big forces that run the world. Bluntly speaking though, these are the lessons that people learned in Humane Response Alliance projects, Adopt-a-Family, and the Justice Task Force. These groups were not helping their members reconnect the caring community or get to know their neighbors better. The groups were not empowering themselves as decision makers in the new "postwelfare" era, either.

To understand the conditions for solidary, empowering civic relationships, it is not enough to ask about rates of group participation or stocks of social capital. It is not enough to ask why those stocks have fallen in America since the early 1970s. It is not even enough to ask what makes people join civic groups. We also should ask what group membership itself means to people, what people define as a good or appropriate group. Customary meanings shape the group conversations that lead to very different kinds of civic action, with different consequences for groups and their wider communities too. We need to bring group meanings and group communication squarely into the debates about civic engagement, instead of resting content with counting groups.

That is why, at the risk of overpacking my study with metaphors, I have distinguished bridges from spirals. The Justice Task Force, Adopt-a-Family, Park Cluster, and the leaders of Humane Response Alliance all wanted more than for people to join more groups—important as that was for starters. They did not define their groups' goals solely in terms of brief encounters, like the ones between adult chaperones and teens at Fun Evenings, or loosely connected network ties, like the Justice Task Force's affiliation with the Living Wage Campaign. Conceiving bridges as distinct kinds of spirals honors the Lakeburg group members' own sense of what they were trying to do. It also makes the best of insights from Tocqueville, Dewey, and Addams—all of whom imagined that civic relationships were about doing things together over time with a variety of people, and not about temporary contacts nor loose networks of the likeminded.

What We Learn from Listening and Watching Closely: Conceptual Contributions

Diverse Customs of Group Life

Tocqueville was right to take mores and habits seriously. Something like Tocqueville's "mores"—customs—do matter greatly for bridge-building and civic empowerment. A cycle of evolving customs and thoughtful talk about group relations propelled the Cluster farther and farther from its origins as a group of volunteers who were helping out in the Park neighborhood.

The trouble is that Tocqueville and latter-day Tocquevillians have underestimated the diversity of civic customs. There is not simply one "civic culture" in the contemporary United States alongside an anticivic culture of privatism, but different sets of customs that encourage some definitions of worthwhile civic activity and discourage others. All of them produce goods that many people would value—compassion, social critique, efficiency, among others. Most do not encourage people to create the bridges that build a greater community.

Was it worth the time to depict these customs closely with a fine brush? Why not paint American civic life in big, broad strokes the way Tocqueville did, inviting comparisons with other nations? The answer is in the details. Seemingly small matters of custom contribute to big differences in shepherding resources, relating to state agencies, and communicating social criticism. If social scientists want to understand the conditions that help ordinary people take more owner-ship of society, we need to do something that may be counterintuitive: We need to recognize small differences in style between earnest, hardworking volunteers like Ned of Park Cluster and earnest, hardworking volunteers like Ken or Betty, also of Park Cluster. Sociologists often point out that the "small" world of every-day interaction has the largest consequences for people's lives. Mundane, taken-for-granted styles of interaction in schools and workplaces, for instance, per-petuate systematic inequalities. So why wouldn't seemingly small differences in customs perpetuate different forms of civic life? The difference between "help-ing out" and "partnership" depends greatly on the customs of civic groups.

A Call for Better Concepts and Further Research on the Meanings of Civic Ties

Different customs are not equally prominent. We need to study them further and chart their relations with surrounding institutions. Of the customs I studied, helping out, or volunteering, is the most widespread and commonsensical in the United States today. We need more theoretical and empirical studies to figure out how it rose to such prominence after the 1960s. I proposed in chapter 3 that the institutionalized social structure of service provision shaped but did not simply call into being the now-customary, widespread understandings of volunteering in the American mainstream. Civic culture does not simply pop out of an insti-tutional machine. The long-standing culture of voluntarism in America likely plays a role too[1]. Better analytic terms would help sociologists understand how the centuries-old, Protestant-influenced culture of "voluntarism" become the modern "volunteerism" of the past several decades . How exactly have these dif-ferent levels of civic culture evolved alongside social-structural transformations?

To understand the prominence of volunteering in America, sociology needs more comparative ethnographic and historical work, too, to complement stud-ies that offer a bird's eye view of national civic and social service arenas. Exist-ing studies often gloss over social actors' own distinctions between "political" and "nonpolitical" public involvement, or else investigate one type of involve-ment in isolation from others, defining it as political or civic by fiat. If the mean-ings of civic ties matter as much as I have argued, than one next research step is to find out how these definitions have evolved in their institutional contexts.

Another step is to ask how and why those definitions vary within and between societies. Some members of the Lakeburg groups drew sharp distinctions be-tween "political" work and "volunteering." But that is not simply a natural thing to do. We need more research to find out which kinds of groups tend to do like-wise. How and why do people define political activity, charity, or service work in opposition to one another, in combination, or in some other relation? The question is striking when so much of citizen action is *potentially* ambiguous in these terms. Cross-national investigation of these questions can also strengthen

our analytic grasp of how culture, social structure, and institutions work together. Sociologists are calling for, and now starting to produce, more nuanced
accounts of how institutional structures and cultural structures or logics work
together or interpenetrate.[2] Studying the evolution and meaning of volunteering promises to clarify these basic conceptual issues while illuminating a huge
civic reality of our time.

Beyond the Social Capital Concept

Capital is not the most helpful metaphor to use if we want to research the meanings of civic ties. Though many studies of social capital in civic life rely on statistics on group membership or individual civic behavior, it is telling that Robert
Putnam's framework implicitly privileged a qualitative definition of social ties.
The framework deserves a great deal of credit for helping researchers chart some
striking trends in civic engagement; it offers an extremely flexible conceptual
tool. Still, the social capital concept does not capture all the Tocquevillian claims
about civic-mindedness. It invites us to think of group participation as a unitary good that can be scaled; more is better. It offers a bird's eye view of big
trends in collective life; that is highly valuable for some research questions. We
should not fall into the trap of asking only those questions about civic engagement that the concept can answer.

   The social capital concept freezes the interactions that create different kinds
of ties and different goods. Having become accustomed to seeing itself as an autonomous group on a complicated social map, Park Cluster took on more projects that reproduced and ratified its newly evolved customs, its practical definitions of networks, norms, and trust. It *talked* reflexively, self-critically about its
role in the Park neighborhood. After the fact, we could say that the Cluster created new bridges because it had "bridging social capital." The process depended
on customs and reflexive conversations—not more meetings or more group
members—and these elude the "capital" metaphor.[3] Adopt-a-Family groups, in
contrast, got practice at pushing society away, devaluing the local social map,
even as the volunteers tried to reach out compassionately. The harder the volunteer groups tried to relate interpersonally to the families, the more inscrutable
the families became. The volunteers knew there were barriers to the relationships they wanted to build. They felt them, feared them, tried bravely to overcome them. But their customs limited their ability to talk reflectively about
them. After the fact, we could say that Adopt-a-Family groups lacked bridging
social capital. But that would not help us understand the fact that the groups
did reach out then undercut their own goals. Some questions require concepts
that illuminate interaction instead of freezing it.

   One of those questions is about the future of civic engagement. As public and
private organizations continue to fuse or cohabit in the civic realm, as government's responsibilities for welfare shrink, and market logic runs more and more

of social life, do citizens need to develop new styles of connectedness? What models of group life, old or new, would keep civic participation vibrant, democratic, or even relevant amidst these changing institutional relationships? This is not the place to review research on restructuring governance, revamping welfare provision, or reinventing democracy, but it is worth pointing out the limits of the social capital concept in this context. Americans may need new forms of social capital that can work effectively with new institutional relationships. But to know anything more about those forms we need close listening and close comparisons, along with sensitive charting of the cultural landscape that enables some styles of group life to thrive while others never take root.

Social Reflexivity or an Invisible Hand?

For some social scientists, the question about what forms of civic engagement will serve the evolving social contract is not so pressing: Society ties itself together when more people join more groups. Political scientist Francis Fukuyama has elaborated one version of this invisible hand theory; his relies on the hand of human nature (1999). Frayed and shrunken social ties will regenerate, he maintains, because the propensity to cooperate is hardwired into the human brain. Fukuyama points out how norms of trust and civility generate spontaneously when morning commuters queue up for rides with drivers headed cityward to work. Drivers and riders figure out not to offend each other, not to bring up politics or religion, not to smoke. When government regulations assist or at least do not thwart our innate tendencies, people generate a more connected, more civil society. Yet, spontaneous commuter solidarity makes an odd model for civic life. Participants agree more on what they cannot do together than what they can. They set a simple, unambiguous end-goal. They talk little. Social ties do not require much pondering in this scenario. It is hard to see how community-strengthening responses to social dilemmas like those posed by welfare reform could develop so silently. Sociologists, and citizens too, need better models, better metaphors that make social complexity visible.[4]

For that reason, even the most well-intentioned proposals to get Americans more involved in life outside the house fall short.[5] Whatever virtues they may have as policy, they make for weak sociology. There is no reason to assume that more joining inevitably creates new civic relationships beyond short-term, detachable liaisons. Political theorist Jean Cohen argues a similar point cogently, that the currently popular social capital concept "allows one to avoid the difficult task of showing that the particular trust built up between specific individuals in one context can be transferred without further ado to other contexts, to strangers, or to society at large" (1999, p. 64).

What harm is there in hoping that more summer camp volunteers and more baby showers for low-income mothers will connect society together in small ways? The danger is that we might overlook the real social divisions, conflicts, and complexity that prompted Donald and Evan to do new kinds of bridge-building—and made the bridges so difficult to build. In a world of diverse people and diverse civic groups and networks, with social service agencies that both empower and limit them, faith in the invisible hand of solidarity is unconvincing.

Yet that faith is widespread. Volunteer recruiters, educators, local leaders and television newscasters regularly say that when Americans sign up and give an hour or two of their time a week, community bonds will strengthen. This invisible hand theory of social bonds tempted Donald, of the URC. He wanted new civic projects to weave ties between churches and neighborhoods, between churches and service agencies. He did not mean only that individual volunteers needed to serve more hurting individuals, much as that also would be a good thing. He assumed that more joining and networking would somehow add up to "reconnecting the caring community." His customary definitions of civic action obscured complex relationships that disconnect the most sincere volunteer efforts from the possibilities for a more solidary community life. Donald and other URC leaders got frustrated by the complexity, and by the county agents on whom they relied for the bigger picture of social ties in Lakeburg, but did not give themselves space to talk through that picture with other URC leaders.

We need more research and more theoretical work to understand why social reflexivity would be rare in local civic groups. It is unconvincing, theoretically and empirically, to argue that social service workers or state employees always are domineering bureaucrats controlling a pliant citizenry, the way an earlier generation of critical theories taught. While the structure of social service squeezed the Lakeburg groups' participation in new service initiatives, it is too simple to say there is an administrative logic of social service that vacuums up reflexivity. Social theorists have argued in fact that some trends in modern, complex societies encourage forms of reflexivity (Giddens 1991; Beck, Giddens, and Lash 1994; Habermas 1987). There is good warrant for developing better terms to understand the conditions of social reflexivity. John Dewey pointed out that people needed to "know" the complexity of modern society, to talk reflexively about it, if they were going to organize it democratically. Dewey had no faith in the invisible hand: "[N]o amount of aggregated collective action of itself constitutes a community" (1927, p. 151). The Lakeburg groups' attempts at doing things together bear Dewey out.

What We Learn about Doing Things Together: Substantive Contributions

Volunteering and Networking: Making Togetherness Abstract

Americans have customary ways of doing things together in public life. We give millions of hours every year to short-term volunteer stints: serving meals at homeless shelters, playing ball with "at-risk" teenagers, giving little kids piggyback rides at summer camp (Guterbock 1997; Wuthnow 1998). Many, many loosely connected networks bring interest groups together, at least on paper, to advocate for single issues. There certainly is no denying that volunteering and networking accomplish a great deal in American civic life. With so much of civic life organized around volunteering and networking, it may seem odd to investigate these forms of group life closely. Isn't it just obvious that these are efficient ways to get things done?

That depends on what civic engagement is supposed to do. If it is supposed to cultivate the art of collaboration with widening circles of people, then neither networking nor volunteering as customarily understood are very efficient. Without question, volunteering and networking produce valuable civic and political goods. In the Lakeburg groups at least, neither lived up to the broad vision of the social spiral argument. This suggests at the least that we should be more cautious and speak with much more nuance about the potential of volunteering and loose networking to build community in America, especially in a time of institutional restructuring.

In projects like Fun Evenings and Summer Fun Camp, volunteers got practice at creating brief liaisons. Volunteers were fun, polite, caring, or forbearing for a few hours with individuals they might not see again or see only several times for a couple of weeks. Loosely connected programs like these can give volunteers meaningful, rejuvenating, emotionally touching experiences; time in the field showed me that volunteering can be all of those good things. What's more, carrying off inoffensive, short-term contacts cheerfully is a social skill. It simply is not the skill that social spiral theorists have had in mind. Lakeburg volunteer projects did not cultivate volunteers' ability to collaborate *with* diverse other people over time. They did not give volunteers practice being interdependent with other people in a wider social world, doing things together. Instead, the volunteers often wondered what they should be doing, with whom.

Monitoring exit doors and dance floors and basketball courts, Fun Evenings volunteers got practice thinking of the teens as members of an abstract category: young people at risk of being taken over by menacing social problems lurking just outside. Volunteers in the Interfaith Shelter learned to be circumspect with shelter guests. They, too, learned to treat the people they served respectfully as abstractions: The shelter training encouraged the volunteers to think of the guests as individuals with human dignity—not a bad lesson!—but not as particular members of society, enmeshed in particular relationships with other people, groups, or institutions. Volunteers learned to present themselves amidst people unlike themselves without doing things *together* with those people. Often they were not doing things together with other volunteers, either.

Loose networking in the Humane Response Alliance cultivated coexistence more than collaboration. Catherine of the Justice Task Force and Polly of Fun Evenings could work under the same network umbrella without having to work *together*. As long as everyone focused on "doing" something and recruiting volunteers, no one was figuring out a bigger picture of doing things *together*—neither in the Urban Religious Coalition nor in Lakeburg's church circles. A few of the HRA's projects survived, but the HRA and Donald's broader vision did not.

Short-term networking around the Park neighborhood school issue created an image of collaboration, an abstraction built on misapprehension. It produced an outside political constituency, on paper, for a cause that many Park residents themselves would not have supported. Well-intended networkers in Lakeburg progressive circles actually threatened bridges between Park neighborhood and people outside it because they did not stop long enough to imagine concretely their relationships with Park parents or the neighborhood center. For the volunteers and networkers *themselves,* volunteering and networking could make togetherness elusive, sometimes frustratingly so. These are not practical ways to build a greater enduring community.

When Social Criticism and Deep Caring Keep Togetherness Elusive

The Justice Task Force and Adopt-a-Family seemingly could not look much more different from each other, but they had at least two things in common. Each pursued an alternative to networking and volunteering, at least early on. Each found their own project of doing things together highly disappointing. When deep caring was floundering, the Adopt-a-Family volunteers seized on abstractions such as "cultural differences" to make sense of their frustrations with the families, and the families became only more perplexing. When the Task Force's Economic Justice workshops were failing to energize Lakeburg church circles, Task Force members burrowed deeper into abstract analyses of corporate domination, passing up chances to draw in new members and build bridges with groups in Lakeburg. Presented with perplexities, each project fled to abstractions, and togetherness remained elusive.

Volunteering and networking ended up, finally, as the customary defaults for Lakeburg groups that had cultivated other styles of community involvement. While the Justice Task Force's project to educate churchgoers about welfare reform shrank "off into a corner somewhere" as Frank put it, members gravitated toward the kinds of loosely connected networks that host a lot of progressive politics in the United States. Some tried to get the group involved in a campaign finance reform network and a prison reform network. When Adopt-a-Family volunteers saw how hard it was to build deep, personal relationships from scratch with former welfare-receiving families, Evan introduced a much more conventional volunteer role for church groups, as adjuncts to social service professionals, armed with an "action plan," before the project dissipated entirely.

The default roles were hard to get around. When I listened in on Park social workers' meetings, the social workers *always* discussed Cluster members in their role as volunteers or as networkers who could round up volunteers. They discussed the Cluster in connection with projects such as collecting Christmas presents for Park children, assembling Thanksgiving baskets for needy Park residents, or cleaning up after the annual Southeast Asian Festival. Cluster representatives present at these meetings never challenged these terms of discussion. Trying to describe the Summer Fun Camp quickly, even Cluster member Ken described the Cluster as a group of volunteer "service providers"—which says little about the partnering sensibility that was increasingly central to the Cluster's raison d'être. Scenes from the field help clarify why scholars have considered the volunteer/networker model to be the dominant form of civic engagement since the 1970s. The Lakeburg groups' experiences suggest it is not easy for community groups to mount alternatives to it.

Yet it may be more and more pressing to innovate alternatives. Plug-in style volunteering makes sense in relation to loosely connected networking. Networking in the way I mean it presupposes expert knowledge but not usually much deliberation or institutional change. But the structure of social service *is* changing; that is why Donald thought it was so urgent to come up with new "public-private partnerships" in the wake of welfare reform and the ongoing shrinkage of government responsibility. The Humane Response Alliance's experiences show that volunteering and networking as customarily understood may not be able to fill new institutional gaps that grow if guaranteed welfare or tax-supported expenditures shrink. The question of new civic alternatives in a postwelfare age deserves much more study; scholars of religion and social welfare are beginning to do just that.[6] If new culture proliferates within the troublesome gaps left by institutions (Swidler 2001), then this is a good time for creative thinking about citizens' roles in social and community service.

The fact that alternatives endure at all tells us, once again, that American civic culture is more than a mere reflection of the dominant organizational structure. Customs have a life of their own. Recall how HRA leaders called for networking and volunteering, while the social service administrator who participated in HRA called for neighborhood dialogues and personal transformation. Sociologists would say customs are "relatively autonomous" from the social structure of social welfare or community service. The customs are crucial conditions of possibility for civic life. But only a few customs strengthen the possibilities for doing things together in a way that Tocqueville, Dewey, or Addams would value most.

Doing Things Together Flexibly: A Cultural Possibility

John Dewey hoped that something like what I call social reflexivity could become customary in American public life. Group-building customs are the inescapable grounds for reflexivity: Citizens do not communicate reflectively in a vacuum. They sustain a group as they reflect. As long as individuals recognize themselves as belonging to a group, they will define an inside and an outside, they will sustain bonds that they usually will try not to break, and they will value some kinds of communication over others. Some customs will allow far more social reflexivity than others, but it seems unlikely that any would set no limits whatsoever.

Park Cluster was a flexible group, in Dewey's sense. Its partnership customs enabled it, in Dewey's words, to "interact flexibly and fully in connection with other groups" (1927, p. 147). So the Cluster wondered what Park residents themselves thought about the proposed neighborhood school that had seemed like such a good idea at the outset. They mulled over the biweekly free meals that had seemed at the start like an unquestionably nice thing for the neighborhood. They became more and more uneasy talking about the good of the neighborhood without neighbors at the table. It became increasingly urgent to figure out how they could work with Charmaine, the neighborhood center director, instead of bypassing her. Fitfully, the Cluster *changed* as a group. They transformed their own style of togetherness as they cultivated new relationships beyond the group.

Civic bridge-building requires more than holding the right values or thinking the right thoughts about diversity or equality. It depends on a style of doing things together reflectively. The style of the group influences what people can believe, say, and do together. People need to know how to create flexible groups, apart from what they know or believe about poor people, welfare policy, or inequality. The Cluster shows that flexible groups remain a cultural possibility, and a practical possibility, even if the dominant institutional relationships squeeze them. Different styles of doing things together very likely have their own cultural histories. Park Cluster members' style of doing things together reminded me of Jane Addams's Hull House generating new civic collaborations in poor, immigrant Chicago. Adopt-a-Family seemed to be reenacting a Christian version of Addams's charity visitor, as it tried to create caring relationships with distant "neighbors." Tracing the histories of these customs is an important task for another study. Still, it makes sense to conceive the customs as enduring elements of civic culture, conditions of possibility for American civic life, rather than purely local inventions.

When Certainty Threatens Community

Who would criticize anyone's steadfast desire to work for the greater good? Yet one of the more subtle lessons I learned in Lakeburg is that certainty can threaten community. The URC liaison to Park Cluster was *sure* that busing Park kids to three schools was intolerable, a bad thing for Park kids and parents; she knew that the school board simply had to come up with another plan. In hot pursuit of a good cause, she nearly snapped the fragile ties between the Cluster and the Park neighborhood center. Catherine and Frank were *sure* that the rich would keep getting richer while the poor lost welfare benefits unless brave social critics could awaken people to the hard truth about corporate interests and the growing economic divide. They alienated the one minority leader who came to the Justice Task Force, a potentially valuable ally who might have given the task force and its prophetic truths air time on his radio program.

In a multicultural, unequal society, the practical art of community-building requires tolerance for ambiguity more than moral certainty. As moral philosopher Zygmunt Bauman put it (1991), solidarity with an "other" requires us to cultivate a taste for ambivalence, tenuousness, *uncertainty*. We feel our way toward a relationship with an other whom we already have committed ourselves to recognize and respect as different from us. Just as Jane Addams came to appreciate perplexity as a learning experience, cosmopolitan citizens today may need to work on assuming less and wondering more.

WHY BUILD BRIDGES?

If Park Cluster is any indication, flexible groups can be frustrating, conflict-provoking, not the easiest groups to spend time in. They pass up some of the goods that other styles of group offer. It takes forbearance to stay in a group whose collective self-understanding may change over relatively little time. On the other hand, flexible groups may create bridge relationships, not simply contacts with outsiders but ongoing relationships. So what good are those relationships?

Reorganizing Civic Responsibility

Bridge relationships between Park Cluster and Park neighborhood organized church money and volunteer time differently than Cluster churches would have done without those relationships. In a small way, bridge relationships empowered Cluster churchgoers as civic actors partnering with county agencies, non-profit organizations, and Park residents. Parish nurses and eviction prevention funds do not add up to profound social change. And Reverend Brice was very likely correct: His church—and others in Lakeburg, for that matter—probably could have contributed a lot more money toward building relationships with the Park neighborhood if they had made those kinds of bridging projects more of a priority. Still, Park Cluster's bridging projects represent a distinctive mode of civic engagement that could be one means, among others, to bettering life in low-income neighborhoods, on residents' terms.

Sociologists William J. Wilson (1987) and Robert Sampson (1999) among others might agree. Both would point out that low-income neighborhoods increasingly lack enough resources to make "community empowerment" into more than an empty slogan without outside assistance. While both call on government and other public agencies to make those resources available, they do not rule out that civic organizations may have roles to play in assuring social welfare, too. Others such as sociologist Theda Skocpol (2000) affirm these roles more directly, and include religious groups as well as a democratically empowered state in their vision of a better social contract.

Cultivating the customs of partnership, religiously based groups might innovate new ways of organizing donations and volunteer time. They would create public goods, goods that result from civic deliberation, instead of services that cultivate the "givers and receivers" relationship that Betty of Park Cluster warned against. Conventional service relationships were just what Donald had criticized in his bid to reconnect the caring community. Both Donald and Evan wanted to encourage new forms of responsibility between church-based groups, service agencies, and people they hoped to serve. While Evan's vision complemented the given terms of welfare reform more easily than Donald's did, neither had aimed to promote service as usual, and both hoped that church-based groups and coalitions would play new civic roles in an evolving social contract.

The 1996 welfare reforms and subsequent "faith-based initiative" of the Bush administration publicized religious groups' roles in the social contract as service providers working in tandem with a shrinking state. History as well as current scenes from the field in Lakeburg show that other definitions of the social contract are possible, in which religious groups help to build up civic relationships, civic solidarity, apart from offering service to clients. As sociologist Theda Skocpol observes (2000, p. 38), Christian and Jewish associations in the United States throughout the nineteenth and twentieth centuries "all were in the business of building horizontal, inclusive ties that strengthened the strand of democratic community in America . . . linking many elite Americans with ordinary white and blue-collar working people" (see also Young 2002). If religious groups continue to hold out that bridging potential, at least at local levels, they may practice a kind of civic responsibility different from either the privatized, individual responsibility enshrined in welfare policy reform (S. Hays 2003) or the administrative responsibility promoted by an earlier, liberal consensus. Skocpol's stirring comments on this third possibility are worth quoting at length:

> In a democratic society, fragmentary efforts to "do for" the poor by the privileged can never be a full substitute for all of the children of God associating—"doing together"—as they struggle to move toward the promised land of a just and loving community, and a more complete democracy. Misguided as some contemporary appeals to cramped versions of religious ideals may be, no one has yet found any substitute for the democratic energy unleashed historically by the best in America's tradition of Biblically inspired associationalism. (2000, p. 47)

Bridging in Politics: Standing With Instead of Speaking For the Other

Reflexive, bridging relationships empower political as well as civic alliances between groups. Failures to bridge do more than weaken alliances, lose campaigns, or hurt feelings; they may squander the good reputation that groups and their leaders spend years accumulating and make the next alliance project that much more difficult. The strategic contacts of the sort a URC leader made during the Park school campaign had different alliance-building potential than ongoing, reflexive bridging efforts, even if both kinds of relationship would count on paper as "bridging social capital." By the time the Lakeburg school board was ready to reconsider the question of a new elementary school in Park neighborhood, Cluster members had decided they needed to find out what Park residents thought, instead of assuming their interests were obvious or uniform. The school issue was part of a larger bridge-building project for them.

Once again, it makes sense to distinguish bridging as a particular kind of spiraling outward. The URC leader worked hard at spiraling out to the Park neighborhood and to school board officials. It is worth pointing out that she did not build bridges with Park the way I defined bridge-building in chapter 2 and the way some Cluster members practiced it: She did not try to create a routinized relationship with an *other*. She identified with residents' presumed interests, rather than taking residents as others whose interests needed to be comprehended first. *They* were *us*. All were united in caring about Park kids, so it was as if there was no perceived gap to bridge.

Subordinate groups, potential bridge-building partners, need to be recognized—granted dignity—as "other" before bridges can be built. Bridgebuilders need to perceive and honor gaps first. Other research shows how subordinate groups sometimes chafe at privileged advocates who imagine they already *know* thoroughly the people on whose behalf they advocate.[7] Wellmeaning advocates like these circumvent the possibility of perplexity. Eager in solidarity, they avoid uncomfortable, transforming encounters with an other.

That does not mean we must celebrate otherness as an end in itself. Critics of identity politics in America have taken sharp aim at radical feminists, Afrocentrists, and multicultural advocates so intent on being affirmed in their particularity that they refuse the possibility of meaningful membership in the larger society.[8] Identity separatists make the same move as some strategic alliance builders: They circumvent the possibility of perplexing encounters that might challenge their assumptions.

It is good sociology to say that a group's sense of otherness is not just a political mistake that rational thinking about interests could correct. Those perceptions are part of how groups constitute themselves as groups and map themselves into the larger social world. Some alliances between relatively disenfranchised groups like low-income minority parents in Park neighborhood and majority groups may require ongoing bridge-building beyond strategic liaisons if those alliances are going to thrive at all. They would need people on both sides who are willing to act and feel like Jane Addams's perplexed cosmopolitan citizen.

In Lakeburg, religious traditions influenced the possibilities for bridge-building in a way I was not expecting. Experience in the field taught me some new things about religion and its relation to reflexivity.

RELIGION AND REFLEXIVITY

Common sense says religion offers people unchanging polestars that guide them, keep them from questioning too much. But listening to ordinary interaction in the Lakeburg groups, I found that religious meanings could complement the critical questioning and tolerance for ambiguity that characterize social reflexivity. It helps to clear away some potential misconceptions of both religion and reflexivity.

Scholarly specialists and citizens alike often take "religion" to mean systematic worldviews or formal belief systems that form people's most basic identities. Given that definition of religion, we might not think to explore the happenstance, informal, quiet expressions of religious sensibility that slip into everyday life—the tags of religious identity that Cluster members used as they went about their work, for instance. These little tags I heard sometimes in Park Cluster may have done more for civic bridge-building than all of Donald's noble pronouncements on religious people's duty to reconnect the caring community.

The Lakeburg groups confirmed what I had imagined at the outset: Sometimes it is much better to ask what people do with religion instead of what religion makes people do or be. I learned that religion makes people neither civic-minded nor anticivic minded. Rather, people carry religion into different kinds of civic activities with very different styles of expression.

The concept of reflexivity easily invites misunderstandings, too. Social reflexivity does not mean talking about social relations in the abstract or analyzing society's institutions at a distance. Social reflexivity means relating self-critically to others, not intellectualizing about relations that happen somewhere else. To be socially reflexive, people have to picture themselves and their groups *in* relationships with some larger social context, and be willing to ponder those relationships critically, even self-critically. That is why, as much as Task Force members criticized capitalism and the "Band-Aid" of compassion, they were not practicing social reflexivity. Arguably, their critique was valuable anyway; the group's *value* for members or the surrounding locale was not at issue in this study. The point here is to get clearer on what social reflexivity is and is not. Task Force members worked at remaining apart from people whose consciousness they wanted to raise, rather than imagining a relationship to them. They practiced social critique; they were not practicing social reflexivity.

If we imagine reflexivity in a religiously identified group, we might think of confession and penitent soul-searching, or else the kind of deep, risky personal sharing that many Americans now associate with spirituality in small support groups and study groups.[9] This kind of reflection is valuable, sacred, to many

people. It is good to note, though, that personal reflection is not the same as social reflexivity—talking about how the civic group setting one is in relates to a
larger social context. Groups that practice personal reflection together may
practice social reflexivity too; it would take a separate study to find out how personal sharing sessions, social reflexivity, and bridge-building may relate to one
another. I did see that even after Religious Anti-racism Coalition members allowed themselves a long session of personal sharing about cultural diversity,
they continued to clash over different, implicit definitions of how to work together. Members shared the ability to talk personally about culture and race and
listened appreciatively to one another's personal stories, but continued having
a hard time bridging differences between mainline and evangelical Protestants
in the RARC.

If people practice social reflexivity, they talk about relationships that often are
harder to see than interpersonal relationships individuals experience privately.
Words can bring to life relationships and obligations that no one literally sees.
Religious traditions offer simple, powerful words that help people to picture obligations and relatedness, words such as "parish" or "neighbor." People may use
those words to keep people out of their circle of togetherness, but they also can
use them to imagine ties to people who are not literally part of a parish, and not
neighbors in a physical sense. In this very practical way, religion *sometimes* may
help groups reflect on, articulate their place in the wider social world. It may
help people cultivate social stewardship, a sense of being embedded in and responsible for society. With that sensibility, civic groups gain a distinctive kind
of power.

Togetherness and the Power to Write the Social Contract

The social spiral argument had two parts. This book has focused mainly on the
most prominent part, the idea that civic groups bring their members into relationships with other people and groups they may not encounter otherwise. The
other part was that civic groups empower citizens to take on responsibilities that
otherwise would belong to state agencies or be left to market forces. I showed
how the HRA, the Justice Task Force, and Adopt-a-Family in different ways
failed to empower or even disempowered their members. It is not just by coincidence that these groups, by their own standards, failed at the projects of doing
things together that I illustrated in the case chapters.

How does togetherness relate to empowerment? We think of strength in
numbers, strength in unity: "The people united will never be defeated," goes a
popular protest chant. Of course a tight unity can give groups the power to win
resources or rights. The Lakeburg groups' experiences taught me another relation between togetherness and power.

When a group's own style of togetherness keeps it from talking reflectively about its place on the larger social map, the group closes down opportunities to collaborate in steering society. It foregoes the power to participate in drawing the lines between governmental, market, and civic relationships. The lines are not natural. A lot of times, they are not obvious. People have to talk about them if they want to redraw them or reimagine the institutions between the lines, and in modest ways that is what both Donald and Evan had hoped to do. Citizens will not exercise the power to help draw those lines if their own forms of togetherness make it seem either threatening or a waste of time to talk about relationships between professionals, networkers, volunteers, and the people they consider beneficiaries.

Aware that they were confronting a new, "postwelfare" age, the Lakeburg groups might have re-visioned relationships between civic and governmental roles in an ongoing, practical, reflective way, out loud. That is what Park Cluster began to do, not by theorizing the relations between state and civil society in the abstract, but by talking thoughtfully, self-critically, about concrete projects that gave church groups more civic responsibility than they had before the discussion began.

Why would civic groups care to exercise this kind of power? Citizens will be subordinates or adjuncts only, rather than *collaborators,* if their groups do not allow them the space to imagine and mull over their responsibilities in the wider world. Citizens might decide their responsibility includes challenging government's shrinking role in social welfare. They may decide they want to affirm the shrinkage or rethink relationships in the social contract entirely. Citizens will not arrive at *any* picture of their role in the social contract if mulling over the options threatens their forms of group togetherness.

Even before the 1996 welfare policy reforms took effect, some lawmakers and political commentators wondered how to encourage religious groups to pick up some of what government was letting go. Others wondered how government should fix the welfare system instead of shrinking or outsourcing it. Fewer people asked a more basic question raised by this historic shift in responsibilities: *Who* should decide what roles government, job markets, religious and other community groups play in addressing human needs? If ordinary citizens play a role, then they must be able to create groups that can talk about the bigger picture and citizens' place in it. If they do not allow themselves that conversation, they are alienated from one of the means of solidarity in a complex society.

The Power of Talking about Culture

Readers restless for social change still might wonder why it is worth taking the time to learn about civic customs and reflexivity. Could the time be better spent studying the consequences of different welfare policies, different institutional arrangements? Shouldn't civic advocates put their time into fighting for government to support civic initiatives? Studies of civic culture, I argue, make an indispensable contribution to civic empowerment.

Culture is one of the conditions of possibility for civic relationships. Of course it takes more than the "right" civic culture to institute empowering, solidarity-building civic relationships. At the same time, neither more money nor more enabling state policies, *crucial as these are,* will be enough to make those relationships thrive. Citizens will have to talk reflectively about the cultural customs that can make bridges hard to build despite builders' best intentions. Social research can help citizens and policy makers reflect critically on customs we otherwise take for granted even if we decry other conditions that contribute to elusive togetherness. For anyone who longs after a more solidary and just society, talking about culture is one very practical thing to do.

Appendix I

THEORY AND EVIDENCE IN A STUDY OF RELIGIOUS

COMMUNITY SERVICE GROUPS

Starting with Theoretical Goals

How can anyone address a time-honored thesis such as the social spiral argument with but a relatively small number of groups from one region? There is more than one answer to the question, because there are different ways to use theory in a participant-observation study. Sometimes we think of participant-observation as a single method with a single goal. It makes more sense to think of participant-observation as a set of techniques that we might use in conjunction with one or more logics of inquiry. My own goals required that I draw on two logics of inquiry, each of which figured more prominently in some stages of the project than others. Elsewhere I have written at greater length on how participant-observers use theory to develop a field research project, from formulating vague initial questions to writing up the research in the form of an argument (Lichterman 2002). This appendix explains my conceptual goals for *Elusive Togetherness,* and how Lakeburg worked as a site for meeting them.

Like many participant-observers, I began this study with curiosity about a subject—religion in American community life. I was critically aware of theories people had used to investigate the subject. Tocqueville's writings on religion and civic life in the United States loomed especially large, and became more puzzling the longer I spent in the URC's community service groups, especially the Justice Task Force and the Humane Response Alliance. The social spiral argument, or the rough version of it that I had in mind during field sorties, did not seem to apply to these two groups. Their monthly meeting discussions were as bewildering to me as they were earnest. If anything, these groups were digging themselves deeper into seclusion, not spiraling outward. There *did* seem to be something about the style of interaction in these groups that influenced their ability, or inability, to build bridges outward. My overriding quest was to understand that "something" better than Tocqueville or his contemporary champions could. As the project proceeded I realized I had two goals, not just one, and I would need to draw carefully on two kinds of guides to participant-observation research.

One of those guides is the "extended case method." This method offers a sound rationale for using field observations to illuminate large theoretical questions. Social researchers rarely want to test theories with only a few cases, and I certainly do not claim to have done that. But following the extended case method, we can *improve* existing theories so that those theories better accommodate our own cases without losing existing insights that our own cases would not challenge (Burawoy 1998; Burawoy et al. 1991). That is what I set out to do in Lakeburg: I hoped to improve on Tocquevillian thinking about civic groups. Clearly, Tocqueville was not simply wrong about how important "habits" or "mores" were in civic groups, but there was much more to say. Tocqueville's own notions grasped better what was puzzling and interesting about the Lakeburg groups than the much less supple if more scientific-sounding concept of social capital. But Tocqueville's insights were not adequate to what I was seeing and hearing. So one of the study's primary goals was to improve or "reconstruct" parts of the social spiral argument, responsibly, in light of what I learned in Lakeburg. That makes this, in part, a "theory-driven" study. I followed the extended case method selectively, borrowing the most from its approach to theory.[1]

The central, logical, and rhetorical move of the extended case method is to analyze the field site at hand in light of social and cultural processes that are larger than the field site; hence the name "extended case." We extend our observations of everyday settings out to macrosocial processes that we specify and historicize as much as possible. We know those processes through one or more preexisting theories, but our field observations in turn reconstruct the theories so that they fit our cases better. I "extended" my cases into a particular socio-historical context—the economically unequal, culturally diverse, organizationally complex, contemporary United States. That is why I decided to look for "bridges" and not just any ties spiraling outward, so that I might improve Tocquevillian thinking in light of contemporary American social realities.

I focused on one theoretical notion in particular. *Civic culture*, as I explained in chapter 2, was the primary macrosocial process that I hoped to address, and theorize more effectively, as I analyzed my Lakeburg field sites. Tocqueville offered a simple theory of American civic culture that has continued to inspire a lot of contemporary research: American civic groups cultivate a culture that encourages people to spiral outward into their communities, counterbalancing privatizing or anticivic habits that Americans might otherwise cultivate. My field sites were suggesting that this theory was highly inadequate though not entirely wrong. I used the seeming anomalies to address the Tocquevillian concept of civic culture in hopes of improving it. And as extended case methodologist Michael Burawoy (Burawoy et al. 1991, p. 9) bids, I turned to other theories that might illuminate my findings and also benefit from improvement themselves.

Two theoretical reconstructions resulted: First, this book shows that there are different sets of cultural customs that enable and constrain what people do in local civic groups, not just one generic "civic culture" and a privatistic antithesis. Civic culture is more differentiated and less broadly solidarity-building in the contemporary United States than Tocquevillian terms can appreciate. Second, the Lakeburg cases contributed to an improvement of contemporary theories of culture: Cultural discourses do not create meaning all by themselves for groups in everyday life. Rather, they are *filtered* through the "style" of the group using the discourse (Eliasoph and Lichterman 2003). Group styles, or what I have termed group-building customs in this book, are themselves part of the larger cultural repertoire that influences the group. They are not made up from scratch. In analytic terms, "culture" is more than one thing, so we need different culture concepts to understand how groups use meanings in everyday life.

Substantive Goals

Some of my aims were more substantive—about the concrete subject-matter of religiously based civic groups, and not only about Tocquevillian theory. Participant-observation, I reasoned, would give me a valuable and little-used window on *how* civic groups institute the bridging ties that matter so much in contemporary scholarship. I thought I should take advantage of the close-up view, and try to figure out what factors inside and outside the groups might matter for bridging work—staying aware all the while that any claims I made about these processes would be limited by Lakeburg's particularities and the size of my own sample. Beyond responding to preexisting theory, then, I wanted to arrive at some *tentative generalizations* about how the social spiral works in the contemporary United States, how bridging would work when it worked.

Few people had addressed the question of the social spiral directly with close observations of civic group life. And long after the start of my study, scholars were still discovering and arguing over what might constitute a "typical" community service project within different religious traditions.[2] Sociologists knew that religiously based community service groups were prominent in American civic life. But only rarely had we looked closely at them and their immediate contexts. An ethnographic study could contribute a lot by portraying everyday interaction in groups not obviously extreme according to prior research, without trying to assess exactly how representative each of the study's groups was.[3]

Given the state of research, it made sense to cast my net widely in one locale. I chose a variety of groups with different aims, in hopes of finding some clear, durable patterns. That is why I chose a self-consciously political group (the Justice Task Force) as well as the other more conventional community service groups that might seem more immediately comparable. That is why I wanted evangelical as well as mainline Protestant groups. As a participant-observer, I could look for patterns "close to the ground" that others might not see or hear, and make very tentative claims that other researchers might investigate further. The tentative generalizations I generated from this study would be no less "theoretical" than the preexisting theories I brought to the project. But these generalizations would be driven more by patterns I discovered in the field than by patterns that preexisting theory encouraged me to see.

Of course I could not control all the potential variables that made the Lakeburg groups different from one another. The groups were comparable in a number of ways, though. The groups and projects affiliated with the Urban Religious Coalition had some, though certainly not all, of the same administrative constraints. They were promoted in the same monthly newsletters to the same audience of URC members and friends. I discovered core group members' social backgrounds in interviews if I did not know already, and in some ways, these were roughly comparable too. Among four major cases in the book—the Humane Response Alliance networkers, the Justice Task Force, the Adopt-a-Family project, and Park Cluster—core members were entirely white with one exception, until two African American Park neighborhood residents became regular participants at Cluster meetings late in the study. The groups shared the same metropolitan region, the same media market, and the same county social services bureaucracy. Among those four major cases, a strong majority of members were working in or retired from white-collar professions; teaching and human service work, broadly defined, were well represented. The two Adopt-a-Family groups differed in that several women core members and one male core member among the two groups were working at home taking care of children. Much as the groups carried out differently defined bridging projects, their social characteristics did not make them wildly incomparable if the goal was to make modest, tentative claims about patterns.

One striking pattern I discovered was that Park Cluster did have some successful bridge-building experiences from its own point of view, while the other groups considered their bridge-building efforts ultimately to have failed, with the possible limited exception of the free meals project in chapter 5. The fact that successful bridge-building was so rare was an "anomaly" that invites us to reconstruct Tocquevillian understandings of civic culture in light of present social-structural and cultural realities. It was that, and I did that. With my observations at hand, I went on to seek out potentially generalizable patterns of interaction that promote bridge-building, as an analytic goal in itself. I moved beyond the logic of the case extension.

I was proposing to generate new[4] if very tentative theory in light of my cases. Social researchers Anselm Strauss and Barney Glaser have written authoritatively on how participant-observers generate new theory from their observations, "grounded theory" as they aptly put it (Stauss 1987; Glaser and Stauss 1967; Stauss and Corbin 1991). They generate theory through the "constant comparative method." Following this method, we focus on people, interactions, or events that are interesting to us in light of our substantive or theoretical interests. I took bridge-building as a substantive interest, even *apart* from its theoretical relevance for Tocquevillian thinking. Alighting upon observations of interest, we name and categorize those observations, and continue researching our field sites *with those categories in mind.* Constantly comparing later observations with earlier ones in our field notes, we hope to discover relationships between people, interactions, or events that help us understand our subject of interest better. We scrutinize parts of "the field" more sharply, in search of patterns. We may add very different field sites into our project, and narrow our gaze upon particular relationships in those sites, in hopes that specific contrasts will help clarify how some relationship of interest works. Through this constant-comparative process, we conceptualize the relationships that we have discovered and build up new, "grounded" theory about how a social process works, rather than starting self-consciously with preexisting theories that we intend to improve.

I discovered in the field that a very particular kind of communication, which I termed social reflexivity, seemed an important concomitant to bridge-building. I discovered that other groups cut off that kind of communication when it emerged. They did not simply lack the ability for reflexivity but seemed in need of keeping it at bay. In Park Cluster I discovered that an important part of reflexivity involved imagination. Holding aloft an imagined relationship had practical consequences for the group. Social reflexivity could lead to ties that, in turn, helped to ratify and reinforce the boundary-drawing and other customs that made reflexivity possible. My "grounded" conceptualizations of how civic groups cultivate or fail to cultivate bridges appear at the end of chapter 6.

In the same spirit the book discusses several "grounded" discoveries about religion in civic life. Mindful of hazards in generalizing too far from these findings, I still consider them very much worth reporting. They deserve further investigation: I discovered that a group might identify as a religious group without speaking much, if any, religious discourse. And from comparing Park Cluster with the three other large projects, I discovered that religion might complement civic bridge-building not by offering emotionally compelling discourses or guiding values but a simple, practical term or two for the bridge-building project.

Combining Goals in One Project

Having conceived this project from the outset as an extended case project, in the field I realized I was in a position to make other kinds of contributions, generating new concepts rather than improving existing ones. So to some extent, I was combining the goals privileged in two *different* methods of participant-observation, balancing my commitments of research and writing time to each. One prominent argument has implied that the logic of the extended case method simply is incompatible with the logic we follow in order to produce grounded theory (Burawoy et al. 1991). I agree that the two logics are not parallel, and lead ultimately toward different conceptual goals. But I offer a somewhat different view on how the two logics relate to each other; I offer these from the standpoint of note-taking in the field and the standpoint of writing up the study.

From the standpoint of note-taking, the extended case method itself *builds on*, while ultimately departing from, the constant-comparative method *as a way of producing and recording observations in the field*. As extended case methodologist Burawoy says, "[e]ach day one enters the field, prepared to test the hypotheses generated from the previous day's 'intervention.' Fieldwork is a sequence of experiments that continue until one's theory is in sync with the world one studies" (1998, pp. 17–18). Trying out field hypotheses and modifying them in light of further observation is exactly what the constant comparative method dictates in the field. That is why, as I have written elsewhere (Lichterman 2002), it is helpful to keep in mind some of the steps of the constant comparative method even in an extended case project. Only, the extended case method puts constant field comparisons in the service of generating a (written) dialogue with existing theory. Producing grounded theory, in contrast, means using constant field comparisons to generate a new theory on a substantive topic—a theory that may be informed by, but not driven from the very start, by preexisting concepts. Put roughly, the extended case method gives its practitioners different *theoretical* goals from those of people who produce grounded theory but assumes a similar, constant-comparative practice in the field. The two methods' field practice diverge as the researcher makes theoretical choices that determine the focus of observation, the content of later research memos, and writeups from the research.[5]

The two logics diverge during the field research because focusing on a substantive topic as a goal in itself invites different comparisons from the ones we might make if the main goal is to create a critical, empirically informed dialogue with a preexisting theory. Extended case methodologists compare cases that differ relatively little in order to zero in on how macrosocial forces work in a particular setting. Grounded theory methodologists, in contrast, sometimes want to study cases that differ markedly from one another in order to find some general patterns (Burawoy 1998, p. 19). Constantly comparing observations, the researcher is led toward different kinds of comparisons, depending on theoretical goals.

One substantive, theoretical goal became bigger as the study progressed: I wanted to conceptualize civic relationships more effectively than other research had done with the concept of social capital. This was not a matter of improving a preexisting concept so much as replacing it with another that highlighted processes that social capital as a concept could not accommodate well at all. I was struck at how much the meanings of ties mattered—something Tocqueville would not have disputed—as I pointed out in chapter 1. And I was struck that "social capital" was diffusing widely in studies that claimed Tocqueville's mantle, disabling researchers from taking civic interaction and meanings as objects of study in their own right. My field observations made it compelling for me to develop an alternative, one that could help to make interaction a bigger focus in contemporary studies of civic life. In this way, I wanted the study to contribute some new conceptualizations that other researchers might use to investigate the same processes.

Why was it acceptable to pursue and balance the two sets of theoretical goals? "Improved" theory and "grounded" theory require us to accept different assumptions about what can count as scholarly knowledge (see Burawoy 1998; Burawoy et al 1991). I argue that a book-length study can make different kinds of arguments, as long as it identifies them as such. An improvement of preexisting theory also may afford a start toward a fresh argument about how social processes, like civic interaction, work, keeping in mind the limits on generalizeability. The extended case method involves the researcher in *two* "running exchanges," one of which goes on between field notes, provisional analysis of field notes, and the next set of field notes—and the other between those analyses and existing theory (Burawoy et al. 1991, pp. 10–11). Apart from the limits of time, energy, and imagination, there is no reason one cannot carry on the second exchange while also burrowing more deeply into the first so as to make a somewhat different contribution to the sociological literature. I did not follow out the extended case method in its entirety; neither did I specify relations between grounded categories such as "bridging" and "imagination" as much as a more deeply developed grounded theory would. I balanced goals to arrive at a multifaceted contribution that I decided would best serve a broad community of scholars.

That brings us to the standpoint of writing up the study. In the end, a participant-observation study is a piece of writing as well as an application of epistemological postulates; the study may matter to many people on the former grounds more than the latter. Participant-observers do not always brace their studies into a single research logic, and certainly they do not always follow any one logic in its entirety.[6] Their studies are nevertheless contributions to scholarly discussion, and sometimes broader citizen discussion too. I created *Elusive Togetherness* with some widely recognized conventions of sociological writing in mind. One of those is that we try to identify our contributions in terms of theories and concepts that are prominent in the research communities we are addressing. I did that by speaking to the ongoing debates about social capital and religion in public life, among other topics, even if that meant departing from the extended case logic that initiated the project. Logics of research that stand in tension with one another in the abstract, especially if taken to their endpoints, are not necessarily incompatible if written carefully into a large study.

Many participant-observers are coming to grips with the simple fact that writing actively propels our constant comparisons, our field notes, our arguments (for instance, Clifford and Marcus 1986; DeVault 1999). Writing is intrinsic to our research practice all the way through our projects, and that means that preexisting theory can enter our projects, self-consciously or not, at any point. Preexisting theories entered this study not only at the start but toward the end. I discovered in the field that social reflexivity was making a difference in the Lakeburg groups' bridge-building abilities; earlier I used a different term for the kinds of interaction I came to identify as social reflexivity. I could hardly ignore that John Dewey and Jane Addams, both of whom propounded the social spiral argument, also valued something like social reflexivity in their own accounts of civic life. I had not focused much on *this* feature of their writings, until I realized that what they would call reflexivity seemed to matter a lot in the field. At that point I realized that these two theorists could help narrate my "grounded" discovery. Certainly I did not have a sample appropriate to testing their own implicit theories. Rather, their concepts helped sensitize me to patterns I discovered in the field (Glaser and Strauss 1967, p. 46; Stauss and Corbin 1990, p. 42), patterns that I then went on to specify as much as possible by comparing the Lakeburg groups. In that way, this study could contribute to the resurgent interest in pragmatist theory as it developed a new, grounded argument about civic interaction.

IMPROVING AND DEVELOPING THEORY IN LAKEBURG

Lakeburg did not have to be a typical city in order to be a good place to investigate the social spiral argument. Any amount of solid new evidence might help improve—not reject, but improve—the social spiral argument in ways that might apply to other cases too. But since I also make tentative claims about how bridging works, how reflexivity and other factors matter, the fact that I studied the process in Lakeburg rather than somewhere else could make a difference. Given my substantive goals, the ideal locale for exploring religiously based civic engagement would have varied kinds of faith-based groups that were active in the community outside their own congregations.

Metropolitan Lakeburg fit the bill nicely in several ways. Between the Urban Religious Coalition and Tumbling Walls, I could compare Christians of very different theological bents addressing welfare reform and racial conflict. In 1997, the Lakeburg telephone book listed 375 "churches," under 67 denominational subheadings. These houses of worship represented the entire Protestant spectrum, from the liberal United Church of Christ, Episcopal Church, and Evangelical Lutheran Church in America, to conservative Assemblies of God and charismatic churches, along with Catholic churches, a Friends meeting, and three Unitarian Universalist societies. This diversity characterized Lakeburg County as well as the city of Lakeburg. Both the Urban Religious Coalition and Tumbling Walls drew active members from churches in the county, not just the city. Touring Lakeburg's churches, a visitor could find skyline-defining cathedrals and storefront fellowships; an old limestone landmark downtown; a for-

mer auto shop, newly converted to divine purposes, a half mile away; or a newly
built megachurch, with an enormous parking lot to match, in an upscale suburban neighborhood near a regional highway.

Lakeburg long-timers often considered Lakeburg a politically liberal city in a
relatively progressive county, urbane by midwestern standards. It is easy—too
easy—to equate political liberalism with freewheeling cosmopolitanism, wari-
ness toward religion, or religious indifference. A survey of Lakeburg County
households found only 17 percent of the respondents would "strongly agree"
that "I would not want my child to attend a school where they said daily
prayers"; the proportion that strongly disagreed with the statement was two and
a half times as great.[7] On the one hand, Lakeburg elected a lesbian Democratic
congresswoman during this study. On the other hand, a Republican primary
candidate was an African American Christian fundamentalist who made the
news regularly. Lakeburg was a place in which the URC director could prevail
upon the county's chief welfare administrator to speak at a meeting of church
volunteers; the welfare chief introduced herself as an Episcopalian. Lakeburg
sported more religious diversity then, and less anti-religious sentiment, than
one might expect of a "progressive" city.

In some ways, Lakeburg was quite an atypical city. City residents were more
educated on average than other Americans. They were more likely to be white.[8]
They were more likely to have white-collar jobs. One would not want to regard
Lakeburg as a mirror of American religious life: In the survey above, 17 percent
of respondents characterized themselves as born-again Christians or evangelicals, while a Gallup poll from 1993 found 46 percent of Americans identifying
as born-again. And while Southern Baptism and other conservative Baptist denominations were represented among Lakeburg congregations, one would not
guess from Lakeburg alone that the Southern Baptist denomination is America's single largest. Unsurprising for the upper midwest, Lutheran congregations
were prominent in Lakeburg—though Episcopal and Presbyterian churches
contributed as many URC core members in the groups I studied. It would be
unwise to generalize from Lakeburg's religious life to religious trends in the
American south.

At least some of Lakeburg's atypical characteristics were virtues for this study.
Lakeburg was in many ways a "best possible case," one that might illustrate the
potential that American culture and institutions offer for outward-spiraling,
bridge-building community service by religious groups. Mainline Protestants
are more associated with outward-looking civic efforts than are evangelicals or
fundamentalists (see Wuthnow and Evans 2002; Ammerman 2002; Chaves,
Giesel, and Tsitsos 2002; Wuthnow 1997c, d). In the broadest terms, mainline
faith is more associated with a questioning, self-reflexive religious identity than
are evangelical or fundamentalist faiths, which affirm religious certainty. If
faith-based groups in the disproportionately mainline Protestant milieu of
Lakeburg strained the social spiral argument and had a hard time building en-

during bridges, then it is reasonable to think that typical groups in more theologically conservative locales would have at least as much difficulty. My challenge to the social spiral argument should be relevant beyond Lakeburg. Or to paraphrase Pastor Ed Lindstrom's comment, if they couldn't do it in Lakeburg, where could anyone do it?

Appendix II

STUDYING CUSTOMS

A Cultural Approach to Group Life

Studying group life is central to the sociological enterprise. There are many different ways to study groups. Mine is a cultural approach. My close-up investigation of the Lakeburg groups helped refine a way of studying group life that had begun to emerge in my own earlier studies. How could I know that the patterns I saw in my groups were general enough to deserve a conceptual framework? How did I know how many kinds of group customs to identify?

I have worked inductively, and collaboratively, to address these questions. Cases from a variety of research projects led toward the concept I call "customs" in this book; the trio of customs introduced in chapter 2 borrowed insights from other studies while accommodating interesting findings that competing frameworks would neglect (Eliasoph and Lichterman 2003). This appendix lays out a few basic insights from studies that influenced the "customs" concept. Then it illustrates how I found customs at work in the Lakeburg groups. Since the aspects of interaction that mattered most in the Lakeburg groups were patterned and durable the most helpful studies were ones that illuminate the relatively durable, cultural features of group life.[1]

Behind the Three Dimensions

Several bodies of research contributed to this cultural approach. The "boundaries" dimension of group-building customs draws upon studies of social identity and symbolic boundaries. These studies show that people carry with them fairly stable images, or cognitive maps, of how their group relates to and is distinct from other groups on the horizon.[2] Groups define themselves in relation to other groups of people who are "like us" and "not like us." I listened for the routine ways that people in the Lakeburg groups mapped their groups into the world of people, groups, communities, or institutions beyond the group—however they imagined that world. Different groups maintained very different social maps.

The "bonds" dimension represents an important insight by scholars of institutional life, that different kinds of institutions or groups define the obligations and connections between members differently. Even organizations similarly structured "on paper" may ascribe different meanings to group ties. I found, as neoinstitutionalists suggest, that those definitions tended to come in "bundles" and lasted from meeting to meeting in the Lakeburg groups.[3]

The "speech norms" dimension draws on the symbolic interactionism of sociologist Erving Goffman, along with linguistic anthropology, ethnography of communication, and related fields.[4] These studies all analyze how groups sustain norms that implicitly tell members what is appropriate speech. I heard members of the Lakeburg groups speaking with very different assumptions about what kinds of speech were appropriate to the group, even though all of these groups were mostly volunteer and all were religiously based in some way. Some of the group settings called for "businesslike" talk about tasks, for instance; some called for prayerful discernment of other people's needs; some elicited righteous anger.

This trio of dimensions is a heuristic device for understanding a group's form of togetherness. The three dimensions emerged from comparing sixteen cases of activist, volunteer, and other community service groups.[5] Repeatedly we found that these three dimensions usefully and adequately identify aspects of "groupy-ness," or togetherness.

Finding Evidence of Customs at Work in Group Interaction

Customs influence the kinds of conversations groups can have. How do I show customs influencing interaction if interaction is also the main indicator of the customs themselves? The customs concept should do more than explain those conversations that I already use as evidence of a custom; otherwise the explanation risks looking like an exercise in chasing one's own tail. The potential problem of circular reasoning here is remedied at least partly because I was lucky to observe most of the Lakeburg groups as they were forming or else reaching important turning points that members themselves would recognize as turning points. So I got to hear the groups settle into customs that endured, even as topics of discussion changed. How did I know how to identify customs at work?

One of the best kinds of evidence for the existence of a group custom is a breach of the custom. So I used group members' interactional "mistakes," avoidances, awkward silences, and irreconcilable misunderstandings as particularly powerful signs that group-building customs were at work (see for instance, Goffman 1961, pp. 7–81; McCall and Simmons 1978, p. 142; Davie 1995, p. 45; Lichterman 1996, chap. 4). Anthropologist Jody Davie's recent research on a Presbyterian women's support group proceeded similarly. She described the little indicators of interactional norms aptly: Newcomers to her women's group might talk too much at first or ask the leader for direct answers to questions. Quick, vague replies and inattention would help them figure out that modest sharing and personal exploration, not instruction, were themselves the group's goals.

An awkward scene from the Justice Task Force gives a good, quick illustration of conversational misunderstandings. Task Force members sometimes clashed intentionally with other volunteers in URC projects, even when the others agreed with them. Not understanding the intent, other volunteers could feel disoriented by these encounters—as if the rug had been pulled out from under them. At a large public meeting of volunteers with the Lakeburg County welfare administrator, for instance, the County Volunteer Coordinator could not understand why Task Force member Kate told the audience about an assumption that well-paying jobs are waiting for anyone who wants to work. The volunteer coordinator figured that Kate was a smart woman and should know it could not be true that plentiful good jobs awaited former welfare recipients. From her end, Kate had intended her statement as ironic commentary, a barb at people who *assume* things like that. The irony, the emphasis on assumptions, got lost in communication across customs—different speech norms in this case—leaving the coordinator perplexed and unable to make any more sense out of what she had heard.

I also listened to the same individuals in different settings, to get more of a handle on the dominant customs in one setting (Eliasoph 1998, 1996; Lichterman 1999). Let me illustrate with an example of boundary-drawing: I heard Catherine of the Task Force tell a Lakeburg nonprofit volunteer coordinator, *after* the end of a Task Force meeting, that "you need to have both volunteering and activism." Yet I had never heard her affirm volunteering and activism with such equanimity in the setting of a Task Force meeting. At meetings, she always emphasized how important it was for people to become critical activists and stop focusing solely on the "wounded" individuals—to "look further upstream" for causes, to use her favorite metaphor. She worked at drawing boundaries between the Task Force and charitable volunteer efforts. The boundaries pertained to the group setting; they did not completely circumscribe Catherine's communication on the topic of volunteering and activism in all settings.

Similarly, I heard two leading Park Cluster members speak about their role very differently in their *church committee meetings* from the way they talked in Cluster meetings. Again, different settings promoted different boundaries, which promoted different kinds of communication. In the Cluster, the two members talked about building relationships between the Cluster and distinct local groups and agencies. In their church outreach committee, their social map was much simpler. They spoke of the Cluster effort as one out of many of their church's projects to "help the needy." They had a pot of money to administer every year, and they followed what their pastor called "the buckshot approach." They tried to spread the funds around to hit as many needy people as possible— blind people in Korea, hungry people in the United States, newly converted Presbyterians without Bibles in Ukraine. Helping an aggregate of needy individuals in Lakeburg or around the world is an unimpeachably good deed. It would be different from spiraling ties to particular groups or neighborhoods and cultivating distinctive relationships with them on their own terms. The church committees I observed, as chapter 7 describes in much more depth, imagined a different social map than the one that implicitly guided a lot of the Cluster's proceedings.

Clashes over how to define a good member or a worthwhile project were also trusty signs of customs at work—different customs in conflict. Arguments between Park Cluster member Ned and other members, for instance, brought the quiet background work of customs into high relief. Ned thought a good Cluster member was someone who worked hard at gathering donations to meet individual needs in the Park neighborhood. Other people in the Cluster appreciated members who helped connect the Cluster to groups outside the neighborhood or helped the Cluster think about long-term neighborhood needs, even if that all took a great deal of open discussion that Ned saw as a waste of time. Arguments between participants in the Humane Response Alliance helped cue me in to different definitions of mutual responsibility in the group—different understandings of social bonds none of which had become dominant yet.

My own mistakes cued me in to customs too. When I told Adopt-a-Family members, for instance, that teachers ignored problem students because of organizational politics, the puzzled looks in my direction and sudden pause in the friendly chatter—along with my own embarrassment—told me I might have violated a speech norm. Later, with more evidence to reflect upon, I realized that was just what had happened. The church group valorized compassionate discernment of individual needs, not social analysis-cum-critique.

The speech norms dimension of customs may seem to reinvite circular reasoning into the picture of how civic groups work. That would be a real risk if I used this concept to explain *particular* comments made in a group and identified the speech norms in play *only* by those very same comments. So I should clarify that "speech norms" refers to *broad categories* of speech. These are not hard to identify in the field (see Bakhtin 1988). Recent studies of religious groups (C. Bender 2003; Davie 1995) use or imply the concept effectively. They show how everyday talk comes in recognizable patterns, genres. The research basis for this dimension is broad, and a couple of examples will help to clarify how I am using it. Communication scholar Gerry Philipsen (1992), for instance, contrasts the hyperbolic, "strutting" speech favored by men in a Chicago working-class neighborhood with circumspect, more egalitarian speech of men from coastal California. Studying the official meetings of a native Australian people, anthropologist Fred Myers (1996) contrasts a roundabout style of discussion with the more "efficient" style associated with Western business meetings. The speech norms concept distinguishes broadly different styles of speech that ordinary speakers can recognize at least implicitly. It does not claim to explain utterances sentence by sentence. It helps us explain why an entire style of speech may get silenced in a group. When I suggested to the Religious Anti-racism Coalition, for instance (chapter 7), that it should discuss who exactly it represented, to which audiences, the facilitator cut me off: It was not hard to see, after the meeting, that I was threatening to make the meeting into a "brainstorming session"—something he enjoyed, but not on meeting time. He assumed this was a task-oriented "business meeting" that should make decisions expeditiously.

THEORIZING THE INFLUENCE OF CUSTOMS: A NEW VIEW

The "customs" concept improves on other ways of linking culture and action that, oddly, bypass the shared patterns that make up "culture" to begin with. Earlier generations of researchers treated civic culture as privately held values or beliefs, the chief residents of internal consciousness.[6] Earlier social science work on culture (for example, Almond and Verba 1963; Parsons and Shils 1951) shared this view. In the United States, it is still common sense to think of culture as a set of inner beliefs and values that people may or may not express, but carry around in their heads. Those earlier studies made a conceptual leap from agents of socialization—church, family, or school, for instance—straight into the individual's psyche, with little attention to *patterns of communication* that shape, mediate, the social messages we learn from others.[7] Now, sociologists ask how patterns of communication facilitate different kinds of civic action and interaction, from global, mass-mediated arenas to face-to-face settings.[8]

In the older approach to civic culture, we might hear Catherine's Justice Task Force decrying the effects of welfare reform and then impute "social justice values" to the group. Then we might use those (assumed) values to help explain what the group did. With the newer focus, we study communication about social justice, communication we can hear at the Task Force's monthly meetings or read in the group's flyers and position statements, instead of imputing formless, abstract values to people's minds. We look for patterns, the vocabularies and the customs shaping communication, and observe how those patterns along with other social forces open up or shut down lines of action for the group. In this newer perspective, cultural forms do not simply reflect realities existing outside culture but have *some* causal force of their own, some power to shape social structure and social action.[9]

It makes sense to think that cultural customs are "deep," as sociologist William Sewell Jr. (1992) would put it. That means they are taken for granted, not so easily manipulable, able to influence other kinds of cultural expression. They act as "constitutive rules" (Swidler 2001; Armstrong 2002), quietly telling group members how to go about what they are doing together as they are doing it.[10] As "deep" culture, customs influence a group's ability to use other kinds of culture: The case chapters show how groups use vocabularies of relationship-building (culture) to mean certain things, according to the customs at hand (also culture). Counterintuitive as it may sound, it is entirely possible for one form of culture to influence another form of culture (Swidler 2001). If group-building customs are deep, taken for granted, then some may be long-standing cultural traditions in themselves. Given other research on styles of speech and styles of politics,[11] it a likely possibility; I plan to investigate it more in a future, cross-national study of civic life.

NOTES

CHAPTER ONE
IN SEARCH OF THE SOCIAL SPIRAL

1. Alexis de Tocqueville 1969 [1835], p. 515.

2. For a representative sample of theory and research, see Alexander 2001b, 2001a, 1995); Berman 1997; Boyte and Evans 1986; Cohen and Arato 1992; Eliasoph 1998; Fullinwider 1999; Jacobs 1996, 2000; Kaufman 2002; Putnam 2000, 1995, 1993; Skocpol and Fiorina 1999; Mark E. Warren 2001; Mark R. Warren 2001; Wood 2002; Wuthnow 1999b,c, 1998, 1996; Young 2002, 2001.

3. The most prominent tradition of inquiry into civic life, as political theorist Mark E. Warren observes (2001), is the Tocquevillian, and Alexis de Tocqueville is one of the main sources of the particular argument about civic groups that I examine in this book. As I will observe below, a variety of viewpoints—liberal, communitarian, radical-democratic—have all drawn on aspects of Tocqueville's thought. There are still other traditions of inquiry into civic life: Learning both from Hegel and Marx's subversion of Hegel, the German critical tradition has kept alive its own hopes for civic groups, or civil society, to resist class domination and cultivate visions of a more just, more democratically driven society (Habermas 1989; Cohen 1982; Cohen and Arato 1992). American sociologist Jeffrey Alexander (2001a, forthcoming) has used Talcott Parsons's notion of the "societal community" to theorize the civic arena in a still different vein, emphasizing the conditions for justice and solidarity.

4. For summaries of these trends, see Wuthnow 1999b, 1998, 1994; Smelser and Alexander 1999; Tarrow 1994; Skocpol 2000, Skocpol and Fiorina 1999; Putnam 2000.

5. For this definition, see Walzer 1992; Cohen and Arato 1992; Shils 1991; Wolfe 1989; Berger and Neuhaus 1977; Etzioni 1996.

6. I will refer below to studies that show civic and state relationships interpenetrating. But think, for example, of a multicultural fair put on by a city-funded arts program or a neighborhood center whose budget depends partly on city funds and federal grants—the Park neighborhood center where I studied Park Cluster, in chapter 6, is a good example. That is why it is best to define civic groups by the kinds of relationships they sustain, the kinds of "hats" people tend to wear there, rather than as part of a distinct sector of society. Emirbayer and Sheller (1999) make a very similar theoretical argument, that we should define the "public" sphere of society in terms of sociable relationships that may intersect with state and market institutions, rather than trying to conceive it as a separate sector; see Cohen and Arato 1992 for a congenial and authoritative theoretical discussion. See also Brown's (1998) helpful illustrations from state-funded AIDS service organizations in British Columbia.

7. Below I'll explain my use of the tags "mainline" and "evangelical."

8. See Ronald Beiner's (1995) statement about the lack of evidence on civic groups. John Wilson (2000) made the observation about studies of consequences in his review of research on volunteering

9. For the Minnesota high schoolers study see Johnson et al. 1998. On service learning, see Blyth, Saito, and Berkas 1997, Myers-Lipton (1998), and Yates and Youniss (1996).

10. As Michael Young (2002, 2001) argues, Tocqueville's writings did not capture the nationwide organization building and networking that was taking off just after his famous visits to the United States.

11. Cohen and Rogers (1992), for instance, have envisioned state-sponsored citizen groups, as have Fung and Wright (2003). Studies of AIDS social services (Brown 1998) in Canada, budget planning meetings in Brazil (Baiocchi 2001), and youth programs in the United States (Eliasoph 2002) all picture these kinds of collaborative efforts that we apprehend clumsily if we imagine civic life to inhabit its own separate space in society.

12. See Wuthnow 1998; Skocpol and Fiorina 1999.

13. For a discussion of how researchers can use participant-observation evidence from one locale to reconstruct theory, see appendix I.

14. Reflective, open, and self-critical discussion is, for many scholars of democracy, a crucial characteristic of good citizenship. These scholars take their inspiration from Jürgen Habermas, who famously called sites for this kind of discussion "the public sphere" (Habermas 1989, 1987, 1974). These scholars (for instance, Habermas 1992, 1989; Fraser 1992; Schudson 1998; Taylor 1995; Hunter 1994; Eliasoph 1998) all emphasize discussion of public or political *issues:* the environment, war, the role of women in society, drug abuse, presidential impeachments, for example. But I am applying their democratic criterion to the ways people in this study talk about relations with other people or groups.

15. See for instance Skocpol 2000, 1999. Robert Putnam also argues (2000) that state policies should legislate incentives for people to develop civic ties.

16. See for instance Tarrow 1994; McAdam, McCarthy, and Zald 1996.

17. See for instance Wuthnow's (1998) argument about the changing meanings of civic involvement in a bureaucratic, social service environment. His argument resonates with a "neoinstitutionalist" emphasis on the scripts or routines that define public life; see DiMaggio and Powell 1991, and for more empirical work on institutionalized scripts, see Clemens 1997 and Becker 1999. Schervish et al. (1995) and McKnight (1995) make an argument parallel to Wuthnow's but in more critical terms. Writing from a different, critical angle, social theorist Jürgen Habermas (1987, 1984, 1976) and other critical theorists (for instance, Offe 1996) would argue that in modern, capitalist societies, the administrative logic of the state stymies or distorts grass-roots efforts by ordinary citizens to create community life in their own ways, according to their own "lifeworld" of shared, communal understandings.

18. Of course there are different streams of communitarian social thought, and not all would put the same emphasis on core values, or even use the phrase. Here I am drawing on Amitai Etzioni's formulation (1996; see also Lehman 2000 for a variety of more and less communitarian responses to Etzioni).

19. For reflexive politics, see Giddens 1991; Habermas 1987; Beck, Giddens, and Lash 1994; Melucci 1996a; Cohen and Arato 1992; for reflexive selfhood, see Melucci 1996b, Giddens 1991; for reflexive religion, see Roof 1999; Besecke 2002.

20. See the discussion of church finances in Wuthnow 1997.

21. In their studies of volunteering, Liebow (1993) and Poppendieck (1998) comment explicitly on the differences in symbolic power between servers and the people served. Poppendieck (1998) argues there are consequences for institutional power, too, at least

in the case of volunteer food giveaway efforts. The longer they last, she says, the more they replace the option of governmentally sponsored food security and become the commonsense answer to hunger. Ostrander's (1984) and Daniels's (1988) portraits of upper-class volunteers display subtle as well as obvious differences in the power of helpers and helped.

22. On empowerment from above, see Fung and Wright 2003; Baiocchi 2001; Krantz 2003; Eliasoph 2004.

23. For instance, see Verba, Schlozman, and Brady 1995; Putnam 2000.

24. See Steensland 2002; for a good overview of how mainline Protestant denominational leaders and spokespersons think about social issues, see Wuthnow and Evans 2002.

25. For reviews of this research, see Lichterman 1995b or Munkres 2003. My own earlier research (1995b) suggested that differing customs, not differing ideologies, frustrated white and minority environmentalists who tried to work together.

26. The formal title of the 1996 welfare reform legislation is the Personal Responsibility and Work Opportunity Reconciliation Act. For quick, useful summaries of the legislation, see Edin and Lein 1997 or Thiemann, Herring, and Perabo 2000.

27. See helpful discussions in Chaves 1999; Greenberg 2000; and Bartkowski and Regis 2003.

28. As one of his first domestic policy initiatives, President George W. Bush established a federal Office of Faith-Based and Community Initiatives. When John DiIulio, former head of the office, described the mission of this initiative, he argued that local faith-based social service groups could strengthen social bonds: "We've become habituated to transacting our moral and social responsibility for the welfare of others through distant others," he said. Instead of helping one another, Americans push one another away, weakening the bonds of interdependence. Faith-based groups could strengthen those bonds, DiIulio implied, and make ordinary citizens more responsible for the fabric of society. The quote and paraphrased statement come from John DiIulio's lecture in the John M. Olin Foundation Lectures on the Moral Foundations of American Democracy, Princeton University, April 27, 2001. This synopsis of his lecture is available at: *www.princeton .edu/webannounce/Princeton—Headlines/Archived/2001/APR—Text.html*

29. Skocpol argued that civic engagement and state-sponsored initiatives complement one another, and that civic empowerment is unlikely to succeed without governmental support. The others agree, to at least some extent; see for instance Wuthnow's (1989) findings that governmental expenditures do *not* depress civic involvement. Etzioni and Fukuyama would see less of a role for the state in civil-society-building than the others here. Etzioni's (1996) argument for a good society considers the main danger of the state to be its potential for overreaching, not shrinking. Tweaking a commonplace expression, he declares "there should (not) be a law" (1996, p. 138) : The state should not legislate where citizens could rely instead on "the moral voice," reminding one another of shared values and informal norms. Fukuyama (1999) gives the state the most restricted role, at least in advanced industrial societies, proposing instead that human nature is the biggest player in any effort to expand social ties after they have shrunk.

30. For Putnam's own figures on declining memberships, see Putnam 2000, 1996, 1995. For the debate about those figures, see Cohen 1999; Edwards and Foley 1997; Wuthnow 1998; Fullinwider 1999; Greeley 1997; Schudson 1998; Skocpol 1996; Skocpol and Fiorina 1999; Bellah et al. 1996. For accounts of Americans who fear that community life is declining, see Wuthnow's (1998) and Wolfe's (1998) interviews, and the fig-

ures in Putnam (2000, p. 25). For a succinct review of the different strands of argument about social togetherness and civic decline, and some sober assessment, see Wuthnow 1999b. Worries about community are not new; see Hewitt 1989 and Bender 1978 for perceptive treatments of Americans' long-standing ambivalence about community. As I pointed out in an earlier book (1996), fears of communal decline are a staple of cultural criticism; see also Long 1984 and Bender 1978. But that is hardly to say that social togetherness is unworthy of inquiry; on the contrary, it should make a close look at the meanings of "togetherness" all the more compelling.

31. Tocqueville (1969[1835]), p. 506. Subsequent page references are given in text.

32. See Goldberg's argument (2001).

33. For social conservatives indebted to Tocqueville, see Berger and Neuhaus (1977). Radical democrats who credit Tocqueville include Cohen and Rogers (1992) and Eliasoph (1998). Proponents of stronger communities who take Tocqueville in a variety of directions include Bellah et al. (1991, 1985); Boyte (1989); Etzioni (1996); and Putnam (2000, 1996, 1993). Liberal theorists who engage Tocqueville's thinking or use it as a jumping-off point include Gutmann (1998) and Rosenblum (1994).

34. Mark E. Warren 2001, p. 29.

35. A review of the different social capital concepts stretches beyond the limits of my study. Putnam's concept has influenced research on civic engagement the most and so I focus on his. For a good discussion of the different social capital concepts, see Lin 2001.

36. In the study of religious groups alone, Putnam's social capital concept is now widespread. See, for instance, Ammerman 1997a; Bartkowski and Regis 2003; Becker and Dhingra 2001; Park and Smith 2000; Chaves, Giesel, and Tsitsos 2002; Cnaan et al. 2002; M. R. Warren 2001; Wood 2002.

37. See Putnam's review of research on these different outcomes (1995, 2000). For a sharp review of some of the social capital literature, see Portes 1998.

38. See, for instance, Putnam 2000; Putnam and Goss 2002; see also Gittell and Vidal 1998.

39. For a variety of causal arguments about social capital, see Berman 1997 for political institutions; Skocpol 2000, 1999 for governmental policy; or Wood 2002 for the cultural context; see Lin's (2001) smart summary of these divergent approaches.

40. Robert Fishman (2004) very helpfully reviews the limits of "capital" as a metaphor for social relationships.

41. The world of social capital inquiries is far too large to be reviewed here. For summaries of some of this theory and research in sociology, see Lin 2001 or Portes 1998. For just two sociological examples of interest, see research by Wilson and Musick (1997) or Greeley (1997) that use the social capital concept to explain people's levels or kinds of volunteering.

42. Saegert, Thompson, and Warren (2001) offer an excellent sample of social capital researchers who build in some way on Putnam's concept as they addresss community development, neighborhood safety, urban political participation, antipoverty programs, and others topics.

43. See Baiocchi 2003; Eliasoph 1998, 1996; Lichterman 1999, 1996; Mansbridge 1983; Mische 2004; Mendelberg 2003; Walsh 2004.

44. See Becker 1998; Bender 2003; Davie 1995; Eliasoph 1998, 1996; Lichterman 2001a, 1999, 1996, 1995a, 1995b; Patillo-McCoy 1998; Polletta (2002).

45. See Liebow 1993; Poppendieck 1998; C. Bender 2003.

46. Examples include Barkan 1979; Benford 1993; Downey 1986; Fantasia 1988; Lancaster 1988; Whittier 1995.

47. On this point, see Fiorenza 2000 or Smith 1998, pp. 196–97.

48. See, for instance, Gorski 2000.

49. Apart from any specific teachings in the Judeo-Christian religions, a "religious" group is usually one that nurtures a noninstrumental, value-driven regard for society. While much of modern life turns on strategizing, bargaining, impressing, or finessing, religious traditions still call people to care about society, about humankind, as ends in themselves. José Casanova elegantly argues (1994) that national religious leaders have become some of the most insistent, and least impeachable, proponents of the common good in modern societies; religious pronouncements against the nuclear arms race and the injustices of capitalism are two good examples. These leaders refuse to reduce the public interest to economic well-being or political expedience. They draw on their religious faith to challenge society as a whole to do what is most humane for society as a whole. It is all the more puzzling, then, that religious community service groups often had a hard time envisioning and creating the new connections that they set out to create.

50. See Gregory 2002; Mathewes 2002; Mongoven 2002.

51. See Ammerman 2002; Thiemann, Herring, and Perabo 2000; Mark R. Warren 2001; Wood 2002, 1999; see also Demerath and Williams 1992.

52. See Putnam 2000, p. 66, and chapter 4 in general.

53. See Becker and Dhingra 2001; Park and Smith 2000; Putnam 2000; J. Wilson 2000; Greeley 1997; Wuthnow 1999c,d, 1991; Verba, Schlozman, and Brady 1995; Wood 2002, 1999; Mark R. Warren 2001; Chaves, Giesel, and Tsitsos 2002.

54. For instance, Greeley 1997; Putnam 2000; Verba, Schlozman, and Nie 1995; Wuthnow and Hodgkinson 1990; Eckstein 2001; J. Wilson and Musick 1999; but see J. Wilson 2000.

55. See Luckmann 1967; Parsons 1967a; Hammond 1992; for critical reviews, see Regnerus and Smith 1998; Casanova 1994; Chaves 1994.

56. For representative studies, see Caplow et al. 1983, Earle et al. 1976, Douglass and de Brunner 1935, or Underwood 1957; for a contemporary example with a helpful overview of the tradition, see Demerath and Williams 1992.

57. For an exhaustive review of studies on faith-based social service groups and their effectiveness, see Byron Johnson, "Measuring the Effectiveness of Faith-Based Organizations: A Systematic Review of the Literature," paper presented at the Woodrow Wilson School of Public and International Affairs, Princeton University, October 8, 2001. For conceptual overviews of contemporary faith-based coalitions or "special purpose" groups, see Warner 1999; Wuthnow 1999c, 1988; Ammerman 1997a, especially pp. 360–367. Chapters by Ammerman (2002) and Chaves et al (2002) in a volume on mainline Protestants' public engagements, edited by Robert Wuthnow and John Evans (2002), present survey and interview findings on community involvement from national samples of congregations. This work adds greatly to our knowledge of congregations' work in their communities; my ethnographic focus on faith-based community projects complements these broad overviews.

58. See DiMaggio et al. 1996; Hunter 1994. Criticisms of the "culture wars" thesis (see, for instance, Williams 1997) have read Hunter's (1991) initial statement of it as claiming that there is widespread polarization in the American population. Hunter (1994) argued

that many Americans' private opinions are muddier, more ambivalent than the polarized public discourses he found in the debate about abortion.

59. See Skocpol 2000; Robert Putnam 2000, especially pp. 408–410; Bane and Coffin 2000; Coffin 2000; Thiemann et al. 2000; Bellah et al. 1991, 1985; see also Bell 1976.

60. Thanks to Charles Mathewes (2002) for putting this so succinctly.

61. For authoritative historical overviews of Protestantism in the U.S., see among many others Marty 1981; Marsden 1991; Roof and McKinney 1987; Wuthnow 1988; Smith 1998.

62. These and other helpful summaries of mainline belief come from the authoritative overviews in Wuthnow and Evans 2002.

63. This sketch draws especially on Smith's (1998) helpful summaries of evangelical belief; see also Hunter's helpful treatment (1983).

64. See, for instance, Wuthnow 1989, 1988; Warner 1988; Marsden 1991; Hunter 1987; Michaelsen and Roof 1986; Roof and McKinney 1987; Kelley 1972.

65. "Citizen-initiated" means that while state employees may have attended meetings and collaborated with a group, the group was not started by or directed by a governmental agency.

66. Regarding the debates about "faith-based social services," sociologist of religion Nancy Ammerman observed (2001) that sociologists still did not know what it meant for a group to be "faith-based," much less what effects the faith basis might have. She called for research on these topics. She (2002), and sociologists Mark Chaves and colleagues (Chaves et al. 2002) recently compiled some of the first, wide-ranging inventories of what exactly American religious groups do "outside church" in their wider communities. As Ammerman has also argued (2003, 1997b), religious identity can be subtle: We cannot simply assume a group is or isn't "religious" from how much its members talk in explicitly religious terms.

67. Social scientists are just starting to follow the ways people invoke religion, wear their religion "hats," in everyday settings outside of houses of worship. See, for instance, Davie 1995; Bender 1997, 2003; Hall 1997; Ammerman 2003.

CHAPTER TWO
STUDYING THE SOCIAL SPIRAL

1. This is a major contribution of the research literature on contemporary social movements. Researchers stress, for instance, that women's private, individual dissatisfactions with their subordinate roles as housewives and social supports for men did not produce organized, collective action—the women's movement of the early 1970s—until women talked through their insights. As they did so, they developed a collective identity as (feminist) *women*, contesting male power, not just as individuals with coincidentally unlucky situations. Sociologists argue more generally that social movements arise only as people communicate their interests—and in doing so, discover what their interests and shared identities are, and what or who their barriers are. I am applying this well-established point to understanding social reflexivity and social bonds: People will not create new relationships between groups and communities intentionally if they never can communicate their sense of what those relationships are. For a sample of the diverse writ-

ings that arrive at the point about communication and social movements, see Melucci 1989; Touraine 1981; Habermas 1989; Fraser 1989; Ferree and Hess 1994; Mouffe 1992; Taylor and Whittier 1992; Calhoun 1994. This insight is strong, too, in earlier writings on public life; for just two classic examples that have influenced sociological theory, see Dewey 1927 and Arendt 1958.

2. See, for instance, Somers 1994; Somers and Gibson 1994; Mische 2003; Mische and White 1998; Emirbayer and Goodwin 1994; Polletta 1999; Stevens 1996; DiMaggio and Powell 1991.

3. See, for instance, Emirbayer and Goodwin 1994; Mische and White 1998.

4. See, for instance, Gould 1991; Mc Adam 1988, 1986; Meyer and Whittier 1994; Diani and McAdam 2003.

5. See Sewell's (1992) clearly written exposition on the topic; see also Kane 1991.

6. In Wuthnow's (2004) reading of Putnam's work on social capital, "bridging" refers especially to relationships between people of different social statuses. See Putnam 2000; Saegert, Thompson, and Warren 2001; Putnam and Goss 2002.

7. Some might say, for instance, that an evangelical Christian volunteer group cannot create a civic-minded relationship because by definition such a group aims to create relationships in Jesus' name, not in the name of citizenly exchange. Not only does such a definition blind us to the community service work that evangelicals do, but it is historically myopic too: Many civic associations and mutual aid groups have done what they do at least partly in Jesus' name.

8. Sirianni and Friedland 2001; Mark R. Warren 2001; Wood 2002; Hart 2001; Demerath and Williams 1992.

9. See, for instance, Gitlin 1995 or R. Bernstein 2003. "Unlearning racism" workshops have traveled American grass-roots activist circles widely. For a sample of the ideologies behind these workshops, see Adair and Howell 1988. For studies that portray people trying to unlearn racism or sexism, see Lichterman 1996 or Munkres 2003.

10. See examples in Lichterman 1996 and Munkres 2003. These conversations can be heard in the "study circles" program fast spreading throughout the United States. Some URC members participated along with other Lakeburgers in study circles, sponsored in part by Lakeburg city government to get ordinary people talking about race relations; over three hundred American locales have organized study circles on some social issue. In study circles, people gather weekly over several months to discuss race or other intergroup relations. Whatever the topic, the circles are designed to bring people from different organizations and different backgrounds together around one table to learn more about each other. Study circle discussion guides suggest that personal sharing sessions are part of the program, along with social reflexivity and public planning. See Study Circles Resource Center (1992, 1994, 1997).

11. At the monthly dialogues, participants specifically were requested to talk only about their own experiences and feelings, on the theory that other kinds of talk might be divisive.

12. For a classic portrait, see the white Freedom Summer activists in McAdam 1988; see also Gitlin 1987.

13. Intellectual biographer Robert Westbrook agrees (1991) that Dewey rested his hopes for democracy on local associations, though Dewey had relatively little to say about how local associations would relate to other associations and institutions in a

Great Community. See the few suggestive lines in Dewey's *Freedom and Culture* (1939, pp. 160–61).

14. Students of church-based social ties say, for instance, that the fact of participating in a religious *group* explains more about members' likelihood of volunteering than members' religious faith on its own. See, for instance, Ellison and George 1994; Wuthnow 1991.

15. This was the exactly the vision of local antitoxics environmentalists in the 1980s and early 1990s, for instance. One leader said it was better for citizen environmentalism to be "nationwide" and knit together on a loose, local mutual-aid principle, rather than "national" and coordinated. See Lichterman 1996.

16. See, for instance, Dewey's prognosis that local communal life in a Great Community will be "alive and flexible as well as stable, responsive to the complex and world-wide scene in which it is enmeshed. While local, it will not be isolated. Its larger relationships will provide an exhaustible and flowing fund of meanings upon which to draw." (1927, pp. 216–17).

17. And a new kind of social scientist would help the process. Working in the public interest, social scientists would inquire into concrete social conditions, disseminate their provisional findings, and work with citizens to solve concrete social problems. On their open-ended journeys of discovery, researchers in this new vein would work with citizens toward creating a national community of shared knowledge (Dewey 1927, pp. 167–68, 177).

18. Dewey credited his friend Addams for teaching that to him (see Charlene Seigfried's introduction to the Illinois edition of *Democracy and Social Ethics* in 2002).

19. See Seigfried's discussion (2002) of the links between Dewey's and Addams's thought.

20. "[W]hile the teaching has included an ever-broadening range of obligation . . . the training has been singularly individualistic. . . . [H]er faculties have been trained solely for accumulation, and she has learned to utterly distrust the finer impulses of her nature, which would naturally have connected her with human interests outside of her family and her own immediate social circle" (2002 [1902], p. 42)

21. Charlene Seigfried discusses some of these contributions convincingly (2002). See also Green 1999, and on cultural radicalism, see Lasch 1966.

22. Classic sources that helped sensitize me to social reflexivity include Dewey 1922, 1927, 1939; Addams 1910, 2002 (1902); and Siegfried 2002. These pragmatist sources still have an important role to play: Contemporary writings discuss reflexivity in general and have been helpful, but do not often identify *social* reflexivity as this study conceives it. Contemporary statements that influenced my approach include Giddens 1991; Habermas 1987; Melucci 1996a; and Beck, Giddens, and Lash 1994.

23. See Tocqueville's discussions of the "mores" or "mental habits" Americans would learn in voluntary associations (1969 [1835], pp. 287, 513–15). Dewey (1922) thought that was possible, especially in a complex society that presented people with diverse, conflicting customs which they might borrow from or combine in new ways. I found there were palpable limits to how much civic group members could combine or transform group-building customs.

24. See the review in Eliasoph and Lichterman 2003; for a classic example, see Becker 1961.

25. Mores, for Tocqueville, included "the different notions possessed by men, the various opinions current among them, and the sum of ideas that shape mental habits" (1969, p. 287).

26. For conceptual underpinnings of Becker's (1999) "cultural models," see DiMaggio and Powell 1991. For the conceptual forebears of Eliasoph's (1998) "civic practices," see especially Bourdieu 1990, 1984, 1977; Goffman 1979, 1961; and Hochschild 1983. For conceptual groundings of my "cultures of commitment" notion, see Bourdieu 1990, 1984, 1977; Bellah et al. 1985; and Hewitt 1989.

27. Becker (1999), for instance, developed a typology with the help of previous writings on the "core tasks" of American religious congregations.

28. My colleague Nina Eliasoph and I make a theoretical and empirical argument (2003) for studying what we call "group style." This book uses the tag "group-building customs" in place of group style, to highlight the resonance with Tocqueville, Dewey, and Addams, and to emphasize something possibly counterintuitive: There are culturally patterned, customary ways to create groups. As we argue, cultural sociologists often have paid more attention to discourses or collective representations than to the forms of groups that use them.

29. See appendix II for more discussion of how I identified customs and their consequences.

30. See Penny Edgell Becker's (1999) similar contrast between the idiocultures concept and one that takes culture more as a structuring force.

31. For a few prominent examples, see Alexander and Seidman 1990; Alexander and Smith 1993; Kane 1997; Rambo and Chan 1990; Sewell 1992; Somers 1995a,b; Steinberg 1999; Swidler 2001, 1986; Tipton 1982; Wuthnow 1984, 1987, 1991, 1992.

32. See the studies in DiMaggio and Powell 1991. For relevant applications, see Becker 1999; Stevens 1996; or Armstrong 2002. For a different school of neoinstitutionalism with some intersecting insights, see Scott, Meyer, and Boli 1994.

33. See, for instance, Bellah et al. 1985, 1996; Hays 1994; Hart 1992, 2001; Teske 1997; Tipton 1982; Witten 1993; Wood 1999, 1994; Wuthnow 1992, 1991, for a few examples.

34. The extremely popular "framing" approach to public discourse turns on the assumption that the definition of public problems is never self-evident, never a simple extrapolation from silent group interests. Social problems, and solutions, get "framed" by activists, the state, or ordinary citizens in everyday conversation. For some germinal statements, see Snow et al. 1986; Snow and Benford 1988; McAdam, McCarthy and Zald 1996; Gamson 1992. Studies of hegemonic discourse pivot on a similar insight, but they add that class interests and state power have much to do with which "framings" become widely circulated and commonsensical. See, for instance, Gramsci 1971; Gitlin 1980; Morley 1980; Kertzer 1990; Lewis 1999. Thirdly, studies of narratives in social history and cultural sociology hold that events in the social world become meaningful, and people become able to act toward them, only when they get articulated in words; the words often take the form of a story. For a representative sample of theory and research, see Somers and Gibson 1994; Kane 1997; Sewell 1980; Ellingson 1991; Jacobs 1996; Wuthnow 1991.

35. Wuthnow (1998) argues that this short-term, task-focused volunteering complements a society in which people change jobs more often and define community in looser, sometimes more virtual, terms. In this society of "loose connections" it makes sense that many people would express their concern for social bonds in loose, sporadic, limited-

term engagements. For close-up studies that portray something like what I call customs in volunteer groups, see C. Bender 2003; Poppendieck 1998; Eliasoph 1998; Liebow 1993; or Ostrander 1984.

CHAPTER THREE

NETWORKERS AND VOLUNTEERS REACHING OUT

1. Interview, November 6, 2000.

2. This quote and the one directly preceding it are from Donald's article "Rebuilding Our Communities: A Spiritual issue," in the URC's bimonthly journal, January–February 1997 (title omitted to preserve anonymity), author's file.

3. For lots of concrete examples, and statistics on church outreach activities, see Ammerman 2002 and Wuthnow 2004; see also Ammerman 1997a; Becker 1999; Chaves, Giesel, and Tsitsos 2002; Cnaan 2002; Roozen, McKinney, and Carroll 1984; Wuthnow 1999d.

4. "Rebuilding Our Communities: A Spiritual Issue," URC's bimonthly journal, January–February 1997, author's file.

5. Lindstrom was pastor of a local Evangelical Covenant church. He characterized his denomination as an offshoot of Lutheranism as practiced in Sweden in the nineteenth century. Theologically, the denomination is more liberal than many independent evangelical churches in the United States.

6. On this conventional, institutionalized understanding of volunteering, see Wuthnow 1998, 1991; Schervish et al. 1995; Eliasoph 1998, 1996. I introduced the social structure of volunteering in chapter 2. On volunteers' limited social imaginations, see Wuthnow 1991.

7. Interview, Novemenber 6, 2000.

8. For the sake of space, I have not described all of the projects associated with Humane Response Alliance. The Alliance coordinated a "safety net task force," whose food pantry support project is introduced below. Short-term shelter services also were discussed at Alliance meetings. The Alliance included a prayer fellowship that prayed for "challenged" neighborhoods in Lakeburg. The social justice, congregational clusters, and Fun Evenings projects represent the Alliance's predominant styles of civic engagement.

9. Philosopher Richard Rorty (1998) has used the term "conversation-stopper" to describe a similar function in public interaction. James Hunter (1994) argues that claims to special insight or a special heritage based on group identity can halt public exchange; in more theoretical terms, Charles Taylor (1994) has argued the same thing. And sociologist Nina Eliasoph has documented (1998) social activists' talk about "self-interest" doing just that: stopping further conversation by appeal to something unquestionable, inviolable.

10. HRA participants told me, in interviews, that they thought the Community Advocates woman really wanted the pantry project for her own network regardless of what HRA might do. By itself, that does not explain why Donald and the others foreclosed on the HRA's initiative to unify churches for civic action and get beyond "turfism," especially since Donald *agreed* with the Community Advocates woman and had said similar things for a long time.

11. Theorists of civil society such as Jürgen Habermas (1989, 1987, 1984) and Jean Cohen and Andrew Arato (1992) are well-known for the argument that the state's ad-

ministrative logic clashes with the collective, open-ended deliberation that people may engage in as citizens in civil society. In Habermas's terms (1987, 1984, 1976) the logic of administrative control has spilled over the proper boundaries of the state and "colonized" everyday life. See also Offe 1996. Communitarians like Etzioni (1996, 1993) make a somewhat similar argument about the state's relation to everyday civic life. They argue that people should rely on morally informed dialogue more than on laws, rights, or regulations to create good communities. Public intellectuals such as John McKnight (1995) and Harry Boyte (1989) counterpose civic initiatives to the top-down power of the state. For a smart counterargument, see Goldberg 2001.

12. Skeptics might figure he was just trying to sound like a nice guy in front of a church audience poised to ask uncomfortable questions. We cannot know for sure. I interviewed Steve along with other welfare personnel. Our open-ended interview gave me a feel for what he thought about church-based community service. I noticed the postcard-sized religious image on his desktop too. I think his talk about increasing communication and fostering spiritual experiences was serious and sincere.

13. I observed two lengthy meetings of the Welfare Coordinating Council (WCC) and also attended a workshop at which the WCC described its efforts to weave a new social safety net. Over one hundred county social workers and community service group leaders at the workshop heard WCC members present the kinds of efforts I am picturing briefly here.

14. "Neoinstitutionalist" scholars argue convincingly that organizational routines have a lot of power in shaping what organizations can plan to do, and how. See DiMaggio and Powell 1991. For a different strain of neoinstitutionalism, see Scott, Meyer, and Boli (1994); the differences are not crucial for my purposes here. For other empirical applications of these insights, see Clemens's work on political lobby groups (1997), and Becker's study of church congregations (1999). The idea that civic groups have somewhat more leeway to construct themselves follows from the definition of "civil society" itself: When we act as members of civil society, it is up to us to define the solidarities and moral limits that make "voluntary" action possible. Tradition, custom, exploratory dialogue, and spontaneity all have a role in the definition. When we act as subjects of the state, or players in the market, in contrast, we act with a lesser degree of creativity and voluntarism because we accept the abstract organizing principles of money or coercive power—much as we still must enact them in some symbolically mediated, meaningful way. See the theorists of civil society cited in chapter 1.

15. Along with the county personnel pictured at this meeting, I heard ten county and city social service professionals at separate, monthly Family Friends meetings. These included public health nurses, youth specialists, school district social workers, and county social workers assigned to the Park neighborhood. These meetings were held so that professionals working in the Park neighborhood could keep up with one another and share ideas for new neighborhood programs. I interviewed five of these social service professionals.

16. Wuthnow's history of the volunteer model (1998) suggests that it arose in tandem with the growth of state agencies after World War II, but does not strongly suggest that one development caused the other. See Schudson 1998 on the Progressive model of good citizenship.

17. It is possible to see already in Tocqueville's (1969 [1835]) characterizations of Americans a task-oriented networker and a can-do volunteer. Of course Tocqueville also

saw religious orders and idiosyncratic crusades that were anything but practical in the contemporary sense.

18. See George Steinmetz's discussion and collection of essays (1999) that present these challenges convincingly.

19. For instance, Putnam 2000; Greeley 1997; Becker and Dhingra 2001; Wuthnow 2004, 1998.

20. Other researchers have not remarked on those nagging uncertainties that I and other volunteers felt about what we should be doing. They do find a similar concern with "doing" itself, a focus on the individual volunteer's own experience, and a dependence on professional coordinators who, in turn, work at making volunteers feel good about their experience in hopes that they might return. See Wuthnow 1998, 1991; Eliasoph 1998; Poppendieck 1998. Eliasoph's analysis of volunteers' group life is particularly close to this one in some ways. It does not detail group customs the way this study does, and it stresses volunteers' relation to politics, not their ability to create bonds between groups and communities.

21. Fun Evenings developed an "idioculture," a set of project-specific understandings, all the while taking part in a broader culture of volunteer customs that all shared a strong family resemblance. Volunteering in other projects helped me understand what was specific to Polly's project and what was broadly characteristic of volunteering in loosely connected networks.

22. It turns out that youth service coordinators (paid by a county program) publicized Fun Evenings at neighborhood centers and schools in town, particular ones in low-income neighborhoods. Kids decided whether or not they wanted to attend; coordinators organized vans and carpools to transport them.

23. When sociologists listen to volunteers talking about what it feels like to volunteer, we usually hear them saying that volunteering makes them feel good, gives them the pride of accomplishment, makes them angry for not being thanked enough, or—more rarely—makes them feel like better members of their communities (Bellah et al. 1985; Daniels 1988; Liebow 1993; Ostrander 1984; Wuthnow 1998, 1991.) Rarely do we hear volunteers feeling unhelpful or feeling that they don't measure up to other volunteers. Yet it makes sense that these worries could bedevil volunteers in a time when volunteering often means being a vaguely defined adjunct to a professional (Wuthnow 1998).

24. For complementary work on how everyday group etiquette constrains thoughtful citizenship, see Eliasoph 1998, 1996. Eliasoph's study highlighted the constraints on political speech.

25. See Putnam 2000; Fukuyama 1999; see also Sztompka's smart discussion (2001) of recent writings on civic trust.

26. Etzioni proposes (1996) that societies need public moral dialogues that help their members articulate "core values" that can organize life in a diverse society. See my response, especially on the question of core values, in Lichterman 2000.

27. See Edwards and Foley's (1997) analysis. See also Jean Cohen's criticisms of "American civil society talk" (1999).

CHAPTER FOUR
CRYING OUT: SOCIAL CRITICS

1. Interview, June 2001.

2. See Putnam 2000; Mark R. Warren 2001; Wood 2002; see also Diani and McAdam 2003.

3. See, for instance, Eliasoph 1998.

4. This is a wide trend in social movement research: Different variants of the "strategic framing" perspective (McAdam, McCarthy, and Zald 1996; Snow and Benford 1988; Snow et al. 1986) all emphasize that people must actively define social problems. Issues do not come readymade. The way activists frame issues influences the collective action they carry out to address those issues. A similar constructionist perspective has of course influenced sociologists' study of social problems outside the field of movement studies, too; see for instance Joel Best's (1990) and Joe Gusfield's (1981) work. Many movement scholars would point out, too, that talking about social problems also entails talk about "who we are" that raises these issues for public consideration. Activists must construct some collective identity; these do not come readymade, either. See Polletta and Jasper's (2001) well-considered review of collective identity studies. Research on public opinion has rested heavily on surveys of attitudes and beliefs (but see Reinarman 1987; Lane 1962). But as Nina Eliasoph argues (1998), people develop new ways of acting on social problems—the problem of toxic waste, for instance—when they talk openly about those problems.

5. See Dawn Moon's (2004) study of how homosexuality as a political topic got processed, or avoided, in church circles she studied. In Steensland's interview study (2002), mainline Protestant denominational leaders express frustration at how their (often liberal) position statements seem little noticed at the local church level—suggesting, again, that progressive politics does not have a large presence in everyday church life.

6. See DiMaggio and Powell 1991.

7. "Dominant" here means the definitions that are enhanced by both material and symbolic power.

8. This has become a truism among students of "collective identity" in social movements; a great deal of empirical work substantiates the point. For prominent statements, see M. Bernstein 1997; Taylor and Whittier 1992; Gamson 1992; Melucci 1989, 1988. See the review in Polletta and Jasper 2001.

9. See my discussion of activist groups as "forums" or sites of the public sphere, in Lichterman 1999.

10. Students of interaction use the popular "frame" idea differently. In some authoritative formulations (Snow and Benford 1988; McAdam, McCarthy, and Zald 1996) the concept denotes a set of definitions that social movement leaders craft strategically to win as many followers as possible. In other formulations (Snow et al. 1986), the picture of frame-wielders' intentions is somewhat more ambiguous, less driven by assumptions about strategic action that shape a lot of social movement scholarship (see Hart 1996 and Lichterman 1999 on this point). In most of these formulations, "frames" sound like cognitive schema made explicit in communication—definitions of the world that people exchange or try to force on one another. In Goffman's seminal writings (1974, for instance), however, "frame" sometimes means the less explicit assumptions or "footing" that people share about what talk itself is for. By this understanding, a lot of social movement framing theory is more about the "picture" than the "frame."

11. See symbolic interactionists McCall and Simmons (1978) and Stone (1962) making this point.

12. See Gitlin's (1987) colorful if not particularly sympathetic treatment. See treatments of the scholarly debates about expressive politics in Breines 1982 and Lichterman 1996.

13. I don't mean to imply that conversation always requires a great deal of common ground. Sometimes two parties do not know exactly what each is talking about, yet they continue trying to communicate. They do work at *establishing* a floor, the opposite of what Justice Task Force members sometimes did. See C. Bender 2003 for lively examples.

14. It has become a large research literature; see for instance McAdam 1988; Friedman and McAdam 1992; for a collection of network perspectives on social movements, see Diani and McAdam 2003.

15. Numerous scholars have pictured this part of community organizing. See, for instance Delgado 1986; Lichterman 1996; Hart 2001; Mark R. Warren 2001; Wood 2002; Krantz 2003.

16. They were indeed: The eight core members all had professional, white-collar jobs or had retired from such jobs.

17. See Wuthnow's (1991) exploration of compassion's meaning: Contemporary American volunteers tend to define compassion as an interpersonal relationship between helper and helped. Wuthnow points out that in its older meaning, compassion implied and depended upon institutional arrangements—a protecting church, among others—without which acts of compassion would not be possible.

18. Eliasoph and Lichterman (2003) point out that group customs, like other forms of culture, have a history and note historical work that bears out that point.

19. For a closer look at third-world solidarity activism and a perceptive analysis, see Munkres 2003.

20. The idea has a noble lineage in secular social theory: Italian political theorist and activist Antonio Gramsci (1971) argued that by repeating radical ideas over and over, in simple language, working-class activists could develop a cultural "bloc" of workers and peasants whose social understandings would challenge those purveyed by capitalist intellectuals and mass culture.

CHAPTER FIVE
CHRIST-LIKE CARE: SOCIAL SERVANTS

1. One of the churches, Lakeside Reformed, organized two groups, each of which took on a family.

2. One of the original seven church groups at the orientation disbanded shortly after its family left the region.

3. See Amy Sherman's (2000) descriptive overview of faith-based organizations that are providing social services in the new (post-1996) welfare policy environment. See the discussion in Chaves 1999.

4. Though less well known than their politically conservative counterparts, evangelical social justice groups have been alive at least since the 1970s. Popular evangelical writer Ron Sider initiated Evangelicals for Social Action in 1973 (see Cochran 2001). Politically progressive evangelicals were prominent in the Call to Renewal, a network, of roughly eighty local groups throughout the United States that promoted a social justice perspective on welfare and poverty, and self-consciously defined itself as an alternative to the Christian Coalition. I studied their Lakeburg affiliate, portrayed in chapter 7 (see also Emerson and Smith 2000).

5. Evan often spoke of "the Church in Lakeburg," or simply "the Church," meaning

Christians as a collectivity. Other evangelical pastors with URC projects whom I met on my rounds spoke of "the Body of Christ" with the same meaning. These were normative visions of Christian unity and corporateness; Evan and others invoked them as a kind of ideal for actual collective efforts by local churches. Their "Church" included believing Christians of all denominational persuasions. Mainline Protestants in this study sometimes resisted being associated closely with evangelicals who used "Christian" in narrow terms to designate someone who practices an evangelical Christianity.

6. See, for instance, C. Smith 1998; Wuthnow 1988; Roof and McKinney 1987; Hunter 1983; Kelley 1972.

7. See, for instance, Becker 1999; Glock and Stark 1965; Roozen, McKinney, and Carroll 1984; Troeltsch 1931; Wood 1999, 1994; Wuthnow and Evans 2002; Wuthnow 1999c,d, 1988; but see Mock 1992; C. Smith 1998; Regnerus and Smith 1998.

8. There were, first of all, the eight church groups that had volunteered in time for the first orientation. There was Adopt-a-Family's advisory board. The church group leaders also met together three times during my study, once with their group members and adopted families.

9. Like other evangelicals I met during this project, Theresa used "the church" to mean Christians in general as a collectivity, not just her own Community in Christ Church.

10. Lamont's comparison of American and French upper-middle-class people (1992) and Varenne's ethnographic study of a Wisconsin town (1977) both find Americans believing social status should be irrelevant when people are interacting.

11. There is little point in summarizing the massive sociological literature on ideology. The briefest overview should suffice: Sociologists' understandings of ideology often take their cue from Marx. But few sociologists now endorse the simplistic readings of Marx that characterize popular, deep-seated ideologies as the product of conspiracies by economic elites to control or dupe "the masses." More subtle treatments emphasize that ideology encompasses commonsense assumptions about the world as well as explicit belief systems (Gramsci 1971; Hall 1977; Hall et al. 1978; Willis 1981); ideologies may be contradictory rather than consistent (Gramsci 1971; Willis 1981; Connell 1983); ideologies are powerful because they shape what we can *say* (and not say) and not just what we *think* privately (Habermas 1987, 1984, 1976; Fraser 1992; Bourdieu 1984; Eliasoph 1998, 1996). My summary characterization of ideology and powerful interests in the main text draws on these insights.

12. This was at the first monthly meeting. I got a stronger sense of the speech genre after bumbling forth with my own rejoinder to this man. I said something about the organizational politics of schools. Other members just looked at me with puzzled sympathy. I hadn't gotten the point.

13. Keith, quoted earlier, had cautioned his church group against assuming that Quenora's family "had nothing," and he wondered aloud about her own social networks. It was a sociologically smart way to think about how low-income people cope with their circumstances. The research literature is large, but see for instance Bourgois 1995; and Stack 1974; or Saegert, Thompson, and Warren 2001; for the limits of relying only on networks inside a single neighborhood, see Sampson 1999. Jerry, who had mentioned the families' "sense of neighborhood" at a meeting of group leaders, said he had studied community development for two years. As he must have found, scholars and practitioners of community development say that the way to improve low-income individuals' lives is to give them opportunities to build on their own local assets and steer their own com-

munities rather than making them clients of outsiders. See for instance McKnight 1995 and Sirianni and Friedland 2001.

14. This is not a typographical error. The women belonged to a church that identified as Catholic and evangelical.

15. See, for instance, Varenne's (1977) observations on how midwestern Americans understood what connects communities and societies.

16. Interviews with some two hundred middle-class Americans in Bellah et al. 1985 suggest this is just the case; see also Wuthnow 1991; Varenne 1977.

CHAPTER SIX
A SOCIAL SPIRAL WINDS OUTWARD: PARTNERS

1. Hmong people arrived in Lakeburg in the 1970s, from southeast Asia, as part of a resettlement deal offered by the U.S. government in exchange for Hmong support of American military objectives during the Vietnam War.

2. They celebrated twice, once with coffee and cake at the Lutheran Home that cosponsored the nurse and once with a more elaborate dessert and sandwich spread a half hour before the start of a regular Cluster meeting. Modest as it was, the nurse project meant a lot to the Cluster.

3. See for instance Berman 1997; Cohen 1999; Edwards and Foley 2001, 1997; or Kaufman 2002.

4. Interview, June 22, 2000. It is worth noting here that Kendra understands the Cluster in terms of her own instrumental goals and volunteers' expressive needs: She thinks in terms of the two variants of individualism that Robert Bellah et al. (1985) found dominant in American public and professional life. She does not say that the Cluster is a good idea because it helps people strengthen community bonds in Lakeburg or because it empowers ordinary citizens to combine efforts with fellow citizens for common goods that few people could oppose.

5. While Ned strongly *preferred* the volunteer mode to partnership, as later scenarios will illustrate, that does not mean he was incapable of participating in a group with some different customs.

6. Interview, June 22, 2000.

7. That wasn't necessarily a safe assumption, and it shows there were limits in the Cluster's ability to talk carefully about other groups.

8. Interview, July 20, 2000.

9. The great majority of Park's residents lived in apartments they rented in two-story buildings built in the two decades after World War II.

10. See the vivid examples of ethnographers' antagonisms toward seemingly narrow-minded volunteers in Kurzman 1991. See also Gouldner's (1967) penetrating comments on sociologists' disdain for "middle dogs" who control underdogs.

11. Confidential documents, "Park Parents School Experiences and Hopes for the Future" and "Bus Transportation Issues/Concerns Related by Park Residents," author's file.

12. Interview, June 20, 2000.

13. The petition had some 120 signatures, from a neighborhood with 350 elementary-school-aged kids and roughly 6,000 residents.

14. She was at least officially a member of the Cluster, and representative from URC, but often left meetings early or came late to report on the school issue. On other issues,

she sounded more like other Cluster members and upheld the value of relationship-building between churches and the neighborhood.

15. For contemporary communitarian thinkers, see Putnam 2000, 1993; Etzioni 1996, 1993; Walzer 1992; for related thinking, see Bellah et al. 1991, 1985; Boyte 1989. For the civic republican tradition, see Arendt 1958; Barber 1984; and of course the writings of Rousseau. Tocqueville's writings on the United States (1969 [1835]) are inspirations for contemporary theorists in both traditions. For pragmatists, see the works of Dewey and Addams noted in chapter 2.

16. A large research literature on social movements makes this point. For recent, synthetic statements, see McAdam, McCarthy and Zald 1996; Tarrow 1994; for classic statements, see McCarthy and Zald 1977; McAdam 1982.

17. As Demerath and Williams (1992) show, these working relationships between local officials and church groups are more common than notions of a strict church/state divide would have it.

18. See, for instance, Habermas 1987, 1976; Cohen and Arato 1992; Cohen 1985; Offe 1996.

19. See Sewell's (1992, p. 13) point that "cultural schemas" eventually wither without resources to embody them. The Cluster's civic-minded map of its place in the larger world would cease being a useful guide if the Cluster always disregarded the civic or governmental entities on the map and focused on getting tasks accomplished and helping individuals, one to one.

20. For an exposition of the logic here, see Boyte 1989; and Mark R. Warren 2001; as well as the writings of Saul Alinsky. See also Lancourt's (1979) comparative study, and illuminating examples of "nonaccountable" politics in Gitlin 1987.

21. To give just one recent and relevant example of this vast sociological tradition, see Kaufman's (2002) argument about the influence of nineteenth-century U.S. civic groups' organizational structure on American political development.

22. See appendix I for a discussion of how and why this study pursues modest theory-generating goals alongside the goal of reconstructing preexisting theory.

CHAPTER SEVEN
DOING THINGS WITH RELIGION IN LOCAL CIVIC LIFE

1. With Adopt-a-Family, it is not clear that a similar but secular group could exist: What sort of group would have *secular* motives for creating deeply interpersonal relationships with strangers?

2. See Ammerman 2003; D. Hall 1997; Pattillo-McCoy 1998; and C. Bender 2003 making this move in ethnographic and historical research. It is the same move that sociologists make when we say that culture includes everyday practices and implicit understandings, as well as more explicit discourses or formal rituals—important as these are.

3. Sociologist of religion Nancy Ammerman commented in 2001 in a professional newsletter that researchers still did not know what exactly distinguished religious or "faith-based" organizations from others.

4. See Wuthnow's (2004) helpful review. Political scientists John Green and Amy Sherman (2002), for instance, rated the explicitness of faith commitments in the organizations they studied, on a scale from completely privatized commitments to openly communicated commitments to active proselytizing of clients. Another team of social

scientists (Smith and Sosin 2001) defined three ways that social service organizations might depend on religious moorings: by running on funding from religious sources, by taking direction from religious leaders, or by allegiance to a religious culture.

5. See Luckmann 1967; Hammond 1992; for critical reviews, see Casanova 1994; Chaves 1994.

6. Scholarship on social identity was one of the main sources for the "boundaries" dimension of customs. See chapter 2; see also Eliasoph and Lichterman 2003.

7. Scholars of social movements make just the same point with a slightly different vocabulary. For a clear and authoritative statement, see Hunt, Benford, and Snow 1994. For a parallel use of this insight to understand local religious groups, see Pattillo-McCoy 1998.

8. The social network scholarship discussed in chapter 2 converges on the same point, that communication is central: Communication, these sociologists said, is not simply an effect of social ties that exist outside communication, but is the medium through which people create ties.

9. I observed three meetings of the Methodist church's outreach committee, at the beginning, middle, and end of a year-long reorganization and revisioning process. I observed two meetings of the Presbyterian church outreach committee and two annual "Outreach Sunday" fairs, at which people involved in the church's varied community projects set up booths in the church basement and solicited new volunteers.

10. For a comprehensive review and assessment of social advocacy by mainline Protestants, see the collected essays in Wuthnow and Evans 2002.

11. Some writers have used the notion of "culture wars" to understand conflicts between other kinds of identity-based groups, not just religious ones. See for instance Gitlin 1995 and Hughes 1993 on gender and racial identity politics in the United States.

12. Ginsburg 1989; DiMaggio, Bryson, and Evans 1996; Williams 1997; Becker 1998.

13. Hunter 1996, 1994, 1991; C. Smith 2000, 1998; DiMaggio, Bryson, and Evans 1996; Ginsburg 1989; Becker 1998.

14. Gamson and Modigliani 1989; Hunter 1994; Benford 1993; Snow and Benford 1988; Snow et al. 1986.

15. See Alexander 2001a; Alexander and Smith 1993; Jacobs 1996, 2000; Kane 1997.

16. See Bellah et al. 1996; Wuthnow 1991; Wood 1994; Witten 1993; K. Hays 1994; Hart 2001.

17. Mark R. Warren (2001) notes that mainline Protestantism's social gospel can support community organizers' campaigns for social justice. The relatively low-income, minority constituencies that tend to predominate in community organizing campaigns (Wood 2002) are less directly connected with mainline Protestantism than with other Christian traditions named here, though.

CHAPTER EIGHT
DOING THINGS TOGETHER: LESSONS
FROM RELIGIOUS COMMUNITY SERVICE GROUPS

1. See, for instance, Swidler's observations (2001) on American voluntarism and the role it plays in solving institutionally given problems.

2. For two fresh departures, see Swidler 2001 and Boltanski and Thévenot 1991.

3. Eventually, more meetings and more group members *resulted* from the transition

toward partnership from conventional volunteering. More frequent meetings and more participants did reinforce the move to partnership, but did not cause it.

4. See my critique of Fukuyama's argument in Lichterman 2001b.

5. In a concluding prospectus for American civic life, Robert Putnam (2000) proposed that Americans make workplaces more family- and community-friendly, that they spend more time with neighbors, less time in front of the television, and become more deeply involved in electoral politics, spiritual communities, and artistic performance.

6. See, for instance, Bane, Coffin, and Thiemann 2000; Bartkowski and Regis 2003; or Wuthnow 2004.

7. See the fascinating ethnographic scenarios and comprehensive literature review in Munkres 2003.

8. See Gitlin 1995; Bernstein 2003; or Hughes 1993.

9. On self-exploration or personal sharing in religious settings, see Roof 1998; Davie 1995; and Wuthnow 1994.

APPENDIX I

THEORY AND EVIDENCE IN A STUDY
OF RELIGIOUS COMMUNITY SERVICE GROUPS

1. In a fully "extended" case study, the researcher becomes very much a part of what she is studying, rather than trying to maintain a certain distance. The researcher aims not only to understand but to change what he is studying. I did not extend my study in these ways. Mine is an extended case study in that I followed the extended case's core moves in order to improve preexisting theory and locate my cases in a specific sociohistorical context.

2. On these two points, see the reviews of relevant research in chapter 1, and for research specifically on evangelicals, chapter 5.

3. Throughout the time I did this study, researchers were still discovering exactly what kinds of community services churches sponsor, how common different kinds are, and what rough proportion of churchgoers are involved in the different kinds. See Ammerman 2002; Chaves, Giesel, and Tsitsos 2002. As Chaves and his colleagues point out, categorizing service projects is not a precise science. A group might be both an "education group" and a "political group," for instance; an interchurch alliance might sponsor a variety of projects under one identity.

4. In the tradition of grounded theory construction, "new" does not mean "uninformed by previous theory and concepts." Rather, it defines discovery more by accumulated findings in the field than by a finding's relation to preexisting theory.

5. Elsewhere, I have discussed the place of writing in ongoing research projects in much more detail (Lichterman 2002). I do not mean to imply that writing or theoretical choices happen only at the end of a research project. My goal here is simply to emphasize that the practices which produce improved theory and the ones that produce grounded theory are not all as different or incompatible as some earlier understandings may lead sociologists to believe.

6. See for instance the long list of studies Burawoy cites (1998, p. 6) as examples of the "rich but inchoate tradition of scholarship in the implicit style of the extended case method."

7. The figures come from a telephone survey of four hundred randomly selected households in Lakeburg County; the margin of error was 4.88 points. I have omitted the source to protect anonymity in my study.

8. In 1994, 43 percent of Lakeburg city residents had a bachelor's degree. Ninety percent were white; 4.2 percent were African American.

Appendix II
Studying Customs

1. The patterned styles of interaction I found are adequately addressed in neither a symbolic interactionism that emphasizes emergent norms and selves nor in a role theory that emphasizes relatively stable relations between roles that are seen as patterned by social structural forces. Synthesizing the two perspectives is a valuable enterprise (Stryker and Statham 1985), but addresses different questions from those that my cases raised about group culture: I found stable patterns of interaction that are instantiated in groups; I propose these belong to a broader cultural repertoire. Neoinstitutionalist conceptualizations capture the stability and breadth of cultural patterns that this book's cases suggest.

2. See, for some excellent examples, McCall and Simmons 1978; Tajfel 1981; Farr and Moscovici 1984; Hewitt 1989; Jenkins 1996; Stets and Burke 2000; Lamont 1999, 1992; Lamont and Fournier 1992; Lamont and Thévenot 2000.

3. For some powerful examples, see DiMaggio and Powell 1991; Morrill 1995; Stevens 2001, 1996; Clemens 1997; Becker 1999; Lichterman 1996.

4. See Goffman 1979, 1961, 1959; see Bergmann 1998; Brenneis and Macaulay 1996; Brenneis and Myers 1984; Fitch 1999; Gumperz 1982a, 1982b; Gumperz and Hymes 1972; Myers 1996; Philipsen 1992; and Rosaldo 1973, 1982 for some examples. See also Bakhtin 1988 on speech genres and Silverstein 1972.

5. The three dimensions emerged inductively, with the help of leads from previous theory and research. Sustained comparisons across six different cases (Lichterman 1996; Eliasoph 1998) revealed that these three dimensions kept arising, over and over, as we tried to make sense of our groups. Thus, through the comparisons we arrived at a tentative, "grounded" understanding of how groups sustain shared grounds for participation (see Glaser and Strauss 1967; Strauss 1987; and Strauss and Corbin 1991 on the discovery of grounded theory). Then we compared the six initial cases with ten other ethnographic cases including ones in this book (Eliasoph 1990; Lichterman 2002, 1999; Eliasoph 2002, 2004) and found, again and again, that the three dimensions adequately covered the definition of good or adequate participation in the groups

6. See Almond and Verba 1963; see critiques by Pateman (1980) and Somers (1995a).

7. See the masterful critique in Somers 1995a; see also Swidler 2001, 1986.

8. For examples, see Somers 1995a; Alexander 2001a; Alexander and Smith 1993; Jacobs 2000, 1996; Kane 1997; Wood 1999, 1994; Hart 2001; Eliasoph 1998; Berezin 1997; Bellah et al. 1996; Calhoun 1994; Schudson 1998; Dayan and Katz 1992; Lichterman 1999, 1996.

9. Sociologists using this perspective say that culture is "relatively autonomous" from social structure. To say culture has a causal force of its own is not to say that class domination, institutionalized hierarchies of gender and race, or state power don't matter! As

William Sewell Jr. has argued (1992), material resources and cultural understandings work together in different ways to produce social structure and action. How *much* cultural forms influence a particular social structure or an event is an empirical question. Alexander and Seidman (1990) offer a good introduction to the meaning of "relative autonomy," and outline some of the varied ways that sociologists have conceived culture's relative autonomy from social structure. For empirical works that draw quite explicitly on a version of the relative autonomy viewpoint, see for instance Alexander and Smith 1993; Wuthnow 1987; Kane 1997; Lichterman 1999; or Wood 1999.

10. We theorize that there is a cognitive basis for group-building customs (Eliasoph and Lichterman 2003), just as there is for other kinds of constitutive rules that quietly tell people or groups how to act. See D'Andrade 1995; Swidler 2001; or Cicourel 1991, 1973.

11. On speech style, see Cmiel 1990. I sketch the history of one political group style, "personalized politics," from the 1950s onward in the United States (Lichterman 1996).

REFERENCES

Abu-Lughod, Lila. 1990. "Can There Be a Feminist Ethnography?" *Women and Performance* 5:7–27.

Adair, Margo, and Sharon Howell. 1988. *The Subjective Side of Politics*. San Francisco: Tools for Change.

Addams, Jane. 1910. *Twenty Years at Hull-House*. New York: Macmillan Company.

———. 2002 [1902]. *Democracy and Social Ethics*. With an Introduction by Charlene H. Seigfried. Urbana: University of Illinois Press.

Alexander, Jeffrey. Forthcoming. *Possibilities of Justice: Civil Society and Its Contradictions*. New York: Oxford University Press.

———. 1982. *Theoretical Logic in Sociology*. Vol. 2, *The Antinomies of Classical Thought: Marx and Durkheim*. Berkeley and Los Angeles: University of California Press.

———. 1988a. *Action and Its Environments: Toward a New Synthesis*. New York: Columbia University Press.

———. 1988b. *Durkheimian Sociology: Cultural Studies*. Berkeley and Los Angeles: University of Caifornia Press.

———. 1995. "The Paradoxes of Civil Society." Social Sciences Research Centre Occasional Paper 16, Department of Sociology, University of Hong Kong.

———. 2001a. "The Long and Winding Road: Civil Repair of Intimate Injustice." *Sociological Theory* 19:371–400.

———. 2001b. "Theorizing the 'Modes of Incorporation': Assimilation, Hyphenation, and Multiculturalism as Varieties of Civil Participation." *Sociological Theory* 19:237–49.

Alexander, Jeffrey, and Steven Seidman. 1990. *Culture and Society: Contemporary Debates*. Cambridge: Cambridge University Press.

Alexander, Jeffrey, and Neil Smelser. 1999. "Introduction: The Ideological Discourse of Cultural Discontent." Pp. 3–18 in *Diversity and Its Discontents*, edited by N. Smelser and J. Alexander. Princeton: Princeton University Press.

Alexander, Jeffrey, and Philip Smith. 1993. "The Discourse of American Civil Society: A New Proposal for Cultural Studies." *Theory and Society* 22:151–207.

Almond, Gabriel, and Sidney Verba. 1963. *The Civic Culture: Political Attitudes and Democracy in Five Nations*. Princeton: Princeton University Press.

Ammerman, Nancy. 1987. *Bible Believers: Fundamentalists in the Modern World*. New Brunswick, N.J.: Rutgers University Press.

———. 1997a. *Congregation and Community*. New Brunswick, N.J.: Rutgers University Press.

———. 1997b. "Golden Rule Christianity: Lived Religion in the American Mainstream." Pp. 196–216 in *Lived Religion in America*, edited by D. Hall. Princeton: Princeton University Press.

———. 2001. "Faith Based Initiatives—Where's the Research?" *Newsletter of the American Sociological Association Section on Sociology of Religion* 7, no. 3 (Spring): 8.

———. 2002. "Connecting Mainline Protestant Churches with Public Life." Pp. 129–58 in *The Quiet Hand of God: Faith-Based Activism and the Public Role of Mainline Protestantism*, edited by R. Wuthnow and J. Evans. Berkeley and Los Angeles: University of California Press.

———. 2003. "Religious Identities and Religious Institutions." Pp. 207–24 in *Handbook for the Sociology of Religion*, edited by M. Dillon. Cambridge: Cambridge University Press.

Arendt, Hannah. 1958. *The Human Condition*. Chicago: University of Chicago Press.

Armstrong, Elizabeth. 2002. *Forging Gay Identities*. Chicago: University of Chicago Press.

Baggett, Jerome. 2000. *Habitat for Humanity: Building Private Homes, Building Public Religion*. Philadelphia: Temple University Press.

Baiocchi, Gianpaolo. 2001. "Activism, Civil Society, and Politics: The Porto Alegre Case and Deliberative Democracy Theory." *Politics and Society* 29:43–72.

———. 2003. "Emergent Public Spheres: Talking Politics in Participatory Governance." *American Sociological Review* 68:52–74.

Bakhtin, M. M. 1988. *Speech Genres and Other Late Essays*. Translated by Caryl Emerson and Michael Holquist. Austin: University of Texas Press.

Bane, Mary Jo, Brent Coffin, and Ronald Thiemann. 2000. *Who Will Provide? The Changing Role of Religion in American Social Welfare*. Boulder, Colo: Westview Press.

Barber, Benjamin. 1984. *Strong Democracy*. Berkeley and Los Angeles: University of California Press.

Barkan, Steve. 1979. "Strategic, Tactical, and Organizational Dilemmas of the Protest Movement against Nuclear Power." *Social Problems* 27:19–37.

Bartkowski, John, and Helen Regis. 2003. *Charitable Choices: Religion, Race, and Poverty in the Post-welfare Era*. New York: New York University Press.

Bass, Dorothy. 1998. *Practicing Our Faith*. San Francisco: Jossey-Bass.

Bauman, Zygmunt. 1991. *Modernity and Ambivalence*. Ithaca: Cornell University Press.

———. 1993. *Postmodern Ethics*. Oxford: Basil Blackwell.

Beck, Ulrich, Anthony Giddens, and Scott Lash. 1994. *Reflexive Modernization*. Stanford, Calif.: Stanford University Press.

Becker, Howard S. 1961. *Boys in White: Student Culture in Medical School*. Chicago: University of Chicago Press.

Becker, Penny. 1998. "Making Inclusive Communities: Congregations and the 'Problem' of Race." *Social Problems* 45:451–72.

———. 1999. *Congregations in Conflict*. Cambridge: Cambridge University Press.

Becker, Penny, and P. H. Dhingra. 2001. "Religious Involvement and Volunteering: Implications for Civil Society." *Sociology of Religion* 62:315–36.

Becker, Penny, and Nancy Eiesland. 1997. "Developing Interpretations." Pp. 15–23 in *Contemporary American Religion: An Ethnographic Reader*, edited by P. Becker and N. L. Eiesland. Walnut Creek, Calif.: AltaMira/Sage.

Beem, Christopher. 1999. *The Necessity of Politics: Reclaiming American Public Life*. Chicago: University of Chicago Press.

Beiner, Ronald. 1995. *Theorizing Citizenship*. Albany: State University of New York Press.

Bell, Daniel. 1976. *The Cultural Contradictions of Capitalism*. New York: Basic Books.

Bellah, Robert. 1987. "Competing Visions of the Role of Religion in American Society." Pp. 219–32 in *Uncivil Religion*, edited by R. Bellah and F. Greenspahn. New York: Crossroad.

Bellah, Robert, Richard Madsen, William Sullivan, Ann Swidler, and Steven Tipton. 1985. *Habits of the Heart: Individualism and Commitment in American Life.* Berkeley and Los Angeles: University of California Press.

———. 1991. *The Good Society.* New York: Alfred Knopf.

———. 1996. *Habits of the Heart: Individualism and Commitment in American Life.* Updated ed. with a new introduction. Berkeley and Los Angeles: University of California Press.

Bender, Courtney. 1997. "Kitchen Work: The Everyday Practice of Religion, Cooking, and Caring for People with AIDS." Ph.D. Dissertation, Department of Sociology, Princeton University.

———. 2003. *Heaven's Kitchen: Living Religion at God's Love We Deliver.* Chicago: University of Chicago Press.

Bender, Thomas. 1978. *Continuity and Social Change in America.* New Brunswick, N.J.: Rutgers University Press.

Bendix, Richard. 1977 [1964]. *Nation-Building and Citizenship.* Berkeley and Los Angeles: University of California Press.

Benford, Robert. 1993. "Frame Disputes within the Nuclear Disarmament Movement." *Social Forces* 71:677–700.

Benhabib, Seyla. 1996. "Toward a Deliberative Model of Democratic Legitimacy." Pp. 67–94 in *Democracy and Difference,* edited by S. Benhabib. Princeton: Princeton University Press.

———. 1999. "Citizens, Residents, and Aliens in a Changing World: Political Membership in the Global Era." *Social Research* 66:709–44.

Berezin, Mabel. 1994. "Fissured Terrain: Methodological Approaches and Research Styles in Culture and Politics." Pp. 91–116 in *Sociology of Culture: Emerging Theoretical Perspectives,* edited by D. Crane. London: Basil Blackwell.

———. 1997. "Politics and Culture: A Less-Fissured Terrain." *Annual Review of Sociology* 23:361–83.

Berger, Peter, and Richard J. Neuhaus. 1977. *To Empower People: From State to Civil Society.* Washington, D.C.: AEI Press.

Bergmann, Jorg. 1998. "Introduction: Morality In Discourse." *Research on Language and Social Interaction* 31 (3 and 4): 279–94.

Berman, Sheri. 1997. "Civil Society and the Collapse of the Weimar Republic." *World Politics* 49:401–29.

Bernstein, Mary. 1997. "Celebration and Suppression: The Strategic Uses of Identity by the Lesbian and Gay Movement." *American Journal of Sociology* 103:531–65.

Bernstein, Richard. 2003. "The Fetish of Difference." Pp. 57–66 in *The Fractious Nation?* edited by Jonathan Rieder. Berkeley and Los Angeles: University of California Press.

Besecke, Kelly. 2002. "Rational Enchantment: Transcendent Meaning in the Modern World." Ph.D. Dissertation, Department of Sociology, University of Wisconsin—Madison.

Best, Joel. 1990. *Threatened Children: Rhetoric and Concern about Child-Victims.* Chicago: University of Chicago Press.

Blyth, D. A., R. Saito, and T. Berkas. 1997. "A Quantitative Study of the Impact of Service Learning Programs." Pp. 39–56 in *Service Learning: Applications from the Research,* edited by A. S. Waterman. Mahwah, N.J.: Lawrence Erlbaum.

Boltanski, Luc, and Laurent Thévenot. 1991. *De la justification: Les economies de la grandeur.* Paris: Gallimard.

Bourdieu, Pierre. 1977. *Outline of a Theory of Practice.* Cambridge: Cambridge University Press.

———. 1984. *Distinction.* Translated by R. Nice. Cambridge: Harvard University Press.

———. 1990. *The Logic of Practice.* Cambridge: MIT Press.

Bourgois, Philippe. 1995. *In Search of Respect: Selling Crack in El Barrio.* New York: Cambridge University Press.

Boyte, Harry. 1989. *CommonWealth: A Return to Citizen Politics.* New York: Free Press.

Boyte, Harry, and Sara M. Evans. 1986. *Free Spaces: The Sources of Democratic Change in America.* New York: Harper and Row.

Breines, Wini. 1982. *Community and Organization in the New Left.* South Hadley, Mass.: J. F. Bergin.

Brenneis, Donald, and Fred Myers, eds. 1984. *Dangerous Words: Language and Politics in the Pacific.* New York: New York University Press.

Brenneis, Donald, and Ronald Macaulay, eds. 1996. *Contemporary Linguistic Anthropology.* New York: HarperCollins.

Briggs, Xavier de Souza. 1998. "Brown Kids in White Suburbs: Housing Mobility and the Multiple Faces of Social Capital." *Housing Policy Debate* 9(1).

Brown, Michael P. 1998. *RePlacing Citizenship: AIDS Activism and Radical Democracy.* New York: Guilford Press.

Burawoy, Michael. 1998. "The Extended Case Method." *Sociological Theory* 16:4–33.

Burawoy, Michael, Alice Burton, Ann Arnett Ferguson, Kathryn Fox, Joshua Gamson, Nadine Gartrell, Leslie Hurst, Charles Kurzman, Leslie Salzinger, Josepha Schiffman, Shiori Ui. 1991. *Ethnography Unbound.* Berkeley and Los Angeles: University of California Press.

Calhoun, Craig. 1994. *Social Theory and the Politics of Identity.* Oxford: Basil Blackwell.

———. 1999. "Symposium on Religion." *Sociological Theory* 17:237–39.

Caplow, Theodore, H. M. Bahr, Bruce A. Chadwick, et al. 1983. *All Faithful People: Change and Continuity in Middletown's Religion.* Minneapolis: University of Minnesota Press.

Carbaugh, Donal. 1988. *Talking American: Cultural Discourses on "Donahue."* Norwood, N.J.: Ablex Press.

Carter, Stephen. 1993. *The Culture of Disbelief.* New York: Basic Books.

Casanova, José. 1994. *Public Religions in the Modern World.* Chicago: University of Chicago Press.

Chaves, Mark. 1994. "Secularization as Declining Religious Authority." *Social Forces* 72:749–75.

———. 1999. "Religious Congregations and Welfare Reform: Who Will Take Advantage of 'Charitable Choice'?" *American Sociological Review* 64:836–46.

Chaves, Mark, Helen Giesel, and William Tsitsos. 2000. "Religious Variations in Public Presence: Evidence from the National Congregations Study." Paper presented at the conference "The Public Role of Mainline Protestantism," Princeton University, June 2–4.

———. 2002. "Religious Variations in Public Presence: Evidence from the National Congregations Study." Pp. 108–28 in *The Quiet Hand of God: Faith-Based Activism and the Public Role of Mainline Protestantism,* edited by R. Wuthnow and J. Evans. Berkeley and Los Angeles: University of California Press.

Cherlin, Andrew. 1999. "I'm O.K., You're Selfish." *New York Times Magazine,* October 17, pp. 44–50.

Cicourel, Aaron. 1973. *Cognitive Sociology.* Harmondsworth: Penguin Books.

———. 1991. "Semantics, Pragmatics, and Situated Meaning." Pp. 37–66 in *Pragmatics at Issue,* vol. 1, edited by Jef Verschueren. Amsterdam and Philadelphia: John Benjamins.

Clemens, Elisabeth. 1997. *The People's Lobby.* Chicago: University of Chicago Press.

Cmiel, Kenneth. 1990. *Democratic Eloquence: The Fight over Popular Speech in Nineteenth-Century America.* New York: William Morrow.

Cnaan, Ram A., with Stephanie C. Boddie, Femida Handy, Caynor Yancey, and Richard Schneider. 2002. *The Invisible Caring Hand: American Congregations and the Provision of Welfare.* New York: New York University Press.

Cochran, Pamela. 2001. "Evangelical Boundaries and the Threat of Biblical Feminism, 1973–Present: A Theological and Institutional History." Ph.D. Dissertation, Department of Religious Studies, University of Virginia, Charlottesville.

Coffin, Brent. 2000. "Where Religion and Public Values Meet: Who Will Contest?" Pp. 121–43 in *Who Will Provide? The Changing Role of Religion in American Social Welfare,* edited by M. J. Bane, B. Coffin, and R. Thiemann. Boulder, Colo.: Westview Press.

Cohen, Jean. 1982. *Class and Civil Society: the Limits of Marxian Critical Theory.* Amherst: University of Massachusetts Press.

———. 1985. "Strategy or Identity: New Theoretical Paradigms and Contemporary Social Movements." *Social Research* 52:663–716.

———. 1999. "American Civil Society Talk." Pp. 55–85 in *Civil Society, Democracy, and Civic Renewal,* edited by R. Fullinwider. Lanham, Md.: Rowman and Littlefield.

Cohen, Jean, and Andrew Arato. 1992. *Civil Society and Political Theory.* Cambridge: MIT Press.

Cohen, Joshua, and Joel Rogers. 1992. "Secondary Associations and Democratic Governance." *Politics and Society* 20:393–472.

Connell, Robert. 1983. *Which Way Is Up? Essays on Class, Sex, and Culture.* Sydney: Allen and Unwin.

Couto, Richard, 1999, with Catherine Guthrie. *Making Democracy Work Better.* Chapel Hill: University of North Carolina Press.

Cuddihy, John. 1978. *No Offense: Civil Religion and Protestant Taste.* New York: Seabury.

D'Andrade, Roy. 1995. *The Development of Cognitive Anthropology.* Cambridge: Cambridge University Press.

Daniels, Arlene Kaplan. 1988. *Invisible Careers: Women Civic Leaders from the Volunteer World.* Chicago: University of Chicago Press.

Davidman, Lynn. 1991. *Tradition in a Rootless World: Women Turn to Orthodox Judaism.* Berkeley and Los Angeles: University of California Press.

Davie, Jody. 1995. *Women in the Presence.* Philadelphia: University of Pennsylvania Press.

Dayan, Daniel, and Elihu Katz. 1992. *Media Events.* Cambridge: Harvard University Press.

Delgado, Gary. 1986. *Organizing the Movement.* Philadelphia: Temple University Press.

Demerath, N. J. 2001. "A Sinner among the Saints: Confessions of a Sociologist of Culture and Religion." Presidential Address, Eastern Sociological Society meetings, Philadelphia, Penn.

Demerath, N. J., and Rhys Williams. 1992. *A Bridging of Faiths: Religion and Politics in a New England City.* Princeton: Princeton University Press.

DeVault, Marjorie. 1999. *Liberating Method: Feminism and Social Research.* Philadelphia: Temple University Press.

Dewey, John. 1922. *Human Nature and Conduct*. New York: Henry Holt.

———. 1927. *The Public and Its Problems*. Denver: Allan Swallow.

———. 1939. *Freedom and Culture*. New York: G. P. Putnam's Sons.

Diamond, Sara. 1989. *Spiritual Warfare: The Politics of the Christian Right*. Boston: South End Press.

Diani, Mario, and Doug McAdam. 2003. *Social Movements: The Network Perspective*. New York: Oxford University Press.

DiMaggio, Paul, Bethany Bryson, and John Evans. 1996. "Have Americans' Social Attitudes Become More Polarized?" *American Journal of Sociology* 102:690–755.

DiMaggio, Paul, and Walter Powell, eds. 1991. *The New Institutionalism in Organizational Analysis*. Chicago: University of Chicago Press.

Douglass, Paul H., and Edmund de Brunner. 1935. *The Protestant Church as a Social Institution*. New York: Harper and Row.

Downey, Gary. 1986. "Ideology and the Clamshell Identity: Organizational Dilemmas in the Anti-nuclear Power Movement." *Social Problems* 33:357–73.

Durkheim, Emile. 1951 [1897]. *Suicide: A Study in Sociology*. Translated by J. A. Spaulding and G. Simpson. New York: Free Press.

———. 1995 [1915]. *The Elementary Forms of the Religious Life*. Translated by K. Fields. New York: Free Press.

Eckstein, Susan. 2001. "Community as Gift-Giving: Collectivistic Roots of Volunteerism." *American Sociological Review* 66:829–51.

Edin, Kathryn, and Laura Lein. 1997. "Work, Welfare, and Single Mothers: Economic Survival Strategies." *American Sociological Review* 61:253–66.

Edwards, Bob, and Michael Foley, eds. 1997. *American Behavioral Scientist* 40 (March–April), special issue, "Social Capital, Civil Society, and Contemporary Democracy."

———. 2001. "Much Ado about Social Capital." *Contemporary Sociology* 30:227–30.

Eliasoph, Nina. 1990. "Political Culture and the Presentation of a Political 'Self.'" *Theory and Society* 19:465–94.

———. 1996. "Making a Fragile Public: A Talk-Centered Study of Citizenship and Power." *Sociological Theory* 14:262–89.

———. 1998. *Avoiding Politics: How Americans Produce Apathy in Everyday Life*. New York: Cambridge University Press.

———. 1999. "'Everyday Racism' in a Culture of Political Avoidance: Civil Society, Speech and Taboo." *Social Problems* 46(4): 479–502.

———. 2002. "Raising Good Citizens in a Bad Society: Moral Education and Political Avoidance in Civic America." Pp. 195–223 in *Meaning and Modernity: Religion, Polity, and Self*, edited by Richard Madsen, William Sullivan, Ann Swidler, and Steven Tipton. Berkeley and Los Angeles: University of California Press.

———. 2004. "Ambiguous Moral Worlds: Everyday Conversation in U.S. Youth Programs." Department of Sociology, University of Wisconsin—Madison and Department of Sociology, University of Southern California. Book manuscript in progress.

Eliasoph, Nina, and Paul Lichterman. 2003. "Culture in Interaction." *American Journal of Sociology* 108:735–94.

Ellingsen, Mark. 1988. *The Evangelical Movement*. Minneapolis, Minn.: Augsburg Publishing.

Ellingson, Stephen. 1995. "Understanding the Dialectic of Discourse and Collective Action: Public Debate and Rioting in Antebellum Cincinnati." *American Journal of Sociology* 101:100–44.

Ellison, C. G., and L. K. George. 1994. "Religious Involvement, Social Ties, and Social Support in a Southeastern Community." *Journal for the Scientific Study of Religion* 33:46–61.

Elshtain, Jean. 1981. *Public Man, Private Woman: Women in Social and Political Thought.* Princeton: Princeton University Press.

Emerson, Michael, and Christian Smith. 2000. *Divided by Faith: Evangelical Religion and the Problem of Race in America.* New York: Oxford University Press.

Emirbayer, Mustafa, and Jeff Goodwin. 1994. "Network Analysis, Culture, and the Problem of Agency." *American Journal of Sociology* 99:1411–54.

Emirbayer, Mustafa, and Mimi Sheller. 1999. "Publics in History." *Theory and Society* 28:145–97.

Epstein, Barbara. 1991. *Political Protest and Cultural Revolution.* Berkeley and Los Angeles: University of California Press.

Etzioni, Amitai. 1993. *The Spirit of Community.* New York: Simon and Schuster.

———. 1996. *The New Golden Rule: Community and Morality in a Democratic Society.* New York: Basic Books.

Fantasia, Rick. 1988. *Cultures of Solidarity: Consciousness, Action, and Contemporary American Workers.* Berkeley and Los Angeles: University of California Press.

Farr, Robert, and Serge Moscovici. 1984. *Social Representations.* Cambridge and New York: Cambridge University Press.

Farrell, James. 1997. *The Spirit of the Sixties: Making Postwar Radicalism.* New York: Routledge.

Ferguson, Ronald, and William Dickens. 1999. "Introduction." Pp. 1–31 in *Urban Problems and Community Development,* edited by R. Ferguson and W. Dickens. Washington, D.C.: Brookings Institution Press.

Ferguson, Ronald and Sara Stoutland. 1999. "Reconceiving the Community Development Field." Pp. 33–75 in *Urban Problems and Community Development,* edited by R. Ferguson and W. Dickens. Washington, D.C.: Brookings Institution Press.

Ferree, Myra Marx, and Beth Hess. 1994. *Controversy and Coalition.* New York: Twyane Publishers.

Fine, Gary Alan. 1987. *With the Boys: Little League Baseball and Preadolescent Culture.* Chicago: University of Chicago Press.

Finke, Roger, and Rodney Stark. 1986. "Turning Pews into People." *Journal for the Scientific Study of Religion* 25:180–92.

Fiorenza, Francis. 2000. "Justice and Charity in Social Welfare." Pp. 73–96 in *Who Will Provide? The Changing Role of Religion in American Social Welfare,* edited by M. J. Bane, B. Coffin, and R. Thiemann. Boulder, Colo.: Westview Press.

Fishman, Robert. 2004. *Democracy's Voices: Social Ties and the Quality of Public Life in Spain.* Ithaca: Cornell University Press.

Fitch, Kristine. 1999. "Pillow Talk?" *Research on Language and Social Interaction* 32 (1 and 2): 41–50.

Flacks, Richard. 1988. *Making History: The Radical Tradition in American Life.* New York: Columbia University Press.

Fraser, Nancy. 1989. *Unruly Practices.* Minneapolis: University of Minnesota Press.

———. 1992. "Rethinking the Public Sphere: A Contribution to the Critique of Actually Existing Democracy." Pp. 109–42 in *Habermas and the Public Sphere*, edited by C. Calhoun. Cambridge: MIT Press.

Friedman, Deborah, and Doug McAdam. 1992. "Collective Identity and Activism: Networks, Choices, and the Life of a Social Movement." Pp. 156–73 in *Frontiers in Social Movement Theory*, edited by A. Morris and C. Mueller. New Haven: Yale University Press.

Fukuyama, Francis. 1999. *The Great Disruption: Human Nature and the Reconstitution of Social Order*. New York: U.S.A. Free Press.

Fullinwider, Robert. 1999. *Civil Society, Democracy, and Civic Renewal*. Lanham, Md.: Rowman and Littlefield.

Fung, Archon, Erik Olin Wright, with contributions by Rebecca Neaera Abers, Gianpaolo Baiocchi, Joshua Cohen, Patrick Heller, Bradley C. Karkkainen, Rebecca S. Krantz, Jane Mansbridge, Joel Rogers, Craig W. Thomas, and T. M. Thomas Isaac. 2003. *Deepening Democracy: Institutional Innovations in Empowered Participatory Governance*. Volume IV of the Real Utopias Project Series. London: Verso.

Galston, William. 1991. *Liberal Purposes: Goods, Virtues, and Duties in the Liberal State*. Cambridge: Cambridge University Press.

Gamson, William. 1992. "The Social Psychology of Collective Action." Pp. 53–76 in *Frontiers in Social Movement Theory*, edited by A. Morris and C. Mueller. New Haven: Yale University Press.

———. 1996. "Safe Spaces and Social Movements." *Perspectives on Social Problems* 8:27–38.

Gamson, William A., and Andre Modigliani. 1989. "Media Discourse and Public Opinion on Nuclear Power: A Constructionist Approach." *American Journal of Sociology* 95:1–37.

Geertz, Clifford. 1973. *The Interpretation of Cultures*. New York: Basic Books.

Giddens, Anthony. 1991. *Modernity and Self-Identity*. Stanford, Calif.: Stanford University Press.

Ginsberg, Faye. 1989. *Contested Lives: The Abortion Debate in an American Community*. Berkeley and Los Angeles: University of California Press.

Gitlin, Todd. 1980. *The Whole World Is Watching*. Berkeley and Los Angeles: University of California Press.

———. 1987. *The Sixties: Years of Hope, Days of Rage*. New York: Bantam Books.

———. 1995. *The Twilight of Common Dreams*. New York: Metropolitan Books.

Gittell, R., and A. Vidal. 1998. *Community Organizing: Building Social Capital as a Development Strategy*. Thousand Oaks, Calif.: Sage Publications.

Glaser, Barney, and Anselm Strauss. 1967. *The Discovery of Grounded Theory*. Chicago: Aldine Publishing Company.

Glendon, Mary Ann. 1991. *Rights Talk: The Impoverishment of Political Discourse*. New York: Free Press.

Glock, Charles, and Rodney Stark. 1965. *Religion and Society in Tension*. Chicago: Rand McNally.

Goffman, Erving. 1959. *The Presentation of Self in Everyday Life*. Garden City, N.Y.: Doubleday.

———. 1961. *Encounters*. New York: Bobbs-Merrill.

———. 1974. *Frame Analysis: An Essay on the Organization of Experience*. New York: Harper and Row.

———. 1979. "Footing." *Semiotica* 25:1–29.

Goldberg, Chad. 2001. "Social Citizenship and a Reconstructed Tocqueville." *American Sociological Review* 66:289–315.

Gorski, Philip. 2000. "The Mosaic Moment: An Early Modernist Critique of Modernist Theories of Nationalism." *American Journal of Sociology* 105:1428–68.

Gould, Roger. 1991. "Multiple Networks and Mobilization in the Paris Commune, 1871." *American Sociological Review* 56:716–29.

Gouldner, Alvin. 1967. "The Sociologist as Partisan: Sociology and the Welfare State." Pp. 35–69 in *For Sociology: Renewal and Critique in Sociology Today*. New York: Basic Books, 1973.

Gramsci, Antonio. 1971. *Selections from the Prison Notebooks*. Translated by Q. Hoare and G. Smith New York: International Publishers.

Greeley, Andrew. 1997. "Coleman Revisited: Religious Structures as a Source of Social Capital." *American Behavioral Scientist* 40 (March–April): 587–94.

Green, John, and Amy Sherman. 2002. "Fruitful Collaborations: A Survey of Government-Funded Faith-Based Programs in 15 States." Washington, D.C.: Hudson Institute.

Green, Judith. 1999. *Deep Democracy: Community, Diversity, and Transformation*. Lanham, Md.: Rowan and Littlefield.

Greenberg, Anna. 2000. "Doing Whose Work? Faith-Based Organizations and Government Partnerships." Pp. 178–97 in *Who Will Provide? The Changing Role of Religion in American Social Welfare*, edited by M. J. Bane, B. Coffin, and R. Thiemann. Boulder, Colo.: Westview Press.

Gregory, Eric. 2002. "Augustine and the Ethics of Liberalism." Ph.D. dissertation, Department of Religious Studies, Yale University.

Gumperz, John. 1982a. *Discourse Strategies*. Cambridge: Cambridge University Press.

———. 1982b. *Language and Social Identity*. Berkeley and Los Angeles: University of California Press.

Gumperz, John, and Dell Hymes, eds. 1972. *Directions In Sociolinguistics: The Ethnography of Communication*. New York: Holt, Rinehart and Winston.

Gusfield, Joe. 1981. *The Culture of Public Problems*. Chicago: University of Chicago Press.

Guterbock, Thomas, and John Fries. 1997. *Maintaining America's Social Fabric: The AARP Survey of Civic Involvement*. Charlottesville: Center for Survey Research, University of Virginia.

Gutmann, Amy. 1998. *Freedom of Association*. Princeton: Princeton University Press.

Habermas, Jürgen. 1974. "The Public Sphere: An Encyclopedia Article." *New German Critique* 3:49–55.

———. 1975. *Legitimation Crisis*. Boston: Beacon Press.

———. 1984, 1987. *The Theory of Communicative Action*. Vols. 1 and 2. Translated by T. McCarthy. Boston: Beacon Press.

———. 1989. *The Structural Transformation of the Public Sphere*. Translated by T. Burger and F. Lawrence. Cambridge: MIT Press.

———. 1992. "Further Reflections on the Public Sphere." Pp. 421–61 in *Habermas and the Public Sphere*, edited by C. Calhoun. Cambridge: MIT Press.

Hall, David. 1997. *Lived Religion in America: Toward a History of Practice*. Princeton: Princeton University Press.

Hall, Peter Dobkin. 1999. "Vital Signs: Organizational Population Trends and Civic Engagement in New Haven, Connecticut, 1850–1998." Pp. 211–48 in *Civic Engagement and American Democracy,* edited by T. Skocpol and M. Fiorina. Washington, D.C., and New York: Brookings Institution Press and Russell Sage Foundation.

Hall, Stuart. 1977. "Culture, the Media and the 'Ideological Effect.'" Pp. 315–48 in *Mass Communication and Society,* edited by J. Curran, M. Gurevitch, and J. Woollacott. Beverly Hills, Calif.: Sage.

Hall, Stuart, C. Crichter, T. Jefferson, J. Clarke, and B. Roberts. 1978. *Policing the Crisis: The State and Law and Order.* London: Macmillan.

Hammond, Phillip. 1992. *Religion and Personal Autonomy: The Third Disestablishment in America.* Columbia: University of South Carolina Press.

Hart, Stephen. 1992. *What Does the Lord Require?* New York: Oxford University Press.

———. 1996. "The Cultural Dimension of Social Movements: A Theoretical Reassessment and Literature Review." *Sociology of Religion* 57:87–100.

———. 2001. *Cultural Dilemmas of Progressive Politics.* Chicago: University of Chicago Press.

Hays, Kim. 1994. *Practicing Virtues: Moral Traditions at Quaker and Military Boarding Schools.* Berkeley and Los Angeles: University of California Press.

Hays, Sharon. 2003. *Flat Broke with Children.* New York: Oxford University Press.

Heelas, Paul, Scott Lash, and Paul Morris. 1996. *Detraditionalization.* Oxford: Basil Blackwell.

Hewitt, John. 1989. *Dilemmas of the American Self.* Philadelphia: Temple University Press.

Hochschild, Arlie. 1983. *The Managed Heart.* Berkeley and Los Angeles: University of California Press.

Hodgkinson, Virginia, and Murray Weitzman. 1996. *Giving and Volunteering in the United States.* Washington, D.C.: Independent Sector.

Hughes, Robert. 1993. *Culture of Complaint: The Fraying of America.* New York: Oxford University Press.

Hunt, Scott, Robert Benford, and David Snow. 1994. "Identity Fields: Framing Processes and the Social Construction of Movement Identities." Pp. 185–208 in *New Social Movements: From Ideology to Identity,* edited by E. Laraña, H. Johnston, and J. Gusfield. Philadelphia: Temple University Press.

Hunter, James D. 1983. *American Evangelicalism.* New Brunswick, N.J.: Rutgers University Press.

———. 1987. *Evangelicalism: The Coming Generation.* Chicago: University of Chicago Press.

———. 1991. *Culture Wars: The Struggle to Define America.* New York: Basic Books.

———. 1994. *Before the Shooting Begins: Searching for Democracy in America's Culture War.* New York: Free Press.

———. 1996. *The State of Disunion: 1996 Survey of American Political Culture.* 2 Vols. Ivy, Va.: In Medias Res Educational Foundation.

———. 2000. *The Death of Character: Moral Education after the Death of God.* New York: Basic Books.

Jacobs, Ronald N. 1996. "Civil Society and Crisis: Culture, Discourse, and the Rodney King Beating." *American Journal of Sociology* 101:1238–72.

———. 2000. *Race, Media, and the Crisis of Civil Society: From Watts to Rodney King.* New York: Cambridge University Press.

Jacobsen, Douglas, and William Trollinger, Jr. 1998. *Re-forming the Center: American Protestantism, 1900 to the Present.* Grand Rapids, Mich.: Eerdmans.

Janoski, Thomas. 1998. *Citizenship and Civil Society*. Cambridge and New York: Cambridge University Press.

Janowitz, Morris. 1952. *The Community Press in an Urban Setting*. Glencoe, Ill.: Free Press.

——. 1975. "Sociological Theory and Social Control." *American Journal of Sociology* 81:82–108.

——. 1978. *The Last Half-Century: Societal Change and Politics in America*. Chicago: University of Chicago Press.

Joas, Hans. 2000. "Procedure and Conviction: On Moral Dialogues." Pp. 37–56 in *Autonomy and Order: A Communitarian Anthology*, edited by E. Lehman. Lanham, Md.: Rowman and Littlefield.

Jenkins, Richard. 1996. *Social Identity*. London and New York: Routledge.

Johnson, M. K., T. Beebe, J. Mortimer, and M. Snyder. 1998. "Volunteerism in Adolescence: A Process Perspective." *Journal of Research on Adolescence* 8:309–32.

Kane, Anne. 1991. "Cultural Analysis in Historical Sociology: The Analytical and Concrete Forms of the Autonomy of Culture." *Sociological Theory* 9:53–69.

——. 1997. "Theorizing Meaning Construction in Social Movements: Symbolic Structures and Interpretation during the Irish Land War, 1879–1882." *Sociological Theory* 15:249–76.

Kaufman, Jason. 2002. *For the Common Good? American Civic Life and the Golden Age of Fraternity*. New York: Oxford University Press.

Kelley, Dean. 1972. *Why Conservative Churches Are Growing*. San Francisco: Harper and Row.

Kertzer, David. 1990. *Comrades and Christians: Religion and Political Struggle in Communist Italy*. Prospect Heights, Ill.: Waveland Press.

Klandermans, Bert. 1992. "The Social Construction of Protest and Multiorganizational Fields." Pp. 77–103 in *Frontiers in Social Movement Theory*, edited by A. D. Morris and C. McClurg Mueller. New Haven: Yale University Press.

Krantz, Rebecca S. 2003. "Cycles of Reform in Porto Alegre and Madison." Pp. 225–36 in *Deepening Democracy: Institutional Innovations in Empowered Participatory Governance*, vol. IV in the Real Utopias Project, edited by A. Fung and E. O. Wright. New York: Verso.

Kurzman, Charles. 1991. "Converting Sociologists: Values and Interests in the Sociology of Knowledge." Pp. 250–68 in *Ethnography Unbound*, edited by Michael Burawoy. Berkeley and Los Angeles: University of California Press.

Kymlicka, Will, and Wayne Norman. 1995. "Return of the Citizen: A Survey of Recent Work on Citizenship Theory." Pp. 283–322 in *Theorizing Citizenship*, edited by R. Beiner. Albany: State University of New York Press.

Lamont, Michèle. 1992. *Money, Morals and Manners*. Chicago: University of Chicago Press.

——. 1995. "The Frontiers of Our Dreams Are No Longer the Same: Cultural Dynamics of Exclusion and Community in France, the United States, and Quebec." In *Self-Determination in Our World*, edited by W. Danspeckgruber and J. Waterbury. New York: Oxford University Press.

——. 1999. *The Cultural Territories of Race: Black and White Boundaries*. Chicago: University of Chicago Press; New York: Russell Sage Foundation.

——. 2002. "The Study of Boundaries in the Social Sciences." *Annual Review of Sociology* 28:167–95.

Lamont, Michèle, and Marcel Fournier. 1992. *Cultivating Differences: Symbolic Boundaries and the Making of Inequality.* Chicago: University of Chicago Press.

Lamont, Michèle, and Virag Molnar. 2001. "How Blacks Use Consumption to Shape Their Collective Identity." *Journal of Consumer Culture* 1:31–45.

Lamont, Michèle, and Laurent Thévenot. 2000. *Rethinking Comparative Cultural Sociology: Repertoires of Evaluation in France and the United States:* Cambridge: Cambridge University Press; Paris: Presses de la Maison des Sciences de l'Homme.

Lancaster, Roger N. 1988. *Thanks to God and the Revolution.* New York: Columbia University Press.

Lancourt, Jane. 1979. *Confront or Concede: The Alinsky Citizen-Action Organizations.* Lexington, Mass.: D.C. Heath.

Lane, Robert. 1962. *Political Ideology.* New York: Free Press.

Lasch, Christopher. 1966. *The New Radicalism in America, 1889–1963: The Intellectual as a Social Type.* New York: A. Knopf.

Lehman, Edward, ed. 2000. *Autonomy and Order: A Communitarian Anthology.* Lanham, Md.: Rowman and Littlefield.

Lewis, Justin. 1999. "Reproducing Political Hegemony in the United States." *Critical Studies in Mass Communication* 16:251–67.

Lichterman, Paul. 1992. "Self-Help Reading as a Thin Culture." *Media, Culture and Society* 14:421–47.

———. 1995a. "Beyond the Seesaw Model: Public Commitment in a Culture of Self-Fulfillment." *Sociological Theory* 13:275–300.

———. 1995b. "Piecing Together Multicultural Community: Cultural Differences in Community-Building among Grassroots Environmentalists." *Social Problems* 42:513–34.

———. 1996. *The Search for Political Community: American Activists Reinventing Commitment.* New York: Cambridge University Press.

———. 1999. "Talking Identity in the Public Sphere: Broad Visions and Small Spaces in Sexual Identity Politics." *Theory and Society* 28:101–41.

———. 2000. "Integrating Diversity: Boundaries, Bonds, and the Greater Community in *The New Golden Rule.*" Pp. 125–41 in *Autonomy and Order: A Communitarian Anthology,* edited by E. Lehman. Lanham, Md.: Rowman and Littlefield.

———. 2001a. "From Tribalism to Translation: Bridging Diversity for Civic Renewal." *Hedgehog Review: Critical Reflections on Contemporary Culture* 3:40–61.

———. 2001b. "Human Nature Fights Back." Review of *The Great Disruption,* by Francis Fukuyama. *The Responsive Community* 11(3):71–75.

———. 2002. "Seeing Structure Happen: Theory-Driven Participant Observation." Pp. 118–45 in *Methods of Social Movement Research,* edited by B. Klandermans and S. Staggenborg. Minneapolis: University of Minnesota Press.

Liebow, Elliot. 1993. *Tell Them Who I Am.* New York: Free Press.

Lin, Nan. 2001. *Social Capital: A Theory of Social Structure and Action.* New York: Cambridge University Press.

Lincoln, C. Eric, and Lawrence H. Mamiya. 1990. *The Black Church in the African-American Experience.* Durham, N.C.: Duke University Press.

Long, Elizabeth. 1984. *The American Dream and the Popular Novel.* New York: Routledge and Kegan Paul.

Luckmann, Thomas. 1967. *The Invisible Religion: The Problem of Religion in Modern Society.* New York: Macmillan.

Lukes, Steven S. 1974. *Power: A Radical View.* London: Macmillan Press.

Mansbridge, Jane. 1983. *Beyond Adversary Democracy.* Chicago: University of Chicago Press.

Marsden, George. 1991. *Understanding Fundamentalism and Evangelicalism.* Grand Rapids, Mich.: Eerdmans.

Marshall, T. H. 1965. *Class, Citizenship, and Social Development.* New York: Anchor.

Marty, Martin. 1981. *The Public Church.* New York: Crossroad.

———. 1997. *The One and the Many.* Cambridge: Havard University Press.

Mathewes, Charles. 2002. *During the World: An Augustinian Theology of Public Life.* Department of Religious Studies, University of Virginia, Charlottesville. Book manuscript.

McAdam, Doug. 1982. *Political Process and the Development of Black Insurgency, 1930–1970.* Chicago: University of Chicago Press.

———. 1986. "Recruitment to High Risk Activism: The Case of Freedom Summer." *American Journal of Sociology* 92:64–90.

———. 1988. *Freedom Summer.* New York: Oxford University Press.

McAdam, Doug, John D. McCarthy, and Mayer N. Zald. 1996. *Comparative Perspectives on Social Movements: Political Opportunities, Mobilizing Structures, and Cultural Framings.* New York: Cambridge University Press.

McCall, George, and Jerry Simmons. 1978. *Identities and Interactions.* New York: Free Press.

McCann, Michael. 1986. *Taking Reform Seriously: Perspectives on Public Interest Liberalism.* Ithaca: Cornell University Press.

McCarthy, John D., and Mayer N. Zald. 1973. *The Trend of Social Movements in America: Professionalization and Resource Mobilization.* New Brunswick, N.J.: Transaction.

———. 1977. "Resource Mobilization and Social Movements: A Partial Theory." *American Journal of Sociology* 82:1212–41.

McCarthy, Kathleen. 1999. "Religion, Philanthropy, and Political Culture." Pp. 297–316 in *Civil Society, Democracy, and Civic Renewal,* edited by R. Fullinwider. Lanham, Md.: Rowman and Littlefield.

McKnight, John. 1995. *The Careless Society: Community and Its Counterfeits.* New York: Basic Books.

Melucci, Alberto. 1988. "Getting Involved: Identity and Mobilization in Social Movements." Pp. 329–48 in *International Social Movement Research,* vol. 1, edited by B. Klandermans, H. Kriesi, and S. Tarrow. Greenwich, Conn.: JAI Press.

———. 1989. *Nomads of the Present.* Philadelphia: Temple University Press.

———. 1996a. *Challenging Codes.* Cambridge: Cambridge University Press.

———. 1996b. *The Playing Self.* Cambridge: Cambridge University Press.

Mendelberg, Tali, and Christopher Karpowitz. 2003. "How People Deliberate about Justice." Revised version of paper presented in the Department of Political Science, University of Wisconsin—Madison, April.

Meyer, David, and Nancy Whittier. 1994. "Social Movement Spillover." *Social Problems* 41:277–98.

Michaelsen, Robert, and W. C. Roof. 1986. *Liberal Protestantism: Realities and Possibilities.* New York: Pilgrim Press.

Minkoff, Debra. 1997. "Producing Social Capital: National Social Movements and Civil Society." *American Behavioral Scientist* 40:606–19.

Mische, Ann. 2003. "Cross-Talk in Movements: Reconceiving the Culture-Network Link." Pp. 258–80 in *Social Movements and Networks*, edited by M. Diani and D. McAdam. London: Oxford University Press.

Mische, Ann, and Harrison White. 1998. "Between Conversation and Situation: Public Switching Dynamics across Network Domains." *Social Research* 65:695–724.

Mitchell, Timothy. 1999. "Society, Economy, and the State Effect." Pp. 76–97 in *State/Culture: State-Formation after the Cultural Turn*, edited by G. Steinmetz. Ithaca: Cornell University Press.

Mock, Alan. 1992. "Congregational Religious Styles and Orientations to Society: Exploring Our Linear Assumptions." *Review of Religious Research* 34:20–33.

Mongoven, Ann. 2002. *Just Love: The Transformation of Civic Virtue*. Department of Religious Studies, Indiana University. Book manuscript in progress.

Moon, Dawne. 2004. *God, Sex, and Politics*. Berkeley and Los Angeles: University of California Press.

Morley, David. 1980. *The "Nationwide" Audience: Structure and Decoding*. London: BFI.

Morrill, Calvin. 1995. *The Executive Way: Conflict Management in Corporations*. Chicago: University of Chicago Press.

Morris, Aldon. 1984. *The Origins of the Civil Rights Movement*. New York: Free Press.

Mouffe, Chantal. 1992. *Dimensions of Radical Democracy*. London: Verso.

Munkres, Susan. 2003. "Activists for Others? How Privileged People Build Alliance Movements." Ph.D. dissertation, Department of Sociology, University of Wisconsin—Madison.

Myerhoff, Barbara. 1979. *Number Our Days*. New York: Simon and Schuster.

Myers, Fred. 1996. "Reflections on a Meeting: Structure, Languge, and the Polity in a Small-Scale Society," Pp. 257–324 in *The Matrix of Language: Contemporary Linguistic Anthropology*. New York: HarperCollins.

Myers-Lipton, Scott. 1998. "Effect of a Comprehensive Service-Learning Program on College Students' Civic Responsibility." *Teaching Sociology* 26:243–58.

Neuhaus, Richard J. 1984. *The Naked Public Square: Religion and Democracy in America*. Grand Rapids, Mich.: Eerdmans Publishing.

Noguera, Pedro A. 2001. "Transforming Urban Schools through Investments in the Social Capital of Parents." Pp. 189–212 in Susan Saegert, J. Phillip Thompson, and Mark R. Warren, eds., *Social Capital and Poor Communities*. New York: Russell Sage Foundation.

Offe, Claus. 1996. *Modernity and the State*. Cambridge: MIT Press.

Ostrander, Susan. 1984. *Women of the Upper Class*. Philadelphia: Temple University Press.

Park, J. Z., and C. Smith. 2000. "'To Whom Much Has Been Given . . . :' Religious Capital and Community Voluntarism among Churchgoing Protestants." *Journal for the Scientific Study of Religion* 39:272–86.

Parsons, Talcott. 1951. *The Social System*. New York: Free Press.

———. 1964. *Social Structure and Personality*. New York: Free Press.

———. 1967a. *Sociological Theory and Modern Society*. New York: Free Press.

———. 1967b. "Full Citizenship for the Negro American?" Pp. 422–65 in *Sociological Theory and Modern Society*. New York: Free Press.

———. 1971. *The System of Modern Societies*. Englewood Cliffs, N.J.: Prentice Hall.

———. 1977. *The Evolution of Societies*. Englewood Cliffs, N.J.: Prentice Hall.

Parsons, Talcott, and Edward Shils. 1951. "Toward a General Theory of Action." Cambridge: Harvard University Press.

Pateman, Carole. 1980. "The Civic Culture: A Philosophic Critique." Pp. 57–102 in Gabriel Almond and Sidney Verba, eds., *The Civic Culture Revisited*. Boston: Little Brown.

Patillo-McCoy, Mary. 1998. "Church Culture as a Strategy of Action in the Black Community." *American Sociological Review* 63:767–84.

Philipsen, Gerry. 1992. *Speaking Culturally*. Albany: State University of New York Press.

Piliavin, Jane. 2003. "Doing Well by Doing Good: Benefits for the Benefactor." Pp. 227–47 in *Flourishing: The Positive Personality and the Life Well Lived*, edited by Corey Lee M. Keyes and Jon Haidt. Washington, D.C.: American Psychological Association.

Pitkin, Hanna F. 1981. "Justice: On Relating Private and Public." *Political Theory* 9:327–52.

Polletta, Francesca. 1999. "'Free Spaces' in Collective Action." *Theory and Society* 28:1–38.

———. 2002. *Freedom Is an Endless Meeting: Democracy in American Social Movements*. Chicago: University of Chicago Press.

Polletta, Francesca, and James M. Jasper. 2001. "Collective Identity and Social Movements." *Annual Review of Sociology* 27:283–305.

Poppendieck, Janet. 1998. *Sweet Charity? Emergency Food and the End of Entitlement*. New York: Penguin Books.

Portes, Alejandro. 1998. "Social Capital: Its Origins and Applications in Modern Sociology." *Annual Review of Sociology* 24:1–24.

Purdy, Jedediah. 1999. *For Common Things: Irony, Trust, and Commitment in America Today*. New York: Alfred Knopf.

Putnam, Robert. 1993. *Making Democracy Work*. Princeton: Princeton University Press.

———. 1995. "Bowling Alone: America's Declining Social Capital." *Journal of Democracy* 6:65–78.

———. 1996. "The Strange Disappearance of Civic America." *American Prospect* 24 (Winter).

———. 2000. *Bowling Alone: The Collapse and Revival of American Community*. New York: Simon and Schuster.

Putnam, Robert, and Kristin Goss. 2002. Introduction. Pp. 3–20 in *Democracies in Flux: The Evolution of Social Capital in Contemporary Society.*, edited by R. Putnam. New York: Oxford University Press.

Rambo, Eric, and Elaine Chan. 1990. "Text, Structure, and Action in Cultural Sociology." *Theory and Society* 19:635–48.

Regnerus, Mark, and Christian Smith. 1998. "Selective Deprivatization among American Religious Traditions: The Reversal of the Great Reversal." *Social Forces* 76:1347–72.

Reinarman, Craig. 1987. *American States of Mind*. New Haven: Yale University Press.

Roof, Wade Clark. 1993. *A Generation of Seekers: The Spiritual Journeys of the Baby Boom Generation*. San Francisco: HarperCollins.

———. 1999. *Spiritual Marketplace: Baby Boomers and the Remaking of American Religion*. Princeton: Princeton University Press.

Roof, Wade Clark, and W. McKinney. 1987. *American Mainline Religion: Its Changing Shape and Future*. New Brunswick, N.J.: Rutgers University Press.

Roozen, David, William McKinney, and Jackson Carroll. 1984. *Varieties of Religious Presence*. New York: Pilgrim Press.

Rorty, Richard. 1998. *Achieving Our Country: Leftist Thought in Twentieth-Century America*. Cambridge: Harvard University Press.

Rosaldo, Michelle. 1973. "I Have Nothing to Hide: The Language of Ilongot Oratory." *Language in Society* 2:193–224.

———. 1982. "The Things We Do with Words." *Language in Society* 11:203–37.

Rosenblum, Nancy. 1994. "Civil Societies: Liberalism and the Moral Uses of Pluralism." *Social Research* 61:539–62.

Saegert, Susan, J. Phillip Thompson, and Mark R. Warren, eds. 2001. *Social Capital and Poor Communities*. New York: Russell Sage Foundation.

Sampson, Robert. 1999. "What 'Community' Supplies." Pp. 241–92 in *Urban Problems and Community Development*, edited by R. Ferguson and W. Dickens. Washington, D.C.: Brookings Institution Press.

Sampson, Robert, Jeffrey Morenoff, and Felton Earls. 1999. "Beyond Social Capital: Spatial Dynamics of Collective Efficacy for Children." *American Sociological Review* 64:633–60.

Sampson, Robert, Stephen Raudenbush, and Felton Earls. 1997. "Neighborhoods and Violent Crime: A Multilevel Study of Collective Efficacy." *Science* 277:918–24 (August 15).

Sandel, Michael. 1982. *Liberalism and the Limits of Justice*. Cambridge: Cambridge University Press.

———. 1996. *Democracy's Discontent*. Cambridge: Harvard University Press.

Schervish, Paul, Virginia Hodgkinson, Margaret Gates, and Associates. 1995. *Care and Community in Modern Society*. San Francisco: Jossey-Bass.

Schudson, Michael. 1994. "The 'Public Sphere' and Its Problems: Bringing the State (Back) In." *Notre Dame Journal of Law, Ethics, and Public Policy* 8:529–46.

———. 1998. *The Good Citizen: A History of American Civic Life*. New York: Martin Kessler Books.

Scott, W. Richard, John W. Meyer, and John Boli. 1994. *Institutional Environments and Organizations: Structural Complexity and Individualism*. Thousand Oaks, Calif.: Sage Publications.

Seigfried, Charlene. 2002. "Introduction to the Illinois Edition." Pp. ix–xxxviii in *Democracy and Social Ethics*, by J. Addams. Urbana and Chicago: University of Illinois Press.

Sewell, William, Jr. 1980. *Work and Revolution in France*. Cambridge: Cambridge University Press.

———. 1992. "A Theory of Structure: Duality, Agency, and Transformation." *American Journal of Sociology* 98:1–29.

Sherman, Amy. 2000. "Should We Put Faith in Charitable Choice?" *Responsive Community* 10:22–30.

Shils, Edward. 1991. "The Virtue of Civil Society." *Government and Opposition* 10:1–20.

Silverstein, Michael. 1972. "Linguistic Theory: Syntax, Semantics, Pragmatics." *Annual Review of Anthropology*: 349–82.

Sirianni, Carmen, and Lewis Friedland. 2001. *Civic Innovation in America*. Berkeley and Los Angeles: University of California Press.

Skocpol, Theda. 1996. "Unraveling from Above." *American Prospect* 25 (March–April 1996).

———. 1999. "Advocates without Members: The Recent Transformation of American Civic Life." Pp. 461–510 in *Civic Engagement in American Democracy*, edited by T.

Skocpol and M. Fiorina. Washington, D.C.: Brookings Institution Press; New York: Russell Sage Foundation.

———. 2000. "Religion, Civil Society, and Social Provision in the U.S." Pp. 21–50 in *Who Will Provide? The Changing Role of Religion in American Social Welfare*, edited by M. J. Bane, B. Coffin, and R. Thiemann. Boulder, Colo.: Westview Press.

Skocpol, Theda, and Morris Fiorina. 1999. *Civic Engagement in American Democracy*. Washington D.C.: Brookings Institution Press; New York: Russell Sage Foundation.

Smelser, Neil, and Jeffrey Alexander. 1999. *Diversity and Its Discontents: Cultural Conflict and Common Ground in Contemporary American Society*. Princeton: Princeton University Press.

Smith, Christian. 1996. *Disruptive Religion: The Force of Faith in Social Movement Activism*. New York: Routledge.

———. 1998. *American Evangelicalism: Embattled and Thriving*. Chicago: University of Chicago Press.

———. 2000. *Christian America? What Evangelicals Really Want*. Berkeley and Los Angeles: University of California Press.

Smith, Christian, with Michael Emerson, Sally Gallagher, and Paul Kennedy. 1996. "The Myth of Culture Wars." *Culture (Newsletter of the Sociology of Culture Section of the American Sociological Association)* 11:7–10.

Smith, Philip. 1998. *The New American Cultural Sociology*. Cambridge and New York: Cambridge University Press.

Smith, Steven Rathgeb, and Michael Sosin. 2001. "The Varieties of Faith-Related Agencies." *Public Administration Review* 61(6): 651–70.

Snow, David. 2001. "Collective Identity and Expressive Forms." Pp. 2212–19 in *The International Encyclopedia of the Social and Behavioral Sciences*, vol. 4, edited by N. Smelser and P. Baltes. Oxford: Elsevier.

Snow, David, and Robert Benford. 1988. "Ideology, Frame Resonance, and Participant Mobilization." *International Social Movement Research* 1:97–217.

Snow, David, E. Burke Rochford Jr., Steven K. Worden, and Robert K. Benford et al. 1986. ""Frame Alignment Processes, Micromobilization, and Movement Participation." *American Sociological Review* 51:464–81.

Somers, Margaret. 1994. "The Narrative Constitution of Identity: A Relational and Network Approach." *Theory and Society* 23:605–49.

———. 1995a. "What's Political and Cultural about Political Culture and the Public Sphere?" *Sociological Theory* 13:113–44.

———. 1995b. "Narrating and Naturalizing Civil Society and Citizenship Theory: The Place of Political Culture and the Public Sphere." *Sociological Theory* 13:229–74.

Somers, Margaret, and Gloria Gibson. 1994. "Reclaiming the Epistemological 'Other': Narrative and the Social Construction of Identity." Pp. 37–99 in *Social Theory and the Politics of Identity*, edited by C. Calhoun. Oxford and Cambridge, Mass.: Blackwell.

Stack, Carol. 1974. *All Our Kin: Strategies for Survival in a Black Community*. New York: Harper and Row.

Steensland, Brian. 2002. "Caring for Creation: Environmental Advocacy by Mainline Protestant Organizations." in *The Quiet Hand of God: Faith-Based Activism and the Public Role of Mainline Protestantism*, edited by R. Wuthnow and J. Evans. Berkeley and Los Angeles: University of California Press.

Steinberg, Marc. 1999. "The Talk and Back Talk of Collective Action: A Dialogic Analysis of Repertoires of Discourse among Nineteenth-Century English Cotton Spinners." *American Journal of Sociology* 105:736–80.

Steinmetz, George. 1999. *State/Culture: State-Formation after the Cultural Turn*. Ithaca: Cornell University Press.

Stets, Jan, and Peter Burke. 2000. "Identity Theory and Social Identity Theory," *Social Psychology Quarterly* 63 (3): 224–37.

Stevens, Mitchell. 1996. "Neoinstitutionalism and Social Movement Research: Hierarchy and Autonomy in the Home Education Movements." Paper presented at the annual meetings of the American Sociological Association, New York.

———. 2001. *Kingdom of Children*. Princeton: Princeton University Press.

Stone, Gregory. 1962. "Appearance and the Self." Pp. 86–118 in *Human Behavior and Social Processes*, edited by A. Rose. Boston: Houghton Mifflin.

Strauss, Anselm. 1987. *Qualitative Analysis for Social Scientists*. Cambridge: Cambridge University Press.

Strauss, Anselm, and Juliet Corbin. 1991. *Basics of Qualitative Research*. Beverly Hills, Calif.: Sage.

Stryker, Sheldon, and Anne Statham. 1985. "Symbolic Interaction and Role Theory." Pp. 311–78 in *Handbook of Social Psychology*, 3rd ed., vol. 1, edited by Garner Lindzey and Elliot Aronson. New York: Random House.

Study Circles Resource Center. 1992, 1994, 1997. The Busy Citizen's Discussion Guide: Facing the Challenge of Racism and Race Relations. 3rd ed. Pomfret, Conn.: Topsfield Foundation.

———. n.d. The Busy Citizen's Discussion Guide: Toward a More Perfect Union in an Age of Diversity. Pomfret, Conn.: Topsfield Foundation.

Swidler, Ann. 1986. "Culture in Action: Symbols and Strategies." *American Sociological Review* 51:273–86.

———. 2001. *Talk of Love*. Chicago: University of Chicago Press.

Sztompka, Piotr. 1999. *Trust: A Sociological Theory*. Cambridge: Cambridge University Press.

Tajfel, Henri. 1982. *Social Identity and Intergroup Relations*. Cambridge: Cambridge University Press.

Tarrow, Sydney. 1994. *Power in Movement: Collective Action, Social Movements, and Politics*. New York: Cambridge University Press.

Taylor, Charles. 1989. *Sources of the Self*. Cambridge: Harvard University Press.

———. 1994. *Multiculturalism: Examining the Politics of Recognition*. Princeton: Princeton University Press.

———. 1995. "Liberal Politics and the Public Sphere." Pp. 183–217 in *New Communitarian Thinking*, edited by A. Etzioni. Charlottesville: University Press of Virginia.

Taylor, Verta, and Nancy Whittier. 1992. "Collective Identity in Social Movement Communities: Lesbian Feminist Mobilization." Pp. 104–30 in *Frontiers of Social Movement Theory*, edited by A. Morris and C. Mueller. New Haven: Yale University Press.

Teske, Nathan. 1997. *Political Activists in America*. Cambridge: Cambridge University Press.

Thiemann, Ronald, Samuel Herring, and Betsy Perabo. 2000. "Risks and Responsibilities for Faith-Based Organizations." Pp. 51–70 in *Who Will Provide? The Changing Role of Religion in American Social Welfare*, edited by M. J. Bane, B. Coffin, and R. Thiemann. Boulder, Colo.: Westview Press.

Tilly, Charles. 2002. *Stories, Identities, and Political Change.* Lanham, Md.: Rowan and Littlefield.

Tipton, Steven. 1982. *Getting Saved from the Sixties.* Berkeley and Los Angeles: University of California Press.

Tocqueville, Alexis de. 1969 [1835]. *Democracy in America.* Edited by J. P. Mayer, translated by G. Lawrence. Garden City, N.Y.: Doubleday.

Touraine, Alain. 1981. *The Voice and the Eye.* Cambridge: Cambridge University Press.

Troeltsch, Ernst. 1931. *The Social Teachings of the Christian Churches.* New York: Macmillan.

Underwood, Kenneth. 1957. *Protestant and Catholic.* Boston: Beacon Press.

Varenne, Hervé. 1977. *Americans Together: Structured Diversity in a Midwestern Town.* New York: Teacher's College Press.

Verba, Sidney, Kay Schlozman, and Henry Brady. 1995. *Voice and Equality: Civic Voluntarism in American Politics.* Cambridge: Harvard University Press.

Wacquant, Loic, and William Julius Wilson. 1989. "The Cost of Racial and Class Exclusion in the Inner City." *Annals of the American Academy of Political and Social Science* 501:8–25.

Walsh, Katherine Cramer. 2004. *Talking about Politics: Informal Groups and Social Identity in American Life.* Chicago: University of Chicago Press.

Walzer, Michael. 1985. *Exodus and Revolution.* New York: Basic Books.

———. 1992. "The Civil Society Argument." Pp. 89–107 in *Dimensions of Radical Democracy,* edited by C. Mouffe. London: Verso.

Warner, R. Stephen. 1988. *New Wine in Old Wineskins.* Berkeley and Los Angeles: University of California Press.

———. 1993. "Work in Progress toward a New Paradigm for the Sociological Study of Religion in the United States." *American Journal of Sociology* 98:1044–93.

———. 1999. "Changes in the Civic Role of Religion." Pp. 229–43 in *Diversity and Its Discontents,* edited by N. Smelser and J. Alexander. Princeton: Princeton University Press.

Warren, Mark E. 2001. *Democracy and Association.* Princeton: Princeton University Press.

Warren, Mark R. 2001. *Dry Bones Rattling: Community Building to Revitalize American Democracy.* Princeton: Princeton University Press.

Warren, Mark R., J. Phillip Thompson, and Susan Saegert. 2001. "The Role of Social Capital in Combating Poverty." Pp. 1–28 in *Social Capital and Poor Communities,* edited by S. Saegert, J. P. Thompson, and M. R. Warren. New York: Russell Sage Foundation.

Westbrook, Robert. 1991. *John Dewey and American Democracy.* Ithaca: Cornell University Press.

White, Harrison. 1992. *Identity and Control.* Princeton: Princeton University Press.

Whittier, Nancy. 1995. *Feminist Generations.* Philadelphia: Temple University Press.

Williams, Rhys. 1995. "Constructing the Public Good: Social Movements and Cultural Resources." *Social Problems* 42:124–44.

———. 1997. *Culture Wars in American Politics.* New York: Aldine de Gruyter.

Willis, Paul. 1981. *Learning to Labor.* New York: Columbia University Press.

Wilson, John. 2000. "Volunteering." *Annual Review of Sociology* 26:215–40.

———. 2001. "Dr. Putnam's Social Lubricant." *Contemporary Sociology* 30:225–27.

Wilson, John, and Thomas Janoski. 1995. "The Contribution of Religion to Volunteer Work." *Sociology of Religion* 56:137–52.

Wilson, John, and Marc Musick. 1997. "Toward an Integrated Theory of Volunteering." *American Sociological Review* 62:694–713.

Wilson, William Julius. 1987. *The Truly Disadvantaged.* Chicago: University of Chicago Press.

———. 1999. *The Bridge over the Racial Divide.* Berkeley and Los Angeles: University of California Press.

Witten, Marsha. 1993. *All Is Forgiven: The Secular Message in American Protestantism.* Princeton: Princeton University Press.

Wolfe, Alan. 1989. *Whose Keeper? Social Science and Moral Obligation.* Berkeley and Los Angeles: University of California Press.

———. 1998. *One Nation after All.* New York: Viking Press.

Wood, Richard L. 1994. "Faith in Action: Religious Resources for Political Success in Three Congregations." *Sociology of Religion* 55:397–417.

———. 1995. "Faith in Action: Religion, Race, and the Future of Democracy." Ph.D. diss. Dept. of Sociology, University of California, Berkeley.

———. 1999. "Religious Culture and Political Action." *Sociological Theory* 17:307–32.

———. 2002. *Faith in Action: Religion, Race and Democratic Organizing in America.* Chicago: University of Chicago Press.

Wuthnow, Robert. 1984. *Cultural Analysis: the Work of Peter L. Berger, Mary Douglas, Michel Foucault, and Jurgen Habermas.* Boston: Routledge and Kegan Paul.

———. 1987. *Meaning and Moral Order.* Berkeley and Los Angeles: University of California Press.

———. 1988. *The Restructuring of American Religion.* Princeton: Princeton University Press.

———. 1989. *The Struggle for America's Soul.* Grand Rapids, Mich.: Eerdmans.

———. 1991. *Acts of Compassion.* Princeton: Princeton University Press.

———. 1992. *Vocabularies of Public Life.* London and New York: Routledge.

———. 1994. *Sharing the Journey.* New York: Free Press.

———. 1996. *Christianity and Civil Society.* Valley Forge, PA: Trinity Press International.

———. 1997. *The Crisis in the Churches: Spiritual Malaise, Fiscal Woe.* New York: Oxford University Press.

———. 1998. *Loose Connections: Joining Together in America's Fragmented Communities.* Cambridge: Harvard University Press.

———. 1999a. "Can Religion Revitalize Civil Society? An Institutional Perspective." Manuscript, Department of Sociology, Princeton University.

———. 1999b. "The Culture of Discontent: Democratic Liberalism and the Challenge of Diversity in Late Twentieth-Century America." Pp. 19–35 in *Diversity and Its Discontents,* edited by N. Smelser and J. Alexander. Princeton: Princeton University Press.

———. 1999c. "Mobilizing Civic Engagement: The Changing Impact of Religious Involvement." Pp. 331–63 in *Civic Engagement in American Democracy,* edited by T. Skocpol and M. Fiorina. Washington D.C.: Brookings Institution Press; New York: Russell Sage Foundation.

———. 1999d. "Reassembling the Civic Church: The Changing Role of Congregations in American Civil Society." Department of Sociology, Princeton University. Manuscript.

———. 2004. *Saving America? Faith-Based Services and the Future of Civil Society.* Princeton: Princeton University Press.

Wuthnow, Robert, and John Evans, eds. 2002. *The Quiet Hand of God: Faith-Based Activism and the Public Role of Mainline Protestantism.* Berkeley and Los Angeles: University of California Press.

Wuthnow, Robert, Virginia Hodgkinson, and Associates. 1990. *Faith and Philanthropy in America.* San Francisco: Jossey-Bass.

Yates, M., and J. Youniss. 1996. "A Developmental Perspective on Community Service in Adolescence." *Social Development* 5:85–111.

Young, Michael. 2001. "Tocqueville's America: A Critical Reappraisal of Voluntary Associations before the Civil War." Paper presented at the annual meetings of the American Sociological Association, Anaheim, Calif.

———. 2002. "Confessional Protest: The Religious Birth of U.S. National Social Movements." *American Sociological Review* 67:660–68.

INDEX